AN HISTORICAL INTRODUCTION TO AMERICAN EDUCATION

Second Edition

Gerald L. Gutek

*Professor of Educational Leadership and
Policy Studies and History
Loyola University of Chicago*

WAVELAND

PRESS, INC.

Prospect Heights, Illinois

To My Wife, Patricia

For information about this book, write or call:

Waveland Press, Inc.
P.O. Box 400
Prospect Heights, Illinois 60070
(708) 634-0081

Copyright © 1991, 1970 by Gerald L. Gutek

ISBN 0-88133-538-X

Printed in the United States of America

7 6 5 4 3 2 1

Contents

Contents

Preface

I n 1971, the first edition of *An Historical Introduction to American Education* was published by the Thomas Y. Crowell Company. While the book enjoyed many printings, there was not a new edition. I appreciate the interest and efforts of Waveland Press in making this revision available. In preparing the second edition, I have attempted to retain the style and features of the book that contributed to its use in teacher education courses. I have worked to maintain its general historical perspective. The section, "Suggestions for Further Reading" that concludes each chapter includes important books in education of historical significance as well as those that are current publications.

The book originated from my teaching of American Education, an introductory course in undergraduate teacher education at Loyola University of Chicago. These historical units formed one dimension in the course. Other units examined more contemporary matters such as school organization and governance, curriculum and instruction, and issues. Based on its origins in classroom use, the book is intended to provide a brief but general survey of the history of American education for introductory courses in teacher education programs. Instructors can use the book to provide the historical perspective that teacher education students need and can select other books or readings of their choice to complete their course design. Each chapter contains a narrative section and selected source readings. The selected documents that illustrate the subject treated in the chapter are included so that students in teacher education programs can examine the primary sources upon which history is based.

Rather than attempting to be a complete history of American education, the book deals with selected topics and movements. For example, Chapter 1 examines the origins of American education in the colonial era, and Chapter 2 treats the impact of the republican ideology on educational ideas in the revolutionary and early national eras. Chapters 3, 4, 5, and 6 examine the historical development of the institutionalization of elementary, secondary, higher, and teacher education in the United States. Chapter 7 examines the contributions of such important educational theorists as Jean Jacques Rousseau, Johann Heinrich Pestalozzi, Friedrich Froebel, Johann Friedrich Herbart, Maria Montessori, and John Dewey. Chapter 8 is an account of the movement for racial and social integration in American education. Chapter 9 comments on trends in the recent past, and Chapter 10 points the reader in the direction of a conclusion.

I hope that the second edition of *An Historical Introduction to American Education* will be useful to students of American educational history, especially those who are preparing to be teachers in our nation's schools.

Gerald Gutek
Loyola University
Chicago, Illinois

Chapter 1

The Colonial Educational Experience

Introduction

The history of American education begins with the efforts of the English colonials to recreate in the New World the school system they had known before. When a school is established, it is a clear indication that the group sponsoring the school means to perpetuate itself by providing its children in a systematized way with the knowledge and values it regards necessary for survival. The colonists' schools thus reflected their desire to stay and conquer the wilderness.

The patterns of settlement in North America varied according to geographical, climatic, and topographical conditions. Along with these diverse patterns, variations also followed in the life style of the different colonial regions. New England in its Puritan conformity, the Middle Atlantic colonies in their pluralism, and the South in its plantations, all reflected the tendency to develop unique characteristics, as the common English experience was altered by the American environment. The variations in educational processes and institutions which began to mark these regions of settlement likewise reflected the imprint of the new environment.

Colonial education was influenced greatly by the cultural heritage that the colonists brought with them from Europe. To understand their ideas about education, it is necessary to examine some of the precedents that existed in

1

Europe. The Renaissance humanism of the fourteenth and fifteenth centuries stressed the classical forms and tradition and the Greek and Latin languages as marks of the educated man. Linked with this classical humanism was a strong concern with religion, which was part of the heritage of the Protestant Reformation and Catholic Counter-Reformation. The religious element emphasized doctrinal education. Another factor in European culture at that time was the accelerated pace of commercial exchange, which increased the value of persons who could read, write, and calculate.

In addition to the formal educational precedents in the European cultural heritage, non-formal social agencies and processes also influenced the colonists' educational attitudes. In both seventeenth-century Europe and America, agencies such as the family, church, farm, and shop exercised a non-formal educational role on the young. In his definitive work on colonial education, Lawrence Cremin regards the family as the essential unit of social organization and informal education in the colonies.[1] In particular, the Puritans of New England regarded their families as the fundamental unit of both religious and civil society. Throughout the North American colonies, the family was the basic social and economic agency.

In early colonial society, the family household was frequently the scene of sustained instruction that was literary as well as vocational. Reading was a daily activity in many colonial households that found parents teaching their children to master the alphabet and religious books. The chores that were performed by children introduced them to the economic activities that sustained the family in the New World. The values imparted by the family were those of religious piety and respect for parents, elders, and civil and religious authorities.[2] It was upon the foundation of the non-formal agencies of the family and the household that the formal educational structures of the school and the college were built.

Both the intellectual inheritance and the commercial revolution made their impact upon colonial education. The Latin Grammar school continued the emphasis on classical education, while the vernacular schools reflected the demands of doctrinal conformity and basic literacy. As the commercial classes grew in numbers and in importance, they demanded a more utilitarian education. Although all of the English colonies in North America shared the tradition of European intellectual and commercial life, certain differences unique to each region developed early in the New England colonies, the Middle colonies, and the Southern colonies.

The New England Colonies

The New England colonies were settled primarily by English Puritans, who based their lives and their beliefs upon the theological doctrines of the Swiss

THE LANDING OF COLUMBUS.

Note. Columbus was the first European that set foot in the new world. He landed in a rich dress, and with a drawn sword in his hand : his men followed, and all kneeled, and kissed the ground they had so long desired to see.

The Landing of Columbus. Bishop Davenport, *History of the United States* (Philadelphia: William Marshall & Co., 1833), p. 7. This illustration from an early nineteenth century history text depicts a romanticized version of Columbus' landing in the New World.

religious reformer, John Calvin. Their educational orientation was also influenced heavily by his writings, for several aspects of Calvinism were especially relevant to education. First, the doctrine of predestination held that only a certain religiously observant elite was destined for salvation, while the unenlightened masses were doomed to hell-fire and damnation. Second, a certain correlation was indicated between property and the good life. The elect were the industrious, and could therefore be known by their external prosperity. This philosophy helped to establish the Protestant ethic as an integral part of American life, which considered hard work and the acquisition of property as positive values. Third, a spirit of religious conformity developed which led to the suppression of dissent from orthodox doctrine as both a theological and political infraction. The Puritans based their government, particularly that of the Massachusetts Commonwealth, upon a theocratic concept of the state. Education was regarded as an instrument by which the believer might become literate in sacred Scripture, Calvinist doctrine, and the general laws of the Commonwealth. Furthermore, education was a means of achieving social and religious stability both individually and communally. The Puritan Fathers believed that their social blueprint, designed in Heaven, needed no reconstruction.

New England colonial education emphasized the conservative aspect of its role by transmitting a heritage which allowed little room for change. Education of that period also conveyed the particular world-view of Calvinist theology. Since a literate clergy and a literate laity were important to Calvinism, reading and writing were emphasized.

Another important feature of New England colonial education was the close relationship of church, state, and school. When the first schools were established they were considered adjuncts of the church-state. This was in sharp contrast to the later American view that the church, school and state should function separately.

Puritan View of the Child

New England colonial education was permeated by a notion of child psychology which maintained that the infant was conceived in sin and born to corruption.[3] According to this theory, children were savage creatures who needed constant upbraiding and discipline to curb their evil inclinations and desires. The New England boy or girl was not regarded as a child, interested in play and games, but was treated as a miniature adult and made to conform to adult behavior and regulations. Consequently, discipline in both home and school was extremely harsh, with corporal punishment a frequent feature of the child's educational experience. In admonishing parents as to the proper nurture of their children, the New England clergyman Jonathan Edwards warned:

Let me now, therefore, once more, before I finally cease to speak to this congregation, repeat and earnestly press the counsel which I have often urged on heads of families here, while I was their pastor, to great painfulness in teaching, warning and directing their children; bringing them up in the nurture and admonition of the Lord; beginning early, where there is yet opportunity, and maintaining a constant diligence in labors of this kind; remembering that, as you would not have all your instructions and counsels ineffectual, there must be government as well as instructions, which must be maintained with an even hand and steady resolution, as a guard to the religion and morals of the family and the support of its good order. Take heed that it not be with any of you as with Eli of old, who reproved his children but restrained them not; and that, by this means, you don't bring the like curse on your families as he did on his.

And let children obey their parents, and yield to their instructions, and submit to their orders, as they would inherit a blessing and not a curse. For we have reason to think, from many things in the word of God, that nothing has a greater tendency to bring a curse on persons in this world, and on all their temporal concerns, than undutiful, unsubmissive, disorderly behavior in children towards their parents.[4]

Puritan Stress on Education

The New England Puritans, like their European Calvinistic counterparts, greatly valued literacy. They believed it an easy matter for Satan to corrupt the ignorant. In order to ensure a literate people, the Massachusetts General Court in 1642 required the parents and guardians of children to attend to their dependents' ability to read and to understand the principles of religion and the laws of the Commonwealth. Although the Law of 1642 provided for education, it did not order compulsory school attendance and maintenance. It is interesting to note that the Massachusetts Law of 1642 closely paralleled the English Poor Law of 1601, which required the apprenticeship of pauper children. This English Law broadened the definition of "poor parents" from those actually receiving charity to those who were deemed unable to support their children. The Poor Law of 1601 contained two major provisions: that taxes be levied on all property owners within a given parish for the support of paupers; and that all poor and dependent children be bound out as apprentices in order to learn a useful trade. Motivated by the Poor Law, the New England Calvinists feared that a class of ignorant citizens would not only be prone to the devil's wiles, but might also become a dependent class draining the state's prosperity.

In 1647, the General Court of Massachusetts enacted the famous "Old Deluder Satan Law," which required every town of fifty or more families to appoint a teacher of reading and writing. Towns of one hundred or more families were to employ a Latin teacher as well, to prepare students for entry to the colonial college. Enacted in 1647, the "Old Deluder Satan Law" read:

> It being one Chiefe project of ye ould deluder, Satan, to keepe men from the knowledge of ye Scriptures, as in former times by keeping ym in an unknowne tongue, so in these lattr times by perswading from ye use of tongues, yt so at least ye true sence & meaning of ye originall might be clouded by false glosses of saint seeming deceivers, yt learning may not be buried in ye grave of our fathrs in ye church and commonwealth, the Lord assisting our endeavors, —

> It is therefore ordred, yt evry towneship in this jurisdiction, aftr ye Lord hath increased ym number to 50 housholdrs, shall then forthwth appoint one wthin their towne to teach all such children as shall resort to him to write & reade, whose wages shall he paid eithr by ye parents or mastrs of such children, or by ye inhabitants in genrall, by way of supply, as ye major part of those yt ordr ye prudentials of ye towne shall appoint; provided, those yt send their children be not oppressed by paying much more yn they can have ym taught for in othr townes; & it is furthr ordered, yt where any towne shall increase to ye numhr of 100 families or householdrs, they shall set up a grammar schoole, ye mr thereof being able to instruct youth so farr as they shall be fited for ye university, provided, yt if any towne neglect ye performance hereof above one yeare, yt every such towne shall pay 5 £ to ye next schoole till they shall performe this order.[5]

Although it is easy to exaggerate the importance of these early school laws, they did establish certain significant points: 1) the state could require education; 2) the state could require towns to maintain teachers; 3) civil authorities could supervise and control schools; 4) public funds could be used to support education. It is an oversimplification to suggest that these laws anticipated the publicly supported and state-supervised schools that were set up later. However, the passage of this legislation does serve to indicate the importance which the Puritans of Massachusetts attached to literacy.

Elementary Education: The New England Town School

The New England town school emphasized the teaching of reading, writing, and religion, which were taught by a master. The primary subject was reading, and it was taught according to the ABC method. The student first learned the letters of the alphabet, then syllables, words, and finally sentences. The first text was the Hornbook, a sheet of parchment covered by a transparent material, which contained the alphabet, vowels, and syllables, the doctrine of the Trinity and the Lord's Prayer.

The most popular of the colonial school books was the famous *New England Primer*. It appeared in 1690 and ran through numerous editions, and was often referred to as the "Little Bible of New England." This slim volume contained twenty-four rhymes to aid children in learning the alphabet. Each letter was illustrated with a little woodcut or drawing. The first of these rhymes was the well-known "In Adam's Fall, We Sinned All." This little phrase illustrates the close relationship between reading and religion that was the hallmark of New England elementary education. The *New England Primer* also contained vowels, syllables, "An Alphabet of Lessons for Youth," "The Dutiful Child's Promises," the Lord's Prayer, the Creed, the Ten Commandments, "The Duty of Children Towards Their Parents," "Names and Order of the Books of the Old and New Testaments," "The Shorter Catechism Agreed Upon by the Reverend Assembly of Divines at Westminster," and a woodcut of Mr. John Rogers burning at the stake in Smithfield as the first Protestant martyr of Queen Mary's reign.[6]

The student was expected to master the contents of this slim list of printed materials by memorizing them. Writing was learned by copying the printed page or by transcribing the lessons dictated by the teacher. The classroom was ungraded with all students housed in the same classroom irrespective of their age. The teacher, who might be anyone from a ministerial student to an indentured servant, controlled the students by means of the harsh discipline prescribed by religious doctrine.

Secondary Education: Latin Grammar School

The Latin Grammar school was attended by the sons of the New England social, political, and religious elite. Children destined for this elite kind of secondary education did not enter the Latin school directly from the town school, but first learned to read and write in English from lessons with a private teacher or tutor. As its name indicates, the Latin Grammar school was a school where Latin and Greek were taught as the languages of the educated class — those persons destined to become the religious and political rulers of New England. Students attending the school were destined for the ministry of the Puritan Church or positions of political leadership in the colonies.

This institution formed a direct link between the new American educational environment and its European antecedents. The emphasis on the classics, Latin, and Greek was a direct carryover from the classical humanistic tradition of the Renaissance; the religious influence stemmed from the Protestant Reformation. Students entered the Latin Grammar school at the age of eight and studied there for another eight years. Instructional materials were drawn from the Latin classics: Cicero, Terence, Caesar, Livy, Virgil, and Horace. The advanced students read the Greek authors Isocrates, Hesiod, and Homer as well. No attention was given to subjects that might be considered immediately utilitarian, such as mathematics, science, history, or modern languages.

Higher Education: The New England College

The New England Puritans were greatly concerned with having an educated ministry whose members read the Scriptures and doctrines. To provide for the higher education of ministers of the Church, Harvard College was established in 1636. The Harvard curriculum embodied the old medieval curriculum of the liberal arts, The Trivium and Quadrivium. Comprised of three major disciplines, the Trivium dealt with grammar, rhetoric, and logic. The four subjects of the Quadrivium were arithmetic, geometry, music, and astronomy. In addition, Hebrew, Greek, and ancient history were offered because they were useful in Scriptural study.

The New England Educational Experience

Several features marked the New England educational experience, as typified by the Commonwealth of Massachusetts: first, education was considered an instrument of both literacy and religious indoctrination; second, it was an essentially conservative means of transmitting a particular cultural heritage; third, it was localized in order to serve the needs of a rural village society. Although the direct influence of the New England town school on later American education is often exaggerated, this unit of educational organization did contribute considerably to the concept of local control. When the common school was established in the nineteenth century, the states delegated substantial powers to local school districts. Although this made education responsive to the citizens in the district, it also produced significant quantitative and qualitative variations from district to district.

 ## Colonial South: A Cultural Matrix

Because the climate favored the growing of staple subtropical crops such as tobacco, rice, sugar, indigo, and later cotton, the large plantation came to dominate the southern landscape. The society that grew up around the plantation was an agricultural one, supported by a growing number of black slaves. Little communication existed between plantations, so the sense of community characteristic of the New England town was not highly developed.

The large plantation also promoted rigid, immobile social class distinctions. Although strong economic rivalries existed between the landowning plantation gentry and the lower socio-economic group, the "poor whites" who had been pushed to the infertile back country, a kind of racially-based coalition developed between these two groups. In contrast to New England, where community values were religiously based, the southern colonies developed a value structure that rested upon a set of social, economic, and moral relationships centering

not all plantation!

around the black slave system and based on the concept of white supremacy.[7] The economic hostility between the plantation owners and the back-country poor whites was submerged by their mutual interest in the slave system and by the desire of both groups to control the black population.

Southern White Gentlemen's Code

The plantation owners represented a leisure class in an agricultural setting who wanted to establish a chivalrous code of life based upon the Cavalier myth.[8] Although historically there is little truth to the notion that the southern gentry were originally displaced aristocrats, many southern plantation owners believed the myth to be a factual account of their ancestry. The education of southern gentlemen contained two major emphases: an ethical code based upon a conception of chivalry; and practical instruction in the management of the basic agricultural unit, the plantation. The merging of a concept of chivalry and a method of plantation management was not necessarily dictated by either logic or economics, but resulted instead from a rather romanticized view of history.

Like leisure classes in other times, southern gentlemen developed an interest and ability in oratory. It is interesting to note that oratorical ability has often had both aristocratic and democratic connotations. Excellence in speech has long been rated highly by leisure classes. Since the days of ancient Athenian democracy, oratorical prowess has also characterized democratic societies. Southern writers frequently referred to the slave-holding South as a latter-day Athens, since Athenian life at the time of Pericles was similarly supported by a large slave population that enabled the free citizens to follow cultural pursuits. The unusual blending of aristocratic and democratic elements in the South produced a generation of orator-statesmen that included Washington, Jefferson, Madison, and Monroe, all of whom were leaders in the early republic's political experience. As an educational exemplar, the orator has served as a model for the well-rounded, liberally educated person who is a persuasive public speaker.

The population patterns which resulted from the plantation economy also made formal education difficult. A small population was scattered over a large land area. Because of the long distances between plantations and the lack of well-defined community life, a good deal of the formal education of the socio-economic elite was provided by tutors.

Because of the problems of establishing a formal structure for transmitting the social code, southern educational patterns also embraced much that was informal. The plantation itself served as an informal school where young men and women could learn "proper manners" by directly imitating their parents. The young man learned the skills of plantation management from his father.

The daughter of the elite family was reared to occupy the exalted social position of mistress of the plantation. As the future wife of a plantation owner, she was trained to carry out the domestic duties of managing the household and the servants. Like her brother she often had the benefits of private tutoring, and learned the social graces from her mother. Children of wealthy families often completed their education by going to European or colonial colleges.

Poor White Education

Although the poor whites, who were usually located on small farms on infertile land, often occupied an economic position inferior to that of the black slave, they learned to feel superior because they were white. Thus a set of mores and folkways based upon the economic and social conditions of a slave society evolved that reinforced the doctrine of white supremacy. Economically restricted by the plantation system, the poor whites lived at a subsistence level, and only fear of the blacks checked hostility to the plantation owner. In the southern backwoods, education was concerned with survival rather than the intricacies of a classical tradition. Education for the poor white boy was informal; he learned through the direct experience of farming and hunting with his father. The girl learned simple domestic tasks from her mother. While such informal lessons served the immediate needs of survival in an inhospitable environment, they produced a class of illiterate people, a condition that inhibited the progress of the South in later years.

Black Education

The education of the black slave was functionally related to the needs of a plantation-based economy. In being uprooted from their native Africa, the blacks were torn from their own culture and thrust into an environment not merely inhospitable but completely alien. As slaves the African blacks were undergoing induction into a society vastly different from that of their homeland. They were forced to adapt from the life of a hunter-herdsman-farmer to that of a plantation laborer. As in the case of the poor white, the slaves' education was direct and informal as they learned the vocational skills of their economic level. Although the field hands only learned the simple agricultural skills, some of the slaves received more specialized training as mechanics, blacksmiths, or domestic servants. Fearful of slave insurrections, the southern plantation owners made no attempt to provide formal education. Literacy in the sense of reading and writing was not available to most of the slaves, although there were a few exceptions.

Formal Education

Thus far formal education in the South has not been considered, for the simple reason that, except for the tutoring provided for the upper-class children of plantation society, it was not readily available. However, certain types of formal education eventually did evolve in some areas of the South.

Influenced by the English Poor Law of 1601, which had required training for the dependent poor, the colonies of Virginia and North Carolina made it compulsory for orphans and pauper children to be apprenticed. Orphans were indentured to masters of specific trades to learn a particular skill. The master, in addition to teaching his trade, was also required to provide instruction in reading and writing.

Another development of more formal education in the South was the establishment of various private denominational schools. These denominational or charity schools were supported by private endowments or gifts. The Anglican missionary society, the Society for the Propagation of the Gospel in Foreign Parts, maintained elementary schools which provided religious instruction, reading, writing, and rudimentary arithmetic. But these attempts to establish formal education were sporadic and never reached the level of organization achieved by the Puritans in New England.

As was the case in England, and the other North American colonies, higher education in the South was restricted to the sons of the upper class. Some members of this elite were sent to England for further education. In 1693 The College of William and Mary was established in Virginia to educate the ministry of the Anglican Church. Originally, it had three departments of instruction: a grammar school, a School of Philosophy, and a Theology School. In 1779 the college was reorganized, and the scope of the curriculum was broadened to include natural philosophy, mathematics, law, medicine, moral philosophy, fine arts, and modern languages.

For most of the population in the South, therefore, colonial education was informal rather than formal. Because of population distribution and the economic system, such formal education as did exist was highly aristocratic and confined to the elite group of white plantation owners. Educational progress in the South lagged behind that of New England because of the lack of a sense of community goals comparable to the religious orientation in New England.

 ## The Middle Atlantic Colonies: Pluralism

Located between New England and the Southern colonies, the Middle Atlantic colonies included New York, New Jersey, Pennsylvania, and Delaware. While New England was characterized by patterns of religious and racial homogeneity and the South by patterns of economic homogeneity, the Middle Atlantic colonies comprised an extremely pluralistic society. Religious pluralism was evidenced by such diverse sects as Dutch Reformed, Anglican, Lutheran, Quaker, Presbyterian, Roman Catholic, and Jewish. The presence of the English, Dutch, Swedes, French, Danes, Jews, Irish, Scottish, and Germans resulted in widely varying racial and linguistic patterns as well. Various economic endeavors included farming, manufacturing, commerce, and related activities.

Because of the diverse traditions, languages, and religions, there was no common fund of shared experience upon which to build a required or extensive educational enterprise. Various linguistic and religious groups attempted to perpetuate themselves through isolation, which each one thought would preserve the elements particular to its culture. Conflicting motives and goals also retarded the growth of institutional patterns of formal education. We have earlier defined education as the process of introducing the immature to their culture; but the middle colonies' experience was complicated by the existence of multiple cultural patterns.

Educational Patterns in New York

Until 1664, New Amsterdam was a Dutch colonial possession. The most powerful religious agency there was the Dutch Reformed Church, a Calvinistic sect which, like its New England counterpart, believed in an educated ministry and laity. While the Dutch West India Company supported education, the church exercised control over it. Under church auspices elementary or reading and writing schools were maintained. After the English seized the colony these schools persisted, as the small Dutch community struggled to preserve its cultural identity against the English influx.

The English established a number of charity schools, supported by the Anglican Church and protected by the colonial governor, where instruction was given in reading, writing, arithmetic, catechism, and religion. The primary emphasis was on the elementary level of education, although a statute was passed to provide for the teaching of Latin and Greek.

Whenever formal institutions fail to respond to economic conditions, nonformal substitutes come into existence. Despite the difficulty of maintaining organized educational institutions, a number of private schools developed. The government's neglect of education encouraged their growth. More and more members of the rising commercial class attended these schools, for special skills were offered that were needed for trading, such as navigation, bookkeeping, and modern languages. The "private venture school" was an educational response to the demand for practical skills and knowledge.

Educational Patterns in Pennsylvania

Pennsylvania followed a pattern similar to New York's; the English Quakers who first established a colony there were soon joined by Scots-Irish Presbyterians and German Pietists. Each group had its own notion of culture and of how to transmit it. Quaker elementary schools stressed religion, reading, writing, and arithmetic. The Quakers rejected the harsh forms of corporal punishment prevalent during that period and gave greater attention to the individual nature of each child. Although the English founded charity schools, the German colonists rejected them as part of an English plot to undermine Germanic culture. Among the German teachers was Christopher Dock, who wrote the first book about education in the New World. As in New York, the absence of strong governmental concern with education caused private venture schools and private tutors to fill the educational gap.

Conclusion

Although certain features were unique to each colonial region, the colonies also shared this early stage of the American educational experience in many ways. Because church and school were intimately connected, the religious influence was strong in all areas where the school served as a formal instructional agency, and much of the educational content was religious. This element persisted into the eighteenth and even into the nineteenth centuries. Also, the society served by the school was predominantly rural and agrarian.

The American colonial educational experience, then, basically consisted of the reconstruction of imported English institutions in light of the New World environment. It also included the failure of some elements of the imported educational tradition to meet environmental challenges. For example, the New England town school was an attempt to offer literacy to the people of the settlement within the immediate societal framework. The Latin Grammar school with its emphasis on Latin and Greek represented a failure of secondary education to adjust to the demands of this new world. However, in a nonutilitarian sense the Latin Grammar school did provide a sense of continuity with the humanistic tradition of the Western world.

When the American colonists rose in rebellion against England, they were beginning to come to grips with the realities of this new environment. The struggles of the revolutionary generation of Americans, discussed in the following chapter, indicate the attempts by American intellectual leadership to fashion and direct an educational experience appropriate to the unique environment they had discovered.

Notes

[1] Lawrence A. Cremin, *American Education: The Colonial Experience, 1607-1783* (New York: Harper and Row, Publishers, 1970), pp. 135-136.

[2] Bernard Bailyn, *Education in the Forming of American Society* (New York: W.W. Norton and Co., 1972), p. 16.

[3] Stanford Fleming, *Children and Puritanism: The Place of Children in the Life and Thought of the New England Churches, 1620-1847* (New Haven: Yale University Press, 1933).

[4] H. Norman Gardiner, ed., *Selected Sermons of Jonathan Edwards* (New York: The Macmillan Company, 1904), p. 148.

[5] Nathaniel Shurtleff, ed., *Records of the Governor and Company of the Massachusetts Bay in New England* (Boston: n.p., 1853), II, 203.

[6] Paul Leicester Ford, ed., *The New England Primer* (New York: Dodd, Mead, and Co., 1899).

[7] In this description of the American South the author has condensed almost 150 years of southern history. Although the large plantation did not emerge immediately, the pattern already existed by the close of the seventeenth century. The southern white code evolved as an expression of racially conditioned mores and folkways in the period between the Revolution and the Civil War.

[8] Some plantation owners considered themselves to be the descendants of the Cavaliers, the English aristocrats who supported the Stuart cause against Cromwell's "Roundheads." According to the "Cavalier myth," these displaced aristocrats emigrated to the American South, where they re-established the old aristocratic way of life in the form of plantation society. Historically, the "Cavalier myth" is more legend than fact.

Selections to Accompany
Chapter 1

The life style of the New England colonist was permeated by the theology of John Calvin. Various ministers of the Gospel in the New World elaborated this theology and recast it in the New England form of Puritanism. Among the most famous of these divines was Jonathan Edwards. Although his writings are complex and deal with a variety of themes ranging from metaphysics to aesthetic experience, Edwards never strayed far from the Puritan intellectual and religious framework. It is important to interpret the New England educational experience in the light of this frame of reference. The selections which follow are taken from Edwards' sermon, ''Sinners in the Hands of an Angry God.''

Jonathan Edwards' Sinners in
the Hands of an Angry God

The God that holds you over the pit of hell, much as one holds a spider or some loathsome insect over the fire, abhors you, and is dreadfully provoked; his wrath towards you burns like fire; he looks upon you as worthy of nothing else, but to be cast into the fire; he is of purer eyes than to bear to have you in his sight; you are ten thousand times so abominable in his eyes, as the most hateful and venomous serpent is in ours. You have offended him infinitely more than ever a stubborn rebel did his prince: and yet it is nothing but his hand that holds you from falling into the fire every moment. 'Tis ascribed to nothing else, that you did not go to hell the last night; that you were suffered to awake again in this world after you closed your eyes to sleep; and there is no other reason to be given why you have not dropped into hell since you arose in the morning, but that God's hand has held you up. There is no other reason to be given why you han't gone to hell since you have sat here in the house of God, provoking his pure eyes by your sinful wicked manner of attending his solemn worship. Yea, there is nothing else that is to be given as a reason why you don't this very moment drop down into hell.

O sinner! consider the fearful danger you are in. 'Tis a great furnace of wrath, a wide and bottomless pit, full of the fire of wrath, that you are held

Source: H. Norman Gardiner, ed., *Selected Sermons of Jonathan Edwards* (New York: The Macmillan Company, 1904), pp. 88-89, 96-97.

over in the hand of that God whose wrath is provoked and incensed as much against you as against many of the damned in hell. You hang by a slender thread, with the flames of divine wrath flashing about it, and ready every moment to singe it and burn it asunder; and you have no interest in any Mediator, and nothing to lay hold of to save yourself, nothing to keep off the flames of wrath, nothing of your own, nothing that you ever have done, nothing that you can do, to induce God to spare you one moment.

• • •

And you that are young men and young women, will you neglect this precious season that you now enjoy, when so many others of your age are renouncing all youthful vanities and flocking to Christ? You especially have now an extraordinary opportunity; but if you neglect it, it will soon be with you as it is with those persons that spent away all the precious days of youth in sin and are now come to such a dreadful pass in blindness and hardness.

And you children that are unconverted, don't you know that you are going down to hell to bear the dreadful wrath of that God that is now angry with you every day and every night? Will you be content to be the children of the devil, when so many other children in the land are converted and are become the holy and happy children of the King of kings?

And let every one that is yet out of Christ and hanging over the pit of hell, whether they be old men and women or middleaged or young people or little children, now hearken to the loud calls of God's word and providence. This acceptable year of the Lord that is a day of such great favor to some will doubtless be a day of as remarkable vengeance to others. Men's hearts harden and their guilt increases apace at such a day as this, if they neglect their souls. And never was there so great danger of such persons being given up to hardness of heart and blindness of mind. God seems now to be hastily gathering in his elect in all parts of the land; and probably the bigger part of adult persons that ever shall be saved will be brought in now in a little time, and that it will be as it was on that great outpouring of the Spirit upon the Jews in the Apostles' days, the election will obtain and the rest will be blinded. If this, should be the case with you, you will eternally curse this day, and will curse the day that ever you was born to see such a season of the pouring out of God's Spirit, and will wish that you had died and gone to hell before you had seen it. Now undoubtedly it is as it was in the days of John the Baptist, the axe is in an extraordinary manner laid at the root of the trees, that every tree that bringeth not forth good fruit may be hewn down and cast into the fire.

Therefore let every one that is out of Christ now awake and fly from the wrath to come. The wrath of Almighty God is now undoubtedly hanging over a great part of this congregation. Let every one fly out of Sodom. *"Haste and escape for your lives, look not behind you, escape to the mountain, lest ye be consumed."*

New England Primer, *which first appeared in 1690, was one of the most popular and widely used textbooks in the colonial elementary school. Known as the "Little Bible of New England," it combined the basic rudiments of literacy and religious education. The selections reprinted here are the rhymes by which the New England school child mastered the letters of the alphabet.*

New England Primer

A
In Adam's Fall,
We sinned all.

B
Thy life to mend,
This Book attend.

C
The Cat doth play,
And after slay.

D
A Dog will bite
A thief at night.

E
An Eagle's flight
Is out of sight.

F
The idle Fool
Is whipped at school.

An Alphabet of Lessons for Youth.

A WISE son maketh a glad father, but a foolish son is the grief of his mother.

B ETTER is a little with the fear of the Lord, than great treasure, and trouble therewith.

C OME unto Christ, all ye who labor and are heavy laden, and he will give rest to your souls.

D O not the abominable thing which I hate, saith the Lord.

Source: *The New England Primer Improved*, or *An Easy and Pleasant Guide to the Art of Reading; to Which is Added the Assembly's Shorter Catechism* (Pittsburgh: United Presbyterian Board of Publication, n.d.). This is a nineteenth century reprinting of the original seventeenth century *Primer*.

G
As runs the Glass,
Our life doth pass.

H
My Book and Heart
Shall never part.

J
Job feels the rod,
Yet blessed his God.

K
Proud Korah's troop
Was swallowed up.

L
The Lion bold,
The Lamb doth hold.

M
The Moon gives light,
In time of night.

Alphabet of Lessons continued.

EXCEPT a man be born of the Spirit, he cannot see the kingdom of God.

FOOLISHNESS is bound up in the heart of a child, but the rod of correction will drive it far from him.

GRIEVE not the Holy Spirit, lest he depart from thee.

HOLINESS becometh the house of God forever, for verily the Lord is a holy God.

N
Nightingales sing
In time of Spring.

O
The royal Oak,
   It was the tree
That saved his
   Royal Majesty.

P
Peter denied
His Lord and cried.

Q
Queen Esther comes
   In royal state,
To save the Jews
   From dismal fate.

R
Rachel did mourn
For her first-born.

S
Samuel anoints,
Whom God appoints.

Alphabet of Lessons continued.

I T is good for me to draw near unto God. I will call upon him as long as I live.

J ESUS himself testified, that a prophet hath no honour in his own country.

K EEP thy heart with all diligence, for out of it are the issues of life.

L IARS will have their part in the lake which burns with fire and brimstone.

M AKE no friendship with an angry man, and with a furious man thou shalt not go.

T

Time cuts down all,
Both great and small.

U

Uriah's beauteous wife
Made David seek his life.

W

Whales in the sea,
God's voice obey.

X

Xerxes the great
Shared common fate.

Y

Youth forward slips.
Death soonest nips.

Z

Zaccheus he,
Did climb the Tree,
His Lord to see.

Alphabet of Lessons continued.

NOW is the accepted time; now is the day of salvation.

OUT of the abundance of the heart, the mouth speaketh.

PRAY to thy Father who is in secret, and thy Father who seeth in secret, shall reward thee openly.

QUIET minds are blessed with contentment.

JOHN ROGERS, minister of the Gospel in London, was the first martyr in Queen Mary's reign, and was burnt at Smithfield, February 14th, 1554. His wife, with nine small children, and one at her breast, followed him to the stake: with which sorrowful sight he was not the least daunted, but, with wonderful patience, died courageously for the gospel of Jesus Christ.

A few days before his Death, he wrote the following Advice to his children.

1 GIVE ear, my children, to my words,
    Whom God hath dearly bought;
Lay up his laws within your hearts,
    And print them in your thought.

2 I leave you here a little book,
    For you to look upon;
That you may see your father's face,
    When he is dead and gone:

3 Who for the hope of heavenly things,
    While he did here remain,
Gave over all his golden years
    To prison and to pain.

4 Where, bound with painful iron bands,
    Inclosed in the dark,
Not many days before his death
    He did compose this work.

5 And for example to your youth,
    To whom I wish all good,
I send you here God's perfect truth,
    And seal it with my blood.

Suggestions for Further Reading

Bailyn, Bernard. *Education in the Forming of American Society: Needs and Opportunities for Study*. New York: W.W. Norton and Co., 1972.

Cremin, Lawrence A. *American Education: The Colonial Experience 1607-1783*. New York: Harper and Row, Publishers, 1970.

Cohen, Sheldon S. *A History of Colonial Education: 1607-1776*. New York: John Wiley and Sons, Inc., 1974.

Fleming, Stanford. *Children and Puritanism: The Place of Children in the Life and Thought of the New England Churches, 1620-1847*. New Haven: Yale University Press 1933.

Ford, Paul L., ed. *The New England Primer*. New York: Dodd, Mead and Co., 1899.

Gardiner, H. Norman, ed. *Selected Sermons of Jonathan Edwards*. New York: The Macmillan Company, 1904.

Greven, Philip J. *Child-Rearing Concepts, 1628-1881: Historical Sources*. Itasca, IL: F.E. Peacock Publishers, Inc., 1973.

Johnson, Clifton. *Old-Time Schools and School Books*. New York: The Macmillan Company, 1904.

Kilpatrick, William H. *The Dutch Schools of New Netherland and Colonial New York*. Washington: Government Printing Office, 1912.

Knight, Edgar W. *A Documentary History of Education in the South Before 1860*. Chapel Hill: University of North Carolina Press, 1949.

Middlekauff, Robert. *Ancients and Axioms: Secondary Education in Eighteenth-Century New England*. New Haven: Yale University Press, 1963.

Morgan, Edmund S. *The Puritan Family: Religion and Domestic Relations in Seventeenth-Century New England*. New York: Harper and Row, Publishers, 1966.

Morison, Samuel Eliot. *The Intellectual Life of Colonial New England*. New York: New York University Press, 1956.

Chapter 2

Educational Patterns and Ideas During a Revolutionary Era

Introduction: Early Federal Period

The American Revolutionary period produced a generation of statesmen, who first broke the ties that bound them politically to the old order and then guided the new nation through the uncharted regions of a republican covenant. The Declaration of Independence and the Constitution gave form and direction to the new political order. The leaders of this revolutionary generation realized that a republic of self-governing citizens would function effectively only if such a government rested on a firm foundation in the education of its citizens. If there was a system of education proper to monarchy, then there was one appropriate to free men. Benjamin Franklin and Thomas Jefferson were foremost among those who sought to assess the condition of education and plan the reforms needed to assure the continuing existence of the United States as a sovereign and independent nation.

After the American Revolution brought the colonial period to an end, the thirteen colonies became integrated in the emerging national consciousness of the early republican period. The United States was an experiment in political forms being cast in a new environment, as new social and political institutions were constructed by the republican government. While the colonial forms of education persisted into the republican era, there was much theorizing over the institutional organization and curricular content that education should adopt as a means of introducing people to a new government and cultural experience. A major part of this theorizing centered about the problem of how to replace the old loyalties with a set of values and commitments based on the new concept of self-government. As the intellectual leaders of an independent and sovereign nation, Jefferson, Franklin and Webster were concerned with developing a feeling of American cultural identity in the nation's citizens and in their offspring. Many of the proposals offered for republican education revealed a strong propensity toward cultural nationalism. The American revolution had won political independence for the thirteen colonies. Now, it was necessary to weld these states into a nation by establishing their cultural independence from Europe and its aristocratic ways.

Under the Articles of Confederation, one of the infant Congress' major problems was that of administering the Northwest Territory. To encourage the settlement of this area, the first Northwest Ordinance was adopted in 1785. This Ordinance called for the territory to be surveyed and divided into townships of six square miles each, which were then subdivided into thirty-six sections. The income derived from the sixteenth section was to be set aside for school funds. Although much of this income was dissipated, the precedent for the establishment of school funds was set. The Ordinance of 1787 encouraged education as "necessary to good government and the happiness of mankind." Although the Ordinances of 1785 and 1787 predated state ratification of the federal Constitution, they contained elements that would have continuing significance for education. The federal government had expressed a concern for the support of educational institutions that anticipated the programs of assistance adopted in the late nineteenth and twentieth centuries.

Although land was reserved for school support, the federal Congress avoided making specific injunctions as to how the funds derived from this land should be administered. This lack of specific directive resulted from widespread fear of centralizing educational powers in a federal authority. Throughout the eighteenth and nineteenth centuries education remained localized and decentralized.

The United States Constitution, ratified in 1789, did not mention education. Under the "reserved powers clause" of the Tenth Amendment in the Bill of Rights, the responsibilities and prerogatives of education remained vested in the individual states of the Union. Following the New England tradition of controlling education through the township, most of the states delegated substantial educational powers to local school districts. Although education remained a state function, local school districts and school boards thus gained

Commencement of Hostilities. Bishop Davenport, *History of the United States* (Philadelphia: William Marshall & Co., 1833), p. 31. Davenport's early nineteenth century history textbook is interesting for its application of the catechetical question and answer method of instruction to the teaching of history.

CHAPTER VII.

COMMENCEMENT OF HOSTILITIES.

Q. What occasioned the battle of Lexington?

A. In April, 1775, Colonel Smith and Major Pitcairn were sent with a body of troops to destroy the military stores which had been collected at Concord, about twenty miles from Boston. At Lexington, the militia were collected to oppose the incursion of the British troops.

Q. Were the Lexington militia successful in their opposition?

A. No: they were dispersed, and eight of their number killed.

Q. When did the battle of Lexington take place?

A. On the 19th of April, 1775: here was shed the first blood in the American Revolution.

Q. What did the Americans do immediately after the battle of Lexington?

A. They commenced the enlistment of regular soldiers.

Q. Where was the congress of Massachusetts in session at the time of the battle of Lexington?

A. At Watertown, ten miles from Boston.

Q. What did it vote?

A. That thirty thousand men should be raised in the New-England colonies.

Washington Before the Revolution. D.H. Montgomery, *The Leading Facts of American History* (Boston: Ginn & Co., Publishers, 1892). Illustrations of the first President of the United States were common in the nineteenth century history textbooks.

WASHINGTON BEFORE THE REVOLUTION.

the initiative in matters of educational support and control. The great qualitative and quantitative variations that have developed since then in American public schools reflect local districts' ability to suppport education.

The absence of provision for education in the Constitution has been used as an argument to block federal involvement by the opponents of federal aid to education. Although the system of local control has persisted, many Americans have become increasingly aware of the importance of education to the nation as a whole. The large-scale federal programs of assistance enacted in the twentieth century are evidence of this.

Plans for an American System of Education

Although the federal government did not create a national system of American education, many writers on education recommended a new approach to schooling in the Republic.

Meanwhile, numerous plans for a national system of education were suggested. While many of the proposals formulated during the early republican era were never actually carried out, the educational theories of such men as Benjamin Rush, Robert Coram, Samuel Knox, and Samuel Smith did contribute to the nineteenth-century development of the common school.[1]

The concepts of "nationalism" and "science" were constant themes in the writings of the American intellectuals of the late eighteenth and early nineteenth centuries. Writers such as Benjamin Rush recognized that a residue of old loyalty to England on the part of many people might delay the development of a sense of identification with the United States. A feeling of nationalism might also be impeded by regional loyalties that were allowed to take precedence over national commitment. The cultivation of a sense of American identity meant the building of a common commitment and loyalty to the United States as all independent and sovereign nation.

The concept of a "scientific attitude" was based upon the intellectual ferment of the eighteen century Enlightenment, which was rooted in the basic conviction that people could discover the laws of the universe through the instrument of science. A "scientific attitude" called for open-minded objectivity and willingness to experiment. Old loyalties and commitments had to be examined and if necessary altered or abolished in the light of scientific discovery. The generation of the revolutionary age believed that "science" applied to social and political relationships as well as to natural and physical reality. If people were willing to experiment and to look to the future rather than to rely on the past, then a better and more progressive society would result. Closely allied to the "scientific attitude" was the notion of "progress." If guided by scientific principles instead of ignorance, then improvement of both people and society would inevitably follow.

The American intellectuals of the revolutionary era fused the concepts of "nationalism" and "science" into an ideal which they believed appropriate for adoption as a guiding principle in the United States. As the Revolution had swept away the old political order, so a revolutionary system of education could likewise remove anti-science prejudices from the American mind. Benjamin Rush, urging a unique brand of education that would reinforce the principle of patriotism, suggested that the federal government should set up an educational structure that would remain flexible enough to absorb constant modifications. Such a national system, Rush said, should be directed toward the building of an attitude distinctively American and scientific.

Robert Coram, in 1791, called attention to the economic basis of educational support. There was a great deal of variation in the ability of local communities to support their schools. Because they were poorly endowed, the rural schools were inferior to the more prosperous urban schools. Stressing the intimate relationship between educational opportunity and social, political, and economic equality, Coram strongly advocated a uniformly supported system of national education. Samuel Knox proposed an educational plan that would combine instruction in classical humanities and American nationalism. Another theorist, Samuel Smith, saw education as providing a means of social control. Smith believed that the United States had a mission to serve as the model of democracy for the rest of the world. These, however, were only various points of emphasis in the plans presented to the American Philosophical Society; actually, there were two major areas of agreement among this group: one, that a national system of education should be used to establish and promote a distinctive American culture; and two, that an educational commitment to the scientific attitude would promote progress.

For Rush, Coram, Smith, and Knox, old-world customs and attitudes clearly failed to provide an adequate foundation for the loyalties and creative intelligence necessary for the proper administration of the new government. Realizing that a system of education was called for that could serve the unique needs of the American people, such philosopher-statesmen as Benjamin Franklin and Thomas Jefferson each formulated plans for the development of such a system. These plans reveal the intimate relationship which both men felt existed between education and the social and political order. Although Franklin's plan was actually proposed before the Revolution, it was a revolutionary plan in that it recognized the unique conditions of the American environment in the light of changing social and economic patterns. Jefferson's plan was introduced during the years of the Revolution, and it demonstrated clearly the emphasis placed on educating the new kind of citizen — men capable of self-government.

Benjamin Franklin. D.H. Montgomery, *The Leading Facts of American History* (Boston: Ginn & Co., Publishers, 1892). Franklin was author of a plan to create an English grammar school in Philadelphia.

BENJAMIN FRANKLIN.

Franklin's Educational Plan

Benjamin Franklin's life has come to be considered as archetypical of the opportunities available to the new class of economic entrepreneurs in North America. Franklin's career reveals a largely self-educated individual and a self-made businessman who succeeded because of his own common sense, inventiveness, and initiative. A inventor, statesman, and home-spun philosopher, Franklin was a person who preferred innovative experimentation to the security of the status quo.

Franklin was the son of Josiah Franklin, a small businessman who manufactured soap in Boston. Benjamin Franklin's formal education consisted of a few private reading and writing lessons and one year in the Boston Grammar School. More important in Franklin's education than formal schooling was his practical training as an apprentice to his brother in the printing business. An avid reader, Franklin's self-education led him to read the books of Locke, DeFoe, Bunyon and other significant authors. In particular, John Locke's empirical theory of knowledge had a strong impact on him. Locke's assertion that ideas were based on direct sensory experience rather than being present innately in the mind was put into practice by Franklin, the scientist and inventor. One of Franklin's guiding principles was that there should be no separation between theory and practice in either life or education. His many educational projects reflected this belief that ideas needed to be tested and judged by their consequences.

As one of Philadelphia's prominent residents, Franklin devoted considerable effort to organizing and participating in societies that contributed to intellectual and social improvement.[2] Franklin helped organize the Junto, a discussion club that debated current scientific, educational, and political ideas. Believing in the importance of self-education, he organized a voluntary subscription society to support a lending library for Philadelphia. In 1743, he helped to organize the American Philosophical Society to stimulate and support research in the natural sciences. For Franklin, these organizations brought together like-minded persons to discuss matters of intellectual, scientific, and political importance. As a person who enjoyed and learned from lively conversation, Franklin was comfortable and intellectually stimulated by the company of gifted scientists and philosophers. At a time when institutions of higher education were dominated by the ancient classical languages and theology, these associations promoted a lively nonformal education that made Philadelphia the leading scientific center of colonial America.

In addition to his scientific interests, Franklin, a public man, also was involved in politics. From 1753 to 1774, he served as the Post Master General of the colonies. In 1774, he proposed the Albany Plan of Union to unite the colonists against the French and Indian threat. While Franklin's plan did not suggest the independence of the colonies, it sought to arouse in the colonists the feelings that they were a common American people, with a distinctive identity rather than colonial provincials living in a disconnected string of minor settlements. Franklin made a major contribution to the United States by his service as the new republic's ambassador to France. Through his tactful diplomacy, he succeeded in gaining French recognition of the United States as an independent and sovereign nation. He also secured a military alliance with France that was crucial in winning the war for independence from Great Britain. As an elder statesman, Franklin was a delegate from Pennsylvania to the Constitutional convention in 1787. He played an important role in devising and winning support for the various compromises that led to the United States' Constitution.

In addition to his scientific activities and record of national service, Franklin was interested in education. His *Poor Richard's Almanack* put forth a lively, common sense, and home spun philosophy of life. The admonitions of Poor Richard epitomized the practical and utilitarian values of frugality, diligence, hard work, and thrift that characterized the rising American middle class of merchants, tradesmen, and entrepreneurs.

Although a self-educated man who learned largely from his own efforts, Franklin valued formal education or schooling. He had a strong antagonism to traditional Latin Grammar schools and colleges which, in their emphasis on the ancient Greek and Latin languages, completely neglected science and other useful subjects. In 1749, Franklin in his *Proposals Relating to the Education of Youth in Pensilvania* announced a plan to establish an English language grammar school in Philadelphia. Franklin's *Proposals* sought to: one, establish a school in which English and not Latin would be used in instruction; two, devise a curriculum that emphasized scientific knowledge and utilitarian skills; and three, prepare students to make useful contributions to society, politics, the occupations, and the professions.

In its theoretical outline, Benjamin Franklin's educational plan combined two basic elements of study, the humanistic and the utilitarian; the relative merits of these twin functions of education still vex administrators today. In his person and in his attitudes Franklin represented the growing middle class of businessmen and professionals who were becoming impatient with the inherited traditions and institutions that favored the landed aristocracy of the old order. The new class wanted an educational system that would serve practical and utilitarian ends. At the same time, Franklin realized that if American education were to reflect the American dream of progress and opportunity for all, it needed to stimulate a feeling of nationalism that would break down the colonial provincialism that had hitherto divided Americans. Franklin also emphasized the need for Americans to develop a scientific outlook to aid in national development.

In 1749, Franklin proposed a curriculum for the education of Pennsylvania youth that, in effect, constituted a program of studies for an English Grammar school as opposed to the old Latin Grammar school.[3] Instead of the narrow classical studies of the Latin Grammar school, his plan called for a broad and practical curriculum that would emphasize both ethical and professional elements. Values were stressed equally with skills and knowledge.

Recognizing the relationship between effective education and the school environment, Franklin's plans for the new English Grammar School included a consideration of the physical facilities. There was to be a library containing books and periodicals, a laboratory with scientific equipment, and workshops for the various trades. Unlike the crude and uncomfortable schools of the eighteenth century, Franklin's proposed school was to be a comfortable, well-lighted, ventilated and heated building. The building, itself, was to be located in a pleasant natural setting with gardens.

The proposed curriculum encompassed many subjects and resembled the modern comprehensive high school. English grammar, classics, composition, rhetoric, and public speaking were a part of language studies; but the important distinction was that classes were to be conducted in English, the vernacular of trade and daily life, rather than in Latin. Utilitarian crafts were also included: carpentry, shipbuilding engraving, printing, painting, cabinetmaking, carving, and gardening. Although Franklin referred to these areas as elementary art works, they were actually vocational skills.

Mathematics was to be offered as a practical subject rather than as strictly theoretical study. Mathematical studies included arithmetic, geometry, astronomy, and accounting. History was to supply students with exemplars or models based upon the lives of famous historical figures. Greek, Roman, English, and colonial history were offered, with emphasis on the moral lessons they supplied.

Although English was the language spoken, and the first one taught, students could elect a second language according to anticipated vocational needs. Latin and Greek might be studied by prospective ministers; Latin, Greek, and French by physicians; French, German, and Spanish by merchants. Other subjects in the curriculum were natural science, agriculture, technology, physical education, and character education.

Franklin's plan for an English school, a revolutionary educational proposal for its times, is historically significant. It proposed an English language alternative to the Latin Grammar school that foreshadowed the nineteenth century academy and the twentieth century high school. His argument for including science and vocational subjects into the curriculum anticipated the direction that American education would take in the late nineteenth and early twentieth centuries.

As an actual operating institution, however, Franklin's school, while it was established, was not given a fair trial. After a short time in operation, the school closed. Most likely, the headmaster, or principal, who conducted the school was unprepared to implement the needed innovations.

In the history of American education, Franklin's proposals reflected the trends of the revolutionary and early national periods and also anticipated the future. His emphasis on scientific and utilitarian subjects and methods were a noticeable departure from the inherited European classical tradition. Franklin's proposals pointed to the creation of a comprehensive educational institution that would provide students with a curriculum appropriate to the economic needs of a developing nation.

Thomas Jefferson's Plan of Education

Unlike Franklin, Thomas Jefferson (1743-1826) enjoyed both social and formal educational opportunities. Born of a prosperous plantation family, in Virginia's Albemarle County in 1743, Jefferson attended the local English vernacular and Latin Grammar schools. His formal education was completed with his graduation from William and Mary College. He was honored as a distinguished man of letters by election to the American Academy of Arts and Sciences, and served as president of the American Philosophical Society from 1797 to 1815. As a leading statesman during the formative republican period, Jefferson held the positions of member of the Virginia legislature, delegate to the Continental Congress, Governor of Virginia, Minister to France, Secretary of State, Vice President and President.[4]

While Thomas Jefferson is usually remembered as the author of the Declaration of Independence and as the third President of the United States, he was an educational theorist as well as a statesman. He often said that his epitaph should refer to only three of his accomplishments: writing both the Declaration of Independence and the Virginia Bill of Rights, and founding the University of Virginia.

In 1779 Jefferson introduced into the Virginia legislature a "Bill for the More General Diffusion of Knowledge."[5] Implicit in his proposal were three assumptions: first, that republican government and democratic decision-making required an educated and literate citizenry; second, that education should be a political rather than a religious function; third, that educational control should be vested in state governments. It was significant that the proposals of both Jefferson and Franklin implied a shift in emphasis from the religiously oriented education of the colonial period to the more secular approach that characterized the later development of American public education.

Thomas Jefferson. Charles F. Horne, ed. *Great Men and Famous Women, IV* (New York: Selmar Hess, Publisher, 1894), p. 257. Jefferson, a future U.S. President, introduced a plan of public education while serving in the Virginia legislature.

School Units in Jefferson's Plan

According to Jefferson's plan, the counties of Virginia were to be subdivided into wards and each ward was to support an elementary school. The school was to provide instruction in reading, writing, arithmetic, and the history of Greece, Rome, England, and America. The teacher was to be supported by the school district. All white children in the district were to attend the ward school for three years of publicly financed elementary education. After three years, the parents could maintain the enrollment of their children in the school by paying tuition. The significance of Jefferson's plan was that each white child in the state was provided with an elementary education, even though it was a limited one.

Jefferson also recommended the establishment of twenty grammar (secondary) schools in the state of Virginia.[6] The supervisor of each district would select the most able student in every elementary school who was unable to pay the tuition for the grammar school. These scholarship students were to continue in the grammar school for two to three years, where they would study Latin, Greek, English, geography and higher mathematics. The most promising student from among this group would then receive an additional six years of education and the rest of the class be dismissed. The highest ranking twenty students, selected annually, would continue as far as the grammar school education extended. At the end of this period, half would be dismissed to become teachers in the elementary schools and the remaining ten would go on to higher studies at the College of William and Mary.

The significance of Jefferson's proposal, which was never enacted, lies in its educational content and perspective. Jefferson wanted education to exercise a sifting function, by selecting the most able citizens through the schools and preparing them for leadership roles in the new society. His proposal contained both democratic and elitist elements: first, it was democratic in that it provided for the education of all (white) children at least on a rudimentary level; second, it recommended a publicly supported and publicly controlled education system; third, it was selective in that it tended to produce an intellectual elite; fourth, although it was an improvement over existing conditions, the educational advantage would remain in the hands of the economically wealthy, in that all of this group could stay in school as long as they wished providing they could pay for their education.

Webster: Pioneer of American Schooling

The career of Noah Webster (1758-1843) as an educator paralleled important trends in educational theory and practice in the United States from the revolutionary era to the establishment of common schools in the nineteenth century. Renowned as the "father of American grammar and the American dictionary," Webster was born in Connecticut and attended the local district school in West Hartford. After completing his higher education at Yale College, he taught in district elementary schools. Although he was later admitted to the bar as an attorney, Webster did not practice law. He devoted his life to promoting an Americanized form of the English language and to writing on educational topics.[7]

Webster was a convinced proponent of American cultural nationalism. For him, cultural nationalism meant that a people, especially the citizens of the new American republic, should develop their own unique forms of culture. Literature, poetry, the arts, and other forms of cultural expression should express national feelings and sentiments. For Webster, the achievement of political independence from Great Britain was only the first step in creating a new nation. The United States had to achieve its cultural independence from the old world of Europe, with its outmoded aristocratic way of thinking. Webster argued enthusiastically for the cultural separation of American from foreign attitudes. A proponent of a "self-conscious" American nationalism, he argued that a system of education should be created in the new republic that would advance a purely American culture. Like the other theorists of the early national period, he claimed that the most effective means of national development required the "general diffusion of science" among the American people.[8]

Webster realized that the thread of unity that had brought the citizens of the various states together in their struggle for independence from Britain was still weak. He believed that a common language would be a potent force in encouraging a sense of national unity to overcome the tendencies to sectional and regional separatism. Webster worked to establish a uniquely American form of the English language that would be uniform throughout the states and regions that comprised the United States. A uniform national language would be, he reasoned, an important instrument in creating a distinctive American character and identity. Webster was an acute observer of the power that language has in transmitting both knowledge and values. He also understood that schools as important agencies for language instruction were both knowledge and value transmitting institutions.

Seeing an important connection between nationalism and political independence, Webster argued that "a national language" was the "bond of national union." He wanted to develop a uniquely American language and literature.[9] Believing that an American identity could be created through a distinctive national language and literature, Webster worked to reshape the English language used in the United States into a uniquely American language. A genuine American language would eliminate the remnants of European usage. It would free American speech from localism and provincialism and promote linguistic uniformity. A uniquely American language would serve as the linguistic mortar of national union. To encourage language uniformity, he believed that his proposed American language needed to become the standard language used throughout the United States. It would have to be taught deliberately and systematically to the young in the nation's schools. As they learned the standard American language, children would also learn to think, believe, and act as Americans.

Once again, Webster, thinking as a school master, realized that the teaching of a standard form of the English language in America required a supply of standardized textbooks that could be used in the schools. He, thus, set out to write a series of such textbooks. To advance his cause for an American language, Webster wanted the textbooks to be free of a pro-British orientation. Webster published his *A Grammatical Institute of the English Language*, containing a speller, a grammar, and a reader in 1783. Later editions were simply called, *The American Speller* and the *Elementary Spelling Book*, commonly referred to as the "Blue-Back Speller" or "Webster's Old Spelling Book."[10]

In his books, Webster sought to develop a standard American pronunciation and an effective method of instructing children in the language. Standard pronunciation, for Webster, meant pronunciation used by the "most accurate scholars and literary gentlemen" which are free of those "odious distinctions of provincial dialects, which are the objects of reciprocal ridicule in the United States."[11] Webster's textbooks, especially his spelling books, were very popular and used in schools throughout the United States. It is estimated that fifteen million copies of his speller were sold by 1837.

The early editions of Webster's textbooks emphasized nationalistic themes. Once the republican ideology was clearly established in the United States, later editions stressed a more conservative value orientation. Webster now saw language and schooling as means of social stability and control rather than of social change.[12] Stressing obedience, loyalty, and duty to established authorities, Webster, now, saw schooling as a means of social control to develop discipline and order. When schools are used as agencies of social control, this means that they impose the beliefs and values of the dominant or ruling class on those who have a lower socioeconomic status.

Webster's textbooks encouraged an emphasis in American schools on public speaking, oratory, and elocution, skills which were esteemed among Americans. The stress on public speaking reflected the general American enthusiasm for the ministry and the legal profession which required oratorical abilities. Oratory, of course, was important in political campaigns in a democratic society.

After twenty-five years of research and writing, Webster completed his great work, the *American Dictionary of the English Language*. Published in 1825, the *American Dictionary* contained 70,000 entries. Webster hoped that his dictionary would correct the errors that originated from a "misunderstanding of words."[13]

Webster was both an educational theoretician and a practitioner. His theory sought to promote sense of cultural nationalism among the recently united and newly independent Americans. Language, for him, was the great vehicle for creating a sense of cultural commonality throughout the states and regions of the new republic. To achieve standardization in schools, he wrote a series of textbooks to aid in the process of language learning.

Conclusion

The educational plans of Franklin, Jefferson, Webster, and the other theorists of the early national period called for a new kind of civic education that was suited to the economic, social, and political needs of the new republic. Although the ideas expressed by these theorists were not put into practice immediately, they reflected a common desire to educate citizens who could effectively participate in a republican society. These plans were designed to build a nation and to bind its people together in a commonly shared political covenant. Franklin's proposal for a more utilitarian curriculum was an early plan to enlist education in the cause of economic development. Jefferson's proposal sought to provide a common education for the general population and to identify an intellectually-capable elite for positions of responsibility in the new republic. Webster worked to develop a common language to raise American's cultural consciousness and unity.

Notes

[1] Allen O. Hansen, *Liberalism and American Education in the Eighteenth Century* (New York: The Macmillan Company, 1926).

[2] For a well-done biography of Franklin, see Edmond Wright, *Franklin of Philadelphia* (Cambridge, MA: Harvard University Press, 1988).

[3] A discussion of Franklin's proposals can be found in the following: John H. Best, ed., *Benjamin Franklin on Education* (New York: Bureau of Publications, Teachers College, Columbia University, 1962); Robert Ulich, *History of Educational Thought* (New York: American Book Company, 1945); and Merle Curti, *The Social Ideas of American Educators* (New York: Littlefield, Adams Co., 1960), which contains sections on both Franklin and Jefferson.

4 For a well-written biography of Jefferson, see Noble E. Cunningham, Jr. *In Pursuit of Reason: The Life of Thomas Jefferson* (Baton Rouge: Louisiana State University Press, 1987).

5 Jefferson's educational ideas are analyzed in Gordon C. Lee, "Learning and Liberty: The Jeffersonian Tradition in Education," *Crusade Against Ignorance: Thomas Jefferson on Education* (New York: Bureau of Publications, Teachers College, Columbia University, 1962).

6 During the colonial and Revolutionary periods, a "grammar school" referred to a preparatory school. This was in contrast to the "elementary" or "vernacular" school which provided the basic tools of reading, writing, and arithmetic. During the nineteenth century, however, the "common school" was so frequently referred to as a "grammar school" that a grammar school education was usually understood as an elementary education. However, for Jefferson, a "grammar school" provided education that was college preparatory in nature.

7 Harry R. Warfel, *Noah Webster: Schoolmaster to America* (New York: Macmillan Co., 1936), p. 9. Also, see Erwin C. Shoemaker, *Noah Webster, Pioneer of Learning* (New York: Columbia University Press, 1936), p. 21.

8 Shoemaker, p. 44, p. 6.

9 Henry Steele Commager, "Schoolmaster to America," in *Noah Webster's American Spelling Book* (New York: Bureau of Publications, Teachers College, Columbia University, 1958), p. 6.

10 Shoemaker, pp. 67-70.

11 Noah Webster, *A Grammatical Institute of the English Language*, Part I (1783) (Menston, U.K.: The Scholar Press, 1968), p. 6.

12 Richard M. Rollins, "Words as Social Control: Noah Webster and the Creation of the *American Dictionary*," *American Quarterly*, XXVIII (Fall 1976), pp. 415-430.

13 Rollins, p. 424.

Selections to Accompany
Chapter 2

Foremost among Benjamin Franklin's convictions about the development of American education was his belief that it was necessary for English to be the language of instruction. Stressing utility, he felt that concentration on Latin and Greek as the languages of learning ill prepared Americans to harness a wilderness environment. Too much time was wasted in the study of dead languages. Second, he believed, like Noah Webster, that the evolution of an American form of English as a common language would serve to provide a greater sense of community in the New World. Third, Franklin felt that English as a common language would facilitate the assimilation of foreign language groups. He believed this to be a matter of special concern for Pennsylvania with its large concentration of German-speaking residents. The selection which follows was first attached as an appendix, written by Franklin, to a sermon preached by the Reverend Richard Peters on January 7, 1751. In it Franklin presented his proposed plan of instruction for an English Grammar school.

Franklin's Idea of an English School

It is expected that every Scholar to be admitted into this School, be at least able to pronounce and divide the Syllables in Reading, and to write a legible Hand. None to be receiv'd that are under ( ) Years of Age.

First or Lowest Class

Let the first Class learn the *English Grammar* Rules, and at the same time let particular Care be taken to improve them in *Orthography*. Perhaps the latter is best done by *Pairing* the Scholars, two of those nearest equal in their Spelling to he put together; let these strive for Victory, each propounding Ten Words

SOURCE: Leonard Labaree et al., eds., *The Papers of Benjamin Franklin* (New Haven: Yale University Press, 1961), IV, 102-8. Reprinted by permission of Yale University Press.

every Day to the other to be spelt. He that spells truly most of the other's Words, is Victor for that Day; he that is Victor most Days in a Month, to obtain a Prize, a pretty neat Book of some Kind useful in their future Studies. This Method fixes the Attention of Children extremely to the Orthography of Words, and makes them good Spellers very early. 'Tis a Shame for a Man to be so ignorant of this little Art, in his own Language, as to be perpetually confounding Words of like Sound and different Significations; the Consciousness of which Defect, makes some Men, otherwise of good Learning and Understanding, averse to Writing even a common Letter.

Let the Pieces read by the Scholars in this Class be short, such as Croxall's Fables, and little Stories. In giving the Lesson, let it he read to them; let the Meaning of the difficult words in it be explained to them, and let them con it over by themselves before they are called to read to the Master, or Usher; who is to take particular Care that they do not read too fast, and that they duly observe the Stops and Pauses. A Vocabulary of the most usual difficult Words might be formed for their Use, with Explanations; and they might daily get a few of those Words and Explanations by Heart, which would a little exercise their Memories; or at least they might write a Number of them in a small Book for the Purpose, which would help to fix the Meaning of those Words in their Minds, and at the same Time furnish every one with a little dictionary for his future Use.

The Second Class to be Taught

Reading with Attention, and with proper Modulations of the Voice according to the Sentiments and Subject.

Some short Pieces, not exceeding the Length of a *Spectator*, to be given this Class as Lessons (and some of the easier *Spectators* would he very suitable for the Purpose). These lessons might be given over Night as Tasks, the Scholars to study them against the Morning. Let it then be required of them to give an Account first of the Parts of Speech, and Construction of one or two Sentences; this will oblige them to recur frequently to their Grammar, and fix its principal Rules in their Memory. Next of the *Intention* of Writer, or the *Scope* of the Piece; the Meaning of each Sentence, and of every uncommon Word. This would early acquaint them with the Meaning and Force of Words, and give them that most necessary Habit, of Reading with Attention.

The Master then to read the Piece with the proper Modulations of Voice, due Emphasis, and suitable Action, where Action is required; and put the Youth on imitating his Manner.

Where the Author has us'd an Expression not the best, let it be pointed out; and let his Beauties be particularly remarked to the Youth.

Let the Lessons for Reading be varied, that the Youth may be made acquainted with good Stiles of all Kinds in Prose and Verse, and the proper Manner of reading each Kind. Sometimes a well-told Story, a Piece of a Sermon, a General's Speech to his Soldiers, a Speech in a Tragedy, some Part of a Comedy, an Ode, a Satyr, a Letter, Blank Verse, Hudibrastick, Heroic, &c. But let such lessons for Reading be chosen, as contain some useful Instruction, whereby the Understandings or Morals of the Youth, may at the same Time be improv'd.

It is requir'd that they should first study and understand the Lessons, before they are put upon reading them properly, to which End each Boy should have an English Dictionary to help him over Difficulties. When our Boys read English to us, we are apt to imagine *they* understand what *they* read because *we* do, and because 'tis their Mother Tongue. But they often read as Parrots speak, knowing little or nothing of the Meaning. And it is impossible a Reader should give the due Modulation to his Voice, and pronounce properly, unless his Understanding goes before his Tongue, and makes him Master of the Sentiment. Accustoming Boys to read aloud what they do not first understand, is the Cause of those even set Tones so common among Readers, which when they have once got a Habit of using, they find so difficult to correct: By which Means, among Fifty Readers we scarcely find a good One. For want of good Reading, Pieces publish'd with a View to influence the Minds of Men for their own or the publick Benefit, lose Half their Force. Were there but one good Reader in a Neighbourhood, a publick Orator might be heard throughout a Nation with the same Advantages, and have the same Effect on his Audience, as if they stood within the Reach of his Voice.

The Third Class to be Taught

Speaking properly and gracefully, which is near of Kin to good Reading, and naturally follows it in the Studies of Youth. Let the Scholars of this Class begin with learning the Elements of Rhetoric from some short System, so as to be able to give an Account of the most usual Tropes and Figures. Let all their bad Habits of Speaking, all Offences against good Grammar, all corrupt or foreign Accents, and all improper Phrases, be pointed out to them. Short Speechs from the Roman or other History, or from our *Parliamentary Debates*, might be got by heart, and deliver'd with the proper Action, &c. Speeches and Scenes in our best Tragedies and Comedies (avoiding every Thing that could injure the Morals of Youth) might likewise be got by Rote, and the Boys exercis'd in delivering or acting them; great Care being taken to form their Manner after the truest Models.

For their farther improvement, and a little to vary their Studies let them now begin to read *History*, after having got by Heart a short Table of the principal Epochs in Chronology. They may begin with Rollin's *Antient and*

Roman Histories, and proceed at proper Hours as they go thro' the subsequent Classes, with the Best Histories of our own Nation and Colonies. Let Emulation be excited among the Boys by giving, Weekly, little Prizes, or other small Encouragements to those who are able to give the best Account of what they have read, as to Times, Places, Names of Persons, &c. This will make them read with Attention, and imprint the History well in their Memories. In remarking on the History, the Master will have fine Opportunities of instilling Instruction of various Kinds, and improving the Morals as well as the Understandings of Youth.

The Natural and Mechanic History contain'd in *Spectacle de la Nature*, might also be begun in this Class, and continued thro' the subsequent Classes by other Books of the same Kind: For next to the Knowledge of *Duty*, this Kind of Knowledge is certainly the most useful, as well as the most entertaining. The Merchant may thereby be enabled better to understand many Commodities in Trade; the Handicraftsman to improve his Business by new Instruments, Mixtures and Materials; and frequently Hints are given of new Manufactures, or new Methods of improving Land, that may be set on foot greatly to the Advantage of a Country.

The Fourth Class to be Taught

Composition. Writing one's own Language well is the next necessary Accomplishment after good Speaking. 'Tis the Writing-Master's Business to take Care that the Boys make fair Characters, and place them straight and even in the Lines: But to *form their Stile*, and even to take Care that the Stops and Capitals are properly disposed, is the Part of the English Master. The Boys should be put on Writing Letters to each other on any common Occurrences, and on various Subjects, imaginary Business, &c. containing little Stories, Accounts of their late Reading, what Parts of Authors please them, and why. Letters of Congratulation, of Compliment, of Request, of Thanks, of Recommendation, of Admonition, of Consolation, of Expostulation, Excuse, &c. In these they should be taught to express themselves clearly, concisely, and naturally, without affected Words, or high-flown Phrases. All their Letters to pass through the Master's Hand, who is to point out the Faults, advise the Corrections, and commend what he finds right. Some of the best Letters published in our own Language, as Sir William Temple's, those of Pope, and his Friends, and some others, might be set before the Youth as Models, their Beauties pointed out and explained by the Master, the Letters themselves transcrib'd by the Scholar.

Dr. Johnson's *Ethices Elementa*, or first Principles of Morality, may now be read by the Scholars, and explain'd by the Master, to lay a solid Foundation of Virtue and Piety in their Minds. And as this Class continues the Reading of History, let them now at proper Hours receive some farther Instructions in Chronology, and in that Part of Geography (from the Mathematical Master) which is necessary to understand the Maps and Globes. They should also be acquainted with the modern Names of the Places they find mention'd in antient Writers. The Exercises of good Reading and Proper Speaking still continued at suitable Times.

Fifth Class

To improve the Youth in *Composition*, they may now, besides continuing to write Letters, begin to write little Essays in Prose; and sometimes in Verse, not to make them Poets, but for this Reason, that nothing acquaints a Lad so speedily with Variety of Expression, as the Necessity of finding such Words and Phrases as will suit with the Measure, Sound and Rhime of Verse, and at the same Time well express the Sentiment. These Essays should all pass under the Master's Eye, who will point out their Faults, and put the Writer on correcting them. Where the Judgment is not ripe enough for forming new Essays, let the Sentiments of a *Spectator* be given, and requir'd to be cloath'd in a Scholar's own Words; or the Circumstances of some good story, the Scholar to find Expression. Let them be put sometimes on abridging a Paragraph of a diffuse Author, sometimes on dilating or amplifying what is wrote more closely. And now let Dr. Johnson's *Noetica*, or first Principles of human Knowledge, containing a Logic, or Art of Reasoning, &c. be read by the Youth, and the Difficulties that may occur to them be explained by the Master. The Reading of History, and the Exercises of good Reading and just Speaking still continued.

Sixth Class

In this Class, besides continuing the Studies of the preceding, in History, Rhetoric, Logic, Moral and Natural Philosophy, the best English Authors may be read and explain'd; as Tillotson, Milton, Locke, Addison, Pope, Swift, the higher Papers in the *Spectator* and *Guardian*, the best Translations of Homer, Virgil and Horace, of *Telemachus, Travels of Cyrus*, &c.

Once a Year, let there be publick Exercises in the Hall, the Trustees and Citizens present. Then let fine gilt Books be given as Prizes to such Boys as distinguish themselves, and excel the others in any Branch of Learning; making three Degrees of Comparison; giving the best Prize to him that performs best; a less valuable One to him that comes up next to the best; and another to the third. Commendations, Encouragement and Advice to the rest; keeping up their Hopes that by Industry they may excel another Time. The Names of those that obtain the Prizes to be yearly printed in a List.

The Hours of each Day are to be divided and dispos'd in such a Manner, as that some Classes may be with the Writing-Master, improving their Hands, others with the Mathematical Master, learning Arithmetick, Accompts, Geography, Use of the Globes, Drawing, Mechanicks, &c. while the rest are in the English School, under the English Master's Care.

Thus instructed, Youth, will come out of this School fitted for learning any Business, Calling or Profession, except such wherein Languages are required; and tho' unaquainted with any antient or foreign Tongue, they will be Masters of their own, which is of more immediate and general Use; and withal will have attain'd many other valuable Accomplishments; the Time usually spent in acquiring those Languages, often without Success, being here employ'd in laying such a Foundation of Knowledge and Ability, as, properly improv'd, may qualify them to pass thro' and execute the several Offices of civil Life, with Advantage and Reputation to themselves and Country.

B.F.

Thomas Jefferson's educational theory reflected the shift in attitude in the United States from a religious viewpoint to a secular one. Jefferson felt that the newly established republic required a body of educated citizens if it was to endure. The selection which follows, "A Bill for the More General Diffusion of Knowledge," was proposed by Jefferson to the legislature of Virginia for the purpose of making education accessible to a larger segment of the population. The significant feature of the proposal was its attempt to provide basic literacy for the white population by guaranteeing three years of education for all white children in the state. Equally important was Jefferson's attempt to prepare an educated leadership by means of a system of state-supported scholarships.

A Bill for the More General Diffusion of Knowledge

Whereas it appeareth that however certain forms of government are better calculated than others to protect individuals in the free exercise of their natural rights, and are at the same time themselves better guarded against degeneracy, yet experience hath shewn, that even under the best forms, those entrusted with power have, in time, and by slow operations, perverted it into tyranny; and it is believed that the most effectual means of preventing this would be, to illuminate, as far as practicable, the minds of the people at large, and more especially to give them knowledge of those facts, which history exhibiteth, that, possessed thereby of the experience of other ages and countries, they may be enabled to know ambition under all its shapes, and prompt to exert their natural powers to defeat its purposes; And whereas it is generally true that that people will be happiest whose laws are best, and are best administered, and that laws will be wisely formed, and honestly administered, in proportion as those who form and administer them are wise and honest; whence it becomes expedient for promoting the publick happiness that those persons, whom nature hath endowed with genius and virtue, should be rendered by liberal education worthy to receive, and able to guard the sacred deposit of the rights and liberties of their fellow citizens, and that they should be called to that charge without regard to wealth, birth or other accidental condition or circumstance; but the indigence of the greater number disabling them from so educating, at their own expence, those of their children whom nature hath fitly formed and

Source: Julian P. Boyd, ed., *The Papers of Thomas Jefferson, Vol. 2: January 1777-June 1779.* Copyright ©1950 Princeton University Press. © 1978 renewed by Princeton University Press. Excerpt, pp. 526-533 reprinted with permission of Princeton University Press.

disposed to become useful instruments for the public, it is better that such should be sought for and educated at the common expence of all, than that the happiness of all should be confided to the weak or wicked:

Be it therefore enacted by the General Assembly, that in every county within this commonwealth, there shall be chosen annually, by the electors qualified to vote for Delegates, three of the most honest and able men of their county, to be called the Aldermen of the county; and that the election of the said Aldermen shall be held at the same time and place, before the same persons, and notified and conducted in the same manner as by law is directed for the annual election of Delegates for the county.

The person before whom such election is holden shall certify to the court of the said county the names of the Aldermen chosen, in order that the same may be entered of record, and shall give notice of their election to the said Aldermen within a fortnight after such election.

The said Aldermen on the first Monday in October, if it be fair, and if not, then on the next fair day, excluding Sunday, shall meet at the court-house of their county, and proceed to divide their said county into hundreds, bounding the same by water courses, mountains, or limits, to be run and marked, if they think necessary, by the county surveyor, and at the county expence, regulating the size of the said hundreds, according to the best of their discretion, so as that they may contain a convenient number of children to make up a school, and be of such convenient size that all the children within each hundred may daily attend the school to be established therein, distinguishing each hundred by a particular name; which division, with the names of the several hundreds, shall be returned to the court of the county and be entered of record, and shall remain unaltered until the increase or decrease of inhabitants shall render an alteration necessary, in the opinion of any succeeding Aldermen, and also in the opinion of the court of the county.

The electors aforesaid residing within every hundred shall meet on the third Monday in October after the first election of Aldermen, at such place, within their hundred, as the said Aldermen shall direct, notice thereof being previously given to them by such person residing within the hundred as the said Aldermen shall require who is hereby enjoined to obey such requisition, on pain of being punished by amercement and imprisonment. The electors being so assembled shall choose the most convenient place within their hundred for building a school-house. If two or more places, having a greater number of votes than any others, shall yet be equal between themselves, the Aldermen, or such of them as are not of the same hundred, on information thereof shall decide between them. The said Aldermen shall forthwith proceed to have a school-house built at the said place, and shall see that the same be kept in repair, and, when necessary, that it be rebuilt; but whenever they shall think necessary, that it he rebuilt, they shall give notice as before directed, to the electors of the hundred to meet at the said school-house, on such day as they shall appoint, to determine by vote, in the manner before directed, whether it shall be rebuilt at the same, or what other place in the hundred.

At every of these schools shall be taught reading, writing, and common arithmetick, and the books which shall be used therein for instructing the children to read shall be such as will at the same time make them acquainted with Graecian, Roman, English, and American history. At these schools all the free children, male and female, resident within the respective hundred, shall be intitled to receive tuition gratis, for the term of three years, and as much longer, at their private expence, as their parents, guardians or friends, shall think proper.

Over every ten of these schools (or such other number nearest thereto, as the number of hundreds in the county will admit, without fractional divisions) an overseer shall be appointed annually by the Aldermen at their first meeting, eminent for his learning, integrity, and fidelity to the commonwealth, whose business and duty it shall be, from time to time, to appoint a teacher to each school, who shall give assurance of fidelity to the commonwealth, and to remove him as he shall see cause; to visit every school once in every half year at the least; to examine the scholars; see that any general plan of reading and instruction recommended by the visiters of William and Mary College shall be observed; and to superintend the conduct of the teacher in every thing relative to his school.

Every teacher shall receive a salary of   by the year, which, with the expences of building and repairing the school-houses, shall be provided in such manner as other county expences are by law directed to be provided and shall also have his diet, lodging, and washing found him, to be levied in like manner, save only that such levy shall be on the inhabitants of each hundred for the board of their own teacher only.

And in order that grammar schools may be rendered convenient to the youth in every part of the commonwealth, Be it farther enacted, that on the first Monday in November, after the first appointment of overseers for the hundred schools, if fair, and if not, then on the next fair day, excluding Sunday, after the hour of one in the afternoon, the said overseers appointed for the schools in the counties of Princess Ann, Norfolk, Nansemond and Isle-of-Wight, shall meet at Nansemond court-house; those for the counties of Southampton, Sussex, Surry and Prince George, shall meet at Sussex court-house; those for the counties of Brunswick, Mecklenburg and Lunenburg, shall meet at Lunenburg court-house; those for the counties of Dinwiddie, Amelia and Chesterfield, shall meet at Chesterfield court-house; those for the counties of Powhatan, Cumberland, Goochland, Henrico and Hanover, shall meet at Henrico court-house; those for the counties of Prince Edward, Charlotte and Halifax, shall meet at Charlotte court-house; those for the counties of Henry,

Pittsylvania and Bedford, shall meet at Pittsylvania court-house; those for the counties of Buckingham, Amherst, Albemarle and Fluvanna, shall meet at Albemarle court-house; those for the counties of Botetourt, Rockbridge, Montgomery, Washington and Kentucky, shall meet at Botetourt court-house; those for the counties of Augusta, Rockingham and Greenbrier, shall meet at Augusta court-house; those for the counties of Accomack and Northampton, shall meet at Accomack court-house; those for the counties of Elizabeth City, Warwick, York, Gloucester, James City, Charles City and New-Kent, shall meet at James City court-house; those for the counties of Middlesex, Essex, King and Queen, King William and Caroline, shall meet at King and Queen court-house; those for the counties of Lancaster, Northumberland, Richmond and Westmoreland, shall meet at Richmond court-house; those for the counties of King George, Stafford, Spotsylvania, Prince William and Fairfax, shall meet at Spotsylvania court-house; those for the counties of Loudoun and Fauquier, shall meet at Loudoun court-house; those for the counties of Culpeper, Orange and Louisa, shall meet at Orange court-house; those for the counties of Shenandoah and Frederick, shall meet at Frederick court-house; those for the counties of Hampshire and Berkeley, shall meet at Berkeley court-house; and those for the counties of Yohogania, Monongalia and Ohio, shall meet at Monongalia court-house; and shall fix on such place in some one of the counties in their district as shall be most proper for situating a grammar school-house, endeavouring that the situation be as central as may be to the inhabitants of the said counties, that it be furnished with good water, convenient to plentiful supplies of provision and fuel and more than all things that it be healthy. And if a majority of the overseers present should not concur in their choice of any one place proposed, the method of determining shall be as follows: If two places only were proposed, and the votes be divided, they shall decide between them by fair and equal lot; if more than two places were proposed, the question shall be put on those two which on the first division had the greater number of votes; or if no two places had a greater number of votes than the others, as where the votes shall have been equal between one or both of them and some other or others, then it shall be decided by fair and equal lot (unless it can be agreed by a majority of votes) which of the places having equal numbers shall be thrown out of the competition, so that the question shall be put on the remaining two, and if on this ultimate question the votes shall be equally divided, it shall then be decided finally by lot.

The said overseers having determined the place at which the grammar school for their district shall be built, shall forthwith (unless they can otherwise agree with the proprietors of the circumjacent lands as to location and price) make application to the clerk of the county in which the said house is to be situated, who shall thereupon issue a writ, in the nature of a writ of ad quod damnum, directed to the sheriff of the said county commanding him to summon and impannel twelve fit persons to meet at the place, so destined for the grammar school-house, on a certain day, to be named in the said writ, not less than five, nor more than ten, days from the date thereof; and also to give notice of the same to the proprietors and tenants of the lands to be viewed, if they be to be found within the county, and if not, then to their agents therein if any they have. Which freeholders shall be charged by the said sheriff impartially, and to the best of their skill and judgment to view the lands round about the said place, and to locate and circumscribe, by certain metes and bounds, one hundred acres thereof having regard therein principally to the benefit and convenience of the said school, but respecting in some measure also the convenience of the said proprietors, and to value and appraise the same in so many several and distinct parcels as shall be owned or held by several and distinct owners or tenants, and according to their respective interests and estates therein. And after such location and appraisement so made, the said sheriff shall forthwith return the same under the hands and seals of the said jurors, together with the writ, to the clerk's office of the said county and the right and property of the said proprietors and tenants in the said lands so circumscribed shall be immediately devested and be transferred to the commonwealth for the use of the said grammar school, in full and absolute dominion, any want of consent or disability to consent in the said owners or tenants notwithstanding. But it shall not be lawful for the said overseers so to situate the said grammar school-house, nor to the said jurors so to locate the said lands, as to include the mansion-house of the proprietor of the lands, nor the offices, curtilage, or garden, thereunto immediately belonging.

The said overseers shall forthwith proceed to have a house of brick or stone, for the said grammar school, with necessary offices, built on the said lands, which grammar school-house shall contain a room for the school, a hall to dine in, four rooms for a master and usher, and ten or twelve lodging rooms for the scholars.

To each of the said grammar schools shall be allowed out of the public treasury, the sum of   pounds, out of which shall be paid by the Treasurer, on warrant from the Auditors, to the proprietors or tenants of the lands located, the value of their several interests as fixed by the jury, and the balance thereof shall be delivered to the said overseers to defray the expence of the said buildings.

In these grammar schools shall be taught the Latin and Greek languages, English grammar, geography and the higher part of numerical arithmetick, to wit, vulgar and decimal fractions, and the extraction of the square and cube roots.

A visiter from each county constituting the district shall be appointed, by the overseers, for the county, in the month of October annually, either from their own body or from their county at large, which visiters or the greater part of them, meeting together at the said grammar school on the first Monday in November, if fair, and if not, then on the next fair day, excluding Sunday, shall have power to choose their own Rector, who shall call and preside at future meetings, to employ from time to time a master, and if necessary, an usher, for the said school, to remove them at their will, and to settle the price of tuition to be paid by the scholars. They shall also visit the school twice in every year at the least, either together or separately at their discretion, examine the scholars, and see that any general plan of instruction recommended by the visiters of William and Mary College shall be observed. The said masters and ushers, before they enter on the execution of their office, shall give assurance of fidelity to the commonwealth.

A steward shall be employed, and removed at will by the master, on such wages as the visiters shall direct; which steward shall see to the procuring provisions, fuel, servants for cooking, waiting, house cleaning, washing, mending, and gardening on the most reasonable terms; the expence of which, together with the steward's wages, shall be divided equally among all the scholars boarding either on the public or private expence. And the part of those who are on private expence, and also the price of their tuitions due to the master or usher, shall be paid quarterly by the respective scholars, their parents, or guardians, and shall be recoverable, if withheld, together with costs, on motion in any Court of Record, ten days notice thereof being previously given to the party, and a jury impannelled to try the issue joined, or enquire of the damages. The said steward shall also, under the direction of the visiters, see that the houses be kept in repair, and necessary enclosures be made and repaired, the accounts for which, shall, from time to time, be submitted to the Auditors, and on their warrant paid by the Treasurer.

Every overseer of the hundred schools shall, in the month of September annually, alter the most diligent and impartial examination and enquiry, appoint from among the boys who shall have been two years at the least at some one of the schools under his superintendance, and whose parents are too poor to give them farther education, some one of the best and most promising genius and disposition, to proceed to the grammar school of his district; which appointment shall be made in the court-house of the county, on the court day for that month if fair, and if not, then on the next fair day, excluding Sunday, in the presence of the Aldermen, or two of them at the least, assembled on the bench for that purpose, the said overseer being previously sworn by them to make such appointment, without favor or affection, according to the best of his skill and judgment, and being interrogated by the said Aldermen, either on their own motion, or on suggestions from the parents, guardians, friends, or teachers of the children, competitors for such appointment; which teachers shall attend for the information of the Aldermen. On which interregatories the said Aldermen, if they be not satisfied with the appointment proposed, shall have the right to negative it; whereupon the said visiter may proceed to make a new appointment, and the said Aldermen again to interrogate and negative, and so toties quoties until an appointment be approved.

Every boy so appointed shall be authorised to proceed to the grammar school of his district, there to be educated and boarded during such time as is hereafter limited; and his quota of the expenses of the house together with a compensation to the master or usher for his tuition, at the rate of twenty dollars by the year, shall be paid by the Treasurer quarterly on warrant from the Auditors.

A visitation shall be held, for the purpose of probation, annually at the said grammar school on the last Monday in September, if fair, and if not, then on the next fair day, excluding Sunday, at which one third of the boys sent thither by appointment of the said overseers, and who shall have been there one year only, shall be discontinued as public foundationers, being those who, on the most diligent examination and enquiry, shall be thought to be of the least promising genius and disposition; and of those who shall have been there two years, all shall be discontinued, save one only the best in genius and disposition, who shall be at liberty to continue there four years longer on the public foundation, and shall thence forward be deemed a senior.

The visiters for the districts which, or any part of which, be southward and westward of James river, as known by that name, or by the names of Fluvanna and Jackson's river, in every other year, to wit, at the probation meetings held in the years, distinguished in the Christian computation by odd numbers, and the visiters for all the other districts at their said meetings to be held in those years, distinguished by even numbers, alter diligent examination and enquiry as before directed, shall chuse one among the said seniors, of the best learning and most hopeful genius and disposition, who shall be authorised by them to proceed to William and Mary College, there to be educated, boarded, and clothed, three years; the expence of which annually shall be paid by the Treasurer on warrant from the Auditors.

Suggestions for Further Reading

Arrowood, Charles F. *Thomas Jefferson and Education in a Republic*. New York: McGraw-Hill Book Co., 1930.

Best, John H., ed. *Benjamin Franklin on Education*, New York: Bureau of Publications, Teachers College, Columbia University, 1962.

Babbidge, Homes D. *Noah Webster: On Being American. Selected Writings, 1783-1828*. New York: Praeger Publishers, 1967.

Blinderman, Abraham. *Three Early Champions of Education: Benjamin Franklin, Benjamin Rush, and Noah Webster*. Bloomington, IN: Phi Delta Kappa Educational Foundation, 1976.

Commager, Henry Steele, ed. *Noah Webster's American Spelling Book*. New York: Bureau of Publications, Teachers College, Columbia University, 1962.

Cunningham, Noble E., Jr. *In Pursuit of Reason: The Life of Thomas Jefferson*. Baton Rouge: Louisiana State University Press, 1987.

Greene, John C. *American Science in the Age of Jefferson*. Ames, IA: Iowa State University Press, 1984.

Hansen, Allen O. *Liberalism and American Education in the Eighteenth Century*. New York: Macmillan Co., 1926.

Heslep, Robert D. *Thomas Jefferson and Education*. New York: Random House, 1969.

Honeywell, Roy J. *The Educational Work of Thomas Jefferson*. Cambridge, MA: Harvard University Press, 1931.

Lee, Gordon C. *Crusade Against Ignorance: Thomas Jefferson on Education*. New York: Bureau of Publications, Teachers College, Columbia University, 1962.

Madsen, David L. *Early National Education: 1776-1830*. New York: John Wiley and Sons, 1974.

Rollins, Richard M. *The Long Journey of Noah Webster*. Philadelphia: University of Pennsylvania Press, 1980.

Shoemaker, Ervin C. *Noah Webster, Pioneer of Learning*. New York: Columbia University Press, 1936.

Wagoner, Jennings L., Jr. *Thomas Jefferson and the Education of a New Nation*. Bloomington, IN: Phi Delta Kappa Educational Foundation, 1976.

Warfel, Harry R. *Noah Webster: Schoolmaster to America*. New York: Macmillan Co., 1936.

Woody, Thomas. *Educational Views of Benjamin Franklin*. New York: McGraw-Hill Book Co., 1931.

Wright, Edmond. *Franklin of Philadelphia*. Cambridge, MA: Harvard University Press, 1988.

Chapter **3**

Evolution of the Common School

Introduction: Currents of Social Reform

The common school represents one of the most important American
contributions to the history of education. It was an equally significant
factor in the cultural, social, and intellectual development of the United
States as a nation. In the common schools of this country, citizens of the new
republic received their first lessons in democracy.

Although the common schools have been defined in various ways, they were
usually elementary, and devoted to the cultivation of literacy, numeracy, and
citizenship. Offering a program combining the skills of reading, writing, and
arithmetic, these predecessors of the contemporary public school educated
generations of Americans to carry out the duties and privileges of life in a
republic. In this way, the common schools helped to weld a democracy that
encompassed many people of various religious, ethnic, and social backgrounds.

During the nineteenth century, the westward migration of the homesteaders
extended the new country's frontiers across the North American continent,
and common schools were established in many of the new settlements. At
the same time the population was increased by successive waves of European
immigrants landing on the eastern shore and either settling in the cities or
joining the journey to the Pacific. For the immigrants and their children, the

common school was an instrument of Americanization which facilitated the learning of a new language and a new way of life.

The dynamic energy created by both the Atlantic immigration and the westward migration contributed to the emergence of the national character. As an instrument of cultural transmission, the common school played a large role in the development of that character.

While the early republican theorists had supplied many of the ideas for later educational experimentation, it was the later generations of educational leaders who established the common school as the agent for both cultural unification and transmission of the society. As the modulations from colony to fledgling republic to industrial nation took place, much of the European tradition was radically altered, and in the march to the Pacific Ocean a number of the inherited practices of European society were transformed. Two of these trends were especially noteworthy: first, the sectarian religious control which had previously dominated educational enterprise was replaced by civil, patriotic, and utilitarian concerns; second, the earlier rigid, closed class structure was swept away by the more democratic fellowship of the frontier.

The course of nationhood was not only perilous, as evidenced by the Civil War; it also involved patient and often extensive transformation. In the early nineteenth century, the United States experienced a period when every area of life was subjected to critical examination by a generation that believed strongly in social reform. In the new zeal for reform, a welter of proposals swept the nation. Temperance, abolition of slavery, women's rights, utopian socialism, penal improvement, and popular education were all advocated. While many of the reforms proved transitory, the demand for public education through common schooling remained to become one of the greatest achievements of American society.

Philanthropic Alernatives to Common Schools

In the early nineteenth century the United States was a developing nation. Business and political leaders recognized that some system of mass education was needed to educate the children of the newly arrived immigrants and factory workers who were converging on the growing cities. Several large cities, such as New York and Philadelphia, experimented with a variety of voluntary or philanthropic kinds of education before adopting common schools. In a voluntary arrangement, interested individuals and groups joined to support a private educational agency without being compelled to do so by the state. A philanthropic endeavor was one in which wealthy benefactors donated money for school support. The philanthropic concept drew its theoretical support from the Protestant notion of stewardship by which persons of wealth and position were expected to contribute to the moral and educational improvement of the lower socioeconomic classes.

Voluntary and philanthropic educational undertakings rested on the premise that education was essentially a private or charity matter. While trying to avoid state intervention, the philanthropists who contributed to voluntary plans of education wanted to provide minimal, basic literacy and character training to children, especially to those of the lower social and economic classes. The most noteworthy attempts at philanthropic education were the subscription society, the Sunday school, the infant school, and the monitorial school.

The members of a subscription society contributed money that was used to support schools and reading rooms. Some subscription societies were formed by businesspeople and industrialists to support schools for the poor. At times, their motives were humanitarian and altruistic; at other times, they sought to use education to socially control a growing urban working class that might threaten the established social order.

The most important philanthropic educational efforts were the Sunday school, the infant school, and the monitorial school. These three approaches to schooling related to the evolution of an industrial society in the early nineteenth century. Industrialization produced social changes that weakened the educative role of the family on its offspring and also posed threats to older forms of religious schooling. These alternative schools were imported from England which was also experimenting with voluntary approaches to mass education.

The Sunday school clearly reflected the impact of industrialization upon children, especially on those of the working classes. In both England and the United States, large numbers of children were employed as cheap laborers in factories, mills, and mines. Since their long work day of often twelve hours made it impossible for them to attend school during the week, some of the children were instructed on Sunday, the one day when the factories were idle. Due to the limited time available and due to the exhausted condition of the children, Sunday school instruction was limited to the basics of reading, writing, religion and character formation. When common schools were established, the secular function of Sunday schools in providing reading, writing, and arithmetic instruction shifted to public education. Abandoning their more general educational function, Sunday schools emphasized religious instruction, especially in the doctrines and practices of the churches that sponsored them. The American School Union which was established to coordinate the activities and provide curricular materials of a religious nature for the various Protestant churches which were members.[1] Today, the Sunday school remains as an arrangement that provides religious education for the children in many Protestant denominations.

The infant school, which enjoyed some popularity, was another response to early nineteenth century industrialization. Since women were employed in factories, the mother's time with her children was reduced. Children could be left in the infant school while their mothers were at work. The infant school concept, a crude prototype of the modern day care center, was developed by Robert Owen (1771-1858), the British industrialist and communitarian socialist, at New Lanark in Scotland.[2] When Owen came to the United States, in 1825, he popularized the infant school. Basically, the infant school was a nursery school arrangement in which the young children, ranging in age from two to six years, were given moral, physical, and intellectual training.

The most popular alternative to the common school was the monitorial school which was also imported from England. Its prominence in the United States illustrates the interchange of educational ideas between America and Europe. In many respects, the nineteenth century American educators were in the position of borrowing educational ideas and institutions from their European counterparts. In England, two rival school societies had been established to promote monitorial education. The British and Foreign School Society followed the version of monitorial education devised by Joseph Lancaster (1778-1838) while the National School Society followed that of Andrew Bell (1753-1832).[3] In the United States, Lancaster's method which promised to educate large numbers of children methodically, efficiently, and cheaply attracted the greatest attention.[4] Lancaster, himself, came to the United States to popularize monitorialism which was inaugurated in New York in 1806 and in Philadelphia in 1807. The Governor of New York, De Witt Clinton, was an enthusiastic proponent of Lancaster and his method.

The basic principles of Lancasterian monitorial education was that a master teacher would train advanced students to teach skills to less advanced students. Since most of the teaching was done by student monitors, the expenses were kept to a minimum. Because large numbers of children attended the factory-like monitorial schools, Lancaster developed a semi-military system to control them. Lessons were broken down into elements, and each phase of instruction was assigned to a particular monitor. The method required that children of relatively equal ability be grouped together so that instruction could proceed uniformly. Each phase of instruction had its appropriate lesson plan. For example, Lancaster divided the students who were learning to read into eight classes: learning the alphabet, learning words or syllables of two letters, three letters, four letters, five letters, reading stories from the Scriptures, reading the Bible, and advanced reading. Instruction in writing and arithmetic were also arranged into groups based on ability levels. To reduce costs even further, inexpensive materials were used. Large wall charts were used instead of books to teach reading; students traced letters on sand tables instead of using pen and paper.

As indicated, the initial popularity of the Lancasterian monitorial system rested on its promise to educate large numbers of children inexpensively. Its very nature, however, confined instruction to the rudimentary skills. Its critics condemned monitorialism as a "parrot method" by which students memorized letters and words but failed to develop the literary and thinking skills needed for personal development and civic competency in a republican society. After enjoying popularity in the early nineteenth century, the monitorial method was discarded. Today, certain variants of monitorial education can still be found. In developing countries that are struggling to conquer illiteracy, the method has been used by literacy teams that teach reading in rural areas. Although the concept of team teaching is much more sophisticated than the monitorial method, certain similarities exist. Team teaching requires the careful scheduling of instructional time that Lancaster worked to achieve. In some colleges and universities, senior professors lecture to large groups of students which are then divided into discussion groups led by teaching assistants. These and other forms of instruction bear some resemblance to the monitorial method.

The use of the various voluntary and philanthropic approaches to mass education both fostered and impeded the movement to publicly supported common schools. In some instances, monitorial schools were rival alternatives that delayed the establishment of common schools. Generally, the philanthropic endeavors provided a stimulus for more extensive universal education.

In contrast to those who sought to use education for social control, others saw popular education as a means of inducing social change. For example, a number of workers' associations were organized in the 1830s to advance the interests of the laboring classes. Many of the leaders of the workers believed that knowledge was power and that the proper kind of education would diffuse knowledge among the ranks of the working classes.[5] Some of the workers' associations established schools and maintained reading rooms for the education of their own members.

One of the leading proponents of workers' education was William Maclure (1763-1840), a scientist, geologist, and philanthropist. In his *Opinions on Various Subjects*, Maclure argued that schools of industry should be established for the American working classes.[6] In these schools, working class children were to be educated to recognize their genuine political and economic interests. Maclure, who opposed the classical studies, devised a curriculum that stressed the basic sciences and their practical application to agriculture and industry. He also encouraged European teachers to immigrate to the United States to introduce the Pestalozzian method which he regarded as the most effective form of education. Maclure was one of the early proponents of the theory that education could be used for social change rather than for social control by the vested interests.

Arguments for Universal Education

An important factor in the movement for universal education was the motivation of the reformers. Many of them were concerned with the people's need for political enlightenment. Democratic processes and procedures required an electorate capable of choosing its officials and an officialdom capable of governing. For both an educated, literate citizenry was a necessity.

Equally important in the demand for universal education was the increasing force of nationalism. Common schools could establish common values and loyalties and weld groups with diverse ethnic and religious backgrounds into a common American identity. In addition to these civic demands, the rising middle and working classes wanted a more utilitarian education which would prepare skilled businessmen and workers. Although the motives of the middle-class businessmen and factory workers may have operated at cross purposes, the means they sought merged in an ill-defined demand for widespread elementary education.

A fourth motive, and one of crucial importance in the struggle for public education, was that Americans viewed education as a means of social improvement and economic advancement. To many Americans, education was something intrinsically good, in and of itself. Americans believed that with equality of educational opportunity established through a public school system, definite social progress could be achieved. Although this view of education is naive, it remains a popular American belief. More realistically, education can serve as an instrument to various ends. If social progress is to result as an educational end, the means to achieve it must be deliberately made a part of the educational process.

An important coalition that supported universal publicly-supported and controlled elementary schooling was made up of clergy and members of Protestant churches such as the Methodists, Baptists, Presbyterians, and Congregationalists. Although doctrinal differences existed among these churches, they had much in common. Their congregations were largely composed of persons of English ethnic origin and language. Persons identified with these churches often held leading political and educational positions. In fact, members of these mainstream Protestant churches tended to identify their ethical beliefs with the very concept of republican self-government. For them, a set of common Protestant Christian beliefs and ethics existed that could form the basis for the moral formation of citizens in the American republic.

Clergy of the mainstream Protestant churches were often leaders in the movement to establish public education in the United States. Churches, such as the Presbyterians which had once supported parochial schools, came to believe that they could rely on public educational institutions. However, they sought to ensure that these public institutions stressed the right kind of values.

Leaders of the mainstream Protestant churches were alarmed by the growing numbers of Catholic immigrants who were coming to the United States in the nineteenth century, especially from Ireland and Germany. This immigraion, they feared, would reduce the Protestant dominance in the United States. Further, it could change the character of the nation. If the children of immirants were educated in public schools that stressed a common set of values derived from a generalized Protestant ethic, then a common Protestant culture might be maintained.[7] In its origins, the early establishment of public schools reflected a very strong Protestant orientation and values. By the end of the nineteenth century, however, this religious orientation would greatly diminish.

While there were many who favored some system of public education, more conservative elements opposed the idea with a variety of arguments. Tax-conscious property owners claimed that it violated the natural sanctity of property rights to tax one man in order to educate another's child. Other opponents saw public education as a movement designed to establish the domination of one political party over another. For example, the political party in power at the time of the school system's establishment might attempt to control the appointment of school teachers and administrators through patronage. Further, the dominant party might seek to inculcate its particular political dogma into the curriculum in order to indoctrinate the young.

Since the common schools were to be publicly supported and controlled, others regarded the campaign for common schools as a socialist conspiracy that was determined to obliterate class distinctions by herding all the children in the nation into one group of institutions. Some religious sects alleged that public schools would be godless, and would dismiss religious values in favor of secular ones. Certain foreign language groups feared that a common school system would obliterate their distinctive languages, customs, and mores.

Proponents of the Common School

The social reformers who viewed public education as a means of realizing the American dream defined the common school as an institution that would provide its students with basic cultural and literary skills. But it was to be more than just another vernacular school in the European sense; it was to be the means of transforming the nation into a cultural sociopolitical entity. Common did not mean lowly or base-born, but expressed the idea of a cultural community in which ideas, experiences, beliefs, aspirations, and values would eventually become uniquely American.

With this view of the common school in mind, prominent defenders mounted podiums in countless meeting halls to plead their cause. Political figures such as Horace Mann, Henry Barnard, James G. Carter, and Thaddeus Stevens argued tirelessly for the enactment of common school legislation. The American Lyceum movement organized by Josiah Holbrook in 1826 took up the appeal to popularize the common school. Educational publications such as William Russell's *American Journal of Education*, Henry Barnard's *Connecticut Common School Journal*, and Horace Mann's *Common School Journal* carried editorials calling for the enactment of common school laws by various state legislatures.

Although the European vernacular primary school differed from the system proposed for the United States, the centralized elementary educational system in Prussia appealed to many Americans. Not many of them admired the militarism of the Prussian example, but they did appreciate its efficiency and organization. Many of the reforms of Pestalozzi and Fellenberg were included as a part of Prussian teacher education. Further, the system boasted such innovations as a uniformly prescribed curriculum, standard teacher certification requirements, and taxation for school support. Calvin Stowe, emulating the report of Victor Cousin to the French government concerning Prussian schools, made a similar one to the Ohio legislature. He concluded by pointing out that if a monarchy could supply universal education for its subjects, a republic such as the United States could do no less for its citizens.

While the movement for compulsory, publicly supported and controlled education varied from state to state and region to region in intensity and effectiveness, some general observations can be made. As early as 1827 the state of Massachusetts made the total support of schools by taxation compulsory. Other states in New England and the Midwest followed that model. The movement to widespread, publicly supported education followed more gradually in the Middle Atlantic states and did not really develop in the South until the Reconstruction period after the Civil War.

A general outline of the process of establishing compulsory common school education can be described in four major phases. First, the state enacted permissive legislation by recognizing school districts as legal units which could each serve as a taxing body, providing that the majority of the people within the district were so agreed. The important point was that, by means of permissive legislation, the school district was recognized as a unit with administrative and taxing powers. In the second phase the state, though it did not require the formation of such districts, encouraged them by providing grants of monies from the general school fund to those districts which agreed to support public schools. The state monies came from permanent school funds derived from the sale of public land, state taxes or lotteries, and allotments from federal revenues. The third phase constituted compulsory but still not completely free public education. While the state now required the formation of school districts, the tax support was often inadequate to provide elementary education for all the children living in the school district. As a result, the districts were obliged to use the rate bill, a charge levied upon parents on the basis of the number of children attending the district school. The tuition payments supplied by the rate bill supplemented funds derived from public sources. The last step was the establishment of compulsory and completely tax-supported public education as increased sources of revenue became available for school support. The growth of industry in the eastern states provided an increased tax base in revenue derived from industrial properties. As more people moved into the western states, the establishment of a stable community life facilitated the collection of revenue for those schools. Occasionally, the surplus income of the federal government derived from the tariff would be distributed among the states and used for the common school fund. As more money became available for school financing, the rate bill was gradually discontinued, and elementary education was opened to children from all social and economic classes.

Horace Mann

One of the leaders in promoting the common school was the educational statesman Horace Mann. He was born in 1796 in Franklin, Massachusetts, and raised as a Calvinist, although he later became a Unitarian. He received his bachelor's degree at Brown University, read law, and was admitted to practice in 1823. In 1827 he was elected to the Massachusetts legislature, where he supported educational reform. In 1838 he was appointed Secretary of the Massachusetts Board of Education. Through his *Annual Reports* and work as editor of the *Common School Journal* he contributed a great deal to the cause of public education in Massachusetts and throughout the nation. After retiring as Secretary of the Board in 1849, he served in Congress, and later became President of Antioch College. He died in 1859 an honored American statesman and educator.

To begin to understand Mann's significance, one must first examine his theoretical posture. He was essentially an eclectic, whose speeches and writings indicate no clearly defined philosophical structure.[8] However, five broad currents of thought permeated his educational theorizing: remnants of Calvinism; American transcendentalism; the republican-democratic ethic; industrial capitalism; and phrenology.[9]

Horace Mann rejected the stern Calvinist predestinarianism of his youth for the gentle, more liberal Unitarianism that attracted other New England intellectuals, such as Ralph Waldo Emerson and Theodore Parker, during the first half of the nineteenth century. Unwilling to accept doctrines based on the innate corruptibility of human nature, he believed that organized education could liberate human intelligence and thus effect both individual and social reformation. Although liberal in his theology, Mann recommended the teaching of a "common Christianity" in the public schools. Still remaining a Calvinist in some ways, he continued to believe in the stewardship theory of wealth. He expected wealthy men to act as economic guardians, using their resources for the public welfare.

A New England intellectual himself, Mann did not escape the transcendentalist idealism of Emerson and the whole philosophical school at Concord. Emersonian idealism provided a means of intellectual escape from the harsh realities of an embryonic industrialism. Transcendentalists believed that the human mind could achieve communion with the Absolute, the Universal Mind or Oversoul, through intuitive self-evaluation and detachment from materialism. Transcendentalist education sought not only to teach purely factual lessons but also to endow education with a deeper and more complex significance. Because knowledge was such a powerful tool for doing good and avoiding evil, Mann wanted the common schools to be instrumental in creating a far-seeing intelligence and a purer morality.

Devoted to the democratic ethic, he saw public, common schooling as an instrument of the American republic. An intimate relationship existed between liberty, self-government and universal education; political and social liberties could be secure only if people were educated enough to make intelligent decisions. The common school was to serve as a school of democracy, a center of civic education, and a training-ground for responsible public service.

In speaking of the relationship of common education to republican institutions, Mann warned:

> The truth has been so often asserted, that there is no security for a republic but in morality and intelligence, that a repetition of it seems hardly in good taste. But all permanent blessings being founded on permanent truths, a continued observance of the truth is the condition of a continued enjoyment of the blessing. I know we are often admonished that, without intelligence and virtue, as a chart and compass, to direct us in our untried political voyage, we shall perish in the first storm; but I venture to add that, without these qualities, we shall not wait for a storm, — we cannot weather a calm. If the sea is as smooth as glass we shall flounder, for we are in a stone boat. Unless these qualities pervade the general head and the general heart, not only will republican institutions vanish from amongst us, but the words prosperity and happiness will become obsolete. And all this may he affirmed, not from historical examples merely, but from the very constitution of our nature. We are created and brought into life with a set of innate, organic dispositions or propensities, which a free government rouses and invigorates, and which, if not bridled and tamed by our actually seeing the eternal laws of justice, as plainly as we can see the sun in the heavens, — and by our actually feeling the

sovereign sentiment of duty, as plainly as we feel the earth beneath our feet, — will hurry us forward into regions populous with every form of evil.[10]

The span of Mann's life coincided with the beginnings of the American system of mass industrial production, and he was well aware that economic and political power was gravitating from the agriculturalist to the industrialist. If the common school concept was to succeed in practical terms, it had to have the support of the growing middle class of businessmen, professionals, and entrepreneurs. Business and industrial property would constitute much of the taxation base needed to finance a common school system.

In framing his appeal for a tax-supported system of common schools, Mann developed a theory of humane and responsible capitalism which greatly resembled the stewardship concept contained in the Protestant ethic. In the course of each generation, certain intelligent and efficient individuals worked so diligently that they accumulated wealth beyond that needed for their own sustenance. As responsible men, these stewards had a moral and a civic responsibility to direct their surplus wealth into investments which would pay social dividends. Mann was thus using the profit motive to argue his theory when he pointed out that investment in public education would contribute to the growth of social intelligence and enable men to exploit natural resources with greater efficiency. Wealth would be increased, and every class would benefit. Although Mann saw abuses in the ruthless capitalism of the nineteenth century, he believed in working with the system rather than against it. In urging the propertied class to support common-school education, he said:

> Does any possessor of wealth, or leisure, or learning, ask, "What interest have I in education of the multitude?" I reply, you have at least this interest, that, unless their minds are enlightened by knowledge and controlled by virtuous principle, there is not, between their appetites and all you hold dear upon earth, so much the defense of a spider's web. Without a sense of the inviolability of property, your deeds are but waste-paper. Without a sense of the sacredness of person and life, you are only a watchdog whose baying is to be silenced, that your house may be more securely entered and plundered. Even a guilty few can destroy the peace of the virtuous many. One incendiary can burn faster than a thousand industrious workmen can build; — and this is true of social rights as of material edifices.[11]

Mann was clearly pointing out to the men of wealth and position that it was in their own self-interest to provide for common school education. Property rights would be best maintained in a social context in which the masses were educated to respect property and encouraged to acquire their own. For example, the various introductory reading texts, such as the McGuffey series, stressed the values of hard work, industriousness, and frugality. Respect for both private and public property ranked high in the values stressed by the common-school teachers of the nineteenth century. The common-school movement in America coincided with the rise of European socialism and anarchism. Mann and others believed that common civic education would serve as a deterrent to the successful importation of anarchism and its spread among the immigrants and native American workingmen.

Mann also accepted an intellectual fad of his day—phrenology. The phrenologists believed that the mind was composed of faculties governing human attitudes and conduct and that character could therefore be modified as the appropriate faculties were either exercised or allowed to atrophy through disuse. Education could therefore build the good society by improving the character of individual children in mechanical ways. This doctrine has been discarded by contemporary educators.

It is clear from Mann's theoretical posture that he never developed a clearly defined philosophy of education. Some parts of his theoretical framework were inconsistent with other elements. His great faith in the power of schooling as an instrument of social progress was naive. Although formal education can contribute to social and individual progress, the school is only one of several social institutions. The effectiveness of a program of formal instruction depends upon the educational commitment made by the total society. Mann's trust in phrenology was unfounded in reality. However, his belief in the improvability of man, in educational opportunity, and in the democratic ethic were sources of inspiration for the widespread acceptance of the common school concept in American education.

Mann's life was devoted to the development of the common school. According to his concept, education was to be state-supported and publicly controlled. He felt that the dual aristocratic system of education was alien to the American concept of equalitarian democracy; the common school would be free and open equally to all. Educational opportunity would be the legacy of every American child regardless of his or her social, religious, and economic background.

The common school would also avoid the stigma attached to state education that had developed with the paupers' and apprentices' schooling provided for by the English Poor Laws. It would be of such excellent quality that all parents would want to send their children to the public elementary school, and eventually it would be superior to private schools. It would also serve as a unifying force, assimilating immigrants, foreign language groups, and other diverse elements in American society into one nation. Through children's association with each other, social class conflicts would be resolved.

As the school represented the interests of the entire community, its expenditures were to be publicly obtained and controlled. As the school board was non-sectarian, its elected officials were to be responsive to the community as a whole rather than to any particular religious, economic, or social class.

An Educated Teaching Profession

As common schools were established, as a result of Mann's struggle for public education, it became necessary to prepare enough competent teachers to staff these institutions. In his surveys of Massachusetts' district schools, Mann found evidence of a very poor level of teaching performed by unqualified and inadequately prepared teachers. To remedy this unfortunate situation, he set up teachers' institutes, established normal schools, and worked for the improvement of teachers' salaries. Teachers' institutes were periodic in-service meetings in which teachers met to discuss their mutual problems and to hear lectures on educational topics. The normal schools were teacher training institutions which specifically prepared prospective teachers in common-school subjects, pedagogy, and instructional methodology. The increase in teachers' salaries was designed to attract more competent individuals to teaching.

To popularize his efforts to improve teaching Mann also applied himself to educational publication. In his *Annual Reports* and *Common School Journal* he attracted public attention to the need for improving the quality and quantity of public school education.

In discussing the education of teachers, Mann asked:

> In order to preserve our republican institutions, must not our Common Schools be elevated in character and increased in efficiency? And, in order to bring our schools up to the point of excellence demanded by the nature of our institutions, must there not be a special course of study and training to qualify teachers for their office? No other worldly interest presents any question comparable to these in importance.[12]

Henry Barnard

A colleague of Horace Mann's in the common school movement, Henry Barnard (1811-1900) served as Secretary of the Connecticut State Board of Education from 1838 to 1842. Among his other formal contributions to education were his service as State Commissioner of the Public Schools in Rhode Island, 1845-1849, Chancellor of the University of Wisconsin, 1858-1860, and United States Commissioner of Education, 1867-1870. Barnard's significance as an educational leader was not confined to his role as an administrator, however. Over much of the nineteenth century he was the most prominent commentator on educational affairs in America. As a journalist and editor, he popularized public education through the *Connecticut Common School Journal* and the *American Journal of Education*. Through his writing and speaking, he kept Americans informed as to the progress and promise of the public school. He also introduced teachers to the ideas of European educational reformers such as Pestalozzi, Froebel, and Herbart.

Barnard's intellectual framework of education embraced four major currents: Christianity, capitalistic individualism, utilitarianism, and Americanism.[13] Barnard associated his entire educational program with Christianity. He opposed the free-thinking and materialistic skepticism of some of the proponents of non-sectarian common-school education. Because of his religious orientation, he felt that education should prepare Christian men and women. The Bible should be used to bring about good character; history and geography were deemed useful subjects in furthering the Christian commitment.

Like Mann's, Barnard's life coincided with the growth of American industrialization. With the growth of cities and the increase in the urban working population came an increase of tenements, slum conditions, child labor, and more sharply felt economic class antagonisms. Barnard, however, espousing *laissez-faire* economic theory, felt that these social dislocations were necessary evils. The American school was to be definitely associated with the principles of economic individualism. Natural laws of supply and demand were operative in the economic realm; as a corollary, social competition was the best means of obtaining social progress.

Barnard's emphasis on a utilitarian curriculum was directly related to the continuing industrialization of American life. The growing tendency toward mass production required the preparation of a class of industrialists who could manage their business affairs intelligently and profitably. It also required a large body of workers who were capable of learning the skills involved in industrial productivity. These needs were essentially economic in character, and Barnard believed that a functional curriculum would satisfy them.

Barnard believed that the common school should further the ends of American patriotism as much as possible. Urging civic education, he stressed love of country, its traditions, heritage, and heroes.

Barnard did not limit himself to theorizing, but also wrote about school practice. The ends of education implied more than mere mastery of the basic literary skills. Although a knowledge of writing and arithmetic was necessary, the proper objectives of education included good health, accurate observation, clear reflection, and the cultivation of morality. Further, emphasis should be placed on the utilitarian aspects of education. The child should never suppose education to be merely a set of abstractions. In Barnard's *First Annual Report* as Secretary to the Connecticut Board of Common School Commissioners in 1838, he gave Connecticut teachers advice on subjects ranging from writing to religion.[14] The primary branches of learning should not be neglected, he wrote, since reading, writing, and arithmetic were the foundations of later schooling and a successful life. The most important subject was the English language, which included spelling, reading, speaking, grammar, and composition. Instead of being confined to long lists of words learned by repetition, spelling should be related deliberately to reading and writing. The practical uses of arithmetic should be stressed. Religious and moral instruction should also be taught.

Concerning teaching as a profession, Barnard warned against the confusion that could result from rapid teacher turnover. The loss of continuity, and therefore of time resulting from changing teachers, tended to retard the progress of the school, he pointed out. Like Mann, Barnard also urged more adequate teacher education, the establishment of normal schools, and increased financial compensation for teachers.

The Country School

By the mid-nineteenth century, the common school pattern had been established in the northern states. After the Civil War, the pattern was then extended to the southern states as well. As new states were admitted to the Union in the western territories across the Mississippi River, they, too, established common school systems. A characteristic of such systems was the country school, often a one-room building, in which children of various ages were taught by a single teacher.

Since the United States' Constitution did not address education, it was reserved to each of the states. The states, which remained the ultimate authority for public education, delegated responsibility for administering and organizing public schools to the local school district. These school districts were governed by elected local boards of education which determined the location of the school or schools, established attendance areas, levied the property tax that supported the school, hired the teacher, set the length of the school year, established the curriculum, and paid the teacher's salary. Fuller, an historian of rural education, has called these districts "laboratories of democracy in which rural Americans learned the importance of their vote, how to make laws, and how to govern themselves."[15]

The one-room rural school house was usually a wooden frame building that was rectangular in design and invariably painted white or red. The building's interior housed several rows of desks for the pupils who were usually seated two to a desk. Both boys and girls, ranging in age from six to seventeen, attended the school. The younger and usually shorter children were seated in the front rows so that they could see the black board which was at the front of the room. Here, the teacher was located often behind a large wooden

Interiors of one-room country schools that are preserved at museum villages. Photograph 1 depicts school at South Park City, Fairplay Colorado; Photograph 2 is of school at Prairie Village, South Dakota; Photograph 3 is of school at Pioneer Arizona, Phoenix, Arizona; Photograph 4 is at Bonanzaville, North Dakota. Photographs by Patricia Gutek.

Representative one-room country schools that are preserved at museum villages. Photograph 1 depicts the Garo school, built in 1879, located at South Park City Museum, Fairplay, Colorado; Photograph 2 is of the Scotch Settlement School, Greenfield Village, Dearborn, Michigan; Photograph 3 is from Prairie Village, South Dakota; Photograph 4 is a school of the 1890s located at Pioneer Arizona, Phoenix, Arizona. Photographs by Patricia Gutek.

desk. The decorations in the room were sparse, consisting of an American flag and portraits of George Washington and Abraham Lincoln. On the school walls might be hung a map of the United States.

In the first half of the nineteenth century, the teachers in the district schools were often young men who taught school while preparing for other careers. With the success of the common school movement, more women entered teaching and gradually came to outnumber men in the teaching force. By the end of the nineteenth century, women dominated the ranks of elementary teachers. Some of the teachers had little more than a common school education themselves. By mid-nineteenth century, however, more and more teachers were graduates of the teacher education schools called normal schools. The teacher was expected to be a moral exemplar for her students. Of rural school teachers, Fuller wrote: "In her high-buttoned shoes and long skirt, black apron and shirtwaist fringed with celluloid collar and cuffs, she was expected to be and she was a symbol of rectitude there on the Middle Boarder and the major figure in the educator's moral uplift movement in the late nineteenth century." [16]

Ireland Grade School, Stonington Township, Christian County, Illinois, 1941.

Lesson XXIX, The Play Ground. Charles W. Sanders, *Sanders' Pictorial Primer* (Chicago: S. C. Griggs & Co., 1866), p. 23. This lesson is from a representative mid-nineteenth century reading book.

PICTORIAL PRIMER.

LESSON XXIX.

boys	rides	with	hoops
girls	cart	their	swing
one	some	guns	jump
flies	ball	swords	rope
kite	train	roll	dolls

THE PLAY-GROUND.

See the boys and girls at play.
One boy flies his kite, and one rides in his cart.
Some play at ball; some train with their guns and swords.
The girls roll their hoops, or ride in the swing.
Some jump the rope, and some play with their dolls.

A Third Grade Language Exercise. C. C. Long, *New Language Exercises for Primary Schools* (New York: American Book Co., 1889), p. 21. A language arts lesson from a late nineteenth century text book.

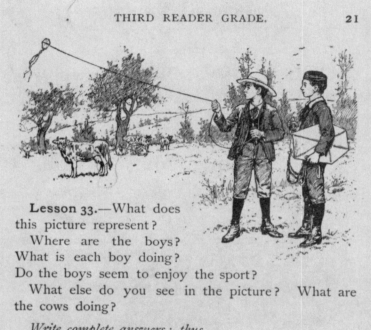

THIRD READER GRADE.   21

Lesson 33.—What does this picture represent?

Where are the boys?
What is each boy doing?
Do the boys seem to enjoy the sport?

What else do you see in the picture? What are the cows doing?

Write complete answers; thus,

A PICTURE.

This picture represents two boys with their kites. I think the boys are in a field because I see grass and trees in the picture. One boy is holding the string of his kite, which is high in the air. The other boy stands at his left, and has a kite under his arm. He is looking at the kite which his companion is flying. The boys seem to enjoy the sport very much.

Back of the boys are trees, under which are several cows. Some of the cows are standing, and some are lying down.

Close your books and write the description of the picture from memory.

In the rural schools, the school day usually began with a prayer or hymn or a patriotic verse. The standard curriculum was reading, writing, arithmetic, spelling, history, and geography. The books used were full of moral lessons and patriotic sentiments. In the early nineteenth century, each student often brought the books that their family owned with them. The teacher would make an assignment from the book and the student would, after memorizing it, recite it. In the post-Civil War period, textbook companies began to publish standardized textbooks for various grade levels. With standardized texts available, teachers were able to use simultaneous group instructions. Among the most popular textbooks used in the country schools were the *McGuffey's Eclectic Readers*. The stories used in the *McGuffey Readers* were intended to instill moral lessons as well as develop reading skills.

Harris and Urban Schools

While the one room rural school presented one version of the common school in the United States, the large urban school was still another version of public education. In the large cities of the United States such as New York, Philadelphia, Boston, Chicago, and Saint Louis, for example, schools were large structures, often of brick construction, that contained a number of classrooms and administrative space for the principal as well. The superintendent of schools, a professional educator who served as chief executive officer presided over the large urban districts which were becoming increasingly standardized and centralized. Attempting to eliminate the inefficiency attributed to rural schools, the urban school administrators sought to operate the urban schools like well-run businesses.

Mann, Barnard, and other common school leaders had worked in an America that was still predominantly rural and small town and that was just beginning to experience the early stages of industrialization. After the Civil War, a great transformation began in American life that would continue into the twentieth century. Industrialization was creating a society that was growing increasingly urban and technological. As a corollary to industrialism, the administration and organization of public schooling became more centralized and systematic, especially in the large cities of the United States. While the one-room school was still a common fixture in the rural areas of the South, Midwest, and Western states, large factory-like schools were being built in the nation's big cities. These large urban schools were built to accommodate several hundred students along with their teachers and principals.

William Torrey Harris (1835-1909) represented the new style of school administrator who appeared after the Civil War, replacing the older generation of common school leaders such as Mann and Barnard. As the major spokesman

Letter Writing. C. C. Long, *New Language Exercises for Primary Schools* (New York:
American Book Co., 1889), p. 44 A letter writing exercise from a late nineteenth century
textbook.

44   LANGUAGE EXERCISES.

LETTER-WRITING.

Lesson 68.—*Copy this letter.   Notice the position, capital-
ization, and punctuation of the different parts.*

> Erie, Pa., Dec. 9, 1890.
>
> Dear Cousin Frank,—
>
> I am so glad that you are to spend your vacation with me. What fun we shall have!
>
> Father has promised me a new sled and a pair of skates. If the weather is cold, we will have a fine time coasting and skating.
>
> Do not fail to come. I will meet you at the station.
>
> Your loving cousin,
>
> Edwin.

of American education in the second half of the nineteenth century, Harris exemplified a style of administration that sought to consolidate and build on the work of the earlier common school leaders. Harris also attempted to direct public schooling in ways that were responsive to America's new industrial and urban realities.

From 1868 to 1880, Harris was the Superintendent of Schools in St. Louis, a growing commercial and industrial metropolis that was experiencing the possibilities as well as the problems of urban growth and development.[17] At the nation's crossroads, St. Louis' location between the North and South gave it a population with both southern and northern sentiments. With a diverse racial and ethnic population, it had a large black community as well as a large number of immigrants, especially German-Americans. In this setting of urban diversity where the one-room rural school was obviously obsolete, Harris established the basic patterns of urban school administration. As he solved the quantitative problems of organizing, classifying, and structuring an urban school system, Harris earned a reputation as an efficient and effective administrator.

As a leader in school administration, Harris was convinced that sound educational policies need to be based on an equally sound philosophy of education. For him, the idealism of the German philosopher, Georg Wilhelm Hegel, and the American transcendentalist, Ralph Waldo Emerson, provided such a philosophy. Idealism gave Harris a rationale that united the older spiritual values with the new industrial ones. Using Hegel's dialectical process, Harris reasoned that a synthesis could be developed that incorporated the positive features of both sets of values. For example, the older spiritual values, based on the Protestant ethic, stressed the importance of diligence, hard work, and perseverance. These older values also carried with them the sense of developing a public responsibility in which wealth would be used for the common good. The newer values, stemming from the process of industrialization, stressed the elimination of needless effort, efficiency in production, and the effective management of time, energy, and resources. The traditional values of the inherited Puritan ethic were well suited to enhance the efficient productivity needed in an industrial society and economy. This synthesis of values could become the philosophy of public education. Under Harris' direction, the schools assumed an active role in preparing the educated workers and managers needed in an industrial economy.[18]

A conservative in his social policy, Harris used his idealist rationale to support and to justify the status quo. He believed that a society had attained a high level of civilization when its social life was organized in institutions such as the family, church, school, and state. These social institutions, he believed, were evolving to higher, more complete, and more complex forms of organization. In such an institutionalized society, the school was an important

Elementary Arithmetic. George M. Philips and Robert R. Anderson, *The Silver-Burdett Arithmetics: Elementary Book* (Boston: Burdett and Co., 1913), p. 1. An elementary arithmetic text that reflects the Pestalozzian emphasis on using objects to teach abstract operations.

ELEMENTARY ARITHMETIC

CHAPTER I

COUNTING, READING, AND WRITING NUMBERS

Counting and Reading Numbers to 9

1. Exercise:

Count the dots in each group.

•	••	•••	••••	•••••
one	two	three	four	five
1	2	3	4	5

••••••	•••••••	••••••••	•••••••••
six	seven	eight	nine
6	7	8	9

Count five; count nine.

Point to the right dots and count *one, two, three, four, five, six, seven, eight, nine.*

Point to four dots; five dots; six dots; nine dots.

Count nine and score thus:

I II III IIII IHI IHI I IHI II IHI III IHI IIII

Point to the right figure, and count *one, two, three, four, five, six, seven, eight, nine.*

Point to the figure that stands for six; five; eight; seven; four; nine.

1

social as well as educational institution. Schools socialized children by providing them with the habits, skills, and knowledge that they needed to participate effectively in an industrial society of growing complexity, specialization, and integration.

Harris' view of the function of the school was based on his conception of the role of social institutions. As society's special agency for promoting civilized life in its younger and more immature members, the school was to cultivate such values as self-discipline, civic commitment, obedience to duly established law and order, and a respect for private property. Taking an essentially reflective view of the school's function, Harris saw it transmitting the cultural heritage to the young so that the time-honored principles of civilization could be passed on and preserved and extended by them. A reflective view of schooling, such as that held by Harris, sees the school as a kind of social mirror that reflects back to society the knowledge and values that it already possesses. In contrast, an originative or reconstructionist orientation argues that the school should create new knowledge and values that will bring about social change.

According to the reflective view of schooling, the school's organization and structure were designed to facilitate the efficient transmission of the curriculum which was the crucial part of its educative mission. Although it would be later defined to encompass all of the students' educational experience, the school curriculum in the nineteenth century referred to the skills, subjects, and values that were comprised in the formal program of instruction. The curriculum, in urban school districts such as Harris' St. Louis, was becoming a carefully graded, structured, organized, sequenced, and cumulative way of organizing knowledge and skills. Since children were organized into grades based on their chronological age, the lessons and materials used in instruction were likewise organized for each grade level. The lessons and materials in reading, writing, arithmetic, and the other subjects were organized according to a sequence that led to a cumulative kind of teaching and learning. Teachers developed and used lesson plans in which a particular unit of subject matter content or a particular skill were taught step-by-step. Each step, in turn, led to a higher level and more complex step. Thus, the urban school, unlike its rural counterpart, was characterized by teaching and learning routines that were part of an educational master plan.

As an educational master planner, Harris developed a curriculum that encompassed the child's entire range of school experiences. Harris became a convinced proponent of Friedrich Froebel's kindergarten concept of early childhood education, which rested on a foundation of philosophical idealism. For Harris, attendance in the kindergarten was to introduce children to group activities and develop readiness for later more academic kinds of learning. After developing these initial skills in the kindergarten, children would then be ready for the elementary school curriculum which Harris, in true idealist fashion, called the "five windows of the soul." Consisting of mathematics, geography, literature and art, history, and grammar, the elementary curriculum would give the children the knowledge base and tool skills needed to participate in human culture. After completing elementary school, students went on to study the more advanced subjects of the secondary school curriculum.

As a school administrator, Harris believed that efficient instructional methods were needed to transmit the curricular subjects effectively. He urged teachers to cultivate industriousness, regularity, punctuality, and discipline in their classrooms and to impress on students the need for incorporating these good working habits into their daily lives.[19] Harris' style of school management and classroom discipline encouraged childrens' conformity to adult standards and to existing social institutions. In St. Louis, Harris stressed strategic planning that involved setting educational objectives and priorities and developing efficient administrative procedures. Harris emphasized meticulous classification and grouping of pupils when dealing with large numbers of students. What emerged was the graded system where the work of each year was organized into a specific grade level that saw students grouped according to their age. The pattern of organizing elementary schools into eight grades, each an academic year in length, and high schools into four years became the standard arrangement in the United States. The graded school in which each grade was taught in a self-contained classroom contrasted with the ungraded pattern found in rural one-room schools where children of all ages were in the same classroom.

In the late nineteenth century, many of the states enacted compulsory attendance laws that required children to attend school until they reached the permitted leaving age. State funding was usually distributed to schools based on the average daily attendance of the students enrolled. To qualify for funding from the states and to make sure that the compulsory attendance laws were being observed meant that school administrators had to compile and maintain statistics on attendance. Further, school administrators such as the superintendent and principal had to make certain that the school buildings were physically safe. They had to concern themselves with problems of lighting, heating, ventilation, and other matters related to the schools' physical facilities. As the nineteenth century came to an end, the result was that school administration had become a complex undertaking. Urban school systems were also showing signs of centralized uniformity and routine.

While he primarily saw the school's mission as preserving existing social institutions and values rather than changing them, Harris also realized that school administrators had to solve new kinds of problems. Throughout the nineteenth century, the education of immigrant children was an important socio-educational issue. Some school administrators believed that the public schools should pursue a rigorous policy of Americanization that eliminated ethnic and cultural differences. Harris, however, took a more moderate stance. While he believed that the public schools should assimilate immigrants into the mainstream of American life, Harris also believed the the assimilative process should be gradual assimilation, he encouraged bi-lingual and bi-cultural educational programs for St. Louis' large German community. While his goal was to bring German-speaking children into the larger English-speaking society, the process would respect their native language and culture.

Because of his successful administration in St. Louis, Harris gained a national reputation. As the United States' Commissioner of Education from 1889 to 1906, he became the authoritative spokesman for American public education. He was a member of the most important educational associations and commissions of the period. He was particularly influential in shaping the policies of the National Education Association which was the largest organization of professional educators in the country.

Harris was a consolidator rather than an innovator. His vision of public education was essentially one in which schools were to transmit existing knowledge and values rather than seeking to change society. His greatest achievement was that of channeling the earlier enthusiasm of the common school proponents into patterns of efficient administration and organization of schools. The work of Harris and other nineteenth century urban school administrators had the consequences of giving American public education the shape that it would have through much of the early twentieth century.

Conclusion

The common school movement represented the foundational stage in the development of the American public school system. The establishment of public elementary school education was the first rung on the structure that became known as the American educational ladder. As a result of the pioneering work of Horace Mann and Henry Barnard, common schools were established by various state legislatures. It was William T. Harris who established the style of the efficient administration of public schools in an industrial and urban society. With the system of common schools as its basic foundation, it was then possible to extend public education upward to the secondary level. Eventually, this process would create a complete system of publicly supported and controlled educational institutions. The origin and establishment of common schools in the United States owes much to the efforts of these educational leaders.

Notes

1 Frank G. Lankard, *A History of the American Sunday School Curriculum* (New York: Abingdon Press, 1927), p. 66.
2 Harold Silver, *Robert Owen on Education* (Cambridge: University Press, 1969), pp. 109-110.
3 Eric Midwinter, *Nineteenth Century Education* (New York: Harper & Row, 1970), pp. 28-29.
4 Carl F. Kaestle, *Joseph Lancaster and the Monitorial School Movement* (New York: Teacher's College Press, Columbia University, 1973), pp. 176-180.
5 Arthur M. Schlesinger, Jr., *The Age of Jackson* (New York: The New American Library, 1958), p. 66.
6 William Maclure, *Opinions on Various Subjects*, I (New Harmony, IN: School Press, 1821), pp. 65-70.
7 The role of evangelical Protestant churches in the common school movement is analyzed in Lloyd P. Jorgenson, *The State and the Non-Public School, 1825-1925* (Columbia, MO: University of Missouri Press, 1987), pp. 31-54.
8 Frank C. Foster, "Horace Mann as Philosopher," *Educational Theory*, X (January, 1960), 925.
9 Merle Curti, *The Social Ideas of American Educators* (New York: Littlefield, Adams, and Co., 1959), pp. 101-38.
10 Horace Mann, *Lectures and Annual Reports on Education* (Cambridge, MA: Published for the Editor by the Cornhill Press of Boston, 1867), p. 151.
11 *Ibid.*, pp. 197-98.
12 *Ibid.*, p. 103
13 Curti, *Social Ideas*, pp. 139-68.
14 John S. Brubacher, *Henry Barnard on Education* (New York: McGraw-Hill Book Company, 1931). Brubacher provides a skillful introduction and editing of Barnard's *Annual Reports*.
15 Wayne E. Fuller, *The Old Country School: The Story of Rural Education in the Middle West* (Chicago: University of Chicago Press, 1982), p. 45.
16 *Ibid.*, p. 201.
17 Selwyn K. Troen, *The Public and the Schools: Shaping the St. Louis System, 1838-1920* (Columbia, MO: University of Missouri Press, 1975), pp. 1-4.
18 *Ibid.*, pp. 161-62.
19 William T. Harris, *Compulsory Education in Relation to Crime and Social Morals* (Washington, DC: Privately printed, 1885), pp. 4-9.

Selections to Accompany
Chapter 3

The first selection is the "First Annual Report of the Board of Education" of Massachusetts. After referring to the work of the Secretary of the Board, Horace Mann, in the report calls attention to some of the specific problems which faced the common schools of the state. As the report comments on construction of school buildings, school committees, teacher education, school libraries, and textbooks, the reader can see for himself the condition of common schools in Massachusetts as of 1837.

First Annual Report of the Board of Education

It is not the province of the Board of Education to submit to the Legislature, in the form of specific projects of law, those measures, which they may deem advisable for the improvement of the schools and the promotion of the cause of education. That duty is respectfully left by the Board, with the wisdom of the legislature and its committees, on whom it is by usage devolved. Neither will it be expected of the Board, on the present occasion, to engage in a lengthened discussion of topics, fully treated in their Secretary's report, to which they beg leave to refer, as embodying a great amount of fact, and the result of extensive observation skilfully generalized. The Board ask permission only to submit a few remarks on some of the more important topics connected with the general subject.

1. As the comfort and progress of children at school depend, to a very considerable degree, on the proper and commodious construction of school-houses, the Board ask leave to invite the particular attention of the Legislature

Source: Horace Mann, *Lectures and Annual Reports on Education* (Cambridge, MA: Published for the Editor by the Cornhill Press of Boston, 1867), pp. 374-82. The first part of the report which deals with the appointment of the Secretary of the Board has been omitted.

to their Secretary's remarks on this subject. As a general observation, it is no doubt too true, that the schoolhouses in most of the districts of the Commonwealth are of an imperfect construction. It is apprehended that sometimes at less expense than is now incurred, and in other cases, by a small additional expense, schoolhouses much more conducive to the health and comfort, and consequently to the happiness and progress of children, might he erected. Nor would it be necessary, in most cases, in order to introduce the desired improvements, that new buildings should be constructed. Perhaps in a majority of cases, the end might he attained to a considerable degree, by alterations and additions to the present buildings. It is the purpose of the Secretary of the Board, as early as practicable, to prepare and submit a special report on the construction of schoolhouses. When this document shall be laid before them, it will be for the Legislature to judge, whether any encouragement can, with good effect, be offered from the school-fund, with a view to induce the towns of the Commonwealth to adopt those improvements in the construction of schoolhouses, which experience and reason show to be of great practical importance in carrying on the business of education.

2. Very much of the efficiency of the best system of school education depends upon the fidelity and zeal with which the office of a school-committee-man is performed. The Board deem it unnecessary to dilate upon a subject so ably treated by their Secretary. The difficulties to be surmounted before the services of able and faithful school-committee-men can be obtained, in perhaps a majority of the towns of the Commonwealth, are confessedly great and various. They can be thoroughly overcome only by the spirit of true patriotism, generously exerting itself toward the great end of promoting the intellectual improvement of fellow men. But it is in the power of the Legislature to remove some of the obstacles, among which not the least considerable is the pecuniary sacrifice involved in the faithful and laborious discharge of the duties of the school committee. The Board have understood, with great satisfaction, that the subject has been brought before the House of Representatives. They know of no reason why the members of school committees should not receive a reasonable compensation, as well as other municipal officers, of whom it is not usually expected that they should serve the public gratuitously. There are none whose labors, faithfully performed, are of greater moment to the general well-being. The duties of a member of a school committee, if conscientiously discharged are onerous; and ought not to be rendered more so, by being productive of a heavy pecuniary loss, in the wholly unrequited devotion of time and labor to the public good.

3. The subject of the education of teachers has been more than once brought before the Legislature, and is of the very highest importance in connection with the improvement of our schools. That there are all degrees of skill and success on the part of teachers, is matter of too familiar observation to need

repetition; and that these must depend, in no small degree, on the experience of the teacher, and in his formation under a good discipline and method of instructions in early life, may be admitted without derogating, in any measure, from the importance of natural gifts and aptitude, in fitting men for this as for the other duties of society. Nor can it be deemed unsafe to insist that, while occupations requiring a very humble degree of intellectual effort and attainment demand a long-continued training, it cannot be that the arduous and manifold duties of the instructor of youth should be as well performed without as with a specific preparation for them. In fact, it must be admitted, as the voice of reason and experience, that institutions for the formation of teachers must be established among us, before the all-important work of forming the minds of our children can be performed in the best possible manner, and with the greatest attainable success.

No one who has been the witness of the ease and effect with which instruction is imparted by one teacher, and the tedious pains-taking and unsatisfactory progress which mark the labors of another of equal ability and knowledge, and operating on materials equally good, can entertain a doubt that there is a mastery in teaching as in every other art. Nor is it less obvious that, within reasonable limits, this skill and this mastery may themselves be made the subjects of instruction, and be communicated to others.

We are not left to the deductions of reason on this subject. In those foreign countries, where the greatest attention has been paid to the work of education, schools for teachers have formed an important feature in their systems, and with the happiest result. The art of imparting instruction has been found, like every other art, to improve by cultivation in institutions established for that specific object. New importance has been attached to the calling of the instructor by public opinion, from the circumstance that his vocation has been deemed one requiring systematic preparation and culture. Whatever tends to degrade the profession of the teacher, in his own mind or that of the public, of course impairs his usefulness; and this result must follow from regarding instruction as a business which in itself requires no previous training.

The duties which devolve upon the teachers even of our Common Schools, particularly when attended by large numbers of both sexes, and of advanced years for learners (as is often the case), are various, and difficult of performance. For their faithful execution, no degree of talent and qualification is too great; and when we reflect that in the nature of things only a moderate portion of both can, in ordinary cases, be expected, for the slender compensation afforded the teacher, we gain a new view of the necessity of bringing to his duties the advantage of previous training in the best mode of discharging them.

A very considerable part of the benefit, which those who attend our schools might derive from them, is unquestionably lost for want of mere skill in the business of instruction, on the part of the teacher. This falls with especial hardship on that part of our youthful population, who are able to enjoy, but for a small portion of the year, the advantage of the schools. For them it is of peculiar importance, that, from the moment of entering the school, every hour should be employed to the greatest advantage, and every facility in imparting knowledge, and every means of awakening and guiding the mind, be put into instant operation: and where this is done, two months of schooling would be as valuable as a year passed under a teacher destitute of experience and skill. The Board cannot but express the sanguine hope, that the time is not far distant, when the resources of public or private liberality will be applied in Massachusetts for the foundation of an institution for the formation of teachers, in which the present existing defect will be amply supplied.

4. The subject of district-school libraries is deemed of very great importance by the Board. A foundation was made for the formation of such libraries, by the Act of 12th April, 1837, authorizing an expenditure by each district of thirty dollars, for this purpose, the first year, and ten each succeeding year. Such economy has been introduced into the business of printing, that even these small sums judiciously applied for a term of years will amply suffice for the desired object. To the attainment of this end, it is in the power of booksellers and publishers to render the most material aid. There is no reason to doubt, that if neat editions of books suitable for Common-School libraries were published and sold at a very moderate rate, plainly and substantially bound, and placed in cases well adapted for convenient transportation, and afterwards to serve as the permanent place of deposit, it would induce many of the districts in the Commonwealth to exercise the power of raising money for school libraries. A beginning once made, steady progress would in many cases be sure to follow. Where circumstances did not admit the establishment of a library in each district, it might very conveniently be deposited a proportionate part of the year in each district successively. But it would be highly desirable that each schoolhouse should be furnished with a case and shelves, suitable for the proper arrangement and safekeeping of books. The want of such a provision makes it almost impossible to begin the collection of a library; and where such provision is made, the library would be nearly sure to receive a steady increase.

Although the Board are of opinion, that nothing would more promote the cause of education among us, than the introduction of libraries into our district schools, they have not deemed it advisable to recommend any measure looking to the preparation of a series of volumes, of which such a library should be composed, and their distribution, at public expense. Whatever advantages would belong to a library consisting of books expressly written for the purpose, obvious difficulties and dangers would attend such an undertaking. The Board deem it far more advisable to leave this work to the enterprise and judgment of publishers, who would, no doubt, find it for their interest to make preparations to satisfy a demand for district-school libraries in the way above indicated.

In this connection the Board would observe, that much good might unquestionably be effected by the publication of a periodical journal or paper, of which the exclusive object should be to promote the case of education, especially of Common-School education. Such a journal, conducted on the pure principles of Christian philanthropy, of rigid abstinence from party and sect, sacredly devoted to the one object of education, to collecting and diffusing information on this subject, to the discussion of the numerous important questions which belong to it, to the formation of a sound and intelligent public opinion, and the excitement of a warm and energetic public sentiment, in favor of our schools, might render incalculable service. The Board are decidedly of opinion, that a journal of this description would be the most valuable auxiliary which could be devised, to carry into execution the enlightened policy of the government, in legislating for the improvement of the schools, and they indulge a sanguine hope that its establishment will shortly be witnessed.

5. The subject of school-books is perhaps one of more immediate and pressing interest. The multiplicity of school-books, and the imperfection of many of them, is one of the greatest evils at present felt in our Common Schools. The Board know of no way, in which this evil could be more effactually remedied, than by the selection of the best of each class now in use, and a formal recommendation of them by the Board of Education. Such a recommendation would probably cause them to be generally adopted; but should this not prove effectual, and the evil be found to continue, it might hereafter be deemed expedient to require the use of the books thus recommended, as a condition of receiving a share of the benefit of the school fund.

The foregoing observations are all that now occur to the Board of Education, as proper to be made to the Legislature, in connection with the improvement of our Common Schools. They beg leave to submit an additional remark on the subject of their own sphere of operations. It is evident, from the nature of the case, that much of the efficiency and usefulness of the Board must depend on the zeal and fidelity of its Secretary, and that it is all-important to command, in this office, the services of an individual of distinguished talent and unquestioned character. No other qualifications will inspire the confidence generally of the people; and without that confidence, it is impossible that his labors or those of the Board should be crowned with success. The Board ask permission to state, that they deem themselves very fortunate in having engaged the services of a gentleman so highly qualified as their Secretary, to discharge the interesting duties of his trust; and they respectfully submit to the Legislature, the expediency of raising his compensation to an amount, which could more fairly he regarded as a satisfactory equivalent for the employment of all his time. The Board also think, that a small allowance should be made for the contingent expenses of the Secretary in the discharge of his duties, such as postage, stationery, and occasional clerk-hire. It is just, however, to add, that this proposal for an increase of salary is made wholly without suggestion on the part of the Secretary.

In conclusion, the Board would tender their acknowledgments to their fellow-citizens, who, by attending on the meetings of the county conventions, or in any other way, have afforded their cooperation in the promotion of the great cause of popular education. At most of these meetings, permanent county conventions for the improvement of education have been organized. Spirited addresses have, in almost every case, emanated from the county meetings, well calculated to impart vigor and warmth to the public sentiment in reference to the cause of education. On the whole, the Board have reason to hope, that an impulse has been given to the public mind on the subject of education, from which valuable effects may be anticipated. It will be their strenuous effort, under the auspices of the Legislature, and as far as the powers vested in them extend, to encourage and augment the interest which has been excited, and they hope, as they shall acquire experience, that their labors will become more efficient. They do not flatter themselves that great and momentous reforms are to be effected at once. Where the means employed are those of calm appeal to the understanding and the heart, a gradual and steady progress is all that should be desired. The schools of Massachusetts are not every thing that we could wish, but public opinion is sound in reference to their improvement. The voice of reason will not be uttered in vain. Experience, clearly stated in its results, will command respect, and the Board entertain a confident opinion that the increased attention given to the subject will result in making our system of Common-School education fully worthy of the intelligence of the present day, and of the ancient renown of Massachusetts.

All which is respectfully submitted by

> Edward Everett,
> George Hull,
> James G. Carter,
> Edmund Dwight,
> George Putnam,
> E.A. Newton,
> Robert Rantoul, Jun.,
> Jared Sparks.

Boston, February 1, 1838

In 1833, Warren Burton's slim volume, The District School As It Was, *appeared. The book recounts the trials and tribulations of a typical nineteenth-century American boy in the district school of New England. While the book is essentially a reminiscence, it presents a classic statement on the condition of education in the common school. In the student's preparation of the grammar lesson depicted here, the stress is placed on rote memorization with little attention to the content of the lesson. The ignorance of the teacher of any of the principles of educational psychology is also evident.*

Grammar—Young Lady's Accidence— Murray—Parsing—Pope's Essay

On my fifth summer, at the age of seven and a half, I commenced the study of grammar. The book generally used in our school by beginners, was called the *Young Lady's Accidence!* I had the honor of a new one. The *Young Lady's Accidence!* How often have I gazed on that last word, and wondered what it meant! Even now, I cannot define it, though, of course, I have a guess at its meaning. Let me turn this very minute to that oracle of definitions, the venerable Webster: "A small book containing the rudiments of grammar." That is it, then. But what an intelligible and appropriate term for a little child's book! The mysterious title, however, was most appropriate to the contents of the volume; for they were all mysterious, and that for years, to my poor understanding.

Well, my first lesson was to get the Parts of Speech, as they are called. What a grand achievement to engrave on my memory these ten separate and strange words! With what ardor I took my lesson from the mistress, and trudged to my seat! It was a new study, and it was the first day of the school, moreover, before the bashfulness occasioned by a strange teacher had subsided, and before the spirit of play had been excited. So there was nothing at the moment to divert me from the lofty enterprise.

Reader, let your mind's eye peep into that old school-house. See that little boy in the second high seat from the front, in home-made and home-dyed pea-green cotton jacket and trowsers, with a clean Monday morning collar turned out from his neck. His new book is before him on the bench, kept

Source: Warren Burton, *The District School As It Was*, Clifton Johnson, ed. (Boston: Lee and Shepard, 1897), pp. 34-41.

open by his left hand. His right supports his head on its palm, with the corresponding elbow pressed on the bench. His lips move, but at first very slowly. He goes over the whole lesson in a low whisper. He now looks off his book, and pronounces two or three of the first, —article, noun, pronoun; then just glances at the page, and goes on with two or three more. He at length repeats several words without looking. Finally, he goes through the long catalogue, with his eye fastened on vacancy. At length, how his lips flutter, and you hear the parts of speech whizzing from his tongue like feathered arrows!

There, the rigmarole is accomplished. He starts up, and is at the mistress's side in a moment. "Will you hear my lesson, ma'am?" As she takes the book he looks directly in her face, and repeats the aforementioned words loudly and distinctly, as if there were no fear of failure. He has got as far as the adverb; but now he hesitates, his eye drops, his lips are open ready for utterance, but the word does not come. He shuts them, he presses them hard together, he puts his finger to them, and there is a painful hiatus in his recitation, a disconnection, an *anti* to the very word he is after. "Conjunction," says the mistress. The little hand leaves the lips, at the same time that an involuntary "Oh!" bursts out from them. He lifts his head and his eye, and repeats with spirit the delinquent word, and goes on without hesitation to the end of the lesson. "Very well," says the teacher, or the hearer of the school; for she rather listened to than instructed her pupils. "Get so far for the next lesson." The child bows, whirls on his heel, and trips to his seat, mightily satisfied excepting with that one failure of memory, when that thundering word, conjunction, refused to come at his will. But that word he never forgot again. The failure fastened it in his memory forever. This pea-green boy was myself the present historian of the scene.

My next lesson lagged a little; my third seemed quite dull; my fourth I was two days in getting. At the end of the week, I thought that I could get along through the world very well without grammar, as my grandfather had done before me. But my mistress did not agree with me, and I was forced to go on. I contrived, however, to make easy work of the study. I got frequent, but very short lessons, only a single sentence at a time. This was easily committed to memory, and would stay on till I could run up and toss it off in recitation, after which it did not trouble me more. The recollection of it puts me in mind of a little boy lugging in wood, a stick at a time. My teacher was so ignorant of the philosophy of mind, that she did not know that this was not as good a way as any; and indeed, she praised me for my smartness. The consequence was, that, after I had been through the book, I could scarcely have repeated ten lines of it, excepting the very first and the very last lessons. Had it been ideas instead of words that had thus escaped from my mind, the case would have been different. As it was, the only matter of regret was, that I had been forming a bad habit, and had imbibed an erroneous notion, to wit, that lessons were to be learned simply to be recited.

The next winter this Accidence was committed, not to memory, but to oblivion; for, on presenting it to the master the first day of the school, he told me it was old-fashioned and out of date, and I must have Murray's Abridgment. So Murray was purchased, and I commenced the study of grammar again, excited by the novelty of a new and clean and larger book. But this soon became even more dull and dry than its predecessor; for it was more than twice the size, and the end of it was at the most discouraging distance of months, if not of years. I got only half way through the verb this winter. The next summer I began the book again, and arrived at the end of the account of the parts of speech. The winter after, I went over the same ground again, and got through the rules of syntax, and felt that I had accomplished a great work. The next summer I reviewed the whole grammar; for the mistress thought it necessary to have "its most practical and important parts firmly fixed in the memory, before attempting the higher exercises of the study." On the third winter, I began to apply my supposed knowledge in the process of *passing*, as it was termed by the master. The very pronunciation of this word shows how little the teacher exercised the power of independent thought. He had been accustomed to hear parse called *pass;* and, though the least reflection would have told him it was not correct, that reflection came not, and for years the grammarians of our district school *passed*. However, it was rightly so called. It *was* passing, as said exercise was performed; passing over, by, around, away, from the science of grammar, without coming near it, or at least without entering into it with much understanding of its nature. Mode, tense, case, government, and agreement were ever flying from our tongues, to be sure; but their meaning was as much a mystery as the hocus pocus of a juggler.

At first we parsed in simple prose, but soon entered on poetry. Poetry — a thing which to our apprehension differed from prose in this only, that each line began with a capital letter, and ended usually with a word sounding like another word at the end of the adjoining line. But, unskilled as we all generally were in the art of parsing, some of us came to think ourselves wonderfully acute and dexterous nevertheless. When we perceived the master himself to be in doubt and perplexity, then we felt ourselves on a level with him, and ventured to oppose our *guess* to his. And if he appeared a dunce extraordinary, as was sometimes the case, we used to put ourselves into the *potential* mood pretty often, as we knew that our teacher could never assume the *imperative* on this subject.

The fact is, neither we nor the teacher entered into the writer's meaning. The general plan of the work was not surveyed, nor the particular sense of separate passages examined. We could not do it, perhaps from the want of maturity of mind; the teacher did not, because he had never been accustomed to anything of the kind in his own education; and it never occurred to him that he could deviate from the track, or improve upon the methods of those who taught him. Pope's *Essay on Man* was the parsing manual used by the most advanced. No wonder, then, that the pupil and pedagogue so often got bewildered and lost in a world of thought like this; for, however well ordered a creation it might be, it was scarcely better than a chaos to them.

In closing, I ought to remark, that all our teachers were not thus ignorant of grammar, although they did not perhaps take the best way to teach it. In speaking thus of this department of study, and also of others, I have reference to the more general character of schoolmasters and schools.

Suggestions for Further Reading

Binder, Frederick M. *The Age of the Common School, 1830-1865*. New York: John Wiley and Sons, 1974.

Brubacher, John S. *Henry Barnard on Education*. New York: McGraw-Hill Book Co., 1931.

Church, Robert L. and Michael W. Sedlak. *Education in the United States: An Interpretive History*. New York: The Free Press—Macmillan Publishing Co., 1976.

Cremin, Lawrence. *The American Common School*. New York: Teachers College Press, Columbia University, 1951.

Cremin, Lawrence. *The Republic and the School: Horace Mann on the Education of Free Men*. New York: Bureau of Publications, Teachers College Press, Columbia University, 1957.

Curti, Merle. *The Social Ideas of American Educators*. New York: Littlefield, Adams and Co., 1959.

Downs, Robert B. *Horace Mann: Champion of Public Schools*. New York: Twayne Publishers, 1974.

Fuller, Wayne E. *The Old Country School: The Story of Rural Education in the Middle West*. Chicago: University of Chicago Press, 1982.

Jorgenson, Lloyd P. *The State and the Non-Public School, 1825-1959*. Columbus: University of Missouri Press, 1987.

Kaestle, Carl F. *Joseph Lancaster and the Monitorial Schools Movement*. New York: Teachers College Press, Columbia University, 1973.

Katz, Michael B. *School Reform: Past and Present*. Boston: Little, Brown and Co., 1971.

Leidecker, Kurt F. *Yankee Teacher: The Life of William Torey Harris*. New York: Philosophical Library, 1946.

Messerli, Jonathan. *Horace Mann: A Biography*. New York: Alfred A. Knopf, 1972.

Midwinter, Eric. *Nineteenth Century Education*. New York: Harper & Row, 1970.

Nasaw, David. *Schooled to Order: A Social History of Public Schooling in the United States*. New York: Oxford University Press, 1979.

Sitton, Thad and Milam C. Rowold. *Ringing the Children In: Texas Country Schools*. College Station: Texas A & M University Press, 1987.

Thursfield, Richard E. *Henry Barnard's American Journal of Education*. Baltimore: Johns Hopkins Press, 1945.

Troen, Selwyn E. *The Public and the Schools: Shaping the St. Louis System, 1838-1920*. Columbia: University of Missouri Press, 1975.

The Evolution of American Secondary Education

Introduction

In the history of American secondary education no single individuals stand out as do Henry Barnard and Horace Mann in the struggle to establish the common elementary school. Nor did the American high school emerge as a result of the same kind of simple, forthright arguments that were part of the struggle for elementary schools. The comprehensive high school resulted from a slow process of evolution which only gradually defined it as the basic institution of American secondary education. This evolutionary process began with the import of the Latin Grammar school from Europe, continued with the appearance of the academy, and culminated in the public high school.

Although the struggle to establish publicly supported and controlled elementary education had been successful in most of the states by the time of the Civil War, public secondary schools did not emerge until the latter half of the nineteenth century. As the public high school rose in importance to become the dominant institution of secondary education, the famous ladder of American educational opportunity was completed. From that point on, American youngsters could proceed from the pre-school kindergarten through the common elementary school to the high school, and eventually complete their education in the state college or university. The establishment of the public high school was therefore a crucial phase in American education, because it represented the completion of the basic public school system.

Although there are various ways of defining secondary education, ranging from the traditional strictly college preparatory to the more widely varied forms of contemporary adolescent education, for the purposes of this discussion secondary education refers to those formal educational experiences, usually encountered during adolescence, which follow completion of elementary education.[1] This broad definition covers both comprehensive general studies and specialized vocational studies.

Concept of the Educational Ladder

The American educational "ladder" describes the single, articulated, and sequential system of schools open to all, regardless of social and economic class or religious affiliation. The ladder concept is the educational counterpart of the Jeffersonian-Jacksonian doctrines of equality of opportunity. In contrast to this educational egalitarianism, the European dual system differentiates secondary students into separate and discrete educational tracks with one set of schools for the leadership elite and another inferior group for the masses of the population.

To review the progress of the ladder concept in American education, three major periods in the history of secondary school development can he defined: first, the colonial period, dominated by the Latin Grammar school; second, the late eighteenth and early nineteenth centuries, dominated by the academy; third, the late nineteenth and twentieth centuries, dominated by the public high school.

Decline of the Latin Grammar School

As indicated in the discussion of colonial education, the Latin Grammar schools provided a college preparatory education for the sons of the upper classes so that they could meet the entry requirements for admission to institutions of higher learning such as Harvard, Yale, and William and Mary. A classical education was recommended for those aspiring to ecclesiastical or political leadership. Knowledge of the Greek and Latin classics was one of the identifying marks of the person of education and breeding. By the seventeenth and eighteenth centuries, the Latin Grammar school had lost much of the humanism of its Renaissance origins and had grown increasingly formalized and sterile. By the time of its establishment in the North American colonies, the curriculum of the Latin Grammar school was a narrow one that emphasized mastery of the grammatical and stylistic mechanics of the ancient Greek and Latin literatures.

Even before the American Revolution, such critics of the Latin Grammar school as Benjamin Franklin objected to the limited curriculum dominating secondary education. In 1749, Franklin had proposed an English Academy in Philadelphia that would offer a more realistic course of study to satisfy the contemporary needs of the people. At the same time a number of private venture schools appeared. These schools, usually conducted by a single master, offered a wide range of subjects and skills such as modern languages, navigation, bookkeeping, and surveying. Although a number of the private venture schools were begun in commercial centers such as New York, Philadelphia, and Charleston, they were sporadic and usually short-lived.

After the American Revolution of 1776 and the beginning of the industrial revolution, the Latin Grammar school fell into disfavor. The popular quest was for a more utilitarian kind of secondary school that would prepare students for the duties of republican citizenship and for an increasingly industrial society. The institution that emerged to fill this need was the academy.

Rise of the Academy

Although the academy was first introduced in the late eighteenth century, it reflected far more the social-cultural-economic *milieu* of the nineteenth century. It was a social institution that typified the optimism of the American people during the enthusiastic period between the Revolution and the Civil War.[2]

The first half of the nineteenth century was a period of great faith in the possibilities of improving the human condition through social reform. The expansive liberalism that characterized this attitude fostered a climate in which the academies could provide increasing educational opportunities by means of open enrollment and relatively non-structured curricula. It was the age of the common man, of frontier individualism, and also of class mobility, for it was no longer necessary to own property in order to vote.

Economically the age was one of "free enterprise," the era of the individual entrepreneur and Jacksonian *laissez-faire*. The academy, privately controlled as it usually was, extended the spirit of the small entrepreneur into education.

The great popularity of the academies was an outgrowth of the wave of spontaneous enthusiasm for formal education that took the form of an unorganized but nonetheless nationwide movement. By 1855 there were 263,096 students in 6,185 institutions.[3]

The academy tended to replace or absorb the Latin Grammar school, because although it had no clear-cut design as the latter did, the academy met the educational needs of a civilization that was both frontier and industrial in character.

In many ways the academy synthesized the functions of the Latin Grammar school and the private venture school. Like the former it offered classical courses designed for college entrance. In addition, like the private venture school, it offered instruction in such practical subjects as accounting, bookkeeping, navigation, modern languages, and surveying, which were terminal courses for many students. The academies were attended chiefly by members of the rising middle class of businessmen, professionals, and entrepreneurs, and curricula were organized around their needs.

Curricula and Administration of the Academy

Generally speaking, the secondary school had four major responsibilities to meet. First, the rise of direct democracy, which resulted from the Revolution and the extension of suffrage, made it necessary for more people to be educated to take part in civic affairs. Second, commercial expansion and the industrial revolution created a demand for people skilled in such subjects as navigation, accounting, and modern languages. In the same way westward expansion of the frontier encouraged the study of surveying. College preparation remained, as it had always been, one of the perennial concerns of secondary education. The American academies reflected these needs in the wide variety of courses they offered, usually under the heading of one of three basic curricula: classical (college preparatory); terminal (English); and normal (teacher education). Within the framework of these three major curricula there were a number of such hybrids as the classical-English, English-scientific, commercial-English, and normal-English. Because of the extreme *laissez-faire* educational context of the academy, there were probably as many varieties of curricular offerings as there were academies.

Circulars for different schools during this era promised the following courses: classics, Latin, Greek, English, oratory, composition, rhetoric, literature, French, Spanish, Portuguese, German, trigonometry, bookkeeping, accounting, surveying, geography, United States history, general history, logic, moral philosophy, astronomy, chemistry, drawing, religion, natural philosophy, geometry, algebra, needlework, phrenology, optics, geology, biology, botany, domestic science, and agricultural principles.

With such a wide variety of courses to offer, the academies' energies were diffused. Some academies attempted to offer all of them, while others restricted themselves to only a few. Some of the teachers were college graduates and competent in their teaching areas, but others were charlatans, merely interested in a quick tuition fee. Methodology was based on the theory of mental discipline and the acquisition of factual information, and was carried out by drill, textbook memorization, recitation, and repetition. The lack of any common standards inevitably produced several weaknesses. There was chaotic proliferation without organization in course offerings, including numerous short courses in subjects sometimes taught for only a few weeks. There was no established system of accreditation for schools. Some of these weaknesses were later inherited by the high school system that succeeded the academies.

The academies were private or semi-public schools controlled by independent, self-perpetuating boards of trustees. Although a few academies did receive local or state grants and subsidies from their inception, the trustees usually sustained the initial expenses of building the academy, hiring the staff, and attracting the students. Tile bulk of support came from the tuition fees paid by the students.

The prosperity of the academy coincided with a period of intense religious individualism. Denominations proliferated and tended to perpetuate themselves through education. Methodists, Episcopalians, Baptists, Roman Catholics, Presbyterians, Congregationalists, and other groups established their own academies in order to teach the principles of their particular religion, prepare students for college, and offer social and vocational education. Many small denominational colleges existing today were originally chartered as academies.

Some academies were downward extensions of state colleges and universities. Many colleges received charters from state legislatures but found no ready supply of adequately prepared students because of the sparseness of secondary education in their areas. For this reason some of them established secondary schools to prepare students for college entrance by offering basic literary skills and classical languages.

Academy Decline

The Civil War eroded some of America's naive optimism. In the post-war period of the 1870s and 1880s, the rather unwieldy academies were increasingly replaced by the more stable institution of the public high school. This trend was in part attributable to the transition in America from a rural society to an urban one. The urban population was able to support an extensive public secondary school because it provided a larger tax base. By the beginning of the twentieth century, the country's economic basis had shifted from the individual to the corporate structure. As economic entrepreneurship gradually yielded to the corporation, the educational counterpart of entrepreneurship, the academy, also declined.[4] The public high school was better equipped to meet the new demands of the increasing city populations and fill the ranks of corporate industry.

Growth of the High School

Although free high schools had existed in the United States since the founding of the English Classical School of Boston in 1821, it was not until the latter half of the nineteenth century that the high school was firmly established as the dominant institution of American secondary education. During the 1880s its numbers began to outrank the academy. According to the report of the United States Commissioner of Education for 1889-1890, there were 2,526 public high schools with an enrollment of 202,063 in contrast to the 94,391 students enrolled in 1,632 private secondary schools and academies.[5]

The rise of the high school was related to the socioeconomic changes that had transformed the United States from a basically rural agrarian nation to an urban industrial one. The new urban life required that people be more highly trained, that they receive better vocational education, and that they concentrate on the specialized activities of an industrial society. One effect of such specialization was that children no longer had the same opportunity of direct experience with life as they had had in simpler rural communities. Urban society also tended to isolate them from direct participation in social life. As a result the schools came to perform the additional function of intermediary between the adult world and the child's world. What adolescents needed was an institution specifically designed to facilitate their introduction to participation in the adult world.

In addition to the shift from rural to urban life, the industrial revolution also stimulated exploration of new areas of knowledge and study. As a result, the basic literacy provided children by the common elementary school was no longer adequate preparation for their intelligent participation in an industrial society. The high school provided broader educational opportunities for youth to assimilate these expanding areas of knowledge.

However, the high school could not have come into existence as an upward extension of the educational ladder without the necessary foundation of the common elementary school, and, could not have expanded as it did until the development of the latter was well advanced.[6] By the 1870s and 1880s, the existence of the common elementary school had become an accepted reality of American life.

The high school movement received additional impetus from the public's growing sensitivity to the needs of children and youth. Child labor legislation took adolescents out of the factories and mills and placed them in school. The greater educational opportunity resulting from compulsory attendance laws was considered a useful means of reducing juvenile delinquency and producing more worthy citizens.

Finally, industrialized urban society was able to support more extensive educational institutions than the rural one had. Mass production techniques created surplus wealth, making possible a larger base of taxation for spending on education.

The struggle to establish high school education for American youth was actually a continuation of the common school movement. The common school movement of the early nineteenth century had established the state's responsibility for tax-supported elementary education, and as the movement to extend that responsibility to the secondary level gained momentum the struggle was re-enacted. However, this time the arguments were raised in the courts rather than in the legislative assemblies.

Although several court cases are relevant to the legal establishment of taxation for high schools, the Kalamazoo Case of 1874 and the decision rendered by Justice Thomas C. Cooley of the Michigan State Supreme Court clearly established the precedent. A group of taxpayers of the Kalamazoo school district initiated a suit to prevent the board of education from levying a tax to support a high school. The claimants argued that the high school curriculum, which was primarily college preparatory, did not merit public support by taxation. Why, they asked, should the majority of taxpayers be coerced into paying for the education of the small minority that was college-bound?

Justice Cooley's decision to uphold the right of the Kalamazoo school district to tax the community for support of a high school was based on the state's obligation not only to provide elementary education, but also to maintain equal educational opportunity for all. Since the state was already maintaining public elementary schools and colleges, he ruled, it would be highly inconsistent for the state to fail to provide the interim stage whereby the student could move from elementary to higher education. Justice Cooley affirmed the right of the school board to tax for the support of this transitional institution.

The Cooley decision had the effect of encouraging state legislatures to pass laws permitting local boards to establish high schools. Later on, following much the same pattern as they had with elementary education, state legislatures first encouraged and then compelled the establishment of high schools. It was finally possible for a student to attend a complete sequence of educational institutions from kindergarten through elementary and high schools to the highest level a university could offer, all within the framework of publicly supported and controlled schools.

Standardizing the Curriculum: The Committee of Ten

The American high school took shape during the period from 1880 to 1920, the same era that saw the basic American social and economic patterns shift from a rural to an urban orientation. In the confusion and conflict that marked the early years of the new institution's development, the most pressing question was that of whom to educate and how best to do it. Was it to be college preparatory, as had been traditionally true of secondary education? Or was the high school to be a terminal institution, specifically designed for those who would be concluding their formal education there? And should it therefore stress traditional college preparatory subjects, or offer more programs in manual, industrial, commercial, and vocational training?

At first the high school appeared to be in danger of repeating the history of its predecessor, the academy, in offering a multiplicity of ill-defined programs of instruction. Often within the same school could be found curricula with such titles as the ancient classical, the business commercial, the shorter commercial, the English terminal, the English science, and the scientific. The confusion caused by such lack of direction demanded solution if the high school was to become an integral step in the American educational ladder.

To deal with this problem of standardization, the National Education Association established the Committee of Ten in 1892. The Committee was composed of representatives from five colleges and universities, one public school principal, two headmasters of private schools, United States Commissioner of Education William T. Harris, and Committee chairman Charles W. Eliot, President of Harvard University.[7] Since the majority of the Committee members were associated with higher education, it could be anticipated that its work would be oriented toward the college preparatory function of the high school.

Chairman Charles Eliot was an important leader in higher education, whose interests also extended to the fields of elementary and secondary education. He was concerned with improving the efficiency of the schools, making economic use of the time the students spent in school, and increasing their freedom of subject choice by the introduction of a system of electives. As head of the Committee, he vigorously guided its studies of the scope and function of secondary education. The Committee of Ten's policies developed around two of Eliot's basic concepts: earlier introduction of the fundamentals of several subjects in the upper elementary grades, and no differentiation between subjects or teaching of college preparatory and terminal students.[8]

The report of the Committee of Ten recommended eight years of elementary and four years of secondary education. For the high school, four separate curricula were recommended: classical, Latin-scientific, modern language, and English. While each curriculum included foreign languages, mathematics, English, science, and history, the major differences were that the modern language curriculum permitted the substitution of modern languages for Latin and Greek and that the Latin-scientific emphasized mathematics and science.

Subjects appropriate to high school study were English and foreign languages such as Latin, Greek, German, French, and Spanish; mathematics such as algebra, geometry, and trigonometry; natural sciences such as descriptive astronomy, meteorology, botany, zoology, physiology, geology, and physical geography; physical sciences such as physics and chemistry. In addition, the intensive study of selected historical periods was recommended. The Committee further recommended that high school students study intensively a relatively small number of subjects for longer periods of time. Every subject was to be taught in the high school in the same way and to the same extent to each student regardless of his further educational aims.

The Report of the Committee of Ten is a revealing document in that it demonstrates the tendency of the higher institution, the college, to dominate the lower, the high school. Although the Committee stated that the high school did not exist exclusively for the purpose of college preparation, its report was more concerned with subject matter designed for college entrance. The Committee justified its orientation with the theory of mental discipline. The recommended subjects, it claimed, could be used profitably by both the terminal and college preparatory students for training their powers of observation, memory, expression, and reasoning.[9]

High School Accreditation

The relationship of the high school to the college was a major problem of institutional articulation in the 1890s, and the aspect affording the greatest concern was that of entrance or admission requirements to the college. In 1895, the North Central Association was established with a combined membership of colleges and secondary schools for the purpose of establishing closer relations in the North Central states.[10]

In 1899, the National Education Association established the Committee on College Entrance Requirements. In an attempt to resolve the long-brewing conflict over the elective principle, which permitted students to make their own choice of subjects, the Committee proposed a set of constant subjects, a core of courses to be required of all students without reference to their educational destination. The remainder of the program was to be elected by each student.[11] The Committee used the term "unit" to describe a subject acceptable for accreditation purposes. A subject studied for four or five periods a week for one school year in secondary school was defined as a "unit" of study. The constants recommended in the core group were four units of foreign languages, two of mathematics, two of English, one of history, and one of science.

In 1902 the Committee on Unit Courses of the North Central Association defined as acceptable a high school which required fifteen units of work for graduation. Each unit was defined as a course covering a school year of not less than thirty-five weeks, taught in four or five periods of at least forty-five minutes per week. Furthermore, all high school curricula and requirements for college entrance were to include as constants three units of English and two units of mathematics.[12]

In a manner similar to the North Central Association, other regional accreditation agencies were established: the New England Association, the Middle States Association, the Northwest Association, the Western Association, and the Southern Association. Historically, the accreditation associations have developed two alternatives to the problems of college entrance requirements. In the East, the College Entrance Examination Board established a system of examinations for college entrance. In the West, graduates of high schools which were accredited by the North Central Association were admitted to college by certification.[13]

Commission on Reorganization of Secondary Education

In 1918, the National Education Association established the Commission on the Reorganization of Secondary Education to re-examine the scope and function of the high school. The Report of the Commission was significant for its recognition of the need for greater articulation of institutions at all levels of education. Under the leadership of chairman Clarence Kingsley, the Commission issued the famous "Cardinal Principles of Secondary Education," which listed the following as objectives of secondary education, although they were applicable to elementary and higher education as well: health, command of fundamental processes, worthy home membership, vocation, citizenship, worthy use of leisure, and ethical character. The major task of the high school was to translate the "Principles" into action.

The Commission also emphasized the function of the high school as an agent of social integration. In recommending the continuance of the comprehensive high school as part of the standard pattern of organization, the Commission expressed the belief that the public secondary school would bring students of varying racial, religious, ethnic, and economic backgrounds into the same institution. If specialized vocational, commercial, or college preparatory high schools were to replace the comprehensive high school, the Commission felt that the public secondary school could no longer perform its task of social integration.

To some observers, the "Cardinal Principles" did not seem to come to grips with the problems of industrial civilization. George S. Counts in *Secondary Education and Industrialism* said that the Commission left untouched the really vital questions raised by the development of an industrial civilization. What was lacking, he felt, was a carefully constructed social theory to guide the operation of the secondary school.[14]

During its development as a social institution a number of people proposed various programs for standardizing the high school in one way or another. Between 1880 and 1920 strong arguments were advanced in favor of maintaining the strictly college preparatory function of the high school. But equally eloquent pleas were tendered for developing the high school as a non-academically oriented terminal institution, "the people's college." Its shaping involved problems of curriculum construction, articulation in relation to other educational institutions, and accreditation.

During the period from 1880 to 1920, the American high school was primarily college preparatory, emphasizing Latin, modern foreign languages, mathematics, science, English, and history. However, a small group of educators led by G. Stanley Hall, objected strongly to the domination of the high school by colleges. In numerous speeches and articles Hall denounced the tendency, saying that the high school should be more concerned with the education of the adolescent.[15] This group sought to extend the "child study" movement upward, regarding the high school as a natural extension from the common (elementary) school. Because of Hall's and others' efforts, some educators began to view the high school as an adolescent school rather than strictly college preparatory. Others, like David Snedden, launched the "social efficiency" movement. "Social efficiency," also a reaction against the high school's orientation toward college, was an assertion of social reform as defined by a utilitarian criterion. According to this group, the inclusion of any subject in the high school curriculum was justified only insofar as it prepared the student to be a citizen, earner, parent, and consumer.

Development of the Comprehensive High School

In 1880, the high school population was numbered at 110,277; by 1920 it was 2,382,542.[16] Despite the increased attendance, educators such as George S. Counts felt that the high school was still a selective institution. A close relationship existed between parental occupation and high school attendance. Furthermore, children of native-born parents attended in greater numbers than those of immigrant parents. In *The Selective Character of American Secondary Education*, Counts concluded that the high school was serving the upper socioeconomic classes. He called for an extension of the quality of opportunity when he urged the opening of the doors of the high school to all students.[17]

William French in *American Secondary Education* found that the selective character of the high school as it existed between 1880 and 1920 was reinforced by three factors: first, there was lacking a secondary education tradition among many of the immigrants from southern and eastern Europe; second, there were hidden costs in the form of books, supplies, transportation, lunches, and clothing; and third, in many rural districts the lack of a solid financial base impeded the establishment of the high school.[18]

By the mid-1920s, the essential contours of the American comprehensive high school had emerged. It was an institution that offered a range of curricula to an adolescent population of differing interests, aptitudes, and inclinations. Although college preparation remained a continuing function of the high school, secondary school educators began to develop more programs for youth whose formal education would end with the awarding of the high school diploma.

As the high school took on its institutional form in the 1920s and 1930s, four basic types of curricular organization could be identified. One, there was the college preparatory or academic program which included courses in English language and literature, foreign languages, mathematics, natural and physical sciences, and history and social sciences. Two, there was the commercial or business program that offered work in bookkeeping, shorthand, and typing; three, there were also industrial, vocational, home economics, and agricultural programs. Four, there was a modified academic program for terminal students who planned to complete their formal education with high school graduation.

Despite some organizational variations, the usual high school pattern was based on a four year attendance sequence that encompassed grades nine, ten, eleven, and twelve and was generally attended by the age group from fourteen to eighteen. There were exceptions, however, in that some reorganized six-year institutions could be found in which students attended a combined junior-senior high school after completing a six year elementary school. The junior high school of two years, seventh and eighth grade, also began to appear in some urban districts.

In 1929 Counts called attention to the factors which were rapidly democratizing secondary education in the United States. These were the presence of more democratic social ideals, the extension of elementary education opportunities, the development of a more highly integrated society, the growing complexity of civilization, increasing overall wealth and income, and lower death and birth rates.[19]

By 1930, the comprehensive American high school was fairly well established as an institution enrolling adolescents from all kinds of backgrounds and offering an entire range of subjects. The increase in high school enrollments from 4,427,000 in 1930 to 9,619,000 in 1960 tells the story of its popular appeal. Despite the controversies which surrounded it as a social institution, the high school seemed to function as an agent of social and cultural integration, a place where students learned studies in common, mixed socially, and participated in common activities.

The purpose, goals, and curriculum of the American high school often have been subject to debate, controversy, and criticism. Part of this ungoing critique of secondary schooling can be attributed to its crucial location in the educational ladder. After completing high school, students have several career paths. For some students, one path leads to entry into the colleges and universities of the higher educational system. For students who end their formal education with the completion of secondary school, another path may lead to careers in the work force. In terms of these various paths to future career destinations, the high school's role has been defined in different ways. To what degree should the high school be a sorting or shifting agency that acts to determine career destinations? Should the high school be organized according to tracks that separate the college-bound and terminal students? If the high school curriculum is rigidly differentiated into tracks, can the institution still serve as a comprehensive agency for social integration? The high school's history contains many episodes of conflict between those who see it performing a selective role in identifying and educating the college bound students and those who see it performing a more socially integrative function as an institution for the education of adolescents.

As an institution, the high school is also delicately poised between the elementary school and the college. For those who view it as an upward extension of the elementary school, the high school is to continue building the basic skills and socialization processes begun in the elementary school years. For those who see it as a downward extension of the college, its function is preparatory for attendance at the higher institution. Depending upon the public economic and political milieu, the high school purposes and curriculum have veered in both directions.

The high school has been subjected to pressure by those who seek to use it for special purposes. During World War I, patriotic pressures caused a drastic reduction in the number of people studying German as a foreign language. At the same time, rejections of inductees for military service due to physical disabilities stimulated programs of physical education. Also in 1917, the federal government sponsored the Smith-Hughes Vocational Education Act, which provided federal funds as grants-in-aid to states offering vocational studies. As an aftermath of World War II, high school educators concerned with the war's disruption of family life and the increase of juvenile delinquency introduced life adjustment programs into the curriculum. In the late 1950s, with the advent of the Russian space satellite Sputnik, critics began to accuse our high school program of being "watered-down" and pedagogically soft.

The Conant Reports

In the late 1950s, James B. Conant, a former President of Harvard University and a highly respected educational leader, sought to answer some of the important questions about the purpose, function, and curriculum of the

American high school. In 1958, Conant's *The American High School Today*, examined the condition of American public secondary education. In particular, his inquiry focused on the public comprehensive high school which he regarded as an institution that was vital to the concept of education in a democratic society. Conant defined a comprehensive high school as providing education for all the youth of a given district; a specialized high school, in contrast, provided either a vocational or an academic curriculum to selected students.[20]

The comprehensive high school sought to achieve three major goals: to provide a general education for all students regardless of future career destination; to provide effective vocational education programs for terminal students; to provide academically sound academic programs for college preparatory students. In the late 1950s, more than half of the students completed their full-time education upon graduation from a comprehensive high school. For these terminal students who were likely to join the work force upon completing high school, it was important to provide a variety of vocational programs. For college preparatory students, academic courses in mathematics, science, social studies, English, and foreign languages were offered. In addition to the objectives and programs of the formal curriculum, the socially comprehensive milieu of the comprehensive high school also intended to have important societal and civic outcomes. Among its important social objectives, the comprehensive high school was to develop democratic ethical sensibilities, civic competencies, and empathy between students from different racial, ethnic, and socioeconomic backgrounds.

Since he regarded the vitality of the comprehensive high school to be of critical importance to American society, Conant made a number of recommendations to revitalize the institution by improving its academic quality. He recommended a core curriculum of general educational requirements for all students that consisted of four years of English, three or four years of social studies, and at least one year of mathematics and science. While completion of the core requirements would take half of each student's instructional time, students could choose elective courses for the remaining half. He also recommended the establishment of well developed counseling services to aid students in choosing elective courses that corresponded to their interests, attitudes, and career goals.

For terminal students, Conant recommended diversified programs to develop marketable skills. In structuring vocational education programs for their particular high school, administrators were advised to conduct a needs assessment to determine the job market in their local community. Programs should be offered in distributive education, agriculture, industry, and trades according to their appropriateness to each community.

In addition to his curricular recommendations, Conant made several recommendations designed to improve instruction. He recommended that more individualized instruction be provided so that educational experience reflected the individual student's needs and interests. To improve the effectiveness and efficiency of instruction, he urged that students be placed in the more highly academic courses according to their ability. He advised high school administrators and teachers that more time should be devoted to English composition. It was imperative that special remedial programs be instituted for students with reading deficits. Academically enriched courses were to be developed for gifted students. As the former U.S. High Commissioner in post-World War II Germany, Conant clearly recognized that the United States had to exercise a greater and more responsible international role. To internationalize the outlook of American students, he recommended that more opportunities be provided to study foreign languages. As a scientist, Conant who was aware of the need to develop improved mathematical and scientific competencies among Americans recommended more course offerings in these important areas.[21]

Conant's findings and recommendations to improve American public secondary education came at a needed time. They followed a decade of vociferous but often rancorous public debate between the defenders of progressive education and a variety of critics about the nature of American education. Often the debate focused on the academic quality of America's high schools. Among the critics, Arthur E. Bestor, a distinguished historian, charged that American high schools had lost much of their intellectual quality due to the infusion of life adjustment courses into the curriculum. Bestor urged that the secondary school curriculum be based on the intellectual disciplines of history, mathematics, science, and literature, which represented the human race's "fundamental ways of thinking."[22] Like Bestor, Hyman Rickover, an admiral in the U.S. Navy, in comparing the academic achievement of American secondary students with their counterparts in Europe found the Americans to be woefully deficient, especially in the key subject areas of mathematics and science.[23] In 1957, the United States' adversary in the Cold War, the Soviet Union, had successfully launched and orbited a space satellite, Sputnik. The Soviet success was attributed to their superiority in science and mathematics over the Americans. In contrast to often emotionally-charged rhetoric of the 1950s, Conant's report presented an objective and reasoned commentary on the American comprehensive high school. While the high school was performing competently, it needed revitalization. Conant's recommendations gave secondary school administrators and teachers a well-documented plan for reforming their institutions. In many ways, Conant succeeded in identifying key areas that formed the basis of some of the reform efforts of the 1980s as well as of the early 1960s.

In the early 1960s, Conant continued his research on American education. His *Slums and Suburbs*, in 1961, alerted Americans to a serious problem that was eroding the quality of high schools in the central areas of many large cities. He found an alarming difference in the quality of life, economic opportunities, and educational quality in the large metropolitan areas of the United States, particularly the affluent suburbs which ringed the large cities and the depressed central core areas of the cities. While the suburban high schools were geared to providing the academic subjects needed for college admission, the inner city schools were deteriorating and serving as a "holding pattern" for disadvantaged youths who either dropped out or graduated but became unemployed.[24] With the high schools of the metropolitan area falling into these two widely different institutional types, the comprehensiveness of the urban secondary schools was eroding. If the erosion of inner city secondary education was not halted, Conant warned that the comprehensive high school, in its ideal form, would be found only in the smaller towns or consolidated rural districts where all of the students attended the same facility.

Conant's findings in *Slums and Suburbs* were prophetic. They identified the symptoms of the serious problems facing large urban school districts that surfaced later in the 1960s and the 1970s. Historically, the development of American public education had tended in the direction of a single, sequenced, and articulated ladder of educational institutions. However, the deterioration of the quality of comprehensive high schools in the large urban areas jeopardized the principle of equality of educational opportunity. While the concept of the American educational ladder might continue in terms of formal structural organization, a dual system of secondary schools might develop. In such a system, the affluent suburban schools would serve the upper socioeconomic classes. The deteriorating inner city schools would serve the economically disadvantaged groups. Such a dual system of schools might erode the sense of commonly shared civic values.

Contemporary Trends

The history of American secondary education demonstrates that the nature and functions of the high school have been shaped by social forces as well as by educational theory and practice. Several trends can be identified that reveal the response of secondary education to the changing circumstances of contemporary American society. The early 1960s were a time of curricular innovation, especially in the development of new programs designed to improve the quality of American secondary education. Committees of scientists, mathematicians, social scientists, and educators, with the support of philanthropic foundations and the federal government, developed innovative curricula such as the new mathematics, the new chemistry, the new physics and the new social studies. The Ford, Rockefeller, and the Carnegie

Foundations committed funds to encourage the development of the new curricula. The federal government through the National Science Foundation also supported the development and dissemination of new curricular and teaching strategies in the sciences and in mathematics. The new curricular designs were developed by academic specialists who sought to incorporate the structure of disciplines and the discovery method into the secondary school curriculum. By the structure of a discipline was meant the identification and the mastery of the crucial concepts and generalizations needed to understand a particular subject. Subjects that were organized on the basis of concepts and generalizations were supposed to free students from memorizing and reciting the myriad factual details that characterized the old curriculum, especially in the sciences. The use of the discovery method as an instructional strategy meant that students were to learn the process for solving problems and working their way through a subject by approximating the laboratory modes of inquiry used by specialists in the discipline. In order to diffuse the new curricula and methods into the high schools, a series of summer workshops and institutes were conducted in which selected teachers studied the new materials and methods so that they could act as agents of educational change and introduce them into their particular schools.

In historical perspective, it can be seen that the various new curricula after a great deal of initial enthusiasm and of publicity had a more limited impact than was predicted at the time. Several pedagogical factors worked to limit the transforming effects of the new curricula. Many of the projects that were the pilot studies for the new curricula were too selective and unrepresentative of the majority of secondary schools. Professional educators who had expert knowledge of the psychology of learning, instructional design and methodology were often only minor figures in the reform movement which was dominated by professors from the academic disciplines. The teachers who were supposed to be change agents in their schools often were isolated in their schools rather than leaders in developing a teacher-based consensus for the new curricula. By the late 1960s, the mood of the country had shifted from a concern about the Americans' performance in mathematics and science against the Soviet Union to other concerns.

By the mid-to-late 1960s, the national mood had shifted to issues of civil rights and racial integration. President Lyndon Johnson's ''Great Society'' programs stressed the regeneration of education in the inner cities of the country, the development of ''head start'' programs for early childhood education, and compensatory education programs to remediate basic deficiencies in learning. By the late 1960s, a growing climate of unrest and activism swept American youth. Part of the unrest was based on opposition to United States' foreign and military policy in Viet Nam. Still other manifestations of the youth movement were attributed to a ''generation gap'' that was creating a psychic and social distance between American young people and the older generation. As the decade of the 1960s came to an end, some commentators and social critics pointed to the growing problem of drug abuse as symptomatic of the alienation of American youth from traditional values.

By the late 1960s, the trend in academic fashions had moved away from the academic curricular innovations that had stressed mathematics and science to a more humanistic approach. Educational critics such as the influential journalist, Charles Silberman, urged a humanistic reform of American secondary education that would give students greater freedom of choice.[25] In response to the movement for more humanistic and open education, secondary educators developed more flexible programs which featured a wide range of elective and "mini" courses.

As a result of the impact of the social change of the late 1960s and early 1970s, secondary school educators were challenged by the continuing need to redefine the purpose of the high school. Was it to be an institution whose primary purpose was academic preparation for college bound youth? Or, was it to be a multi-purpose institution that sought to meet the social, psychological, emotional, and economic needs of American adolescents? In responding to these questions, many secondary school administrators and teachers responded affirmatively to both questions. While they continued to maintain the high school's comprehensive social and educational tradition, they also continued the process of continuing institutional redefinition.

In the early 1970s, a decline in basic academic skills and competencies generated marked concern on the part of some professional educators and the public. Evidence suggested that the academic aptitude of college bound students had deteriorated since the early 1960s. In particular, this concern focused on a fourteen year decline of scores of high school students on the Scholastic Aptitude Test, or SAT. The College Entrance Examination Board appointed an advisory panel, chaired by Willard Wirtz, to investigate this decline.

In *On Further Examination*, in 1977, the Advisory Panel reported the results of its investigation.[26] The panel's conclusions were significant not only for American high schools but for educational institutions throughout the country. While the panel identified no one cause or single explanation for the decline in test scores, it reported that the problem was a complex one that related schooling to its social context. The panel identified a number of basic social changes that had taken place in American society that had ramifications for schooling and for academic achievement. For example, the numbers of high school students entering college had increased dramatically since the early 1950s when only about twenty-five percent of the graduates entered college. By 1970, nearly half of all high school graduates entered college. The growing population of college students changed the composition of the college population and altered the previous patterns of academic selectivity. Also, the curricular changes of the late 1960s and the proliferation of elective and "mini" courses reduced the concentration on basic subject matter courses whose content had emphasized English, science, and mathematics. The impact of television viewing had reduced the time that students spent on reading, homework, and academic pursuits. The social turbulence of the late 1960s also had unsettling effects on educational institutions. While the panel's report was inconclusive about specific remedies, it anticipated and pointed the way to what would be a searching re-examination of American secondary education in the 1980s.

In the 1980s, the purpose, function, and curriculum of the high school once again was the focus of public attention and debate. A key event in precipitating the national discussion over secondary school reform was the publication of *A Nation at Risk: The Imperative for Educational Reform* by the National Commission on Excellence in Education, which had been appointed by Terrel Bell, the Secretary of Education. According to the Commission, "13 per cent of all 17-year-olds" and "40 per cent" of minority youth could be classified as functional illiterates. Further, the general decline of performance of America students on standardized achievement tests revealed by "a virtually unbroken decline from 1963 to 1980" on the College Board's Scholastic Aptitude Tests pointed to the consistent decline of American secondary students in English, mathematics, and science.[27] To reform the high school curriculum in order to remedy these academic deficiencies, the Commission recommended:

> . . . that State and local high school graduation requirements be strengthened and that, as a minimum, all students seeking a diploma be required to lay the foundations in the Five New Basics by taking the following curriculum during their four years of high school: (1) 4 years of English; (2) 3 years of mathematics; (3) 3 years of science, (4) 3 years of social studies; and (5) one-half year of computer science. For the college bound, 2 years of foreign language in high school are strongly recommended in addition to those taken earlier.[28]

During the 1980s, two important national reports examined the condition of American secondary education: Ernest Boyer's *High School: A Report on Secondary Education in America* and Theodore Sizer's *Horace's Compromise: The Dilemma of the American High School*. These reports, based on in-depth examinations of representative American high schools, made important recommendations for reforming secondary education.

Boyer, in *High School: A Report on Secondary Education in America*, using an approach similar to Conant's monumental study of American secondary education in the late 1950s, examined the condition of the high schools of the 1980s. Boyer, like Conant, was a respected American educational leader.

He was a former U.S. Commissioner of Education and President of the Carnegie Foundation for the Advancement of Teaching. His report, *High School*, supported by the prestigious Carnegie Foundation, was based on the findings of a team of educators who studied the administration, curricula, instruction, teachers and students in fifteen public high schools which had been selected as a cross section of American secondary education.[29]

Boyer found that many high schools did not have a "clear and vital" vision of their mission. As a result, boards of education, administrators, and teachers were unable to formulate widely shared "common purposes" and to set "educational priorities." To create a unifying mission, Boyer recommended that American high schools subscribe to four overarching goals to assist their students to: 1. Develop critical thinking and effective communication skills by mastering language; 2. "Learn about themselves, the human heritage" and their "interdependent world" through a core curriculum resting on "consequential" and "common" human experiences; 3. Prepare "for work and further education through" elective courses that develop "individual aptitudes and interests;" 4. Fulfill "social and civic obligations through school and community service."[30]

Based on these goals, Boyer proposed a secondary curriculum called the "core of common learning" which consisted of the following subjects:

> Language which included the writing of basic English, speech, literature, foreign language, and the arts.
>
> History which included American history, Western civilization, and non-Western studies.
>
> Civics which included the study of the classic political ideas and the structure and functions of contemporary governments.
>
> Science which is divided into the physical and biological sciences.
>
> Mathematics.
>
> Technology and health.
>
> A seminar on an independent project dealing with a significant contemporary issue.[31]

Boyer's recommended "core of common learning" for all students and an individualized elective program for each student resembled Conant's earlier recommendation for a core curriculum of general educational requirements and elective courses based on the individual student's needs and aptitudes. While both Boyer's and Conant's identification of required core courses in English language, history and social studies, science, and mathematics were similar, Boyer's recommended curricular core placed greater emphasis on mathematics and science. Stressing the need for intellectual and social integration, Boyer's stress on social service and an independent research project on a significant contemporary issue were new elements.

Like Boyer's *High School, Horace's Compromise*, a report from a Study of High Schools, headed by Theodore R. Sizer, also focused on the condition of American secondary education.[32] A former headmaster of Phillips Academy and a former Dean of Harvard's Graduate School of Education, Sizer sought to integrate the humanistic approaches of the late 1960s with the renewed emphasis on academic competencies of the 1980s. Like the earlier Conant report and Boyer's report, Sizer used intensive field study to survey selected representative high schools. Sizer developed the following recommendations to reform American secondary education:

1. Since too many high school administrators and teachers underestimated their students' potentials and had exaggerated adolescent inexperience, they needed to raise their expectations for student performance and accountability.

2. The high school diploma should be awarded on the students exhibition of an "agreed-on level of mastery" rather than by accumulating credits in a list of unrelated subjects.[33]

3. The high school curricula and instruction should emphasize important concepts and modes of inquiry rather than an extensive coverage of detailed information of subjects taught in isolation from each other.[34]

Rather than prescribing a curriculum of mandated subjects to be studied for specific time periods, Sizer identified three important questions which high school administrators and teachers were to answer regarding the students who graduated from their institutions:

1. Are they capable of the self-instruction needed to "observe and analyze a situation or problem."

2. Are they decent human beings?

3. Can they effectively use the principal modes of inquiry and observation of the major academic disciplines?[35]

Based upon these focusing questions, Sizer recommended that high schools be reorganized into four departments: Inquiry and Expression, Mathematics and Science, Literature and the Arts, and Philosophy and History.

Sizer also identified spheres of learning designed to advance students' achievement. The first sphere of learning was to develop the students' skills of reading, writing, speaking, listening, measuring, estimating, calculating, and seeing as the basics of schooling. The most effective method of developing these skills was by coaching in which teachers constructively criticized students' work to improve their performance.[36]

The acquisition of knowledge, the second learning sphere, involved the use of the pedagogical narrative, a mode of explaining by lecture, textbooks, films, and other means of transmitting knowledge. For this sphere, Sizer developed the following guidelines:

1. Students deficient in the essential ''standards of literacy, numeracy, and civic understanding'' should continue to work to improve these necessary skills.
2. According to the principle that curricular choice depended on priorities, students, teachers, families, and communities were to follow their preferences.
3. Subject matter should relate, support, and develop skill learning.
4. Subject matter should be connected to students' interests, lead to a destination, and be integrated with other subjects and experiences.

The development of the powers of discrimination and judgment by provocative questioning was Sizer's third sphere of learning. For effective dialogue to occur, small seminar discussions were recommended as the most effective instructional setting and method.[37]

Of the proposals that were made to reform secondary education in the 1980s, Sizer's appeared to be the most tranformative in nature. If implemented his proposal would integrate curriculum and instruction in high schools from a number of separate areas into four large departments that encompassed and integrated the range of human knowledge. By relating spheres of learning to areas of knowledge, he also integrated content and method. In retrospect, Sizer's proposals appeared to resurface certain important educational designs of the early 1960s such as the importance of structures of disciplines and the use of the inquiry method. The use of coaching as a method of learning basic skills was well suited to remedy the deficiencies that limited later learning. Finally, he, unlike other educators who saw reform as prescribing specific courses, sought to maximize freedom of choice wherever possible.

Conclusion

The history of American secondary education needs to be viewed in the context of the major political, social, and economic changes that the United States experienced. The initial introduction of secondary education in North America in the institutional form of the Latin Grammar school reflected the European reverence for the classical languages and literature of ancient Greece and Rome. Mastery of these languages led to entry into college for a small group of selected young men. The academy of the nineteenth century, a product of the age of Jacksonian populism and expansionism, served to broaden access to secondary school for more young people. Its unstructured and often disorganized approach to secondary education limited the academy's usefulness for a nation that was beginning to experience an industrial transformation.

The late nineteenth century saw the high school emerge to become the dominant institution in which Americans provided a secondary education to their young men and women. Located between the elementary school and the college or university, the high school, throughout its history, has been subject to pressures from above and below. The changing attitudes of Americans about what knowledge is of most importance is reflected in the various reforms that have shaped the high school curriculum. When important social and economic changes are taking place in the United States you can expect to see them reflected in the high schools' curriculum.

Notes

[1] William M. French, *American Secondary Education* (New York: The Odyssey Press, 1957), p. 24.

[2] Theodore R. Sizer, *The Age of the Academies* (New York: Bureau of Publications, Teachers College, Columbia University, 1964), p.1.

[3] *Ibid.*, p. 12.

[4] *Ibid.*, p. 41.

[5] Edward Krug, *The Shaping of the American High School* (New York: Harper & Row, 1964), p. 5.

[6] George S. Counts, *Secondary Education and Industrialism* (Cambridge: Harvard University Press, 1929), p. 26.

[7] *Report of the Committee on Secondary School Studies* (Washington, DC: Government Printing Office, 1893).

[8] Krug, *The Shaping of the American High School*, p. 17.

[9] French, *American Secondary Education*, pp. 113-14.

[10] Calvin O. Davis, *A History of the North Central Association of Colleges and Secondary Schools* (Ann Arbor, MI: The North Central Association of Colleges and Secondary Schools, 1945), p. 7.

[11] Krug, *The Shaping of the American High School*, pp. 141-42.

[12] Davis, *A History of the North Central Association...*, p. 49.

[13] Krug, *The Shaping of the American High School*, p. 146.

[14] Counts, *Secondary Education and Industrialism*, pp. 51-52.

[15] Krug, *The Shaping of the American High School*, pp. 84-85.

[16] French, *American Secondary Education*, p. 100.

[17] George S. Counts, *The Selective Character of American Secondary Education* (Chicago: The University of Chicago Press, 1922), p. 152.

[18] French, *American Secondary Education*, pp. 101-2.

[19] George S. Counts, "Selection as a Function of American Secondary Education," *National Education Association Proceedings*, LXVII (1929), p. 597.

[20] James B. Conant, *The American High School Today* (New York: McGraw-Hill Book Co., 1959), pp. 7-8.

[21] *Ibid.*, pp. 44-76.

[22] Arthur E. Bestor, Jr., *The Restoration of Learning* (New York: Alfred A. Knopf, 1955), p. 4.

[23] Hyman G. Rickover, *Report on Russia: Hearing Before the House Committee on Appropriations — 86th Congress* (Washington, DC: U.S. Government Printing Office, 1959), p. 3.

[24] James B. Conant, *Slums and Suburbs* (New York: McGraw-Hill Book Co., 1961).

[25] Charles E. Silberman, *Crisis in the Classroom: The Remaking of American Education* (New York: Random House, 1975).

[26] *On Further Examination: Report of the Advisory Panel on the Scholastic Aptitude Test Score Decline* (New York: College Entrance Examination Board, 1977).

[27] National Commission on Excellence in Education, *A Nation at Risk: The Imperative for Educational Reform* (Washington, DC: U.S. Government Printing Office, 1983), pp. 8-9.

[28] *Ibid.*, pp. 23-31.

[29] Ernest L. Boyer, *High School: A Report on Secondary Education in America* (New York: Harper & Row, 1983), p. 111.

[30] *Ibid.*, pp. 66-77.

[31] *Ibid.*, p. 117.

[32] Theodore R. Sizer, *Horace's Compromise: The Dilemma of the American High School* (Boston: Houghton Mifflin Co., 1984) is a report from the study of high schools co-sponsored by the National Association of Secondary School Principals and the Commission on Educational Issues of the National Association of Independent Schools.

[33] *Ibid.*, pp. 33-34.

[34] *Ibid.*, p. 89.

[35] *Ibid.*, p. 131.

[36] *Ibid.*, p. 99.

[37] *Ibid.*, pp. 109-119.

Selections to Accompany
Chapter 4

Two documents, the Report of the Committee on Secondary School Studies *and the* Cardinal Principles of Secondary Education, *were crucial in defining the nature and program of the high school as the secondary institution of American education. The Committee on Secondary School Studies, known as the Committee of Ten, was appointed by the National Educational Association in 1892. The Committee, guided by Chairman Eliot, submitted its report in 1893. The selections below illustrate the desire of the Committee that instruction in the subject areas begin at an earlier age, that more subjects be offered, and that the same methods of teaching be used for college preparatory and terminal students. Table I illustrates the four model curricula recommended by the Committee for high school students.*

Report of the Committee
on Secondary School Studies

Anyone who reads these nine reports consecutively will be struck with the fact that all these bodies of experts desire to have the elements of their several subjects taught earlier than they now are; and that the Conferences on all the subjects except the languages desire to have given in the elementary schools what may be called perspective views, or broad surveys, of their respective subjects — expecting that in later years of the school course parts of these same subjects will be taken up with more amplitude and detail. The Conferences on Latin, Greek, and the Modern Languages agree in desiring to have the study of foreign languages begin at a much earlier age than now, — the Latin Conference suggesting by a reference to European usage that Latin be begun

Source: *Report of the Committee on Secondary School Studies* (Washington, DC: Government Printing Office, 1983), pp. 14-17, 46-47.

from three to five years earlier than it commonly is now. The Conference on Mathematics wish to have given in elementary schools not only a general survey of arithmetic, but also the elements of algebra, and concrete geometry in connection with drawing. The Conference on Physics, Chemistry, and Astronomy urge that nature studies should constitute an important part of the elementary school course from the very beginning. The Conference on Natural History wish the elements of botany and zoology to be taught in the primary schools. The Conference on History wish the systematic study of history to begin as early as the tenth year of age, and the first two years of study to be devoted to mythology and to biography for the illustration of general history as well as of American history. Finally, the Conference on Geography recommend that the earlier course treat broadly of the earth, its environment and inhabitants, extending freely into fields which in later years of study are recognized as belonging to separate sciences.

In thus claiming entrance for their subjects into the earlier years of school attendance, the Conferences on the newer subjects are only seeking an advantage which the oldest subjects have long possessed. The elements of language, number, and geography have long been imparted to young children. As things now are, the high school teacher finds in the pupils fresh from the grammar schools no foundation of elementary mathematical conceptions outside of arithmetic; no acquaintance with algebraic language; and no accurate knowledge of geometrical forms. As to botany, zoology, chemistry, and physics, the minds of pupils entering the high school are ordinarily blank on these subjects. When college professors endeavor to teach chemistry, physics, botany, zoology, meteorology, or geology to persons of eighteen or twenty years of age, they discover that in most instances new habits of observing, reflecting, and recording have to be painfully acquired by the students, — habits which they should have acquired in early childhood. The college teacher of history finds in like manner that his subject has never taken any serious hold on the minds of pupils fresh from the secondary schools. He finds that they have devoted astonishingly little time to the subject; and that they have acquired no habit of historical investigation, or of the comparative examination of different historical narratives concerning the same periods or events. It is inevitable, therefore, that specialists in any one of the subjects which are pursued in the high schools or colleges should earnestly desire that the minds of young children be stored with some of the elementary facts and principles of their subject; and that all the mental habits, which the adult student will surely need, begin to be formed in the child's mind before the age of fourteen. It follows, as a matter of course, that all the Conferences except the Conference on Greek, make strong suggestions concerning the programmes of primary and grammar schools, — generally with some reference to the subsequent programmes of secondary schools. They desire important changes in the elementary grades; and the changes recommended are all in the direction of increasing simultaneously the interest and the substantial training quality of primary and grammar school studies.

If anyone feels dismayed at the number and variety of the subjects to be opened to children of tender age, let him observe that while these nine Conferences desire each their own subject to be brought into the courses of elementary schools, they all agree that these different subjects should be correlated and associated one with another by the programme and by the actual teaching. If the nine Conferences had sat all together as a single body, instead of sitting as detached and even isolated bodies, they could not have more forcibly expressed their conviction that every subject recommended for introduction into elementary and secondary schools should help every other; and that the teacher of each single subject should feel responsible for the advancement of the pupils in all subjects, and should distinctly contribute to this advancement.

On one very important question of general policy which affects profoundly the preparation of all school programmes, the Committee of Ten and all the Conferences are absolutely unanimous. Among the questions suggested for discussion in each Conference were the following:

7. Should the subject be treated differently for pupils who are going to college, for those who are going to a scientific school, and for those who, presumably, are going to neither?

8. At what age should this differentiation begin, if any be recommended?

The 7th question is answered unanimously in the negative by the Conferences, and the 8th therefore needs no answer. The Committee of Ten unanimously agree with the Conferences. Ninety-eight teachers intimately concerned either with the actual work of American secondary schools, or with the results of that work as they appear in students who come to college, unanimously declare that every subject which is taught at all in a secondary school should be taught in the same way and to the same extent to every pupil so long as he pursues it, no matter what the probable destination of the pupil may be, or at what point his education is to cease. Thus, for all pupils who study Latin, or history, or algebra, for example, the allotment of time and the method of instruction in a given school should be the same year by year. Not that all the pupils should pursue every subject for the same number of years; but so long as they do pursue it, they should all be treated alike. It has been a very general custom in American high schools and academies to make up separate courses of study for pupils of supposed different destinations, the proportions of the several studies in the different courses being various. The principle laid down by the Conferences will, if logically carried out, make

TABLE I

Year	CLASSICAL Three Foreign Languages (one modern)		LATIN-SCIENTIFIC Two Foreign Languages (one modern)	
I	Latin	5 p.	Latin	5 p.
	English	4 p.	English	4 p.
	Algebra	4 p.	Algebra	4 p.
	History	4 p.	History	4 p.
	Physical Geography	3 p.	Physical Geography	3 p.
		20 p.		20 p.
II	Latin	5 p.	Latin	5 p.
	English	2 p.	English	2 p.
	German (or French) begun	4 p.	German (or French) begun	4 p.
	Geometry	3 p.	Geometry	3 p.
	Physics	3 p.	Physics	3 p.
	History	3 p.	Botany or Zoology	3 p.
		20 p.		20 p.
III	Latin	4 p.	Latin	4 p.
	Greek	5 p.	English	3 p.
	English	3 p.	German (or French)	4 p.
	German (or French)	4 p.	Mathematics (Algebra 2) (Geometry 2)	4 p.
	Mathematics (Algebra 2) (Geometry 2)	4 p.	Astronomy ½ yr. & Meteorology ½ yr.	3 p.
		20 p.	History	2 p.
				20 p.
IV	Latin	4 p.	Latin	4 p.
	Greek	5 p.	English (as in Classical 2) (additional 2)	4 p.
	English	2 p.	German (or French)	3 p.
	German (or French)	3 p.	Chemistry	3 p.
	Chemistry	3 p.	Trigonometry & Higher Algebra or History	3 p.
	Trigonometry & Higher Algebra or History	3 p.	Geology or Physiography ½ yr. and Anatomy, Physiology & Hygiene ½ yr.	3 p.
		20 p.		20 p.

TABLE I (*cont.*)

Year	MODERN LANGUAGES Two Foreign Languages (both modern)		ENGLISH One Foreign Language (ancient or modern)	
I	French (or German) begun	5 p.	Latin, or German or French	5 p.
	English	4 p.	English	4 p.
	Algebra	4 p.	Algebra	4 p.
	History	4 p.	History	4 p.
	Physical Geography	3 p.	Physical Geography	3 p.
		20 p.		20 p.
II	French (or German)	4 p.	Latin, or German or French	5 or 4 p.
	English	2 p.	English	3 or 4 p.
	German (or French) begun	5 p.	Geometry	3 p.
	Geometry	3 p.	Physics	3 p.
	Physics	3 p.	History	3 p.
	Botany or Zoology	3 p.	Botany or Zoology	3 p.
		20 p.		20 p.
III	French (or German)	4 p.	Latin, or German or French	4 p.
	English	3 p.	English (as in others 3) (additional 2)	5 p.
	German (or French)	4 p.		
	Mathematics (Algebra 2) (Geometry 2)	4 p.	Mathematics (Algebra 2) (Geometry 2)	4 p.
	Astronomy ½ yr. & Meteorology ½ yr.	3 p.	Astronomy ½ yr. & Meteorology ½ yr.	3 p.
	History	2 p.	History (as in the Latin-Scientific 2) (additional 2)	4 p.
		20 p.		20 p.
	French (or German)	3 p.	Latin, or German or French	4 p.
	English (as in Classical 2) (additional 2)	4 p.	English (as in Classical 2) (additional 2)	4 p.

TABLE I (*cont.*)

IV					
German (or French)	4 p.		Chemistry	3 p.	
Chemistry	3 p.		Trigonometry & Higher Algebra	3 p.	
Trigonometry & Higher Algebra 3 or History 3	3 p.		History	3 p.	
Geology or Physiography ½ yr. and Anatomy, Physiology, & Hygiene ½ yr.	3 p.		Geology or Physiography ½ yr. and Anatomy, Physiology, & Hygiene ½ yr.	3 p.	
	20 p.			20 p.	

a great simplification in secondary school programmes. It will lead to each subject's being treated by the school in the same way by the year for all pupils, and this, whether the individual pupil be required to choose between courses which run through several years, or be allowed some choice among subjects year by year.

The Commission on the Reorganization of Secondary Education of the National Education Association made its report in 1918. In urging the reconstruction of the high school program, the Commission attempted to define the aims and purposes of secondary education. The result of this deliberation was the Cardinal Principles of Secondary Education, *which became the basis of the program for the American secondary school.*

Cardinal Principles
of Secondary Education

This commission, therefore, regards the following as the main objectives of education: 1. Health. 2. Command of fundamental processes. 3. Worthy home-membership. 4. Vocation. 5. Citizenship. 6. Worthy use of leisure. 7. Ethical character.

The naming of the above objectives is not intended to imply that the process of education can be divided into separated fields. This can not be, since the pupil is indivisible. Nor is the analysis all-inclusive. Nevertheless, we believe that distinguishing and naming these objectives will aid in directing efforts; and we hold that they should constitute the principal aims in education.

The Role of Secondary Education
in Achieving These Objectives

The objectives outlined above apply to education as a whole—elementary, secondary, and higher. It is the purpose of this section to consider specifically the role of secondary education in achieving each of these objectives.

For reasons stated in Section X, this commission favors such reorganization that secondary education may be defined as applying to all pupils of approximately 12 to 18 years of age.

1. *Health*. Health needs can not be neglected during the period of secondary education without serious danger to the individual and the race. The secondary school should therefore provide health instruction, inculcate health habits, organize an effective program of physical activities, regard

SOURCE: *Cardinal Principles of Secondary Education: A Report of the Commission on the Reorganization of Secondary Education, Appointed by the National Education Association* (Washington, DC: Government Printing Office, 1918), pp. 10-16.

health needs in planning work and play, and cooperate with home and community in safe-guarding and promoting health interests.

To carry out such a program it is necessary to arouse the public to recognize that the health needs of young people are of vital importance to society, to secure teachers competent to ascertain and meet the needs of individual pupils and able to inculcate in the entire student body a love for clean sport, to furnish adequate equipment for physical activities, and to make the school building, its rooms and surroundings, conform to the best standards of hygiene and sanitation.

2. *Command of fundamental processes.* Much of the energy of the elementary school is properly devoted to teaching certain fundamental processes, such as reading, writing, arithmetical computations, and the elements of oral and written expression. The facility that a child of 12 or 14 may acquire in the use of these tools is not sufficient for the needs of modern life. This is particularly true of the mother tongue. Proficiency in many of these processes may be increased more effectively by their application to new material than by the formal reviews commonly employed in grades seven and eight. Throughout the secondary school, instruction and practice must go hand in hand, but as indicated in the report of the committee on English, only so much theory should be taught at any one time as will show results in practice.

3. *Worthy home-membership.* Worthy home-membership as an objective calls for the development of those qualities that make the individual a worthy member of a family, both contributing to and deriving benefit from that membership.

This objective applies to both boys and girls. The social studies should deal with the home as a fundamental social institution and clarify its relation to the wider interests outside. Literature should interpret and idealize the human elements that go to make the home. Music and art should result in more beautiful homes and in greater joy therein. The coeducational school with a faculty of men and women should, in its organization and its activities, exemplify wholesome relations between boys and girls and men and women.

Home-membership as an objective should not be thought of solely with reference to future duties. These are the better guaranteed if the school helps the pupils to take the right attitude toward present home responsibilities and interprets to them the contribution of the home to their development.

In the education of every high-school girl, the household arts should have a prominent place because of their importance to the girl herself and to others whose welfare will be directly in her keeping. The attention now devoted to this phase of education is inadequate, and especially so for girls preparing for occupations not related to the household arts and for girls planning for higher institutions. The majority of girls who enter wage-earning occupations directly from the high school remain in them for only a few years, after which home making becomes their life-long occupation. For them the high-school period offers the only assured opportunity to prepare for that lifelong occupation, and it is during this period that they are most likely to form their ideals of life's duties and responsibilities. For girls planning to enter higher institutions— our traditional ideals of preparation for higher institutions are particularly incongruous with the actual needs and future responsibilities of girls. It would seem that such high-school work as is carefully designed to develop capacity for, and interest in, the proper management and conduct of a home should be regarded as of importance at least equal to that of any other work. We do not understand how society can properly continue to sanction for girls high-school curriculums that disregard this fundamental need, even though such curriculums are planned in response to the demands made by some of the colleges for women.

In the education of boys, some opportunity should be found to give them a basis for the intelligent appreciation of the value of the well-appointed home and of the labor and skill required to maintain such a home, to the end that they may cooperate more effectively. For instance, they should understand the essentials of food values, of sanitation, and of household budgets.

4. *Vocation*. Vocational education should equip the individual to secure a livelihood for himself and those dependent on him, to serve society well through his vocation, to maintain the right relationships toward his fellow workers and society, and, as far as possible, to find in that vocation his own best development.

This ideal demands that the pupil explore his own capacities and aptitudes, and make a survey of the world's work, to the end that he may select his vocation wisely. Hence, an effective program of vocational guidance in the secondary school is essential.

Vocational education should aim to develop an appreciation of the significance of the vocation to the community, and a clear conception of right relations between the members of the chosen vocation, between different vocational groups, between employer and employee, and between producer and consumer. These aspects of vocational education, heretofore neglected, demand emphatic attention.

The extent to which the secondary school should offer training for a specific vocation depends upon the vocation, the facilities that the school can acquire, and the opportunity that the pupil may have to obtain such training later. To obtain satisfactory results those proficient in that vocation should be employed as instructors and the actual conditions of the vocation should be utilized either within the high school or in cooperation with the home, farm, shop, or office. Much of the pupil's time will be required to produce such efficiency.

5. *Civic education* should develop in the individual those qualities whereby he will act well his part as a member of neighborhood, town or city, State, and Nation, and give him a basis for understanding international problems.

For such citizenship the following are essential: A many-sided interest in the welfare of the communities to which one belongs; loyalty to ideals of civic righteousness; practical knowledge of social agencies and institutions; good judgment as to means and methods that will promote one social end without defeating others; and as putting all these into effect, habits of cordial cooperation in social undertakings.

The school should develop the concept that the civic duties of men and women, while in part identical, are also in part supplementary. Differentiation in civic activities is to be encouraged, but not to the extent of loss of interest in the common problems with which all should cope.

Among the means for developing attitudes and habits important in a democracy are the assignment of projects and problems to groups of pupils for cooperative solution and the socialized recitation whereby the class as a whole develops a sense of collective responsibility. Both of these devices give training in collective thinking. Moreover, the democratic organization and administration of the school itself, as well as the cooperative relations of pupil and teacher, pupil and pupil, and teacher and teacher, are indispensable.

While all subjects should contribute to good citizenship, the social studies — geography, history, civics, and economics — should have this as their dominant aim. Too frequently, however, does mere information, conventional in value and remote in its bearing, make up the content of the social studies. History should so treat the growth of institutions that their present value may be appreciated. Geography should show the interdependence of men while it shows their common dependence on nature. Civics should concern itself less with constitutional questions and remote governmental functions, and should direct attention to social agencies close at hand and to the informal activities of daily life that regard and seek the common good. Such agencies as child-welfare organizations and consumers' leagues afford specific opportunities for the expression of civic qualities by the older pupils.

The work in English should kindle social ideals and give insight into social conditions and into personal character as related to these conditions. Hence the emphasis by the committee on English on the importance of a knowledge of social activities, social movements, and social needs on the part of the teacher of English.

The comprehension of the ideals of American democracy and loyalty to them should be a prominent aim of civic education. The pupil should feel that he will be responsible, in cooperation with others, for keeping the Nation true to the best inherited conceptions of democracy, and he should also realize that democracy itself is an ideal to be wrought out by his own and succeeding generations.

Civic education should consider other nations also. As a people we should try to understand their aspirations and ideals that we may deal more sympathetically and intelligently with the immigrant coming to our shores, and have a basis for a wiser and more sympathetic approach to international problems. Our pupils should learn that each nation, at least potentially, has something of worth to contribute to civilization and that humanity would be incomplete without the contribution. This means a study of specific nations, their achievements and possibilities, not ignoring their limitations. Such a study of dissimilar contributions in the light of the ideal of human brotherhood should help to establish a genuine internationalism, free from sentimentality, founded on fact, and actually operative in the affairs of nations.

6. *Worthy use of leisure.* Education should equip the individual to secure from his leisure the recreation of body, mind, and spirit, and the enrichment and enlargement of his personality.

This objective calls for the ability to utilize the common means of enjoyment, such as music, art, literature, drama, and social intercourse, together with the fostering in each individual of one or more special avocational interests.

Heretofore, the high school has given little conscious attention to this objective. It has so exclusively sought intellectual discipline that it has seldom treated literature, art, and music so as to evoke right emotional response and produce positive enjoyment. Its presentation of science should aim, in part, to arouse a genuine appreciation of nature.

The school has failed also to organize and direct the social activities of young people as it should. One of the surest ways in which to prepare pupils worthily to utilize leisure in adult life is by guiding and directing their use of leisure in youth. The school should therefore, see that adequate recreation is provided both within the school and by other proper agencies in the community. The school, however, has a unique opportunity in this field because it includes in its membership representatives from all classes of society and consequently is able through social relationships to establish bonds of friendship and common understanding that can not be furnished by other agencies. Moreover, the school can so organize recreational activities that they will contribute simultaneously to other ends of education, as in the case of the school pageant or festival.

7. *Ethical character.* In a democratic society ethical character becomes paramount among the objectives of the secondary school. Among the means for developing ethical character may be mentioned the wise selection of content and methods of instruction in all subjects of study, the social contacts of pupils with one another and with their teachers, the opportunities afforded by the organization and administration of the school for the development on the part of pupils of the sense of personal responsibility and initiative, and above all, the spirit of service and the principles of true democracy which should permeate the entire school — principal, teachers, and pupils.

Specific consideration is given to the moral values to be obtained from the organization of the school and the subjects of study in the report of this commission entitled "Moral Values in Secondary Education." That report considers also the conditions under which it may be advisable to supplement the other activities of the school by offering a distinct course in moral instruction.

The following selection is the recommendation of the National Commission on Excellence in Education for the reform of secondary education requirements that appeared in A Nation at Risk: The Imperative for Educational Reform *in 1983. The report was a factor in stimulating several of the states to increase their high school graduation requirements.*

Recommendation A of the National Commission on Excellence in Education

Recommendation A: Content

We recommend that State and local high school graduation requirements be strengthened and that, *at a minimum, all* students seeking a diploma be required to lay the foundations in the Five New Basics by taking the following curriculum during their 4 years of high school: (a) 4 years of English; (b) 3 years of mathematics; (c) 3 years of science; (d) 3 years of social studies; and (e) one-half year of computer science. For the college bound, 2 years of foreign language in high school are strongly recommended in addition to those taken earlier.

Whatever the student's educational or work objectives, knowledge of the New Basics is the foundation of success for the after-school years and, therefore, forms the core of the modern curriculum. A high level of shared education in these Basics, together with work in the fine and performing arts and foreign languages, constitutes the mind and spirit of our culture. The following Implementing Recommendations are intended as illustrative descriptions. They are included here to clarify what we mean by the essentials of a strong curriculum.

Implementing Recommendations

1. The teaching of *English* in high school should equip graduates to: (a) comprehend, interpret, evaluate, and use what they read; (b) write well-organized, effective papers; (c) listen effectively and discuss ideas

SOURCE: The National Commission on Excellence in Education. *A Nation at Risk: The Imperative for Educational Reform* (Washington, DC: U.S. Department of Education, 1983), pp. 24-27.

intelligently; and (d) know our literary heritage and how it enhances imagination and ethical understanding, and how it relates to the customs, ideas, and values of today's life and culture.

2. The teaching of *mathematics* in high school should equip graduates to: (a) understand geometric and algebraic concepts; (b) understand elementary probability and statistics; (c) apply mathematics in everyday situations; and (d) estimate, approximate, measure, and test the accuracy of their calculations. In addition to the traditional sequence of studies available for college-bound students, new, equally demanding mathematics curricula need to be developed for those who do not plan to continue their formal education immediately.

3. The teaching of *science* in high school should provide graduates with an introduction to: (a) the concepts, laws, and processes of the physical and biological sciences; (b) the methods of scientific inquiry and reasoning; (c) the application of scientific knowledge to everyday life; and (d) the social and environmental implications of scientific and technological development. Science courses must be revised and updated for both the college-bound and those not intending to go to college. An example of such work is the American Chemical Society's "Chemistry in the Community" program.

4. The teaching of *social studies* in high school should be designed to: (a) enable students to fix their places and possibilities within the larger social and cultural structure; (b) understand the broad sweep of both ancient and contemporary ideas that have shaped our world; and (c) understand the fundamentals of how our economic system works and how our political system functions; and (d) grasp the difference between free and repressive societies. An understanding of each of these areas is requisite to the informed and committed exercise of citizenship in our free society.

5. The teaching of *computer science* in high school should equip graduates to: (a) understand the computer as an information, computation, and communication device; (b) use the computer in the study of the other Basics and for personal and work-related purposes; and (c) understand the world of computers, electronics, and related technologies.

In addition to the New Basics, other important curriculum matters must be addressed.

6. Achieving proficiency in a *foreign language* ordinarily requires from 4 to 6 years of study and should, therefore, be started in the elementary grades. We believe it is desirable that students achieve such proficiency because study of a foreign language introduces students to non-English-

speaking cultures, heightens awareness and comprehension of one's native tongue, and serves the Nation's needs in commerce, diplomacy, defense, and education.

7. The high school curriculum should also provide students with programs requiring rigorous effort in subjects that advance students' personal, educational, and occupational goals, such as the fine and performing arts and vocational education. These areas complement the New Basics, and they should demand the same level of performance as the Basics.

8. The curriculum in the crucial eight grades leading to the high school years should be specifically designed to provide a sound base for study in those and later years in such areas as English language development and writing, computational and problem solving skills, science, social studies, foreign language, and the arts. These years should foster an enthusiasm for learning and the development of the individual's gifts and talents.

9. We encourage the continuation of efforts by groups such as the American Chemical Society, the American Association for the Advancement of Science, the Modern Language Association, and the National Councils of Teachers of English and Teachers of Mathematics, to revise, update, improve, and make available new and more diverse curricular materials. We applaud the consortia of educators and scientific, industrial, and scholarly societies that cooperate to improve the school curriculum.

Suggestions for Further Reading

Boyer, Ernest L. *High School: A Report of Secondary Education in America*. New York: Harper & Row, Publishers, 1983.

Commission on the Reorganization of Secondary Education. *Cardinal Principles of Secondary Education*. Washington, DC: U.S. Government Printing Office, 1918.

Conant, James B. *The American High School Today*. New York: McGraw-Hill Book Co., 1959.

Conant, James B. *The Revolutionary Transformation of the American High School*. Cambridge: Harvard University Press, 1959.

Conant, James B. *Slums and Suburbs*. New York: McGraw-Hill Book Co., 1961.

Counts, George S. *Secondary Education and Industrialism*. Cambridge: Harvard University Press, 1929.

Counts, George S. *The Selective Character of American Secondary Education*. Chicago: University of Chicago Press, 1922.

Davis, Calvin O. *A History of the North Central Association of Colleges and Secondary Schools*. Ann Arbor: The North Central Association of Colleges and Secondary Schools, 1945.

Fish, Kenneth L. *Conflict and Dissent in the High Schools*. New York: Bruce Publishing Co., 1970.

French, William M. *American Secondary Education*. New York: The Odyssey Press, 1957.

Grant, Gerald. *The World We Created at Hamilton High*. Cambridge: Harvard University Press, 1988.

Gross, Ronald and Paul Osterman. *High School*. New York: Simon and Schuster, 1971.

Hampel, Robert. *The Last Little Citadel: American High Schools Since 1940*. Boston: Houghton Mifflin, 1986.

Krug, Edward A. *The Shaping of the American High School*. New York: Harper & Row, Publishers, 1964.

Krug, Edward A. *The Shaping of the American High School, 1920-1941*. Madison: University of Wisconsin Press, 1972.

National Commission on Excellence in Education. *A Nation at Risk: The Imperative for Educational Reform*. Washington, DC: U.S. Government Printing Office, 1983.

National Education Association. *Report of the Committee of Ten on Secondary School Studies*. New York: American Book Co., 1894.

On Further Examination: Report of the Advisory Panel on the Scholastic Aptitude Test Score Decline. New York: College Entrance Examination Board, 1977.

Ravitch, Diane and Chester E. Finn, Jr. *What Do Our 17-Year Olds Know? A Report of the First National Assessment of History and Literature*. New York: Harper & Row, Publishers, 1987.

Roberts, Arthur D. and Gordon Cawelti. *Redefining General Education in the American High School*. Alexandria, VA: Association for Supervision and Curriculum Development, 1984.

Powell, Arthur G., Farrar, Eleanor and David K. Cohen. *The Shopping Mall High School*. Boston: Houghton Mifflin, 1985.

Sizer, Theodore R. *The Age of the Academies*. New York: Teachers College Press, Columbia University, 1964.

Sizer, Theodore R. *Horace's Compromise: The Dilemma of the American High School*. Boston: Houghton Mifflin Co., 1984.

The Evolution of American Higher Education

Introduction

Higher education in the twentieth century has experienced phenomenal growth, as more and more Americans attend institutions of higher learning than ever before in the nation's history. Mixed emotions of unrest, uncertainty, enthusiasm, and zeal have accompanied this evolution from the quiet exclusive ivy colleges to the modern multiversity's combination of teaching, research, service, and scholarship.

While American institutions of higher learning now range from small liberal arts colleges with only a few hundred students to the great state universities with enrollments of tens of thousands, all of these colleges and universities share a common heritage. This chapter seeks to trace the development of higher learning in America from its origins in the colonial and early national periods through the founding of the state and land grant colleges to the modern university of the twentieth century.

The Colonial College

In the English speaking colonies of North America, the patterns of higher education originally followed those of the two major English universities,

Oxford and Cambridge. Attended by the sons of wealthy families, the English universities offered liberal arts education and the professional studies of law, medicine, and theology, of which the latter was most highly respected. In addition to educating scholars, lawyers, doctors, and theologians, Oxford and Cambridge were expected to prepare the cultured, well-rounded "gentleman." Higher education as practiced in England was class-based and designed for the elite, not for the masses of population.

The English university, like most of the other institutions of higher education in Western Europe, derived its basic structure from the medieval universities of Paris, Salerno, and Bologna. Their essential curriculum was liberal arts as contained in the trivium of grammar, rhetoric, and logic, and the quadrivium of music, astronomy, geometry, and mathematics. Latin was the language of instruction. After completing the liberal studies, the medieval student specialized in one of the professional areas: theology, law, or medicine. The methodology used in the medieval university was the scholasticism developed by Abelard and Saint Thomas Aquinas.

The Renaissance of the fourteenth and fifteenth centuries emphasized the importance of humanistic studies. The scholars of this period stressed Greek and Ciceronian Latin as the languages of the educated man. With the advent of the Protestant Reformation religion became the dominant force as various sects sought to use higher education as a means of building doctrinal commitment by training an educated ministry. The colonial conception of higher education, as transmitted to the New World from England, was derived from the scholasticism of the medieval university, the classical emphasis of Renaissance humanism, and the educational zeal of the Protestant Reformation.

The Puritans of Massachusetts emphasized the necessity of safeguarding the Church in the New World through the tutelage of an educated ministry. Because of their influence, on October 28, 1636, the Massachusetts General Court enacted the legislation which created Harvard College, and at the same time appropriated an initial endowment of 400 pounds for its support. Harvard's original curriculum consisted of the same traditional liberal arts that had been offered in the medieval universities. The function of the college in the clergy's education was evidenced by the emphasis placed on the ancient languages of Hebrew, Greek, and Latin, which were needed for scriptural scholarship. The foundation upon which the entire program of studies rested was Calvinist theology.[1]

In the colonial South, the plantation-owning class of Southern gentlemen sent their sons to England for higher studies in the humanities and professional training. In Virginia, demand for an institution of higher learning led to the royal charter establishing the College of William and Mary in 1693. Thomas Jefferson's interest in higher education later contributed to the reorganization of William and Mary's curriculum in 1779 to include natural philosophy, mathematics, law, anatomy, medicine, moral philosophy, fine arts, and modern languages.

In the Middle Atlantic colonies, Princeton was chartered in 1746 in New Jersey as the educational institution of the Presbyterians. King's College, which became Columbia, was chartered in 1754 to serve the Anglicans of New York, but it soon acquired a reputation for being tolerant in admission and liberal in curriculum. The University of Pennsylvania was chartered in 1779.

By the early eighteenth century Harvard was beginning to be influenced by the liberal thought that eventually characterized the dominant commercial class of Boston. Theological discussion at the college bore the imprint of Deism. As a protest against Harvard's liberal theology, more orthodox Congregationalists established their own institution at New Haven in 1701 to preserve the established religious doctrines, and Cotton Mather persuaded Elihu Yale to supply the first endowment. By the outbreak of the American Revolution, Dartmouth in New Hampshire, Brown in Rhode Island, and Rutgers in New Jersey were also established colleges in North America.

Although each of the colonial colleges had its own particularities, they all required that applicants for admission be versed in Latin and Greek. These requirements sustained the Latin Grammar school as the only secondary institution that supplied the classical language preparation considered so important by the colleges. In addition, Hebrew was also offered by the colleges because it aided study of the Holy Scripture. The eighteenth-century colonial college curriculum resembled the following:

First Year: Latin, Greek, logic, Hebrew, and rhetoric.
Second Year: Greek, Hebrew, logic, and natural philosophy.
Third Year: Natural philosophy, metaphysics, and moral
               philosophy.
Fourth Year: Mathematics, and review in Latin, Greek, logic, and
               natural philosophy.[2]

Enrollment in the colonial colleges was small and came from the economically and socially favored classes. Financial support was meager and the quest for funds always a problem. Despite the authoritarianism exercised by the institutions, the students even then complained about food, lodging, and the quality of instruction.

The Scottish University Influence

While the American colonial colleges were shaped by the English universities of Oxford and Cambridge, the concept of higher education that developed in Scotland also influenced American higher education.[3] In the years immediately prior to the American Revolution, there was a significant immigration of Scots and Scotch-Irish to North America. The Presbyterian ministers who accompanied these immigrants were committed to the establishment of academies and colleges in the New World. In Scotland, universities such as Saint Andrews, Glasgow, Aberdeen, and Edinburgh were centers where education was directed to utilitarian social service, scientific research, and reform. The Scottish universities also attracted a number of Americans who came to complete their higher education. Benjamin Rush, a founder of American medical education, was among these students. Rush studied medicine at Edinburgh and then returned to introduce the new learning into his teaching at the College of Philadelphia and the University of Pennsylvania.

The College of New Jersey, founded in 1742, was an institution of higher learning that particularly reflected the educational ideas of the Scottish universities. While its curriculum retained the classics and a commitment to reformed theology, the program of studies at New Jersey was broadened to include courses in science, geography, astronomy, moral philosophy, and mathematics. There was also an emphasis on sense realism as a method of learning that encouraged observation and experimentation rather than relying on deductive reasoning as commonly was done in the waning years of the colonial period. Sloan has identified four major contributions that derived from the Scottish university influence in America. One, the college was viewed as a location of a genuine academic and scientific community. Two, the college was envisioned as mediator between the claims of science and religion. Three, the initial efforts were undertaken to develop an educational theory that related to the special needs of the American environment. Four, the first appearances of a modern college curriculum could be glimpsed.[4]

Early National Period

Although institutions of higher learning were neglected during the Revolutionary War, the success of the American cause stimulated enthusiasm for a uniquely American form of education. The establishment of a national university under federal auspices was proposed during the debates in the Constitutional Convention. Although Washington, Jefferson, and Madison supported it, the proposal was defeated. Throughout his career Washington continued to urge the establishment of such an institution. His first Inaugural Address referred to it, and his will contained a bequest to be used in financing one. Jefferson unsuccessfully pleaded the same cause during his administration, too.

Though a national university was not established, the early period following independence witnessed an enthusiasm for the founding of colleges. Private colleges continued to function, and numerous state colleges were chartered in the west and south as well. While the colleges on the Atlantic seaboard shifted away from strict adherence to the religious orthodoxy of their founders, the new denominational colleges that followed in the wake of frontier settlement maintained the Protestant commitment to train an educated ministry.

The early state colleges were usually located in small towns. Many of the locations were not easily accessible and were determined by political expediency rather than by carefully considered planning. College preparatory schools were usually lacking, and the colleges often had to maintain their own secondary departments. Libraries, staff, and facilities were weak. Usually, after a brief burst of educational enthusiasm, the relationship between state legislatures and the state colleges was poor.

The University of Virginia, chartered in 1819, was one of the first major institutions to deviate in organization, control, and curriculum from the older pattern of higher education found in the private colonial college. The University of Virginia exemplified several factors typical of the state university: first, public control and support; second, a scientific rather than a classical curriculum; third, student election of subjects rather than a prescribed course of study; fourth, a high level of instruction; fifth, nonsectarianism.[5] These factors could be found to varying degrees in most of the state-established and state-maintained universities such as Indiana, founded in 1820, Michigan, 1837, Wisconsin, 1848, and others prior to the Civil War.

Denominational Colleges

In addition to the state governments, the various religious denominations established institutions of higher education. As the frontier moved west, ministers of the various religious denominations often accompanied the migration of their congregations. Frequently, ministers and priests led the westward advance as missionaries, and some of them stayed to serve the small towns which soon dotted the Midwest and West.

The religious revivals that swept the country during the first half of the nineteenth century created waves of evangelistic ardor. One of the characteristics of revivalism was the way the exercises reflected the religious commitments of each preacher. Because of this religious personalism, many small groups split away from their parent denominations during the pre-Civil War period. Two factors operated to involve the religious denominations in higher education: first, American Protestants, like their European counterparts, usually valued an educated ministry, and even denominations at first suspicious of "too much education" came to agree with them; second, the proliferation of religious groups brought about a competition between them. The denominational college was a popular means of educating the faithful and of building religious commitment in both the ministry and the congregation.

However, the college did not restrict itself to religious education but also offered the liberal and practical subjects. Furthermore, many of these small colleges had to prepare their own students at the secondary level, which stimulated the growth of the academies. Presbyterians, Congregationalists, Roman Catholics, Methodists, Lutherans, Christian Disciples, Baptists, Episcopalians, Quakers, and Mormons were among the sects which founded a number of small liberal arts colleges.[6]

The Dartmouth College Case

As the number of colleges increased and the states became involved in higher education, it was necessary that the private colleges' independence from state control be guaranteed; the precedent was set in the famous Dartmouth College case of 1819. The controversy over the control of Dartmouth College developed from the intense political rivalry between the Federalists, who controlled Dartmouth's board of trustees, and the Jeffersonian Democratic-Republicans, who controlled the New Hampshire state legislature. In 1816 the Democratic-Republican majority in the legislature attempted to take control of Dartmouth, change the charter, annul the original provisions, and establish a new institution called the University of New Hampshire. The Federalist-controlled board of trustees contended that the action of the state legislature was unconstitutional. Daniel Webster argued the case before the United States Supreme Court and won a decision favorable to the board of trustees affirming the original charter. According to Chief Justice John Marshall, the charter granted by King George III was of contractual nature; and under the United States Constitution, the binding force of contracts could not be impaired. In his decision Marshall upheld the sanctity of the Constitution's contract clause and applied it to the Dartmouth case, restoring the college to the board of trustees and returning it to its earlier status as a private educational institution.

The Dartmouth College decision of 1819 had far-reaching significance for both educational and national development. It protected the continued existence of the independent, privately controlled college, and ended state efforts to establish control over such institutions by legislative action. Concerning national enterprise, the Dartmouth decision established the precedent for the inviolability of the commercial contract. At the same time it strongly sanctioned the duality of higher education in the United States, which has produced two great academic systems, one private and the other state-supported. Further, the Dartmouth case illustrated the intimate relationship between education and national life. No institution, not even higher education, can escape political and social conflict. Educational institutions are related to and affected by other political, social, economic, and religious institutions.

New State Universities

As a result of the combined effects of the Dartmouth College decision's protection of private higher education and the demands of the westward-moving population, new state universities were established in the early nineteenth century. As such western areas as the Northwest Territory and the Louisiana Purchase were organized and then admitted as states, their respective governments sought to establish their own state universities; their efforts were encouraged by the federal government's policy of granting land from the national domain for education.

The precedent of land grants for education had been established by the Ordinances of 1785 and 1787, which were enacted by the Continental Congress prior to the ratification of the Constitution.[7] The Ordinance of 1785 reserved the sixteenth section of each township of the Northwest Territory for education, and the Ordinance of 1787 expressed a federal commitment to encourage "schools and the means of education." The use of the abundant frontier land as a source of financial aid to education was an obvious step for the national government to take since it did not require increased taxation.

The establishment of state universities was further encouraged by the federal land grant policy, which granted two townships of land for institutions of higher learning to each state as it entered the Union. Ohio was the first to benefit from this policy, and the Ohio Enabling Act, which contained a provision for land grants to higher education, set a pattern that was followed by other states as they were admitted to the Union. During the 1850s this precedent was cited in the arguments favoring the adoption of a system of land grant colleges and universities. Although several state universities already benefited from the income derived from grants of land by the federal government, it was not until after the enactment of the Morrill Act in 1862 that the "land grant" colleges and universities were established specifically to further agricultural and industrial studies.

Land Grant Institutions

In addition to the land grant provisions contained in the various enabling acts under which states were admitted to the Union, by the middle of the nineteenth century the federal government had also become involved in a number of special educational activities related to higher education.[8] These projects were intended to achieve specific objectives rather than serve as aid to higher education in general. The military academies at West Point and Annapolis, for instance, were established to train army and naval officers and contribute directly to the national defense. In 1857, Columbia Institute for the Deaf, later named Gallaudet College, was established with federal assistance. After the Civil War, Howard University was established to provide higher education for the newly freed slaves. These various ventures of the federal government into higher education were not parallel movements, but they were all aimed at solving particular educational problems. The policy of specific areas of assistance was followed until the 1960s when general programs of aid to education were enacted by Congress.

The movement for the land grant college and university during the 1850s represented a phase of American educational history which again reflected the interaction of growing social, economic, and political pressures upon education. The land grant movement, culminating in the Morrill Act of 1862, is a clearcut example of education as a civilizational instrument intimately related to social forces.

During the first half of the nineteenth century, the emphasis on classical and professional curricula inherited from the European educational tradition continued to dominate American colleges which were generally impervious to change and innovation. The *Yale Report* of 1828, largely the work of that institution's President Jeremiah Day, was an example of the attitude that blocked curricular change. Stressing the classics and mathematics as the foundation of a superior education, the *Yale Report* emphasized that the training and exercise of mental faculties was the proper function of higher education. Farmers' and laborers' pleas for agricultural and industrial instruction and research were ignored by the established colleges and universities, as higher education continued to neglect the needs of a pioneer people on the verge of a great technological transformation.

Allan Nevins, in *The State Universities and Democracy*, wrote that the quest for equal opportunity was the motivating force behind the land grant college movement.[9] This equalitarian impulse echoed the earlier appeals of Horace Mann and Henry Barnard for educational democracy. The farmers and laborers who were members of the agricultural and industrial organizations of the 1850s and 1860s believed that genuine equality of opportunity depended on an education which would facilitate improvement of their economic condition. Although the common school had contributed to economic and social mobility in an earlier period, public elementary education by itself was an inadequate guarantee of mobility in an era of increasing technological specialization. Finding the existing liberal arts colleges unresponsive to their needs, the members of the agricultural and industrial organizations believed that a new institution of higher education was required. Thus, a coalition of farmer, laborer, and industrialist formed to advance the cause of the land grant college.

The idea of the industrial college was first developed by Jonathan Baldwin Turner, who in the early 1850s outlined a plan for a state industrial university in Illinois and asked the federal government for a land grant to be used to establish it. Turner believed that such an institution would help the working classes understand the technological age. In 1853, the Illinois legislature petitioned Congress to endow such a system.[10] Following the example of the earlier land grants to the states, Justin S. Morrill, a Vermont Congressman, introduced a land grant act to encourage agricultural and mechanical instruction without excluding the other scientific and classical studies. Morrill's act encompassed three broad goals: protest against the domination of higher education by the classics; development of practical instruction at the collegiate level; and vocational preparation of the agricultural and industrial classes.

The passage of the First Morrill Act in 1862 represented the culmination of a legislative struggle that extended back five years. When Congress initially passed it, President Buchanan, a strict interpreter of the Constitution, vetoed it. When the bill returned to the President's office in 1862, the more liberal Abraham Lincoln willingly gave his signature. The Morrill Act granted each state 30,000 acres of public land for each Senator and Representative it had in Congress according to the apportionment of the census of 1860.[11] The income from this land was to support at least one college whose primary purpose was agricultural and mechanical instruction. In states lacking adequate acreage of public land, the grant was given in federal scrip, i.e., certificates based upon the public domain which could be sold by the state. The proceeds which accrued were then used to establish the land grant college. It is significant that the federal government, in the case of the Morrill Act, extended the context of federal aid to higher education from the concept of the specifically directed grant to the more general purpose of aiding agriculture and industry.

The Second Morrill Act, passed in 1890, provided a direct cash grant of $15,000, to be increased annually to a maximum of $25,000, for the support of land grant colleges and universities. This Act also provided for similar institutions for blacks in states prohibiting their enrollment in existing land grant institutions. It should be noted that the federal government attached requirements to this aid specifying that land grant colleges provide instruction in agricultural and mechanical subjects and in military training. As the United States emerged as a world power, it needed a larger body of trained military officers than could be provided by the military academies. This provision strengthened the Reserve Officer Training Corps.

Although the Morrill Acts resulted from many pressures, they were essentially a response to the rapid industrial and agricultural growth of the United States in the nineteenth century. Agricultural societies and working-men's associations had supported higher learning to advance this technological revolution still further.

The growth of the land grant colleges in the post-Civil War era coincided with the Populist movement in American politics. After enjoying prosperity during the war the farmers of the 1870s and 1880s faced declining prices, deflated currency, and periodic agricultural depressions. Hoping to improve their economic and political position, the agriculturalists banded together in societies such as the Grange and the Farmers' Alliances. By the late 1880s and 1890s, significant numbers of farmers formed the agriculturalist political coalition called the Populist Party. The equal educational opportunity provided by the land grant colleges was a corollary to the Populists' demands that American economic and political life be made more democratic. Although American Populism had its strength among the farmers and was a last major assertion of rural interests against the growing urbanization of the United States, the business and industrial interests, though opposed to agrarian radicalism, also supported the land grant college movement as an invaluable instrument in industrializing America. Although the farmers and industrialists cooperated in urging a practical curriculum suited to popular needs, agricultural interests dominated. They exerted strong pressures on the land grant colleges established in rural areas to develop a ''science of agriculture.''

Since the passage of the First Morrill Act over a hundred years ago, land grant institutions have been established throughout the United States. In a number of states, these agricultural and mechanical colleges have become part of the state university system. Examples of such universities are Maine, founded in 1865, Illinois and West Virginia in 1867, California in 1868, Nebraska in 1869, Ohio State in 1870, and Arkansas in 1871. More recent examples are the University of Puerto Rico, founded in 1903, and the University of Hawaii, founded in 1907. In addition to the land grant universities there were also a number of agricultural and mechanical colleges established as separate institutions, such as Purdue University, founded in 1869, the Agricultural and Mechanical College of Texas in 1871, and the Alaska Agricultural College and School of Mines in 1922. Seventeen southern states established separate land grant colleges for blacks under the provisions of the Second Morrill Act of 1890. As this partial listing illustrates, there were great differences in the character and location of the land grant institutions.

In *American Higher Education*, Brown and Mayhew have referred to the similarities and diversities among land grant colleges and universities. For example, land grant colleges emphasize agriculture as a blending of the scientific and practical. They also provide areas of study that are closely related to agriculture, such as home economics and veterinary medicine. Maintaining their commitment to industry, the colleges stress technology, engineering, and applied science. In addition to their agricultural and industrial programs, these institutions provide instruction in the liberal arts and sciences and in teacher education. Many of them have developed large extension programs as well to make education available to as many people as possible in each state.[12]

Since land grant institutions serve particular needs of the people in each state, they have developed differences. Some land grant universities have become great research centers by developing a full complex of graduate and professional schools. For example, the faculties of the University of California at Berkeley, the University of Wisconsin, and the University of Illinois include distinguished scholars and scientists engaged in research and scholarship. Several land grant universities are among the highest in the number of graduate and professional degrees granted.[13] The land grant concept as it was developed over a hundred years ago is still dynamic; today it has been extended to urban life. As the nation has changed, the land grant colleges and universities have changed with it.

Formation of the University

The history of American higher education is the story of long, continuous interaction between transplanted European concepts and the American environment. For example, the liberal arts college was derived from the English system and was primarily concerned with undergraduate instruction. It granted a bachelor's degree which marked the recipient as a generally educated non-specialist.

The modern American university has resulted from the imposition of the German graduate school upon the four-year undergraduate college. The nineteenth-century German universities, which emphasized *Lehrfreiheit und Lernfreiheit*, freedom to teach and freedom to learn, had a great influence on American higher education between the Civil War and World War I. Universities such as Berlin, Halle, Gottingen, Bonn, and Munich encouraged scholarly research. A university's graduate faculty, whose members usually held doctorates of philosophy, would guide the research by the instructional methods of seminar, laboratory, and lecture.

In the late nineteenth century many American professors completed their education with a period of residence in a German university. Upon their return to the United States, they sought to transform American higher education into the German pattern. For example, Daniel Coit Gilman of Johns Hopkins and Charles W. Eliot of Harvard worked to make their institutions centers of graduate study and research.[14] The Johns Hopkins University, founded in Baltimore in 1876, became the prototype of the American university inspired by its German counterpart. Here instruction took the form of lectures to large groups and seminars in which a professor and a limited number of graduate students pursued advanced study and research. The methods of Johns Hopkins were emulated by the graduate schools at Harvard, Yale, Columbia, Princeton, and Chicago.[15] Abraham Flexner, a noted student of higher education also inspired by the German university, urged scholars and scientists to be conscious of four major concerns: the conservation of knowledge and ideas; the interpretation of knowledge and ideas; the search for truth; the training of students to carry on this work.[16] Thus, the German emphasis on scholarship and research came to dominate the American university as the graduate faculty devoted themselves to the pursuit of truth and the advancement of knowledge.

The American university took shape and reached its present state of definition in the late nineteenth century. The focal point of the university was the undergraduate college of liberal arts and sciences, which eventually came to be surrounded by the graduate college and the professional schools of law, medicine, agriculture, education, engineering, nursing, social work, theology, dentistry, commerce, and other specialized areas.

This period also saw a tremendous expansion of the undergraduate curriculum. Libraries were enlarged as instruction in science increased, the study of modem languages was introduced, and English, American history, economics, and political science were gradually included. Preprofessional courses, and later whole programs, were introduced at the expense of the general liberal arts studies.

Charles Eliot

Charles Eliot's career as President of Harvard University from 1869 to 1909 reveals how a major American university was transformed from an institution that was dominated by a prescribed classical curriculum into one that met the specialized needs of a modern technological society.[17]

A Harvard graduate, Eliot had been educated in the classics, mathematics, and chemistry. While touring Europe in 1863, Eliot visited French and German universities and polytechnical institutes. Impressed with the academic specialization of these European institutions, Eliot, upon returning to the United States, urged American universities to adopt certain aspects of European higher education. He also encouraged American universities to avoid academic isolation and to respond to the changing technological needs of a modernizing nation.

During his forty years as Harvard's President, Eliot's style of leadership shaped both his own university and American higher education as well. Traditionally, college and university presidents had been selected from the ranks of distinguished clergymen who administered their institutions in a paternalistic fashion. Believing that such paternalism was an obsolete relic of the pre-industrial past, Eliot saw his role to be the chief executive of a highly complex educational corporation.[18] He emphasized greater administrative efficiency, higher academic standards, and greater freedom of choice for students. As chairman of the National Education Association's Committee of Ten, Eliot also sought to develop closer relationships between colleges and universities and elementary and secondary schools.

As a champion of academic freedom of choice, Eliot introduced the elective concept at Harvard in the 1870s. Students were free to choose or to elect a certain number of courses rather than follow a totally prescribed curriculum. The elective principle, Eliot believed, would facilitate undergraduate specialization. It would encourage the development of new specialized fields by permitting professors to teach in their areas of expertise rather than in mandatory general courses. The principle of electivism also provided a form of student evaluation of instructors and courses.

Eliot was regarded as one of America's leading educational statesmen. He worked to make American higher education more responsive to the needs of a modernizing nation. Eliot saw the role of the modern university to be the preparation of the highly trained specialists that a technological society needed.

Curricular Controversies

As colleges and universities responded to technological change, the curriculum of American higher education expanded to include more professional, specialized, and technical courses. The contemporary American university often offers such varied degree programs as business administration, nuclear physics, animal husbandry, hotel and restaurant management, fashion design, and computer programming as well as the traditional arts, sciences, and humanities. As has been true in secondary education, the purpose and curriculum of higher education has been subject to spirited debate and controversy.

While some educators endorsed American higher education's growing utilitarianism and specialization, others claimed that these tendencies were eroding the central academic purpose of colleges and universities. Among the severest critics of specialized programs have been humanities professors. Irving Babbitt, in particular, was a convinced opponent of Eliot's legacy of electivism at Harvard. Babbitt reiterated the philosophy that the study of the classics would prepare a genuinely educated leader of cultivated taste and disciplined judgment.[19] For Babbitt, the essential purpose of higher education was to transmit the enduring values from generation to generation through a general liberal education.

Robert M. Hutchins, President of the University of Chicago from 1930 to 1945, like Babbitt, was a critic of specialization in higher education. In *The Higher Learning In America*, Hutchins attacked the confused purposes of higher education which he attributed to a preoccupation with financial gain, a distorted conception of democracy, and an erroneous notion of progress.[20] The modern university, Hutchins claimed, had lost its integrating purpose, the pursuit of truth when it tried to satisfy the shifting demands of philanthropists, business, football-oriented alumni, politicians and other special interest groups. Opposing what he called the "service station" institution, Hutchins wanted a university whose exclusive purpose was the pursuit of intellectual truth. Hutchins alleged that many American universities had surrendered to a distorted utilitarianism which emphasized financial gain as the most desirable outcome of college degree. A pervasive anti-intellectualism had developed from the emphasis on the purely utilitarian at the expense of theoretical and speculative studies. Believing that theoretical knowledge was essential to develop the human being's rationality, Hutchins wanted to refocus the university's faculty's activities on the pursuit of truth. Over-specialization had caused professors to concentrate on purposes that were too narrow. Such professorial specialists were able to communicate only within their specialty rather than taking part in the general intellectual discourse that made a university a true community of scholars.

Critics of Babbitt's and Hutchins' philosophy see them advocating an ivory tower retreat that isolated the university from the actual needs of society. Rather than concentrating on solely intellectual pursuits, the advocates of specialization believe the university should meet the demands of the modern era and educate people who are competent in specialized technologies and sciences.

The Transformation of Higher Education

After World War II ended in 1945, American higher education began a great transformation, a cycle of growth that would continue uninterrupted until the 1970s. This great transformation began when Congress enacted the Servicemen's Readjustment Act of 1944, known popularly as the G.I. Bill. While the legislation's primary purpose was to provide greater career opportunities to returning war veterans and to ease their transition to civilian life, the G.I. Bill had the consequence of being a massive federal aid program to higher education. Through its provisions, the federal government subsidized tuition, educational materials and fees, and living expenses for veterans who were attending approved educational institutions. From 1944 through 1951, 7,800,000 veterans received educational benefits; 2,232,000 of whom attended colleges or universities.[21]

While Americans had enjoyed greater access to higher education than the citizens of most western nations, opportunities to attend college or university were still limited in the period before the end of World War II. The cost of attending college and highly selective admission requirements were factors that limited enrollments. Also important in keeping enrollments low was an informal social tradition that saw higher education as reserved to members of the more affluent socioeconomic classes. As a result of the G.I. Bill, these inherited stereotyped views of higher education were eroded. In many ways, the veterans inaugurated the era of the non-traditional student as college and university professors developed new teaching strategies for students whose age and experience differed from the college age population of the past. The veterans were older, more experienced, and more highly motivated than the undergraduates of the past. The opportunity to attend colleges and universities became available to a larger and more varied socioeconomic group than ever before in the nation's history.

As a result of growing enrollments, colleges and universities needed more classrooms, laboratories, larger libraries and collections, and a greatly increased faculty. Along with greater state efforts, the federal government contributed to financing the needed expansion of higher education. Recognizing the need for federal aid to higher education, President Kennedy stated in 1963:

> Now a veritable tidal wave of students is advancing inexorably on our institutions of higher education, where the annual costs per student are several times as high as the cost of a high school education, and where these costs must be borne in large part by the student or his parents. Five years ago the graduating class of the secondary schools was 1.5 million; 5 years from now it will be 2.5 million. The future of these young people and the nation rests in large part on their access to college and graduate education. For this country reserves its highest honors for only one kind of aristocracy — that which the Founding Fathers called "an aristocracy of achievement arising out of a democracy of opportunity." [22]

President Kennedy's assessment of the need for federal aid to higher education blended the quantitative and qualitative dimensions of education. His phrase "a democracy of opportunity" demonstrated a determination to continue to provide greater access to institutions of higher learning for more students. Kennedy's term "an aristocracy of intellect" reflected a Jeffersonian-like resolve that, despite its increasing enrollments, American higher education would maintain standards of excellence.

The Higher Education Facilities Act of 1963 provided grants to colleges and universities for the construction of academic facilities. Congress provided an annual appropriation of $230,000,000 for the years 1963 through 1966. For the period 1967-1968, Congress set the amount of the funding. Under the provisions of the Act, any institution of higher education was eligible to apply for a construction grant for an academic facility. This feature of the Act made private and church-related institutions eligible for aid. In religious institutions, however, the facility built with the aid had to be used for non-religious purposes such as instruction or research in the sciences, mathematics, foreign languages or engineering.

During President Johnson's administration, the Higher Education Act of 1965 was enacted. This major federal aid to higher education law provided assistance to a variety of higher education programs. Among them were assistance to libraries, to developing colleges and universities, and grants to qualified high school graduates who might be unable to attend college due to financial need.

The federal role in the expansion of higher education in the post-World War II era had mixed motives. The rise of the United States to world power and the tensions generated by the Cold War with the Soviet Union gave higher education an important role in contributing to national security. The federal government, through the National Science Foundation, was particularly interested in encouraging instruction and research in mathematics, science, and technology. Simultaneously, the federal government, especially during the Johnson administration, sought to continue the impetus to make higher education more accessible to more Americans, especially members of minority who had been under-represented in the past.[23]

Emergence of the Multiversity

Clark Kerr, a former President of the University of California, astutely identified the forces that were changing the character of American higher education. In his important analysis, *The Uses of the University*, Kerr examined two major currents that had reshaped American universities. The first current of change resulted from the combined stimulus of the Morrill Act's land grant movement which created the large state universities and the German research model with its emphasis on graduate education. The second current of change emanated from the expansion that followed World War II. Since 1945, American universities have educated masses of students and engaged in federally-sponsored research that related to the national interest. According to Kerr, the product of these two historical forces was the restructuring of the inherited university into a "multiversity," an institution that was "unique in world history." [24]

In 1963, Kerr described the University of California, where he had served as President as representative of the new model, the "multiversity." At that time, the University of California had an operating budget of nearly half a billion dollars. It spent nearly $100 million for construction, had over 40,000 employees, conducted operations in over 100 locations, and had overseas projects in more than fifty foreign nations. It offered 10,000 courses to a student body that was expected to reach 100,000.[25]

Several characteristics distinguished the "multiversity" from the older university. An obvious distinction was its massiveness. It had a larger physical plant, enrolled thousands of additional students, and had a much larger faculty.

However, a subtle but pervasive change had altered the institution's character and purposes. While the older university model was based on the medieval conception that it should be a community of scholars, the newer university which Kerr called a "multiversity," had many spheres of interest and competitors for power. As a result of his efforts to administer a "multiversity," Kerr was able to identify the major competitors for power: one, the students who through the elective system influenced the fields that the institution would develop; two, the faculty who through its governance of admission requirements, course and program approval, degree requirements, and appointments to its ranks exercised a determining role in shaping institutional structures; third, boards of trustees, state commissions of higher education, and other public officials such as the governor and the legislator, who through their allocation of funds exercised a crucial power over the institution; fourth, special interests such as agricultural, business, labor, and educational organizations which exerted informal pressures for particular programs.[26] In addition to these competitors for power, the institution's administration was becoming a separate bureaucratic entity that was growing apart from both faculty and students.

The Rise of Strategic Planning

By mid-twentieth century, one of American higher education's distinguishing characteristics was its massive size. The 1960s continued the cycle of quantitative growth that began in the previous decade. Institutions of higher education received increasingly larger allocations in state budgets. State commissions of higher education in the late 1950s and 1960s turned increasingly to the concept of strategic planning to determine the course of future growth and development. During the period of growth, planners dealt with such matters as determining the location of new colleges and universities, avoiding program duplication between often competing state institutions, and providing more access to higher education for urban and under-represented groups in the state.

State Master Plans

The concept of strategic planning was new to many state officials and college and university administrators. Historically, American higher education, even in the public sector, was decentralized. This decentralization produced great variations among the institutions in administration, size, organization, faculty, curricula and standards. While this diversity created wide choices for students, it also contributed to costly duplication of resources and efforts.

The efforts of those who sought to coordinate higher education in the states were complicated by a number of historical and demographic factors. In the early nineteenth century when many state institutions had been established, the population was predominately rural. State legislatures which had the responsibility for locating colleges tended to favor sites, often in small towns, that were convenient for rural populations. In the later nineteenth and early twentieth centuries, the United States experienced a large growth in its urban population. Many large urban areas found themselves underserved by state institutions of higher education. State planners had to take these complex issues into consideration as they dealt with the development of higher education.

In order to make a concerted effort at coordinating the development of higher education, many of the states developed master plans. The example of California, a leader in the movement, can be used to describe the role of planning at the state level. California established a Coordinating Council for Higher Education in 1959 that was charged with planning the orderly growth of higher education in the state. California's Coordinating Council was responsible for advising the governing boards of state colleges and universities and state officials on such matters as capital expenses and budgets, differentiation between the institutions, recommending program changes, and recommending the location of new facilities.[27] Through coordinated planning, California developed a tri-level public system of higher education that consisted of community colleges, colleges, and the University of California. Other states such as Ohio, New York, Illinois, Indiana and Florida established boards or commissions of higher education that performed functions in their states that were similar to California.

During the thirty-year period from 1945 to 1975, American higher education experienced great growth. From 1949 to 1964, college and university enrollments almost doubled. In 1949, there were 2,445,000 students enrolled. In 1964, enrollments registered a 96 per cent increase with 4,988,000 students in attendance.[28] In 1970, 8,580,000 students were attending colleges and universities. Five years later in 1975, enrollments reached 11,184,000. [29] The sheer increase in the numbers of students posed serious problems for strategic planners in higher education.

To meet the needs of the millions of students enrolled during the 1950s, 1960s, and early 1970s, educational planners, administrators, and state boards of higher education looked to largely quantitative solutions. The answer to more students was more buildings, more resources, and more faculty. Large scale construction was undertaken to provide additional classrooms, libraries, laboratories, and dormitories. Graduate programs expanded to prepare the new faculty needed. By the early 1970s, American higher education had become a massive educational enterprise.

While enrollments continued to rise after 1975, the increase was less dramatic than in previous decades. In 1980, enrollments in colleges and universities were 12,096,000. In 1986, they were 12,504,000. [30] In the late 1970s and 1980s, higher education planners found themselves in an era of uncertainty. A declining birth rate and the economic inflation of the 1970s apparently caused a leveling off in the college and university population. The period of tremendous growth had ended but the dramatic enrollment declines projected by some experts did not occur. A new group of "non-traditional" students had begun to attend college. These new students often were not of the traditional college age. Many were employed persons who were preparing for career changes or retired persons pursuing their own academic interests rather than professional programs. The 1980s also saw more women enrolled in programs in law, medicine, and business which had been male-dominated fields in the past. The 1980s were a decade of curricular reform and efforts to improve the academic quality of programs. The issues that had once been defined in quantitative terms now needed to be redefined in terms of improving the quality of the academic experience.

Junior and Community Colleges

During the expansive period of growth for American higher education that followed World War II, the junior college took on a special importance. The various state master plans, especially those of California, New York, Florida, and Illinois, emphasized a new and expanded role for two-year colleges. This expanded role transformed the concept of the two-year junior college into the community college, a distinctive American institution of post-secondary education. While the junior college was regarded as either an upward extension of the high school or a downward extension of the four-year college, the community college developed its own institutional identity. Since mid-twentieth century, community colleges have become an important component of mass higher education. This section of the chapter examines the history of one of the most recent additions to the American educational ladder, the community college.

In the late nineteenth century, university presidents such as Henry A. Tappan of Michigan, William W. Follwell of Minnesota, David Starr Jordan of Stanford, and William Rainey Harper of Chicago, sought to develop the research emphasis of their institutions by locating the first two years of undergraduate education elsewhere. Such a move, they believed would permit the faculty to spend more time on specialized research and advanced graduate education. In 1892, President Harper of the University of Chicago divided the undergraduate program into two divisions: the first two years were to be spent in the Academic College and the last two in the University College.

In 1896, these divisions were renamed the "junior college" and the "senior college." The terminology of a "junior college" subsequently was used to refer to other two-year institutions.[31]

As an institution, however, the junior college did not win immediate widespread support. Administrators approached the concept of a separate two-year college somewhat cautiously. The pioneer venture in establishing the junior college was made in 1901 in Joliet, Illinois, with the founding of the Joliet Junior College. Under the direction of Superintendent J. Stanley Brown, high school graduates were encouraged to take post-graduate work without additional tuition.[32] Although Brown's primary aim was to provide courses which would enable students to enter four-year colleges with advanced standing, terminal courses quickly became part of the program as well. In imitation of the venture at Joliet, junior colleges were established throughout the nation.

During the 1920s, 1930s, and 1940s, the number of junior colleges steadily increased, for various reasons. During this period, however, the junior college growth did not provide the relief for the university that Harper and Jordan had anticipated. Some four-year colleges retrenched their programs to two years during the depression period in order to survive. Some technical high schools and institutes were converted to junior colleges. In these and similar instances, junior colleges were being formed from schools already in operation, rather than being founded from the beginning as institutions specifically designed to relieve the overextended universities. During the 1920s and 1930s, there was a slow but consistent increase in the number of two-year colleges. In 1922, there were 207 junior colleges. By 1939, the number of such institutions had reached 575.[33]

As with any new institution, it was difficult at first to define the function of the junior college. As indicated, the two-year college was first conceived by university presidents as a means of diverting the responsibility for educating first- and second-year undergraduates to other institutions. According to this concept, the junior college would offer general liberal arts courses. In 1925, the American Association of Junior Colleges expanded its definition of the institution by stating that its members would offer two years of collegiate instruction of a quality equivalent to the first two years of a four-year college. In addition, the junior college curriculum would serve the social, civic, religious, and vocational needs of the community in which the college was located.[34] Despite this multifaceted definition of its function, the aims of the junior college were ill-defined and differences of opinion persisted. Were liberal arts and sciences to be offered, or were semiprofessional, terminal programs to be set up? As in the case of the high school, the institution that evolved combined both functions.

During the late 1920s and 1930s, junior colleges began to place greater emphasis on vocational and technical training programs. These programs were usually classified as terminal programs since they were the student's culminating experience in an institution of formal education. One of the most extensive programs of terminal or semiprofessional education was introduced at the Los Angeles Junior College, which offered fourteen separate terminal programs in 1929, its inaugural year.[35] Other junior colleges throughout the country also increased the number of terminal programs they offered.

A number of factors were at work in the growing emphasis on semiprofessional and technical education. In 1917 Congress passed the Smith-Hughes Act, which provided federal aid for vocational education. Although this legislation was primarily intended for such programs in the secondary schools, the incentives it provided encouraged vocational education in junior colleges in states where they were considered an extension of secondary education. During the 1920s a large number of educators subscribed to the doctrine of social efficiency, which held that each subject of study could be justified only in terms of its contribution to economic and social utility. During the depression of the 1930s, widespread unemployment stimulated vocational education as many individuals sought to improve their occupational skills. Since World War II, automation has required higher levels of technical competence.[36] Additional leisure time has also encouraged more adult study programs.

Today's community college is a multifunctional institution. It still provides the first two years of collegiate studies, upon completion of which students may transfer to four-year institutions. The student living at home and working part-time may thus obtain a relatively inexpensive education. The community college has responded to the need for technically trained individuals who can perform subprofessional services. It provides adult education by offering vocational, adult, and liberal arts courses. As a community college, it is a cultural, educational, and civic center for the people in the area which it serves. The term ''community college'' indicates the close relationship between the college and the community.

In many of the states which have adopted master plans for higher education the community college is a vital component of the state educational system, providing the first two years of education to students who later transfer to other four-year colleges. This has alleviated some of the pressures of massive student enrollment which strained four-year college facilities. The community college has also provided college education for many students who might have otherwise lacked the opportunity.

California was a leader in developing a state-wide system of community colleges. The first enabling legislation in California for establishing junior colleges was passed in 1907 when the legislature authorized high school districts to offer post-graduate courses. In 1917, the first state financial assistance was provided. In 1921, the legislature authorized the formation of junior college districts.[37] *The Master Plan for Higher Education in California, 1960-1975* proposed diverting enrollments from the state colleges and universities to the public community colleges.[38] The existence of an extensive community college system in California made possible both a selective admission policy at the university while facilitating more liberal access to the state's many public two-year institutions.

Florida also developed an extensive system of community colleges. In 1955, Florida's legislature provided funds for existing junior colleges and authorized appointment of a community college council to make recommendations for future community college development. In 1956, this council recommended establishment of a state-wide system of community colleges to provide a broad range of educational programs. In addition to California and Florida, New York, Texas, and Illinois developed extensive community college systems. By the mid-1960s, development of such state-wide systems had taken place throughout the United States.

The post-World War II era with its massive enrollment increases and efforts at state planning were particularly significant for the growth of two-year community colleges. In 1950, there were 524 two-year colleges in the United States. By 1960, the number of such institutions had reached 582. In 1970, there were 886 two-year colleges. Ten years later, in 1980, their numbers had increased to 1,112. As the 1980s ended, there were more than 1,240 two-year colleges in the nation.[39].

Along with the increase in the number of two-year institutions, there also came a corresponding increase in their student enrollments. In 1975, 3,970,119 students were attending two-year colleges. By 1980, the number of students enrolled had climbed to 4,526,287. As the 1980s ended, enrollments in these institutions were 4,776,000.[40] Clearly, the community college had become an important rung in the American ladder of educational institutions.

The Student Activism of the 1960s

While the 1960s were a time of massive growth of colleges and universities, they were also marked by student alienation. The symptoms of student discontent revealed themselves in the early 1960s with students' complaints against the administrative bureaucracy and impersonality of the large institutions of higher education that had developed as a result of the cycle of growth. From the mid-1960s onward until the end of the decade, the symptoms of discontent developed into student unrest, protest, and activism on many college and university campuses. Many students enlisted in a series of causes that ranged from such broad issues as opposition to United States' policy in the conflict in Viet Nam, to the ending of racial and sexual discrimination, and the eradication of poverty to such limited objectives as ending parietal hours and abolishing grades. At times, student protest resulted from specific campus-based issues and was directed against institutional authorities; at other times, the colleges and universities were the base of more generalized efforts at social reform. In the 1960s, the language related to student activism included such phrases as "the generation gap," the "raising of consciousness," the "counter-culture," "youth alienation," "non-negotiable demands," and the "greening of America."

A significant event in the history of what was termed the "new radicalism" occurred in 1962 when the Students for a Democratic Society, SDS, met at Port Huron in Michigan. [41] The SDS issued a manifesto urging the radical restructuring of American society along the lines of a participatory democracy. Among the objectives of the SDS were the extension of social welfare programs, an equitable redistribution of wealth, and an end to the American presence in Viet Nam. The SDS strategy called for confrontation with university administrators that would cause neutral or uncommitted students to join their cause. It also wanted to use the university as a base for bringing about radical social and political change. At its peak, the SDS could muster nearly 100,000 students. In 1970, the SDS splintered into contending ideological factions such as the Weathermen, an anarchistic group which espoused using violence to bring about social change, and the Progressive Labor group which was devoted to neo-Marxist doctrines and strategy. In the early 1970s, the SDS membership dropped dramatically and the organization ceased to be a force on American college campuses.

The Student Nonviolent Coordinating Committee, SNCC, was also an important organization for students, both black and white, who worked for civil rights for blacks.[42] SNCC's activities for civil and voting rights for blacks brought students to the South where they joined local black organizations in voter registration drives and sit-ins at segregated restaurants, waiting rooms, and other facilities. In some ways SNCC was a training ground where student activists learned the strategies of social protest that they would use later on their own campuses. However, when SNCC moved increasingly in the direction of a black power course of action, white students were either unwelcome or uncomfortable in the organization.

In 1964, national attention focused on the University of California at Berkeley, where the student Free Speech Movement, FSM, confronted the university administration over campus political activity. Led by Mario Savio, the FSM's initial objective was to persuade the university administration to grant it space to solicit members and raise funds for off-campus political causes. From this initial point of confrontation, the FSM broadened its challenge to a more generalized questioning of the University as an educational agency.

It began to attract students who were alienated by the impersonality and bureaucracy of what had been termed a "multiversity." The FSM used strategies that would be imitated at other college campuses such as confrontations with police and the occupation of campus buildings. In this early stage of the student activism of the 1960s, several factors became apparent that would be imitated in other confrontational situations. One, student activist leaders would begin with several demands. During negotiations with university administrators they tended to broaden and increase the demands so that the conflict became more generalized, less specific, and ongoing. Two, the response of university administrators was often unclear and uneven, ranging from appeasement, to conciliation, to stand off, to confrontation. Three, the faculty was often divided on the issues. While faculty members debated the issues, university administrators had to deal with the student activists alone. Four, the entire process received intensive media coverage, especially by television.

Some observers of higher education saw the unrest at the University of California and other institutions as a sign of student alienation. In his description of the "multiversity," Clark Kerr called it "a confusing place for the student" who has "problems of establishing his identity and sense of security within it."[43] To identify the causes of student alienation, the University of California's Academic Senate established a Select Committee on Education. In its report, *Education at Berkeley*, the Select Committee found that students felt they were participants in a great national and international development that had reached a crisis in higher education. The report identified the major reasons for this crisis as the changing role of the university in modern society, the accelerating proliferation of knowledge, rising social expectations, and the emergence of a new generation of students. All of the important sectors of the modern university — professors, students, knowledge, and society — were undergoing an unprecedented state of change. According to the authors of the Report, the modern university faced the complex challenge of preserving its own integrity and stability while accepting change.[44]

To reduce student feelings of the impersonality of the institution, the Select Committee recommended using more seminars, tutorials, and smaller classes to bring students into closer contact with faculty members. These more personally direct ways of organizing instruction were intended to reduce the predominance of the large lecture in which a professor might lecture to hundreds of students. Two other recommendations — a student role in institutional policy-making and more topical or problem-focused courses — were prophetic of trends that would occur at institutions throughout the country. Many colleges and universities appointed students to the various institutional policy-making committees. The curriculum was restructured to include a large number of problem-oriented courses to replace the introductory survey courses which had hitherto generated large course enrollments.

In addition to the Free Speech Movement at Berkeley and the SDS, a variety of student organizations appeared in the 1960s. As student activism accelerated, it nurtured a number of diverse groups that supported a variety of causes. The student activists used different tactics in the various universities. At times, they sponsored teach-ins against American involvement in the war in Viet Nam and against racial and sex discrimination. They also engaged in a series of actions designed to close the university to recruiters for the armed services or for corporations that held military contracts. In some institutions, such as Columbia University, student activists seized and occupied university offices and buildings.

1968 was a climactic year for the student movement. Many college students were attracted to the candidacy of Senator Eugene McCarthy, a liberal anti-war spokesman, who was seeking the Democratic Party's presidential nomination. Some commentators saw the pro-McCarthy "children's crusade" as a factor in President Johnson's decision not to seek re-election. When the Democratic National Convention met in Chicago in the summer of 1968, a violent confrontation took place between the Chicago police and anti-war demonstrators. The failure of Senator McCarthy to win the Democratic Presidential nomination caused many activists to return to their campuses to pursue the politics of polarization or to drop out of higher education. From 1968 through 1970, student unrest and demonstrations continued.

The cycle of student protest and demonstrations reached a tragic climax at Kent State University on May 4, 1970. Here, some students had joined a national student strike to protest President Nixon's decision to send American troops into Cambodia. Protestors had set fire to the campus ROTC building and had prevented firemen from fighting the fire. Ohio's governor responded by ordering National Guard troops to the campus. During a confrontation which involved name-calling and some rock-throwing, guardsmen fired into a crowd of students and killed four of them. The tragic incident at Kent State sent shock waves throughout the nation. After some sympathy demonstrations and counter-demonstrations, the mood on the campuses grew increasingly reflective. Student activism came to an end.

The 1970s marked the end of large scale student activism on the nation's college and university campuses. Students seemed to lose their interest in social and political activism. President Nixon's decision to disengage American military forces from Viet Nam removed a focal issue and the anti-war aspect of the movement dissipated. Even before the last American troops left South Viet Nam in 1973, the new generation of students showed that the campuses would be quiet. Still another factor in the decline of student activism was the splintering of student organizations, such as the SDS into small doctrinaire groups. The violence of the Weatherman faction caused many students to regard such groups as fringe organizations. Finally, the most important cause in ending the period of intense student activism was the mood of the students themselves. Economic changes in American society such as inflation of the early 1970s and the recession of the late 1970s caused many students to look to their own careers and future economic security rather than social issues. Students were now seeking admission into high status fields such as medicine, law, and business that promised financial rewards in greater numbers.

The student activism of the 1960s has had widely varying interpretations. Some commentators saw the movement as the product of upper and middle class youth who lacked specific vocational or professional goal orientations. Others saw the "new radicals" of the 1960s as the children of the old radicals of the 1930s who were acting out the roles that their parents had performed some thirty years before. Critics such as Sidney Hook saw the more extremist tactics of disrupting classes as an instrument of coercion that jeopardized academic freedom. Hook called for combatting the mood of irrationalism in order to preserve the "absolute intellectual integrity of our classrooms and laboratories" and of "our teaching and research against any attempt to curb it."[45]

The 1970s and 1980s

The twenty year period from 1970 to 1990 produced different circumstances and trends for higher education than the previous era of growth that occurred from 1945 to 1969. When the 1970s began, many of the characteristics of American higher education were now in place. At the end of the 1980s, there were more than 3,000 colleges and universities in the United States. These institutions ranged from two-year community colleges, to four-year liberal arts colleges, to large research universities. Of these institutions, 1,500 were public institutions and the rest were under private control.[46] As the twentieth century entered its last decade, an extensive system of community colleges had been established throughout the nation. State universities had grown into massive institutions for teaching and research.

The early 1970s showed signs that the pace of growing enrollments might slow and indeed might be reversed. Because of a decline in the traditional college age population of individuals in the 18- to 24-year range, experts in higher education predicted a serious enrollment decline. Due to the enrollment of more nontraditional students and higher participation rates, the numbers of college students increased but the rate of growth was smaller. For example, colleges were now enrolling more part-time students, more individuals over the age of 25, and larger numbers of women. Blacks and Hispanics who had registered increased attendance gains in the 1970s, still continued to lag behind whites in college attendance rates. By the end of the 1980s, the college enrollment rate for blacks was 33 percent and for Hispanics it was 29 percent.[47]

A serious problem was the spiraling of the costs required for a college education. Tuition, fees, and related costs rose dramatically in the 1980s at a rate that exceeded the general rate of inflation. The high cost of a college education placed a tremendous burden on middle and lower economic class families. Although enrollments did not decline in the 1980s as predicted, there were fears that the cost factor would limit the access of many students to four-year institutions.

During the late 1970s and 1980s, students enrolled more heavily in programs in business, technology, and preprofessional courses for law and medicine than in the arts and humanities. The number of degrees earned in liberal arts and in education declined while those in business, computer science, and engineering increased. An especially important trend was that more women were now enrolled in programs that had once been male-dominated. In the period from 1971 through 1986, the proportion of degrees awarded to women in business and management increased from nine to 46 percent at the bachelor's level. Women also earned an increasing proportion of degrees in the physical and computer sciences.[48] By the 1980s, the undergraduate curriculum in many institutions was being revised in response to what was called the decade of reform. Many institutions were now rejecting what had once been the earlier reforms of the 1960s. The wide student choices of that era were replaced in the 1980s by the return of the core curriculum, a prescribed sequence of courses required of all students. The requirements of the core curriculum generally included courses in the humanities, the social sciences, English, and mathematics and science. Many of the national reports on the condition of American higher education voiced alarm at the declining numbers of students enrolled in mathematics and science programs. Colleges responded by increasing the requirements in these areas.

Conclusion

The higher learning in the United States is a product of both transplanted institutional concepts that originated in Europe and concepts that arose in the American environment. While the colonial college followed the Oxford and Cambridge pattern of offering a classical curriculum to a small elite group of males, the state colleges and universities that arose after the American Revolution broadened the context of higher education. The federal system of land grants, especially in The Morrill Act, worked to create new institutions that emphasized the agricultural and scientific fields needed in a developing nation. The entry of the German research model contributed to the development of the research university.

In the post-World War II era, a massive growth of American higher education institutions occurred. A fully articulated system of community colleges, four-year colleges and universities, and large research institutions developed in the United States. From the time of the Dartmouth College case to the present, a healthy pluralism in higher education has existed in the United States where private, independent, and religious institutions co-exist with public and state institutions.

In the 1990s, American higher education will need to respond to the problems of improving the quality of its programs, especially in mathematics and sciences. It will need to maintain the vitality of the arts and humanities as important core subjects in undergraduate education. A concerted effort will be needed to contain the costs of higher education so that able students are not denied entry to colleges and universities because of economic need.

Notes

[1] For the history of Harvard, see Samuel Eliot Morison, *The Founding of Harvard College* (Cambridge, MA: Harvard University Press, 1935) and *Three Centuries of Harvard* (Cambridge, MA: Harvard University Press, 1936).

[2] Frederick Rudolph, *The American College and University: A History* (New York: Alfred A. Knopf, 1962), pp. 25-26.

[3] Douglass Sloan, *The Scottish Enlightenment and the American College Ideal* (New York: Teachers College Press, Columbia University, 1971).

[4] *Ibid.*, p. 225.

[5] John S. Brubacher, "A Century of the State University," in William Brickman and Stanley Lehrer, eds., *A Century of Higher Education: Classical Citadel to Collegiate Colossus* (New York: Society for the Advancement of Education, 1962), pp. 70-71.

[6] For a discussion of the evolution of denominational higher education, see Allan O. Pfnister, "A Century of the Church-Related College," in Brickman and Lehrer, *A Century of High Education*.

[7] The reader is referred to Chapter 2 for a more detailed treatment of the Ordinances of 1785 and 1787 and their provisions for land grants to education.

[8] For additional reading on the federal government's role in education, see Hollis P. Allen, *The Federal Government and Education* (New York: McGraw-Hill Book Company, 1950); Richard G. Axt, *The Federal Government and Financing Higher Education* (New York: Columbia University Press, 1952); Homer D. Babbidge and Robert M. Rosenzweig, *The Federal Interest in Higher Education* (New York: Columbia University Press, 1962).

[9] Allan Nevins, *The State Universities and Democracy* (Urbana: University of Illinois Press, 1962), p. 17.

[10] *Ibid.*, p. 14.

11 Benjamin F. Andrews, *The Land Grant of 1862 and the Land-Grant College* (Washington: Government Printing Office, 1918), pp. 7-8.

12 Hugh S. Brown and Lewis B. Mayhew, *American Higher Education* (New York: The Center for Applied Research in Education, 1965), pp. 26-27.

13 *Ibid.*, p. 24.

14 *Ibid.*, p. 29.

15 Abraham Flexner, *Universities: American, English, German* (New York: Oxford University Press, 1930), pp. 73-74.

16 *Ibid.*, p. 6.

17 Hugh Hawkins, *Between Harvard and America: The Educational Leadership of Charles W. Eliot* (New York: Oxford University Press, 1972), pp. 30-32.

18 *Ibid.*, p. 52.

19 Irving Babbitt, *Democracy and Leadership* (Boston: Houghton Mifflin Co., 1952), p. 302.

20 Robert M. Hutchins, *The Higher Learning In America* (New Haven: Yale University Press, 1936).

21 Diane Ravitch, *The Troubled Crusade: American Education, 1945-1980* (New York: Basic Books, 1983), p. 14. Also, see Robert Havighurst, Walter Easton, John Baughman, and Ernest Burgess, *The American Veteran Back Home* (New York: Longmans, Green and Co., 1951).

22 John F. Kennedy, *Message from the President of the United States Relative to a Proposed Program for Education* (H.R. No. 54, January 29, 1963), p. 5.

23 For the history of federal aid to education during the Kennedy and Johnson administrations, see Hugh Davis Graham, *The Uncertain Triumph: Federal Education Policy in the Kennedy and Johnson Years* (Chapel Hill, NC: The University of North Carolina Press, 1984).

24 Clark Kerr, *The Uses of the University* (Cambridge, MA: Harvard University Press, 1963), pp. 86-87. The term "multiversity" was coined by Kerr to designate the massive institutions that resulted from these forces. These institutions officially were still called universities.

25 *Ibid.*, pp. 18-19.

26 *Ibid.*, pp. 20-28.

27 T.R. McConnell, *A General Pattern for American Public Higher Education* (New York: McGraw-Hill Book Co., 1962), pp. 152-156.

28 James W. Thornton, *The Community Junior College* (New York: John Wiley and Sons, 1966), pp. 7-8.

29 *Digest of Education Statistics 1989* (Washington, DC: U.S. Government Printing Office, 1989), p. 174.

30 *Ibid.*, p. 174.

31 James W. Thornton, *The Community Junior College* (New York: John Wiley and Sons, 1966), pp. 46-48.

32 Elbert K. Fretwell, Jr., *Founding Public Junior Colleges* (New York: Bureau of Publications, Teachers College, Columbia University, 1954), pp. 11-12.

33 Leland L. Medsker, *The Junior College: Progress and Prospect* (New York: McGraw-Hill Book Co., 1960), p. 12.

[34] Thornton, *The Community Junior College*, p. 45.

[35] *Ibid.*, pp. 51-52.

[36] *Ibid.*, p. 53.

[37] Leland L. Medsker, *The Junior College: Progress and Prospect* (New York: McGraw-Hill Book Co., 1960), p. 210.

[38] McConnell, *A General Pattern*, p. 114.

[39] *Digest of Education Statistics 1989* (Washington, DC: U.S. Government Printing Office, 1989), p. 217.

[40] *Ibid.*, p. 179.

[41] There is an extensive literature on the "new radicalism" of the 1960s. For example, see Paul Jacobs and Saul Landau, *The New Radicals: A Report with Documents* (New York: Random House, 1966); Priscilla Long, ed., *The New Left: A Collection of Essays* (Boston: Porter Sargent, 1969); Seymour M. Lipset and Gerald M. Schaflander, *Passion and Politics: Student Activism in America* (Boston: Little, Brown, and Co., 1971); Kirkpatrick Sale, *S.D.S.* (New York: Random House, 1973); Jim Miller, *Democracy Is in the Streets: From Port Huron to the Siege of Chicago* (New York: Simon and Schuster, 1987); Todd Gitlin, *The Sixties: Years of Hope, Days of Rage* (New York: Bantam Books, 1987).

[42] Clayborne Carson, *In Struggle: SNCC and the Black Awakening of the 1960s* (Cambridge, MA: Harvard University Press, 1981).

[43] Kerr, *The Uses of the University*, p. 42.

[44] Charles Muscatine, et al., *Education at Berkeley: Report of the Select Committee on Education* (Berkeley: University of California Printing Department, 1966), pp. 3-4.

[45] Sidney Hook, *In Defense of Academic Freedom* (New York: Pegasus, Bobbs-Merrill Co., 1971), p. 19.

[46] Curtis O. Baker, ed. *The Condition of Education 1989: Postsecondary Education*, Vol. II (Washington, DC: U.S. Government Printing Office, 1989), p. 32.

[47] Baker, ed. *The Condition of Education*, II, pp. 1-2, 8.

[48] *Ibid.*, p.22.

Selections to Accompany
Chapter 5

The Dartmouth College case of 1819 represents a significant decision of the Supreme Court in the area of higher education. The case grew out of a controversy between the president and board of trustees of Dartmouth against the state legislature of New Hampshire over the control of the college. The decision of Chief Justice John Marshall on behalf of the trustees' right to independent control served to protect both the existence of the private college against state encroachment and the sanctity of contract as guaranteed by the Constitution.

The Dartmouth College Case

This court can be insensible neither to the magnitude nor delicacy of this question. The validity of a legislative act is to be examined, and the opinion of the highest law tribunal of a state is to be revised; an opinion which carries with it intrinsic evidence of the diligence, of the ability, and the integrity with which it was formed. On more than one occasion this court has expressed the cautious circumspection with which it approaches the consideration of such questions, and has declared that in no doubtful case would it pronounce a legislative act to be contrary to the constitution. But the American people have said, in the constitution of the United States, that "no state shall pass any bill of attainder, ex post facto law, or law impairing the obligation of contracts." In the same instrument they have also said "that the judicial power shall extend to all cases in law and equity arising under this constitution." On the judges of this court, then, is imposed the high and solemn duty of protecting, from even legislative violation, those contracts which the constitution of our country has placed beyond legislative control, and, however irksome the task may be, this is a duty from which we dare not shrink. . . .

SOURCE: *The Trustrees of Dartmouth College v. William H. Woodward*, 4 Wheaton, U.S. 518, 4 L. ed 629.

It can require no argument to prove that the circumstances of the case constitute a contract. An application is made to the crown for a charter to incorporate a religious and literary institution. In the application it is stated that large contributions have been made for the object, which will be conferred on the corporation as soon as it shall be created. The charter is granted, and on its faith the property is conveyed. Surely in this transaction every ingredient of a complete and legitimate contract is found. . . .

That education is an object of national concern, and a proper subject of legislation, all admit. That there may be an institution founded by government, and placed entirely under its immediate control, the officers of which would be public officers, amenable exclusively to government, none will deny. But is Dartmouth College such an institution? Is education altogether in the hands of government? Does every teacher of youth become a public officer, and do donations for the purpose of education necessarily become public property, so far that the will of the legislature, not the will of the donor, becomes the law of the donation? These questions are of serious moment to society, and deserve to be well considered. . . .

Almost all eleemosynary corporations, those which are created for the promotion of religion, of charity, or of education, are of the same character. The law of this case is the law of all. In every literary or charitable institution, unless the objects of the bounty be themselves incorporated, the whole legal interest is in trustees, and can be assessed only by them. The donors or claimants of the bounty, if they can appear in court at all, can appear only to complain of the trustees. In all other situations they are identified with, and personified by, the trustees, and their rights are to be defended and maintained by them. Religion, charity, and education are, in the law of England, legatees or donees, capable of receiving bequests or donations in this form. They appear in court, and claim or defend by the corporation. Are they of so little estimation in the United States that contracts for their benefit must be excluded from the protection of words which, in their natural import, include them? Or do such contracts so necessarily require new modeling by the authority of the legislature that the ordinary rules of construction must be disregarded in order to leave them exposed to legislative alteration?

All feel that these objects are not deemed unimportant in the United States. The interest which this case has excited proves that they are not. The framers of the constitution did not deem them unworthy of its care and protection. They have, though in a different mode, manifested their respect for science by reserving to the government of the Union the power "to promote the progress of science and useful arts by securing, for limited times, to authors and inventors the exclusive right to their respective writings and discoveries." They have so far withdrawn science and the useful arts from the action of the state governments. Why, then, should they be supposed so regardless of contracts made for the advancement of literature as to intend to exclude them from provisions made the security of ordinary contracts between man and man? No reason for making this supposition is perceived. . . .

In the view which has been taken of this interesting case, the court has confined itself to the right possessed by the trustees, as the assignees and representatives of the donors and founders, for benefit of religion and literature. Yet it is not clear that the trustees ought to be considered as destitute of such beneficial interest in themselves as the law may respect. . . .

But the court has deemed it unnecessary to investigate this particular point, being of opinion, on general principles, that in these private eleemosynary institutions the body corporate, as possessing the whole legal and equitable interest, and completely representing the donors, for the purpose of executing the trust, has rights which are protected by the constitution.

It results from this opinion that the acts of the legislature of New Hampshire which are stated in the special verdict found in this case, are repugnant to the constitution of the United States, and that the judgment on this special verdict ought to have been for the plaintiffs. The judgment of the state court must therefore be

Reversed.

The Morrill Act of 1862 is one of the crucial documents in the evolution of American higher education. The Act resulted from the pressure of political, social, and economic forces to extend the concept of equality of educational opportunity to higher education. The Morrill Act was introduced by United States Representative Justin Morrill of Vermont and signed in 1862 by President Abraham Lincoln. The text of the Act follows.

Morrill Land-Grant Act of 1862

An Act Donating public lands to the several States and Territories which may provide colleges for the benefit of agriculture and the mechanic arts.

Be it enacted by the Senate and House of Representatives of the United States of America in Congress assembled, That there be granted to the several States, for the purposes hereinafter mentioned, an amount of public land, to be apportioned to each State a quantity equal to 30,000 acres for each Senator and Representative in Congress to which the States are respectively entitled by the apportionment under the census of 1860: *Provided*, That no mineral lands shall be selected or purchased under the provisions of this act.

Sec. 2. *And be it further enacted*, That the land aforesaid, after being surveyed, shall be apportioned to the several States in section or subdivisions of sections, not less than one-quarter of a section; and wherever there are public lands in a State subject to sale at private entry at $1.25 per acre, the quantity to which said State shall be entitled shall be selected from such lands within the limits of such State; and the Secretary of the Interior is hereby directed to issue to each of the States in which there is not the quantity of public lands subject to sale at private entry at $1.25 per acre to which said State may be entitled under the provisions of this act land scrip to the amount in acres for the deficiency of its distributive share, said scrip to be sold by said States and the proceeds thereof applied to the uses and purposes prescribed in this act, and for no other use or purpose whatsoever: *Provided*, That in no case shall any State to which land scrip may thus be issued be allowed to locate the same within the limits of any other State or of any territory of the United States; but their assignees may thus locate said land scrip upon any of the unappropriated lands of the United States subject to sale at private

SOURCE: Benjamin F. Andrews, *The Land Grant of 1862 and the Land-Grant College* (Washington DC: U.S. Government Printing Office, 1918, *Bulletin,* 1918, No. 13), pp. 7-8.

entry at $1.25 or less an acre: *And provided further*, That not more than one million acres shall be located by such assignees in any one of the States: *And provided further*, That no such location shall be made before one year from the passage of this act.

Sec. 3. *And be it further enacted*, That all the expenses of management, superintendence, and taxes from date of selection of said lands previous to their sales and all expenses incurred in the management and disbursement of moneys which may be received therefrom shall be paid by the States to which they may belong, out of the treasury of said States, so that the entire proceeds of the sale of said lands shall be applied, without any diminution whatever, to the purposes hereinafter mentioned.

Sec. 4. *And be it further enacted*, That all moneys derived from the sale of the lands aforesaid by the States to which the lands are apportioned, and from the sales of land scrip hereinbefore provided for, shall be invested in stocks of the United States or of the States, or some other safe stocks, yielding not less than 5 per centum upon the par value of said stocks; and that the moneys so invested shall constitute a perpetual fund, the capital of which shall remain forever undiminished, except so far as may be provided in section fifth of this act, and the interest of which shall be inviolably appropriated by each State which may take and claim the benefit of this act to the endowment, support, and maintenance of at least one college, where the leading object shall be, without excluding other scientific and classical studies and including military tactics, to teach such branches of learning as are related to agriculture and the mechanic arts in such manner as the legislatures of the States may respectively prescribe in order to promote the liberal and practical education of the industrial classes in the several pursuits and professions in life.

Sec. 5. *And be it further enacted*, That the grant of land and land scrip hereby authorized shall be made on the following conditions, to which, as well as to the provisions hereinbefore contained, the previous assent of the several States shall be signified by legislative acts:

First. If any portion of the fund invested as provided by the foregoing section, or any portion of the interest thereon, shall by any action or contingency be diminished or lost, it shall be replaced by the State to which it belongs, so that the capital of the fund shall remain forever undiminished; and the annual interest shall be regularly applied without diminution to the purposes mentioned in the fourth section of this act, except that a sum, not exceeding 10 per centum upon the amount received by any State under the provisions of this act, may be expended for the purchase of lands for sites or experimental farms whenever authorized by the respective legislatures of said States;

Second. No portion of said fund, nor the interest thereon, shall be applied, directly or indirectly, under any pretense whatever to the purchase, erection, preservation, or repair of any building or buildings;

Third. Any State which may take and claim the benefit of the provisions of this act shall provide, within five years, at least not less than one college, as prescribed in the fourth section of this act, or the grant to such State shall cease; and said State shall be bound to pay the United States the amount received of any lands previously sold, and that the title to purchasers under the States shall be valid;

Fourth. An annual report shall be made regarding the progress of each college, recording any improvements and experiments made, with their costs and results, and such other matters, including State industrial and economical statistics, as may be supposed useful; one copy of which shall be transmitted by mail free, by each to all the other colleges which may be endowed under the provisions of this act, and also one copy to the Secretary of the Interior;

Fifth. When lands shall be selected from those which have been raised to double the minimum price in consequence of railroad grants, they shall be computed to the States at the maximum price, and the number of acres proportionally diminished;

Sixth. No State, while in a condition of rebellion or insurrection against the Government of the United States, shall be entitled to the benefit of this act;

Seventh. No State shall be entitled to the benefits of this act unless it shall express its acceptance thereof by its legislature within two years from the date of its approval by the President.

Sec. 6. *And be it further enacted*, That land scrip issued under the provisions of this act shall not be subject to location until after the first day of January, 1863.

Sec. 7. *And be it further enacted*, That land officers shall receive the same fees for locating land scrip issued under the provisions of this act as are now allowed for the location of military bounty land warrants under existing laws: *Provided*, That maximum compensation shall not be thereby increased.

Sec. 8. *And be it further enacted*, That the governors of the several States to which scrip shall be issued under this act shall be required to report annually to Congress all sales made of such scrip until the whole shall be disposed of, the amount received for the same, and what appropriation has been made of the proceeds.

Approved, July 2,1862.

In 1971, The Task Force on Higher Education in its Report on Higher
Education *identified several of the major problems facing higher education
in the United States. The section of the report that follows in the selection
is historically significant in that it identifies and examines issues relating to
the access of minority students in institutions of higher learning. It is
particularly important in urging the reforms that have improved access to
higher education for blacks and women.*

The Unfinished Experiment in Minority Education

The year 1966 marked the beginning of a major undertaking to incorporate
members of ethnic minorities into the mainstream institutions of American
higher education. Prior to the 1960s, the higher education of many minorities
was ignored, and that of blacks was primarily the province of the 4-year black
colleges. Today, prodded by the civil rights revolution and concern for the
disadvantaged, colleges and universities, from the most to the least selective,
in all regions, profess a responsibility to meet the educational needs of
minorities.

We as a nation are thus engaged in the most far-reaching reform in higher
education of the postwar period, one that tests the capacity of our institutions
to transform themselves to serve all students better. Yet, to date, only a few
studies evaluating the results are available.

The information on the participation of blacks — poor as it is — is better than
that for other minorities. Black students also tend to be the recipients of the
strongest feelings toward minority students — both of good will and hostility.
Because black students have been the pathbreakers, how the experiment in
minority education is judged will largely be the question of how well black
students do, how they are seen, and how they see themselves.

Thus, it is primarily black students whom critics of minority programs have
had in mind in implying that such programs have lowered the academic
standards of institutions and seriously diminished the value of degrees; that
soaring minority enrollments have denied places to more highly qualified
students; and that admission of large numbers of ill-prepared (and consequently
frustrated) minority students has contributed heavily to campus unrest. In each
case, available facts simply do not substantiate these implications.

SOURCE: Task Force on Higher Education, *Report on Higher Education* (Washington
DC: U.S. Government Printing Office, 1971), pp. 43-56. Footnotes appearing in the
selection have been deleted.

Soaring enrollments. The impression has sometimes been created that colleges are overcommitted to minorities and that quotas of 10 to 12 percent are common. Blacks, as a percent of total enrollment, are barely holding their own; they average only 3 percent of enrollment in predominantly white institutions.

Cheap degrees. Open admissions have been held responsible for lowered standards—yet open admissions have been the practice at some State universities for many years. Different criteria have clearly been used for admissions of some minority students, but there is little or no evidence of any change in degree standards. The career performance of blacks seems roughly comparable to that of other students.

Minority students and disruption. Minority students have indeed been responsible for some campus disruptions, and these seem to have made a particular impression on the public mind, but more intensive coverage of student unrest has revealed that black students, by and large, are concerned with acquiring an education; the typical disrupter is white and middle-class.

The need for a factual appraisal of such charges as they relate to black students should not, however, obscure the fact that members of other minority groups are entering higher education in increasing numbers. They are fewer, to be sure, and, in the case of Spanish-surnamed Americans and American Indians, their rates of participation in higher education are also lower than those for blacks. As a result, data providing a coherent picture of their progress are even harder to obtain. We emphasize the data concerning blacks in higher education because those are the best data available. It is not intended to suggest that other minorities and disadvantaged whites have the same needs as blacks; or that a program successful for one will work for another; or that programs for other groups should have a lower priority.

The difficulty in appraising the involvement and achievement of members of minorities is not alone the result of inattention to the facts on the part of those who are hostile. Those friendly to minority students have not been anxious to establish the facts. Proponents of the programs have avoided sober assessments of their true cost, the dropout rate, and the magnitude of the adjustment required of all parties—the institutions, the minority students, and their fellow students. Determination to profess loyalty to the idea has sometimes choked off needed debate and constructive criticism. We think it essential, despite the obvious difficulties, to estimate the degree of success so far.

Black Access to Higher Education

The simple measure of the status of blacks in higher education is enrollment; yet it can be one of the most misleading. In a confidential memorandum that reached the press, Counsellor Daniel Patrick Moynihan advised President

Nixon: "Negro college enrollment rose 85 percent between 1964 and 1968, by which time there were 434,000 Negro college students. (The total full-time university population of Great Britain is 200,000.)" Such a comparison implies substantial progress in educating minorities. In fact, in total enrollment, the gains appear much less substantial. According to the Bureau of the Census *Current Population Survey*, black enrollment as a percent of the total actually declined from 1964 to 1966. Since then it has been rising, but very gradually (see table 2).

Table 2.—*Recent black participation in higher education as a percentage of total enrollment*

[Figures in thousands]

	Total enrollment	Total black enrollment	Blacks as a percentage of total enrollment
1964	4,643	234	5.0
1965	5,675	274	4.8
1966	5,999	282	4.7
1967	6,401	370	5.8
1968	6,801	435	6.4
1969	7,435	492	6.6

It is possible that these figures overstate black participation. Other studies show that black enrollment may be lower than Census figures indicate. In any case, while blacks have lately shared in the growth of enrollments, they have not gained in proportion to their numbers. Whereas black students constitute 12 percent of the college-age population, they still constitute only 6.6 percent of college students. Whereas black student enrollment rose by about 250,000 in the past 5 years, nonblack student enrollment rose by 2,500,000; that is, blacks accounted for only 9 percent of the enrollment growth.

To measure access, one must also consider the kinds of institutions and the programs that students attend. At least until very recently, half the black students have attended predominantly black colleges. Enrollment at these has been growing relatively slowly. The significant change since 1966 has been in the predominantly white colleges because their black enrollments previously were minimal. While the percentage of the total enrollment at these "white" institutions still averages only 3 percent, it is visible and growing, creating a sense of barriers coming down in all sections of the country.

All types of preponderantly white institutions have shared in this change, but unevenly. Many private colleges and universities and a few major State universities have taken a leadership role, with or without formal minority student programs, and have black enrollments of 4 to 8 percent. But the largest total numbers of students (and percentages of enrollments) have been at the other end of the institutional spectrum — at the urban, open admission, community colleges and 4-year colleges.

Another dimension of access is the degree to which minority students are willing, able, and encouraged to enroll in all of the different curricular programs of the institution. Black students are concentrated in a few majors, principally in business, education, the social sciences, and the non-M.D. health professions. While the lack of adequate preparation in many fields can be compensated for, a weak background in mathematics and science is a recalcitrant barrier to minority students who would otherwise like to major in science and engineering. Unless some improvement can be made in the secondary schools blacks attend, the number of blacks in medicine, science, and engineering will remain low.

Achievement

Assessors of the effectiveness of the experiment in minority higher education must be wary of unconsciously reflecting or inadvertently serving the ideological interests of partisan observers on both sides.

Data on the academic achievement of blacks — as measured by grades and persistence rates — are even more fragmentary and conflicting than those on access. Most of the evidence available from various colleges shows that the average grades of blacks are somewhat lower than the average grades of all students. There is a danger that we may obscure an important point in discussing the "average" of black students. Not all are risk students. Many have grades and test scores that *exceed* regular admission criteria.

The normal selection criteria for admission to college — high school grades and Scholastic Aptitude Test scores — are reasonably reliable predictors of performance in colleges for blacks and for students generally. Since both measure competence in traditional academic work, and since many blacks have had little exposure to good schools, it is not surprising that high school grades and SAT scores are, as a whole, significantly lower for black entrants than they are for college entrants. However, there is some limited evidence that blacks who persist in their studies perform somewhat better in college than would have been predicted on the basis of these measures.

We investigated whether "grade-bending" in favor of black and other minority students occurs — which would tend to discount some of the achievement noted above. In canvassing faculty in a variety of colleges, we found that it does. As other groups have found for years (athletes perhaps the most notably), some minority students have learned that certain courses are easy grade opportunities. However, in large universities where class size and impersonal grading procedures operate to control against grade-bending, the achievement of blacks is not markedly different from that where smaller classes are the rule. We suspect that, as minority students become a more routine part of the campus scene, faculty members will gradually come to treat them as they do any other students. The evidence does not suggest that present grade-bending either seriously affects academic standards or is permanently entrenched.

In this appraisal we did not reopen the more fundamental debate as to whether grades adequately measure the achievement or the value of education. There is an interesting new piece of evidence, however. Brown University recently studied the postcollege achievement of high-risk students (all students, not just minorities, whose entering SAT scores were 100 points or more below the norm) and found no discernible differences from the achievement of its regular entrants. The results of this study are reinforced by the general feeling expressed to us by a number of graduate school deans, faculty, and admissions officers that a remarkably capable group of young blacks from high-risk programs are now seeking admission to graduate schools, and that, when they graduate with bachelor's degrees, they tend to do well in postgraduate education.

Another measure of achievement is the number of black students who persist to the completion of a degree. The data again are mixed. Many universities show persistence rates for blacks that are lower than the average of all students; a few show higher rates. One clear finding, however, is that blacks at selective institutions have much higher persistence rates than those at unselective institutions. In part, this happens because better students are admitted to selective schools; in part, because students at selective institutions have a high expectation of success, whereas at unselective institutions, dropping out is the norm. Talks with faculty at community colleges where a disproportionate amount of enrollments is black indicate a difficult problem. A great many black students register and attend classes at the semester opening, but their numbers dwindle rapidly until, within a month or so, only relatively few are left.

Special programs tailored to the needs and problems of minority students can make a difference. One of the best, CUNY's SEEK Program, has had a 50 percent dropout rate during its 1st year. While that rate seems disappointing, considering the effort at pretraining, tutoring, and counseling, it can be viewed as encouraging when one considers the poor preparation of the students involved and the high dropout rates for *all* students in the same institutions.

On the whole, we conclude that large numbers of black students can perform close to the existing standards at all types of colleges and universities. With well-run special programs, high-risk students are more likely to stay in college. Persistence rates for blacks at many institutions will approach the average for all students, but, at the least selective colleges, dropout rates remain discouragingly high. Grades will likely continue to be lower. This fact may not have much bearing on those who persist to graduation, however, in terms of later careers.

If the national experiment in minority education is to be valid—and if it is to make further progress—educators must begin to understand what it means to *be* a minority student. Differences in cultural background are becoming more apparent (and may even be getting wider as more "high-risk" students enter), and recognition of these realities is mandatory if we are to respond intelligently to what minority students need. In our conversations with minority students and those who deal with them, we began to deepen our own understanding about some points that must be widely disseminated.

Historically upwardly mobile groups have looked to educational institutions as the principal avenue of social mobility—and the generalization holds for today's minority students in their attitude toward college access. In addition, minority students as a group aspire to more years of education than do whites. Today, when college is more important to mobility than ever before, and when family pressures to succeed are so intense, this force on minority students is a crucial factor in minority education.

What distinguishes minority students from other groups that have used higher education as an avenue of mobility is that today's minorities can never really leave their communities. "Going to college" has always carried with it a measure of "you can't go home again"; but today's minorities have to live with the converse—that you can't leave your ethnic or racial identity behind.

This conflict of being caught between two cultures—that of the ethnic and racial community on the one hand and that of the national social structure on the other—forms the basic dilemma of minority education in contemporary American society.

The pressure on minority students from their own communities is not simply a matter of personal achievement. For, while these young people are often viewed as "disadvantaged" by society at large, they are viewed as extraordinarily "advantaged" by their own communities—and they must bear the dual role of paupers *and* princes. Their successes and failures are community successes and failures.

At the same time, the pressure to succeed in college for many minority students is also a pressure to give up not only community ties but also community dialects, habits, and values—and at just the time when the ethnic community is determined to emphasize and cultivate these traits as signs of a newfound pride and self-esteem. Yet few faculty and administrators with whom we have discussed these issues seem to appreciate what a cruel dilemma this is, or what a hostile and threatening environment the campus can be for a minority student. Some institutions are grappling with this dichotomy through such devices as ethnic study programs or, on a broader scale, community programs. We see no easy path ahead for its resolution.

The Depth of Public Commitment

Commitment to the ideals of minority access to higher education is essential, but it is not enough—and least useful of all is a purely rhetorical commitment. In some measure, it is a matter of how much we are willing to invest. From our discussion with educational officers and the limited data available, it is obvious that the estimates made a few years ago of the cost of achieving effectively equal educational opportunity substantially understated the true amounts. It was a brave beginning back in the mid-sixties. But now the glamour has worn off and we are able to see more realistically the dimensions of the task ahead.

Barriers to Women

The higher education community prides itself on its leading role in the fight to end intolerance in American society. Yet with regard to women, colleges and universities practice a wide range of discriminatory practices. These institutions view women primarily as wives and mothers and their education as preparation for these functions.

The Task Force has identified three major types of barriers which block full participation by women in higher education: first, overt discrimination by faculties, deans, and others acting in official capacities; second, practical institutional barriers, such as rigid admission and residence requirements, and a lack of campus facilities and services, which makes participation in higher education incompatible with many women's other interests and activities; and third, the ingrained assumptions and inhibitions on the part of both men and women which deny the talents and aspirations of the latter.

The unique role of higher education gives it extraordinary leverage to either help or hurt women's chances for equality of opportunity. When colleges and universities deny women the chance to gain skills and credentials, they increase the likelihood that women will not receive equal opportunities in all other social institutions for the rest of their lives.

Higher education exerts another kind of leverage as well. Colleges and universities take upon themselves the task of forming and sanctioning the attitudes and practices which educated people will thereafter consider reasonable. If it is fairness which they sanction, all women are helped; but if it is discrimination they sanction, all women are hurt, educated or not.

The Present Extent of Inequality

Comparisons of the participation and attainment of men and women in higher education reveal a clearly unequal pattern.

> Although, in high school, women earn better grades and higher test scores than men, fewer enter college, and they attain only 41.5 percent of the bachelor's and first professional degrees.

> Although women in college earn better undergraduate records than men, fewer enter graduate school.

> Most of the degrees earned by women are in a few fields of study, such as education, the humanities, and the health professions. Thus, aggregate figures on attainment of women exaggerate their opportunities in higher education.

> Even within those fields considered acceptable, women are confined to subordinate functions. While virtually all the nursing graduates are women, they represent only eight percent of graduating physicians.

If there were any assurance that the denial of equality is rapidly becoming a thing of the past, there could perhaps be some complacency. But it is not merely residual; in some ways, it is increasing. The proportion of 18- and 19-year-old males enrolled in higher education increased 20 percent between 1950 and 1966, but the participation of females increased only 11 percent. The percentage of master's degrees obtained by women reached its peak in 1930 at 40.4 percent and declined to 38 percent in 1968, while the percentage of doctor's degrees obtained by women reached its peak in 1930 at 15.4 percent, and was down to only 12.6 percent in 1968.

We believe that it is not the case that opportunities exist for women which they simply decline to exercise. Rather, we find that there are specific barriers which block their progress and which will not disappear without conscious effort.

Discrimination Against Women as Students

The first such barrier is outright discrimination against women as students, especially at the graduate level. Although few admissions officers or members of graduate fellowship committees would confess to discrimination on the basis of race, many openly argue that women should be denied opportunities because they are women. For example, the Academic Senate of the University of California, Berkeley — an institution renowned for its commitment to civil liberties — recently received the following report of an interview between a social science department chairman and a woman candidate for graduate study:

> "I suppose you went to another college?"
>
> > "I attended U.C. Berkeley."
>
> "But you didn't finish?"
>
> > "I was graduated with a B.A."
>
> "Your grades weren't very good?"
>
> > "I was named to Phi Beta Kappa in my junior year and was graduated *summa cum laude*."
>
> "You have to have 16 to 18 units of X. You don't have that, do you?"
>
> > "As my transcript shows, I had 18 units of X, mostly A's, one or two B's."
>
> "I'm going to disallow all 18 because they were so long ago. You understand that, don't you? There's no point in trying to replace the undergraduate course in order to qualify. You could not do it part-time; you would have to take 18 units in one year. Then you would probably not get into graduate school. If you did, you would meet so much hostility that I doubt if you would stay in. Most women do not finish their work, and we couldn't take a chance on you. We don't want women in the department anyway, and certainly not older women. This may be unfair to you in light of your record, but we just are not going to chance it."

Women's Education as a "Poor Investment"

In order to justify discrimination against women in higher education, the argument is often made that their education is a poor investment of educational resources. The argument has two parts: first, it is argued that women are much less likely to complete their training than men; second, it is argued that women who do complete their training are much less likely to use it because they are likely to marry, become housewives, and give up any idea of a career.

Both parts of the argument have much less basis in fact than is usually supposed. What basis there is seems clearly attributable to artificial obstacles that unnecessarily stand in the way of women completing and using their education, rather than to some innate disposition of women regarding their educational and career goals.

The facts tend to contradict the view that women are poorer risks than men in their disposition to complete training. The percentage of entering undergraduate students who graduate in 4 years is about 15 percent higher for women than for men. As for graduate students, the record for completion is so poor for male students in the fields of the humanities and social sciences (the fields most open to women) that it is absurd to make comparisons unfavorable to women. The available data suggest, if anything, that women do about the same as men: women constituted 30 percent of graduate and professional students in 1967, but earned 35.8 percent of the master's and first professional degrees awarded in 1968.

Two points may account for the impression department chairmen seem to have that women are less likely to complete their training. First, in our society, most women move where their husbands' educational and career opportunities take them. The result is that women must often transfer from one institution to another to complete their training. Women thus *are* less likely to complete their training at the institution where they began. If, in some field, they are less likely to ever complete it, this might be attributed in large measure to the unwillingness of accessible institutions to accept them as transfer students and give them the support which a nontransferring male student would receive as a matter of course.

The second part of the "poor investment" argument seems also unsupported by the facts. In 1968, 42 percent of all women of working age were in the labor force. Women who complete their training do, in fact, tend to use it, and the more training they have, the higher are their rates of participation. Fifty-four percent of the women who have bachelor's degrees are in the labor force, and 71 percent of those who have 5 or more years of higher education are working. More than 90 percent of women who received doctorates in 1957-58 were employed in 1964, and 79 percent of them had not interrupted their careers in the intervening years. Moreover, there is a strong correlation between the number of years of higher education and the likelihood that a woman will be working in her field of major study, i.e., the field where educational resources have been most intensively invested in her training. Nor do women Ph.D.'s let marriage interfere with their productivity. Those who are employed full time publish slightly more than either men Ph.D.'s or unmarried women Ph.D.'s.

Discrimination Against Women in Academic and Professional Life

In one sense, the "poor investment" argument is self-fulfilling. The normal incentives of prestige and money for active participation in professional fields are, to an important extent, withheld from women, especially married women.

Higher education discriminates against women as employees even more than it does as students. A 1966 Office of Education study estimated that, on college faculties, women comprised 32 percent of instructors, 20 percent of assistant professors, 15 percent of associate professors, and 9 percent of full professors. A substantial part of these differences is due to the fact that women are made to wait longer for promotion. Women who do achieve the rank of full professor wait 2 to 5 years longer than men in the biological sciences, and as much as 10 years longer in the social sciences. Moreover, married women must, overall wait 5 to 10 years longer than single women.

In professional and business life there is similarly less economic reward. Starting salaries tend to be lower. A survey conducted in November 1969, regarding jobs and salaries expected to be offered by 206 companies to June 1970 college graduates, showed a differential in the salary offer to be made to men and women with the same college majors in a wide variety of fields.

Women can only look forward to dropping still further behind as their careers progress. The difference in median salaries for men and women is more than $3,000 in chemistry, physics, mathematics, economics, and the biological sciences. Women similarly average lower salaries than men in each of the academic ranks. In this sense, then, women's education is a poorer investment than men's, for they are denied the same income as a return on investment. They do, however, earn much better salaries, compared to other women, the more years of higher education they have completed.

A common myth is that opportunities for women in American society, though not equal, are opening up and that discrimination is steadily declining. When we see that the share of master's and doctor's degrees earned by women was higher between 1920-1940 than it was during the decade of the 1960s; and that women's median salary income, as a percent of men's, decreased by 5.7 percent from 1955 to 1968 (from 63.9% to 58.2%); and that the plight of the woman in education and the job market has not improved, but worsened; and when we add to this the information that there are fewer women elected to public office at all levels today than during those same previous decades, we get an overall view that the American woman is not only failing to hold her own, but is losing ground.

The Lockstep and the Lockout

The prevailing college and university structure presents an array of practical hurdles for women. The problems of access and the educational lock-step that we have noted create barriers that are particularly difficult for women. The fact that these barriers exist today is due, in part, to a failure to analyze and understand the needs of women and, in part, to a lack of consensus that they should be removed.

Rigid policies and practices pressure women into making a choice between marriage and children or advanced study and a career, causing many women to lose out permanently. Women who take time out to marry and work or to raise children for several years find it extremely difficult to return to academic life. Residence requirements, the inability to transfer credits, insistence on full-time study, lack of child-care facilities, and inadequate health services are most frequently cited as problems that keep women from undertaking or completing their undergraduate and graduate studies. Women are frequently discriminated against in obtaining fellowships and travel grants and such amenities as married-student housing.

A recent AAUW survey exploring sex discrimination on the college campus reveals that only 5 percent of the schools reporting provide any kind of day-care services for children of students. Evidently, colleges that are willing to spend enormous sums on athletic facilities, used principally by men, recoil at the thought of establishing such facilities as a nursery where women can leave their children in order to attend classes.

One inevitable and damaging result of this combination of discrimination and lack of adequate facilities is that women students are encouraged to conclude that they should think of themselves only as potential wives and mothers, or, at best, as teachers or nurses. Several studies confirm that even very talented women students are affected by what Mary Bunting, the president of Radcliffe, has called the "climate of unexpectation" for women, and that their aspirations decline as they go through college.

Society's Assumptions About Women

The most formidable barrier to full participation by women in higher education is the assumptions of both men and women about the role of women in our society. These assumptions are internalized by individuals and incorporated into the structure of our institutions without being obvious. Instead, they appear to be the natural outgrowth of what society believes to be women's proper responsibilities.

An important fact about the barrier created by these assumptions is that there is, as yet, no consensus that it should be removed. While some Americans regard discrimination against women as gross injustice and detrimental to the whole society, others see it as a perfectly natural division of social roles based upon inherent differences between men and women. There is today a deep concern about the decline of family life as the main focus of American society. Consequently, any discussion of equalizing opportunities for careers for women unleashes powerful and deeply held feelings among many people.

It is becoming apparent that the prevailing view of women's appropriate role in society has been based on ignorance and misunderstanding, on a failure to think of women as individuals with intellects which need stimulation and egos which need satisfaction, as among men. We are belatedly realizing that when women's minds are awakened by an excellent education, they are not going to be completely fulfilled by merely being gracious shadow-figures for their husbands, if they choose to marry. Lack of outside, independent interests often has a detrimental effect on the husbands and children of able, intelligent women as well as on the women themselves. As with minorities, the corrosive effect of repression and lack of opportunity for women goes far beyond the individual.

Colleges and universities have an unparalleled opportunity to affect the status of women. Their role in the transmission of values and the preparation of men and women for careers makes this opportunity a responsibility that these educational institutions must not ignore if they are to be responsive to the needs of society.

Suggestions for Further Reading

Altbach, Philip G. *Student Politics in America: An Historical Analysis*. New York: McGraw-Hill Book Co., 1974.

Babbidge, Homer D. and Robert M. Rosenzweig. *The Federal Interest in Higher Education*. New York: Columbia University Press, 1962.

Babbitt, Irving. *Democracy and Leadership*. Boston: Houghton Mifflin Co., 1952.

Brickman, William F. and Stanley Lehrer, eds. *A Century of Higher Education: Classical Citadel to Collegiate Colossus*. New York: Society for the Advancement of Education, 1962.

Brunner, Henry S. *Land-Grant Colleges and Universities, 1862-1962*. Washington, DC: U.S. Government Printing Office, 1962.

Gitlin, Todd. *The Sixties: Years of Hope, Days of Rage*. New York: Bantam Books, 1987.

Graham, Hugh D. *The Uncertain Triumph: Federal Education Policy in the Kennedy and Johnson Years*. Chapel Hill, NC: University of North Carolina Press, 1984.

Grobman, Arnold B. *Urban State Universities: An Unfinished National Agenda*. New York: Praeger, 1988.

Hawkins, Hugh. *Between Harvard and America: The Educational Leadership of Charles W. Eliot*. New York: Oxford University Press, 1972.

Hook, Sidney, *In Defense of Academic Freedom*. New York: Bobbs-Merrill Co., 1971.

Kerr, Clark. *The Uses of the University*. Cambridge: Harvard University Press, 1963.

Miller, Jim. *Democracy Is in the Streets: From Port Huron to the Seige of Chicago*. New York: Simon and Schuster, 1987.

Pearson, Carol S., Shavlik, Donna L. and Judith G. Touchton. *Educating the Majority: Women Challenge Tradition in Higher Education*. New York: MacMillan Co., 1988.

Roche, John F. *The Colonial Colleges in the War for American Independence*. Millwood, NY: Associated Faculty Press, 1986.

Sloan, Douglas. *The Scottish Enlightenment and the American College Ideal*. New York: Teachers College Press, Columbia University, 1971.

Tewksbury, Donald G. *The Founding of American Colleges and Universities Before the Civil War*. New York: Bureau of Publications, Teachers College, Columbia University, 1932.

Thornton, James W. *The Community Junior College*. New York: John Wiley and Sons, 1966.

Thwing, Charles F. *A History of Higher Education in America*. New York: Appleton, 1906.

Tiedt, Sidney W. *The Role of the Federal Government in Education*. New York: Oxford University Press, 1966.

The Evolution of American Teacher Education

Introduction

With the institutional growth of the American educational system and widespread popular acceptance of publicly supported and publicly controlled schools, a parallel interest in teacher education developed. The leaders of both the common school and high school movements realized that the success of the "ladder concept" in education depended on an available supply of qualified teachers. Educational statesmen such as Mann and Barnard urged the establishment of institutions to train teachers. This chapter deals with the evolution of American teacher education from the pioneer writings of Samuel Hall in the 1830s to the clearly defined programs offered today. The development of normal schools, teachers' colleges, and professional education as a discipline are integral phases in the history of teacher education.

Colonial and Early National Periods

During the colonial period, teachers varied greatly in their personal and educational qualifications. As explained in an earlier chapter, colonial education was administered through vernacular schools, secondary, and higher institutions. The vernacular school was designed for the masses, the Latin Grammar school and colonial college for the leadership classes. Coinciding with this early bifurcation, there was also a sharp differentiation among the teachers themselves. Teachers in the lower schools were often poorly educated and possessed, at best, only a rudimentary knowledge of the basic skills of reading, writing, and arithmetic. Some of them were bond-servants; others were students of the ministry or the law who kept school to support themselves until they were able to enter their preferred profession.

Teacher selection and certification varied from colony to colony. In New England, school committees certified the appointment of the teacher with the approval of the town minister. In the parochial schools of the middle colonies, the society or the church that supported the school approved his appointment. In the southern plantation areas, tutors were selected by individual families for their own employment. Generally speaking, the certification of the elementary teacher was based primarily on the candidate's religious and political orthodoxy and after that on his skill in teaching reading, writing, arithmetic, and religion.

During the colonial period, teaching was largely a male-dominated vocation. There were some early childhood schools, called "dame schools," which were conducted by women in their homes. Schools, conducted in more institutionalized settings under the control of local towns and districts or churches, were staffed by men. Male-dominance of elementary teaching began to erode with the common school movement in the early nineteenth century. As common schools were established, more women became elementary school teachers.

The master of the Latin Grammar school, for whom a knowledge of Latin and Greek was necessary, was usually a college graduate. A respected member of the colonial community, he was accorded a higher social distinction than the elementary teacher.

During the Revolution the emphasis on the war effort diverted attention from educational efforts to the pressing task of defeating the English army. Whatever money was available was applied to the military needs of the Continental Army rather than toward maintaining or building new schools. In the unsettled political and social conditions that followed the Revolution, the most immediate problem was the establishment of the Republic, and education continued to be neglected. As interest in schools was eclipsed, the status and training of teachers also declined. It was not until the common school revival of the early nineteenth century that the training of teachers was seriously undertaken.

The Common School and Teacher Education

During the first half of the nineteenth century, elementary education became significant again in the United States in the form of the common school system. The proponents of universal education realized that the success of public education depended upon a body of qualified teachers. Among the first to contribute to the literature of teacher education in the United States was a Congregational minister, Samuel Hall, who conducted a private academy for the preparation of teachers. In 1830 he became head of the normal department at Phillips Andover Academy, where he lectured on the "art of teaching." His book, *Lectures to School-Masters on Teaching*, 1833, reveals the condition of elementary education in New England during the early years of the nineteenth century.

The School Examination. Charles Carleton Coffin, *Building the Nation* (New York: Harper and Brothers, 1882), p. 65. The public examination of students by members of school board was a common practice in nineteenth century public schools.

Hall first surveyed the weaknesses plaguing the common school itself. Political and religious divisions within school districts weakened the community support necessary for good schools. Many communities were unwilling to finance their schools adequately and supply them with needed equipment. The wealthy classes enrolled their children in private schools and neglected the common school. Hall also found serious deficiencies in the qualifications of many teachers.[1] He believed that improved teacher education would aid the common school movement, and urged the establishment of institutions devoted to teacher preparation in the necessary branches of literature, the science of teaching, and the modes of school government.[2]

The table of contents of Hall's book indicates his conception of a "science of education." Among the topics he treated are: the importance, character, and usefulness of common schools; obstacles to their usefulness; qualifications of teachers; management and government of a school; teaching of spelling, reading, arithmetic, geography, English grammar, writing, history, and composition; gaining the attention of students; location and construction of school houses; beginning the first day of school.[3]

In his discussion of teacher qualifications, Hall mentioned seven major attributes: first, common sense: the ability to appraise conditions realistically, and through judgment and discrimination to exercise propriety; second, uniformity of temper; third, a capacity to understand and gauge character; fourth, decision of character: pursuit of a uniform course without dissuasion from action he judges correct; fifth, affection for the respect and good will of the students; sixth, just, moral discretion; seventh, the necessary literary qualifications: reading, spelling, writing, grammar, arithmetic, geography, and American history.[4]

In writing about the early history of teacher education, Henry Barnard noted four significant pamphlets which appeared in 1825: Thomas H. Gallaudet's "Plan of a Seminary" for the Education of Instructors of Youth"; James Carter's "Essays on Popular Education," containing a particular examination of the schools of Massachusetts, and an "Outline of an Institution for the Education of Teachers"; and Walter R. Johnson's "Observations on the Improvement of Seminaries of Learning."[5] In addition to these indications of concern with the problems, Governor De Witt Clinton urged the New York legislature to study the best methods of securing highly trained common school teachers.

Among the proponents of teacher education during the era of common school revival, James G. Carter deserves special interest. As a member of the Massachusetts legislature, Carter had joined Horace Mann in advocating the common school cause. Convinced that instruction could be improved only by competent teachers, he urged that they be prepared in normal schools devoted exclusively to teacher education. Carter made a fourfold recommendation which he believed should be followed in establishing normal schools:

1. Selection of a board of commissioners to represent the public interests in teacher education.
2. Appointment of a principal, as head of the normal school, and of a staff of assistant professors to prepare the prospective teachers.
3. Establishment of a library of books on the science of education.
4. Establishment of a demonstration school for children of different ages pursuing various studies.

Carter stressed the establishment of a model school as part of the normal school. In the model school, the prospective teacher could gain needed experience in actual teaching:

> After the young candidate for an instructor, therefore, has acquired sufficient knowledge for directing those exercises and teaching those branches which he wishes to profess, he must then begin his labors under the scrutinizing eyes of one who will note his mistakes of government and faults of instruction, and correct them. The experienced and skillful professor of the science will observe how the mind of the young teacher acts upon that of the learner. He will see how far and how perfectly they understand each other, and which is at fault if they do not understand each other at all.[6]

As a member of the Massachusetts legislature, Carter also sponsored the bills creating the State Board of Education. Horace Mann, who was named first secretary of the Board in 1837, saw the normal school as a new instrument for the advancement of humanity. He was convinced that the existence of the common school was dependent upon the success of the normal school.[7]

As a result of the groundwork laid by Carter and Mann, Governor Edward Everett of Massachusetts signed the bill authorizing the establishment of three normal schools in the towns of Lexington, Barre, and Bridgewater. These early schools offered a curriculum consisting of reading, writing, grammar, arithmetic, geography, spelling, composition, vocal music, drawing, physiology, algebra, philosophy, methodology, and Scriptural reading. As Massachusetts had been the leader in the common-school revival, it also came to lead in teacher education.

Adoption of the Normal School

Other states imitated the pattern which Massachusetts had set. New York first attempted unsuccessfully to educate teachers for the common schools in the existing academies. By 1844, however, New York's legislature had authorized a normal school for the "instruction and practice of teachers of common schools.'' The New York State Normal School was established at Albany. David Perkins Page, the head of the school, significantly contributed to teacher education by stressing training in both theory and practice. His book, *Theory and Practice of Teaching or the Motives and Methods of Good School-Keeping,* 1847, became a standard work in teacher education.[8] Page stressed the idea of practice teaching in a model school, believing teacher education to be inadequate without a period of actual teaching experience under classroom conditions.

Henry Barnard, like Horace Mann, recognized the reciprocal relationship between the success of the common school and that of the normal school. In the *Connecticut Common School Journal,* he compiled a body of educational literature called *Normal Schools, and Other Institutions, Agencies, and Means Designed for the Professional Education of Teachers,* 1851, which included a number of articles, essays, and other writings dealing with teacher education. In this work he summarized the weaknesses impeding the normal school movement in the United States: students were accepted by normal schools without proper preparation and without sufficient testing of their aptitude for teaching; the majority of pupils did not remain in the normal schools long enough to be adequately prepared in subjects and in methods; there were few endowments or scholarships available to aid qualified students financially; there was a lack of trained normal school professors; and the normal schools tried to accomplish more than their means permitted.[9]

The midwestern and western states quickly followed the eastern states in the establishment of normal schools. By 1875 the normal school was accepted throughout the United States. State governments established normal schools by acts of legislature, determined their number, and contributed to the construction of a physical plant. Location of the school was usually determined by spirited bidding among interested communities, one of which would often donate a site for the school.

The course of studies in the normal school was customarily given over a two-year period. The curriculum consisted of a review of the basic common school subjects, lectures on schoolkeeping, and experience in practice teaching in a model school under the direction of the normal school's faculty.

Although normal school programs of teacher education were criticized frequently, these institutions advanced the idea of professional preparation for teachers. Their very existence disputed the common American notion that anyone could teach. They also served as a transitional institution which later developed into the teachers' college. The faculties of the normal schools produced a professional literature which promoted the evolution of a theoretical framework for education. The model school became a distinctive characteristic of teacher education. Perhaps one of the most important contributions of the normal school was the concept that teacher preparation was intimately related to the needs of the public school and the public welfare.

Transition to Teachers College

In the post-Civil War era, colleges and universities gradually recognized the importance of teacher education. The development of the high school as a public secondary institution contributed to this belated recognition. Increasing high school enrollments at the turn of the century also created a greater demand for qualified secondary school teachers. By then, two other changes were already taking place to fill the need: the normal schools were evolving from two-year institutions into four-year degree-granting colleges, and a small number of colleges and universities were establishing chairs of pedagogy. However, some academic traditionalists in the colleges and universities still resisted the entry of professional education into higher education. Where education was first accepted, it was not given the status of an independent discipline but was included as a part of the department of philosophy or psychology. Despite the opposition of traditionalists in the liberal arts, colleges and universities slowly added departments or colleges of education. In 1873, the University of Iowa established the first permanent chair of pedagogy; The University of Wisconsin followed in 1879, Indiana and Cornell in 1886, and in 1892 Teachers College became a part of Columbia University. By 1900, colleges and universities had assumed responsibility for teacher education.

As the colleges and universities entered the field of teacher education, the normal schools were becoming teachers' colleges. By 1900 the growing number of high schools enabled many normal schools to require a high school diploma for admission. Between 1911 and 1920, nineteen state normal schools became teachers' colleges; by 1930, sixty-nine had made the transition.[10] The transformation usually included the following steps: raising the entrance requirements to include high school graduation; enriching the curriculum by adding liberal arts subjects to the courses on professional education and methodology; lengthening the program of studies from two to four years; including work in the theory of education; securing the privilege to grant degrees through state legislative action; and improving faculties. After World War II, many state legislatures permitted teachers' colleges to shift their status to that of the general purpose college, which could grant degrees in other fields besides professional education.

Professional Education

There is considerable controversy today concerning the most desirable program of teacher preparation. Much of it centers around the nature and status of the teaching profession. The question of the professional status of teachers is partly left over from archaic conceptions about teaching. The commonly held belief that an extended period of teacher training is unnecessary,[11] which was attacked by George Counts in *The Social Foundations of Education,* originated during frontier times when untutored farmers organized schools. As areas of knowledge became increasingly sophisticated, however, more than mere training in literacy became necessary.

In 1890, the Superintendent of Schools in New York, Andrew Draper, addressed himself to the problem of improving the professional status of teachers. He found that education had been prevented from becoming a recognized profession by the ease with which one could obtain the right to teach, the laxity of conditions governing teacher employment, the demands placed on normal schools to restrict themselves primarily to candidates for elementary work, and the small number of teachers who were trained graduates.[12] To improve the quality of teaching and to elevate its status, Draper outlined a program of professional preparation which embraced educational psychology, philosophy of education, history of education, and educational methodology. In urging broad scholarship, he said:

> . . . a teaching profession cannot he established on a basis which only covers the work of the common schools. The mere knowledge that is to be conveyed to the child is not all that is required on the part of the teacher. A teaching profession will be controlled by the same inexorable laws as hedge about the other professions. In advance of professional training there must he a scholarship foundation, adequate in extent, and sufficiently well laid to place individual teachers, not a few, but all of them, on an equal footing, and in comfortable relations with the ministers and physicians, and architects and engineers, and which will make sure that the mental equipment of the collective body is at no disadvantages in comparison with that of the entire body of persons composing the other professions.[13]

The work of Draper and other educational leaders contributed to the emergence of a body of professional literature which examined both the theoretical and practical aspects of education. During the 1880s and 1890s, American educators were stimulated by the pedagogical treatises of the German philosopher, Johann Herbart, whose work is discussed more fully later in this book. Herbart had attempted to structure a teaching methodology according to psychological principles. The American Herbartians, led by Frank and Charles McMurry, Charles De Garmo, C. C. Van Liew, and Elmer Brown, introduced Herbart's concepts of apperception, correlation, concentration, cultural epochs, and interest to American teachers. The Herbartians contributed to the enrichment of the elementary school curriculum by including literature, history, and nature study as a part of the school's program. They also wrote textbooks on teaching methods which were widely used in teacher education.

An Elementary School in the 1940s. Lower grade in the Penasco School, December 1941, U.S. Department of Agriculture, Bureau of Agricultural Economics, Photo by Rusinow. National Archives Collections.

In 1892, the National Herbartian Society was organized to advance the study of education as a discipline.

In the scientific movement in education, the development of statistical methods for measurement and testing was greatly aided by E. L. Thorndike's work, *An Introduction to the Theory of Mental and Social Measurements,* 1904. J.M. Rice contributed to scientific measurement as well, with his tests designed to study spelling achievement.

As systems of education expanded and school districts grew larger, professional educators found themselves involved in intricate problems of school administration. Problems of supervision, administration, public relations, financing, and school law led to special courses in school government.

In addition to the improvements in the scientific and administrative aspects of education, its history and philosophy continued to be taught as part of the fundamental knowledge necessary for teachers. These courses were designed to explore the most basic problems of the profession, such as the aims and purposes of education, the function of the school, and the relationship of the school to society.

Teacher Education In The Twentieth Century

By the twentieth century, the basic patterns of teacher education had been fully developed. In the century's early decades, several important forces had shaped the emerging structures of teacher education. One, public elementary and secondary schooling had been completely universalized in the United States. The public elementary and secondary schools with their consistently growing student enrollments required an increasing supply of professionally prepared teachers. Colleges and universities responded to this national need by developing degree programs in teacher education. Two, the certification of teachers was done in the various states by boards of teacher certification or other similar state agencies. The certification requirements of the states were reflected in the teacher education programs in the nation's colleges and universities. Three, extensive research had been done on the problems of teaching and learning, on curriculum and instruction, on school administration and supervision, and on the psychological, sociological, historical, and philosophical foundations of education by professors in departments and colleges of education. This research had developed into an extensive knowledge base that could be used in designing and structuring teacher preparation programs. Four, educational practitioners, the classroom teachers, had organized into a number of professional associations such as the National Council for the Social Studies, the National Association of Teachers of Mathematics, the National Education Association, and other groups. The conferences and publications of these associations brought insights from practice into teacher preparation programs. While the twentieth century programs were a great improvement over those of the nineteenth century, significant variations in their design and quality still existed.

Despite continuing state and institutional variations, teacher education programs generally consisted of four major areas. One, general education courses were required for both elementary and secondary school teachers. Two, there was a major concentration of courses in the teaching area. If the student was preparing to be an elementary teacher, these courses would reflect the subjects and skills found in the elementary school curriculum. However, if the student was preparing to be a secondary school teacher, then he or she enrolled in an academic subject major. Three, there were foundational and methodological courses in professional education. Four, there were a variety of clinical or field experiences which culminated in supervised practice teaching.

Depending upon the particular requirements of the college or university, the general education requirement usually occupied between one-third to one-half of the course work in the four-year bachelor degree program. The general education requirement, designed to provide prospective teachers with a liberal arts and science core, included courses in English language and literature, history and social sciences, physical and biological sciences, the humanities, and mathematics. For some institutions, especially those conducted by religious denominations, courses in philosophy and religious studies might also be required. Some colleges and universities also required completion of foreign language courses. The student's choice of electives completed the individual student's program.[14]

In the late 1960s as many colleges and universities moved away from concentrated core programs in the liberal arts, humanities, and sciences, the general education component of teacher education programs was weakened. In the 1980s, however, there was a renewed emphasis on reconstituting strong liberal arts core requirements by colleges and universities, state teacher certification boards, and professional educational associations.

It was in the area of specialization that the preparation of elementary teachers generally differs from that of secondary teachers. For prospective elementary teachers, preparing to teach grades one through six, the courses in this area were designed to provide preparation in the subjects and skills found in the elementary school curriculum. For example, courses were offered in the methods and materials in the teaching of reading, language arts, children's literature, arithmetic, social studies, earth and life sciences, art, music, and physical education.[15]

The preparation of elementary teachers has been subject to recurrent criticisms and has often been redesigned. Critics generally contend that the preparation of elementary teachers has over-emphasized courses in methodology and neglected more intellectually rigorous academic subject matter. Defenders of elementary education programs contend that the courses in instructional design, strategies, and methodologies are a very important component in realistically preparing teachers. Courses in instructional design and methodology prepare teachers to integrate insights from educational psychology and learning theory, content areas, and the skills needed in the elementary classroom.

The preparation of secondary teachers in subject matter specialization also has been controversial. Later in the chapter, some of the major controversies in this area will be examined. In the conventional teacher education programs that were in place by mid-twentieth century, prospective secondary teachers studied as an academic major those subjects found in the high school curriculum. For example, secondary education students majored in English language and literature, foreign languages, mathematics, history and the social sciences, chemistry, physics, biology, and other subjects taught in high schools. In their preparation as well as in their practice, secondary teachers have needed to master both the academic subject that they plan to teach as well as developing the strategies for effective teaching.

By the 1950s, teacher education programs also contained a sequence of courses in professional education that was largely foundational and methodological. The foundations of education were divided into two components: the cultural and social foundations and the behavioral foundations. In the cultural and social foundations were found such courses as the history, philosophy, and sociology of education. The history and philosophy of education had been consistently present in teacher education since the establishment of the normal schools in the early nineteenth century. In twentieth century teacher education programs, these courses continued to provide students with the historical and philosophical perspectives that were foundational to education. For example, the history of education examined the development of schools, curricula, teaching, and learning over time. Philosophy of education examined the basic purposes of education. Sociology of education examined the structure and function of schools in relationship to social class, mobility, change, and other issues. In some institutional programs, the foundations were taught as separate courses. In other institutions, the foundations were organized into inter-disciplinary courses that focused historical, philosophical, and sociological knowledge and insights on educational issues and problems.

Courses in the behavioral foundations centered largely on educational psychology, tests and measurements, and statistics. These courses were designed to expose students to knowledge about child and adolescent growth and development, learning theory, and the assessment of student progress. Courses in educational psychology, in particular, provided the concepts that could be used in organizing instruction according to students' readiness and ability levels.

The professional sequence as it had developed by the 1950s also included courses in curriculum, instructional design, teaching strategies, and methodology. These courses were designed to provide prospective teachers with a repertoire of strategies that could be used in actual classroom instruction. In these courses, prospective teachers were to learn how to design a unit of instruction. They involved such activities as organizing a particular subject such as the social studies into lessons that were organized according to students' readiness, needs, previous knowledge, and future learning.

Teacher education programs in the twentieth century continued to emphasize the importance of clinical and field experiences for prospective teachers. In the early nineteenth century normal schools, those aspiring to be teachers did their practice teaching in demonstration schools. By the 1950s, teacher education programs contained a sequence of field and clinical experiences designed to introduce prospective teachers to the realities of teaching in public elementary and secondary schools. The field experiences, often in the form of visits to public schools to observe experienced teachers, acquainted students in teacher education programs with a variety of instructional settings. The culminating clinical experience involved the prospective teacher in teaching in a public school setting under the guidance of a co-operating teacher and a supervising professor.

While the foregoing description of teacher education programs at mid-twentieth century is highly generalized, it provides an overview for interpreting later developments, issues, and controversies in the field. As teacher education prepares to enter the twenty-first century, the programs that were standardized in the twentieth century provided the basis for further development and reform.

Patterns of Teacher Certification

The patterns of teacher certification, the granting of a license to prospective teachers attesting to some degree of competence, have been closely related to teacher education. As public education became more common and more important in the nineteenth century, a number of governmental agencies assumed control of teacher certification. As described earlier, during the eighteenth century religious and political conformity were more important requirements than pedagogical competence. By the nineteenth century, districts, towns, townships, and counties were all licensing teachers, and a confusing number of certificates existed. Such licensing agencies usually administered some kind of examination to determine the competence of applicants for teaching positions who lacked educational preparation or experience. Often, normal school graduates were certificated without examination.

In the latter half of the nineteenth century, state superintendents or departments of education took over the function of teacher certification. Gradually, each state developed its own licensing program through which it controlled who entered the teaching profession. While this was an improvement over certification being granted by numerous local agencies, each state still applied its own qualifications.

The requirement of public schools that teachers possess bachelor's degrees appeared only very late in the nineteenth century. In 1896, Utah was the first state to require a degree for high school teaching. Gradually, other states followed. By 1920, ten states required a college degree for secondary school certification. By 1950, every state required it as a standard qualification of the beginning high school teacher.[16] Elementary teaching lagged behind; only after World War II did the majority of states require the bachelor's degree for any kind of certification.[17] California was the first, in 1963, to require a minimum of five years of college for any standard teaching credentials; other states have followed since then.

State patterns for teacher certification have become increasingly complex. The nature of professional preparation varies as do the number and kinds of certificates granted, and the duration of their validity. Despite differences, the following practices are common: centralization of certification authority in state departments of education; issuance of certificates for definite subjects or specified grade levels; minimum requirement of a bachelor's degree for certification; and requirement of specific courses in professional education and a definite number of courses in the teaching field.

The complexities of teacher certification have been severely criticized. In 1946, the National Education Association established the National Commission on Teacher Education and Professional Standards (the TEPS Commission), which was to continually reexamine teacher selection, recruitment, preparation, certification, in-service training, and general advancement of educational standards. Through the efforts of this Commission and other professional education organizations, the National Council for Accreditation of Teacher Education (NCATE) was established in 1952 to accredit programs of teacher education offered by colleges and universities. Upon invitation, NCATE evaluates each institution meeting the following criteria: first, it must already have been accredited by the proper regional accrediting agency and by the appropriate state department of education; second, it must be a non-profit institution of higher learning offering not less than four years of college work leading to the bachelor's degree; third, it must offer a four-year curriculum for the preparation of either elementary or secondary teachers, or both, or offer graduate programs in education.[18] Sponsors of NCATE procedures advocate the Council as a national organization for the evaluation and accreditation of qualified teacher education programs. The states would then automatically license all graduates who have successfully completed the accredited programs. By 1965, twenty-four states had agreed to accept NCATE accreditation for teacher certification, which has significantly contributed to the tendency to standardize teacher certification. NCATE detractors allege that it is inflexible and has overemphasized requirements not justified by research.

The Educational Debates of the 1950s

During the 1950s, an important national debate took place which focused attention on both the quality of American public education and the preparation of teachers for the public schools. Proposals for "reforming" teacher education often occur within the context of more general recommendations for bringing about change in public education.

In the 1950s, critics alleged that academic standards in the nation's public schools had been lowered by a "soft pedagogy" that had been introduced by progressive and life adjustment educators. The critics' challenge was also important for teacher education in that they believed that the inadequacies that they perceived in public education could be remedied, in part, by changing the way in which teachers were prepared. In replying to the critics, defenders of the system contended that American public schools in the post-War era were educating more students at a higher level of quality than had ever been attempted anywhere in the world. The educational issues of the 1950s were related to the social, political, economic, and international context of that period. An examination of the climate of the 1950s sets the debate in its historical perspective.

When World War II ended in 1945, the United States experienced a period of pervasive social change and readjustment. The war's aftermath had generated fundamental social changes in American life. The population was larger, more affluent economically, and more mobile. Pre-war patterns of life associated with either the large cities or rural areas were altered by the emerging phenomenon of suburbia. New housing was constructed in the growing suburbs that developed in concentric patterns around the major cities. The migration of large numbers of former city dwellers to the suburbs produced a need for the construction of new schools. The high birth rate of the late 1940s and the 1950s caused a dramatic increase in school enrollments. Through the 1950s, there were shortages of trained teachers and available classroom space. In addition to these demographic changes, it was believed that traditional values were eroding. The term "juvenile delinquent" was often used to describe teenagers who were rebelling against conformity to the status quo.[19] To cope with such rapid social change, some educators suggested the life adjustment education be introduced into the public school curriculum and into teacher education programs.

In 1947, the United States Office of Education established the Commission on Life Adjustment for Secondary School Youth.[20] The general orientation of the life adjustment philosophy was directed to the education of adolescents for whom college preparation or vocational training was neither feasible nor appropriate. Although never precisely defined, the proponents of life adjustment education claimed its intent was to prepare American youth to live democratic and personally and socially satisfying lives. Life adjustment educators stressed participation in personal, social, and community activities as well as the study of academic subjects. For example, life adjustment courses might include such units as finding a job, being a careful consumer, attracting friends, use of leisure time, hobbies, and other topics. Many of these units were a departure from the more academic subjects that were traditionally found in the secondary school curriculum.

Among the leading educational critics of the 1950s was Arthur E. Bestor, an historian and leader in the Council for Basic Education. Bestor's *Educational Wastelands* claimed that life adjustment education encouraged an anti-intellectualism that detracted from the study of the basic intellectual disciplines of language, mathematics, science, and history.[21] His *Restoration of Learning* continued his critique of American public education and suggested proposals for its reform.[22] Bestor recommended that the school curriculum should be reformed to emphasize basic intellectual disciplines. Believing that many teacher preparation programs lacked intellectual content and rigor, he argued that teachers should be prepared in academic subject matter rather than courses in educational methodology.

A major event occurred in 1957 when the Soviet Union, America's adversary in the Cold War, successfully launched Sputnik, a space satellite that orbited the earth. Many Americans, who regarded the Soviet Union as technologically backward, were stunned by the Soviet successes in space. This event, part of the international scenario of the Cold War, precipitated a national storm of criticism directed against the lack of quality in American public education.

Educational critics, such as Admiral Hyman G. Rickover, saw education as a potentially potent weapon that related to America's national defense. In his comparisons of European and American education, Rickover concluded that American schools were academically inferior.[23] Charging that American public schools were failing to identify and challenge academically talented students, he urged the development of programs for intellectually gifted students. Rickover urged greater emphasis on foreign languages, mathematics, and science to improve the academic quality of American education and to meet the Soviet challenge.

Still other criticisms came from political conservatives such as Max Rafferty who charged that progressive and life adjustment educators had undermined the moral fiber of American life.[24] To restore traditional values, Rafferty urged that American public schools should return to a curriculum of basic subjects, to discipline, and to a patriotic form of civic education.

During the 1950s, the arguments of the critics of American public education and the counter-arguments of its defenders reached a fever peak. According to the critics, American public schools had deteriorated in their academic quality. Anti-intellectual programs of life adjustment and progressive education had weakened instruction in the basic intellectual disciplines of history, mathematics, science, and foreign languages. They also charged that the lack of challenging academic standards in the public schools had produced educational mediocrity; that the concentration on education courses in teacher preparation had produced incompetent teachers; and that European systems of education were academically superior to American schools.

Professional educators, public school administrators, and teachers' organizations challenged the validity of the critics' arguments. Defenders of the system argued that comparisons of American public schools to European educational systems were invalid. The critics, they said, had ignored the fact that only a very small percentage of Europeans attended academic schools because of long standing social class divisions and highly selective procedures that denied admission to most of the age specific population. The system's defenders claimed that American public schools in the post-World War II era were educating more children than ever before in the nation's history. Although it might be true that educational facilities were insufficient to meet the needs of the growing number of students, blame should not be attributed to public school administrators and teachers. Rather, they contended that more funding was needed to improve facilities and increase the number of trained teachers. The defenders of the system also claimed that many of the critics were misinformed or uninformed about research in educational psychology, the development of instructional techniques and media, and the use of educational innovations. Finally, the defenders contended that the open enrollment pattern of public schools guaranteed equality of educational opportunity and that attention to the interests, needs, and problems of children and adolescents was based on sound educational research, theory, and practice.

In the 1980s, history tended to repeat itself when another national debate about the quality of American education occurred. Stimulated by *A Nation at Risk* and other myriad national reports, a new generation of critics contended that American public schools had deteriorated academically.[25] Among the criticisms of the 1980s were: American students were deficient in mathematical and language skills; the academic superiority of foreign educational systems had weakened the United States' economic and technological superiority; American students were inadequate in science; many teachers were inadequately prepared to provide effective instruction in the needed academic subjects. The general direction of the critics of the 1980s, like those of the 1950s, was for reforms of teacher education that emphasized a greater concentration on academic disciplines and a reduced emphasis on courses in professional education, especially in instructional methodology.

Educational Innovation

During the early 1960s, speeches, articles, and books loudly and boldly proclaimed that the United States was on the verge of an educational revolution.[26] In retrospect, the claims that a revolution was taking place in education were exaggerated. Nevertheless, the 1960s witnessed significant innovations in curriculum, school organization, and instructional materials and methods. The impact of these educational innovations on teacher education can be examined as an episode in the recent history of American education.

The curricular innovations of the early 1960s were primarily the work of mathematicians and scientists in colleges and universities who designed a number of programs variously known as the "new mathematics," the "new physics," and the "new social studies." Underlying the various curricular reforms was the learning theory of Jerome Bruner which emphasized the structure of disciplines and the use of the inquiry or discovery method.[27] The movement for curriculum revision began in the science fields of physics, mathematics, biology and chemistry and then reached into history, the social studies, and other areas. Committees of scholars and scientists attempted to identify the structures of the academic disciplines. Their general effort was designed to replace the stress on information and facts in the various subjects with the key concepts needed to understand a discipline such as chemistry or physics. Stressing the inquiry or discovery method, the designers of the new curricula also sought to restructure instructional methods to approximate the processes used by scientists and scholars in their academic research.

Concurrent with the curricular emphasis on the learning of conceptual structures in the academic disciplines, there was also a stress on the inquiry method by which students were to discover the important generalizations by using the research techniques of the scientist or scholar. Rather than relying on the direct presentation of basic principles by having them stated in textbooks or by teachers, the students were to investigate topics or problems and reach their own conclusions. The curricular innovations of the 1960s received support from the federal government which funded special institutes and workshops for teachers through the National Defense Education Act. Private philanthropic organizations such as the Carnegie Corporation and the Ford Foundation also supported the movement for new curricula. Commercial publishers also promoted the movement by designing and marketing "learning packages" that featured the new programs.

The new curriculum of the 1960s had an effect on teacher education. Although professors of education were involved in designing new programs, the major impact for change came from professors in the academic disciplines. At the time, the academic innovators were unaware or neglected already existing research on learning that was an established part of the literature of teacher education. Some of the critics of the new curricula felt that it had been introduced without sufficient attention being paid to the experience of classroom teachers. To others, the apparent sophistication of the new curricular programs masked a superficiality that neglected needed information and skills. Nevertheless, the concerted efforts of the private corporations, the federal government, and the commercial publishers created a new curricula that had an impact on teacher education.

While the academic committees of scientists and scholars in the subject matter fields were introducing new curricula, professional educators devised innovative patterns of school organization. One such innovation was the "nongraded school" which was designed to remove the lockstep inflexibility of the graded system by eliminating the conventional grade labels that were attached to children. According to the proponents of the "nongraded school," it was important to devise organizational patterns in which students could progress at their own individual rate of learning. In a nongraded school, for example, academically talented students could progress at a faster rate from basic to more advanced work. Those who needed special or remedial attention could move at a rate that was appropriate for them.

In the early 1960s, team teaching attracted national attention as a major educational innovation. Defined as an "effort to improve instruction by the reorganization of personnel," team teaching involved two or more teachers planning and working together in the instruction of the same group of students.[28] The effective use of team teaching involved the organizing of a school faculty and staff into a close working relationship and often required redesigning the structure and scheduling of a school. Team leaders, cooperating teachers, and instructional aides needed to be organized into coordinated instructional teams. Students had to be regrouped into flexible divisions such as large sections, small discussion groups, and individualized study arrangements.

The early experimentation with team teaching was conducted by the School and University Program for Research and Development at Harvard University, the Claremont Graduate School Team Teaching Program in California, and the Wisconsin School Improvement Program. J. Lloyd Trump, who headed the Committee on Staff Utilization of the National Association of Secondary School Principals, was one of the articulate advocates of team teaching.[29] Trump's concept of team teaching was a broad one that required careful planning and implementation. He recommended that forty percent of instruction should occur in large group sections, forty percent in individualized study, and twenty percent in small group seminars. The full implementation of Trump's plan called for flexible scheduling and often new designs in school architecture.

Team teaching also altered conventional teacher education programs. While every teacher did not have to be highly proficient in all subjects, all teachers involved in team teaching needed a thorough understanding of the entire educational process. Members of the teaching team needed to be prepared to work effectively with their colleagues in planning, organizing, presenting, and evaluating instruction. One beneficial effect of team teaching was to reduce the isolation of teachers from their colleagues. It also permitted and encouraged teachers to develop special areas of competence and expertise.

In retrospect, it is debatable if team teaching had the profound impact that its proponents predicted. The enthusiasm generated for team teaching in the early 1960s caused it to be introduced by some administrators who did not understand its full implications. In some schools, a crude version of team teaching was introduced in which two teachers merely shared the same classroom. Also, at times, the organization of team teaching was a mechanical affair that was untouched by the new curricular designs of the period.

The 1960s also saw the development of new instructional technologies such as educational television, programmed learning, and computer based instruction. Educational television is an example of the successful instructional use of the new technology. Early in the 1950s, educators had begun to experiment with educational television. In 1957, Alexander J. Stoddard initiated the National Program in the Use of Television in the Schools which was financed by the Ford Foundation's Fund for the Advancement of Education. In 1961, the six-state Midwest Program on Airborne Television Instruction, located at Purdue University, began to broadcast lessons to schools and colleges from high-flying airplanes. A major open circuit effort was the "Chicago College of the Air" which televised credit courses over WTTW, the educational television channel in Chicago. In 1965, a National Center for School and College Television was established at Indiana University with a grant from the United States Office of Education. This Center was designed to serve as a central source of information about educational television. By the late 1960s, more than ten million students received part of their formal education via television. The use of television also had a direct impact on teacher education. In methods courses, for example, prospective teachers who had their classes videotaped could have an instant critique of their teaching as they watched themselves on television monitors when the tape was replayed.

The educational revolution of the 1960s also focused attention on the so-called "teaching machines" with programmed and computer-based instruction. Programmed instruction was designed to bring students to concept formation through a series of carefully graduated steps that provided them at the same time with a means of instant self-evaluation. Since the students were able to recognize their successes and errors as rapidly as they made them, they could proceed at their own learning rate. Programmed instruction was particularly adaptable to the study of subjects that could be reduced easily to elemental steps. Programs in grammar, foreign languages, logic, and mathematics were developed. The use of electronic computers was also an innovation of the late 1960s and 1970s. Electronic computers made it possible to store, classify, record, and retrieve large amounts of information. Among the pioneers in computer based instruction were the System Development

Corporation, International Business Machines, and the Generalized Academic Simulation Programs at the Massachusetts Institute of Technology.

By the mid-1960s, new and different directions were being forged in American education as new curricula were developed, new patterns of school organization were introduced, and new technological instruments were designed for classroom use. While many schools were transformed by the innovations of the 1960s, other schools either ignored the innovations or adopted them in ways that were far removed from what the innovators had intended. The climate of the late 1960s was not the same as that of the beginning of the decade. The innovations had not produced the sweeping transformation that their promoters had promised. In fact, the mood of the late 1960s revealed a general discontent with the existing patterns of schooling. This was particularly true in the inner city schools attended largely by children of minority groups such as blacks and Hispanics. Teacher education programs now included courses on the education of the urban child and on bi-lingualism.

The late 1960s and the early 1970s saw the emergence of new educational critics who wrote a twentieth century version of Rousseau's romantic and child-centered *Emile*. While Bestor and other critics of the 1950s had charged the public schools with failing to cultivate intellectual disciplines, critics of the new genre argued that schools were too formal, bureaucratic, and inflexible. For example, Bel Kaufman's best-selling novel, *Up the Down Staircase*, recounted a dedicated young teacher's frustrations at the hands of an unfeeling and rigid school administration.[30] A series of books came from the pens of angry critics of American schooling such as Herbert Kohl, Jonathan Kozol, George Dennison, and John Holt.[31] The romantic critics were generally anti-institutional and urged that children should be free to follow their own curiosity, interests, and needs. Teachers were to guide the learning process in an enthusiastic, interesting, and exciting way.

The cause of informal and open learning gained a major impetus when Charles E. Silberman's *Crisis in the Classroom* appeared in 1970.[32] Silberman's book, based on his research as director of the Carnegie Corporation's Study of the Education of Educators, advanced the thesis that American public schools had become overly formal. Excessive routine and formality had created devitalized and often inhumane schools that were governed by mindless bureaucracy. For Silberman, the remedy was to create more open, informal, and humanistic schools. He argued that the British Primary School, or integrated day school, presented a model that could be adapted to American elementary education. The informal open classrooms would encourage teachers to follow and guide learners' interests. At the secondary level, American high schools were to be reformed by eliminating unnecessary rules and regulations, by allowing more student input, and by a substantial curriculum revision that stressed the structure of academic discipline.

Silberman and other advocates of open learning and humanistic education stimulated an American interest in the British Primary School.[33] Although it took various forms, the British Primary School rested on the philosophy that children learned most effectively through a direct involvement with their immediate environment in which they were free to pursue their own interests with the guidance of teachers. Rather than following the scheduled time sequences of the more traditional and formal school, the British Primary approach stressed longer blocks of time where the children worked individually or in small groups at a wide range of activities. The British Primary School quickly gained a following among enthusiastic American educators who began to implement it as open space education.

During the late 1960s and early 1970s, the open education movement steadily gained ground in the United States. A noteworthy example of the implementation of open education occurred in North Dakota where a number of small schools were converted into informal or open schools. Throughout the country, school districts inaugurated open classrooms or open space schools. In some cases, the open school theory was applied correctly and produced the desired educational consequences. In other situations, the open space concept was introduced hastily by educators who failed to understand its full pedagogical implications. As a result, certain open space situations merely became a large room or open area in which several teachers taught in a conventional manner.

Accountability was still another concept that gained wide currency in professional educational literature and in teacher education in the early 1970s. The basic meaning of accountability was that the various components of an educational system such as schools, administrators, and teachers should be responsible for what children learn. The working assumption was that a higher quality of education could be obtained by making professionals responsible for their product.[34] If teachers were to be accountable for their students' achievement, then the objectives of instruction needed to be stated in specific terms that were verifiable. Public school administrators who were charged with the responsibility of being accountable for student achievement began to devise lists of behavioral objectives for various skills and subject matters. If students achieved the specific objectives stated for a learning area, then it was assumed that the requirements of accountability were being met. The accountability movement has had some impact on teacher education in that prospective teachers began to study the methods of devising and of fulfilling behavioral objectives. Programs in school administration also began to include courses in management by objectives.

By the mid-1970s, the pendulum of educational change had begun to swing away from innovation to basic education. The "back-to-basics movement" began among parents and non-professionals and then began to influence professional educators. Essentially, the back-to-basics advocates argued that the school curriculum needed to emphasize basic skills and subjects. There was a fear that essential skills of reading, writing and arithmetic were being neglected. Along with the attention to the basic skills and subjects, the back-to-basics advocates urged a return to discipline and order in the classroom with the teacher restored to a position of authority.

A leading force in the back-to-basics movement was the Council for Basic Education organized in 1956 to work for an increased emphasis on the fundamental intellectual disciplines in the public schools. The Council advocated that students receive instruction in the basic intellectual disciplines of English, mathematics, science, history, foreign languages and the arts.[35]

Federal Aid to Education

The late 1950s and 1960s were a period in which the federal government through its financial assistance brought about change in schooling and teacher education. After World War II, several national and international trends generated increased federal funding for education. During President Eisenhower's administration, from 1952 to 1960, it was argued that federal support was needed for educational programs, especially in mathematics and science, that related to the national defense. For President Kennedy, the educational needs of the 1960s required federal support to construct more facilities in higher education and provide more educational opportunities for gifted children. The policies of Lyndon Johnson, a former teacher who wanted to be known as the "Educational President," reflected a Jacksonian tendency to equalize educational opportunity and a New Deal propensity to encourage federally-funded social welfare and educational programs. The years of the Cold War, the New Frontier, and the Great Society saw more federal involvement in funding education. In the 1970s and 1980s, the federal interest in education continued but funding was reduced. Although President Reagan gave his efforts to educational reform, he believed that support of education was primarily a state and local responsibility. The inflationary period of the 1970s and the large federal budget deficits of the 1980s also reduced federal funding.

The National Defense Education Act (NDEA), passed in 1958 in response to the concerns generated by Sputnik, made federal funds available to upgrade teacher competency in science, mathematics, foreign languages, and counseling. The principal motivation for the Act grew out of a concern that the Soviet Union might surpass the United States in the crucial areas of mathematics and science. Foreign language instruction also received an impetus as a result of the NDEA. Funds were provided for the establishment of language laboratories in many school districts.

In his educational message of 1962, President Kennedy advised Congress that teacher education programs needed to incorporate the important advances that had occurred in the discovery and transmission of knowledge. While the special institutes for teachers supported by the National Science Foundation and the Office of Education helped to provide keep a limited number of teachers up-to-date in their fields, Kennedy wanted to extend the opportunities for attending these institutes to more teachers. He believed a definite need existed to raise standards in both course content and instructional methods in teacher educational programs. In urging that colleges and universities be given federal support in improving their teacher education programs, Kennedy stated:

> ...the key to educational quality is the teaching profession. About 1 out of every 5 of the nearly 1,600,000 teachers in our elementary and secondary schools fails to meet full certification standards for teaching or has not completed 4 years of college work. Our immediate concern should be to afford them every possible opportunity to improve their professional skills and their command of the subjects they teach.[36]

Although Kennedy encouraged general aid to education legislation, it was not enacted until 1965 when President Lyndon Johnson proposed aid to elementary, secondary, and higher education. The enactment of the Johnson legislation marked a temporary shift in congressional attitude toward educational funding by the federal government. Prior to 1965, Congress had aided specific programs rather than enact general aid to education legislation. For example, vocational education was supported by the Smith-Hughes Act of 1917 and mathematics and science education was aided by the National Defense Education Act of 1958. The Elementary and Secondary Education Act (ESEA) of 1965, in contrast, provided more general aid for elementary and secondary schools.

The Elementary and Secondary Education Act was related to Johnson's "Great Society" programs and to the "war on poverty." In particular, the "war on poverty" sought to provide job training for economically disadvantaged youth, restore vitality to the inner cities of large urban areas, and provide assistance to schools in poverty impacted areas. For example, the ESEA contained the following provisions: Title I, "Federal Assistance for Local Education Agencies for the Education of Children of Low-Income Families," was designed to develop and support programs to aid economically and educationally disadvantaged children. Title II provided funds to purchase library books, textbooks, periodicals, magnetic tapes, phonograph records, and other educational materials. Title III provided for the establishment of model schools, pilot programs, and community centers to supplement the offerings of local school districts in such areas as continuing adult education, guidance and counseling, remedial instruction, special educational services, enriched academic programs, and health. Title IV sought to improve educational research, the dissemination of information to teachers and teacher education institutions, and the establishment of regional laboratories. Title V sought to assist the departments of education of the various states to administer the new programs.

For President Johnson, federal aid to education was an important strategy in the "war on poverty." To break the cycle of poverty, federal support was given to programs to improve inner city schools and to provide job training for disadvantaged youth. In 1965, the Head Start Programs were inaugurated to provide enriched early childhood experiences for disadvantaged children. In 1968, special programs were developed by the U.S. Office of Education to familiarize professors of education with the special needs and problems of inner city schools.

During the Carter administration, the Department of Education was established in 1979 with the Secretary of Education as a member of the Cabinet. The Reagan administration, from 1981 to 1989, pursued a general policy of stimulating and encouraging educational reform rather than supporting federal aid. The publication of *A Nation at Risk: The Imperative for Educational Reform* called for an emphasis on academic subject matter, especially mathematics and science. It also made a seven part recommendation to improve the preparation of teachers:

1. Prospective teachers "should be required to meet high educational standards, to demonstrate an aptitude for teaching, and to demonstrate competence in an academic discipline."

2. Teachers' salaries should be increased and "should be professionally competitive, market-sensitive, and performance-based." Further, effective evaluation systems should be used to identify and reward superior teachers.

3. School boards should issue eleven month contracts to teachers to provide time for professional and curriculum development.

4. School districts should develop career ladders for teachers.

5. Alternative entry into teaching for teachers of mathematics and science should be developed.

6. Incentives, such as grants and loans, should be used to attract high qualified students into teaching.

7. Master teachers should be involved in designing teacher education

programs and in supervising teachers in the early stages of their professional careers.[37]

Broadening The Educational Mainstream

The recent history of education in the United States has seen several movements and trends that have broadened educational opportunities for more children and adolescents. Members of racial and ethnic minority groups and persons with handicaps whose educational opportunities had been restricted by traditional and discriminatory practices enjoyed a greater access to education than ever before in American history. The 1960s and 1970s were a period of broadening the mainstream of American educational institutions to more people. The impact of greater educational opportunities was most pronounced in three areas: the education of students with handicaps, bi-lingual education, and multi-cultural education. Developments in these three fields had an impact on how schools were organized, on how instruction was planned and delivered, and how teachers were prepared.

The right of children with handicaps to an equal educational opportunity was affirmed in 1974 in a case that was heard in the U.S. District Court in Pennsylvania. The court ruled that the state of Pennsylvania was obligated "to place each mentally retarded child in a free, public program of education and training appropriate to the child's capacity." The court's decision was based on the right of children with handicaps to treatment and education according to the Fifth and Fourteenth Amendments to the Constitution. Especially important in the judicial reasoning was the "due process" provision of the Fourteenth Amendment which guarantees that persons cannot be deprived of equal protection of the laws without due process.

In 1975, Congress enacted PL 94-142, The Education for all Handicapped Children Act, which had important consequences for public education and teacher preparation. According to the Act, persons with handicaps had a "fundamental right" to a "free appropriate public education." The law required that "individualized education programs" were to be developed for handicapped children and that educational services were to be provided in the "least restrictive" environment. An individualized education program, or IEP, a plan for the child's education that included learning specific objectives, was to be developed to guide the child's progress. The Act also required that children with handicaps were to be educated in the least restrictive environment. This meant that such children were to be instructed or "mainstreamed" in regular classroom settings. They were to be educated in special settings only for the amount of time needed to provide appropriate services.

For teacher education programs, PL 94-142 generated far-reaching changes. Greater sophistication in diagnosing and an earlier identification of handicaps increased the numbers of children who were to receive special education services. The demand for special education teachers increased. Colleges and universities developed and expanded their special education teacher preparation programs.

The Law's provision requiring "mainstreaming" of children with handicaps into the regular classroom brought about changes in how elementary and secondary teachers were prepared. Teachers in what became known as the "regular" classroom needed to develop strategies and skills for educating children with handicaps in regular classroom settings. To provide such teacher preparation, departments and schools of education redesigned their programs.[38] This often meant that the professors of education, too, had to develop the needed knowledge base and skills to provide such an education to prospective teachers.

Teacher Organizations

Educators, like other professionals, have formed organizations to promote and protect their interests. Today, the two major national organizations that represent teachers' interests are the National Education Association, NEA, and the American Federation of Teachers, AFT. While the NEA and the AFT both promote the cause of education and of teachers, they differ in how they are organized and in their strategies for accomplishing their goals.

The National Education Association, the older of the two national teachers' organizations, originated in 1857 when a small group of educators met in Philadelphia to establish the National Teachers Association. In 1870, the National Teachers Association was reorganized as the National Education Association. The general purpose of the NEA was to promote the cause of public education and to advance the interests of educators.

The NEA, with 1,700,000 members, is the largest organization of educators in the world.[39] It is a confederation of affiliated state and local educational associations that includes departments, commissions, divisions, and committees that relate to a large spectrum of educational activities and interests. The NEA sponsors numerous publications. Among them are *Today's Education* and the *NEA Reporter*. Among the organization's members can be found teachers, administrators, professors, and other educators.

The NEA is governed by an assembly of delegates chosen by member state and local associations. As the Association's legislative body, the assembly establishes the broad policies that govern it as well as its national agenda. The NEA board of directors acts as an executive body that implements the policies established by the assembly.

In addition to its larger membership of classroom teachers, a number of specialized educational organizations have affiliated with the NEA. Among them are the American Association of Elementary-Kindergarten Educators, the American Association of Industrial Arts, the American Association of School Administrators, the Music Educators National Conference, the National Science Teachers Association, and other similar organizations.

As a large confederation of educational associations, the NEA performs a wide range of services for its members. For example, it publishes professional magazines and books, sponsors research, defends teachers from the violation of academic freedom and tenure, promotes a favorable climate of public opinion for education, and lobbies for legislation designed to improve the status of teachers.

The American Federation of Teachers, AFT, organized in 1916, is affiliated with the American Federation of Labor-Congress of Industrial Organizations, AFL-CIO. The vast majority of its 675,000 members are classroom teachers. The Federation's goals are closely identified with improving the salaries, working conditions, and status of teachers. Affiliated with the nation's largest labor organization, the AFT has used the organizational strategies of the American labor movement.[40]

The AFT is composed of state federations which are, in turn, made up of the local federations within that state. The governing body of the AFT is its annual convention. Its executive body consists of the president and a number of vice-presidents who are elected for two-year terms. In addition to the general improvement of education, the AFT has the following specific objectives: one, to gain recognition of the right of teachers to organize, negotiate, and bargain collectively with school districts; two, to work for improved teachers' salaries and working conditions; three, to secure better health and retirement benefits for teachers. The AFT also publishes *American Teacher,* a monthly newspaper, and *American Educator,* a monthly magazine.

Since the 1950s, a serious rivalry has developed between the NEA and AFT to organize and represent teachers. NEA advocates contend that teachers can best accomplish their objectives by working with other educators in their own professional organization. They also claim that full professional strength can be mobilized most effectively through the broad range of affiliations that the NEA provides. In contrast, the AFT believes that its affiliation with the AFL-CIO, the largest labor union in the country, has strengthened the bargaining position of teachers. This affiliation, the leaders of the AFT asserts, brings teachers the support of the AFL-CIO and provides locals of the AFT with the support of the local trade and union councils.

Both the NEA and AFT have been active in recruiting teachers as members of their organizations and in organizing them into local units. Both organizations use collective bargaining strategies and have resorted to strikes when negotiations with boards of education have reached an impasse.

Conclusion

The history of American teacher education, like the general history of American education, is closely tied to the national, social, political, and economic currents of which it is a part. In the colonial era, teaching was part of social and religious milieu in which teachers were employed according to their conformity to the doctrines of the various denominations that supported schools. An important development in the preparation of teachers occurred during the common school movement in the nineteenth century. The establishment of normal schools as institutions specifically designed to prepare teachers for elementary schools was the first systematic effort to develop teacher education programs. The normal school experience was then followed by the establishment of departments and schools of education in colleges and universities.

Teacher education programs are closely related to the certification requirements of the states. These requirements were established to provide some degree of uniformity in the certification of teachers. Today, the various states grant approved program status to those institutional programs that meet their requirements for certification. Regional accreditation associations and the National Council on Accreditation of Teacher Education, NCATE, also work to safeguard the quality of teacher education programs.

Teacher education programs have been the subject of public scrutiny and have been controversial. Periodically, there have been concerted attacks on the extent to which courses in professional education and instructional methodology should be part of the preparation of teachers.

Teachers have formed national organizations such as the National Education Association and the American Federation of Teachers which work to promote the general interests of education and the objectives of the teaching profession.

The developments and trends that are a part of the history of teacher education have had an impact on the preparation of today's teachers. To appreciate the role of the teaching profession in American life, an understanding of the development of teacher education is crucial.

Notes

[1] Samuel Hall, *Lectures to School-Masters on Teaching* (Boston: Carter, Hendee and Co., 1833), pp. 20-21.

[2] *Ibid.*, p. vi.

[3] *Ibid.*, pp. x-xii.

[4] *Ibid.*, pp. 33-35.

5 Henry Barnard, *Normal Schools, and Other Institutions, Agencies, and Means Designed for the Professional Education of Teachers* (Hartford: Case, Tiffany, and Company, 1851), p. 7.

6 James G. Carter, "Outline of an Institution for the Education of Teachers," 1825, in Barnard, *Normal Schools*. pp. 78-81.

7 Charles Harper, *A Century of Public Teacher Education* (Washington, DC: National Education Association, 1939), p. 22.

8 David P. Page, *Theory and Practice of Teaching or the Motives and Methods of Good School-Keeping* (New York: A. S. Barnes and Co., 1885).

9 Barnard, *Normal Schools*, p. 8.

10 Paul Woodring, "A Century of Teacher Education," in William Brickman and Stanley Lehrer, eds., *Century of Higher Education* (New York: Society for the Advancement of Education, 1962), p. 158.

11 George S. Counts, *The Social Foundations of Education* (New York: Charles Scribner's Sons, 1934).

12 Andrew S. Draper, *A Teaching Profession: An Address Before the Massachusetts State Teachers' Association, at Worcester, Massachusetts, November 28, 1890* (Albany: Weed, Parsons, and Co., 1890), p. 5.

13 *Ibid.*, p. 10.

14 Walter K. Beggs, *The Education of Teachers* (New York: The Center for Applied Research in Education, Inc., 1965), pp. 26-27.

15 *Ibid.*, pp. 30-32.

16 *Ibid.*, p. 50.

17 *Ibid.*, pp. 50-51.

18 *Ibid.*, pp. 74-75.

19 James Gilbert, *A Cycle of Outrage: America's Reaction to the Juvenile Delinquent in the 1950s* (New York: Oxford University Press, 1986).

20 U. S. Office of Education, *Life Adjustment for Every Youth* (Washington, DC: U.S. Government Printing Office, 1948); also, see Franklin R. Zeran, *Life Adjustment Education in Action* (New York: Chartwell House, Inc., 1953).

21 Arthur E. Bestor, Jr., *Educational Wastelands: Retreat From Learning in Our Public Schools* (Urbana: University of Illinois Press, 1953).

22 Arthur E. Bestor, Jr., *Restoration of Learning: A Program for Redeeming the Unfulfilled Promise of American Education* (New York: Alfred A. Knopf, 1955).

23 H. G. Rickover, *Education and Freedom* (New York: E. P. Dutton and Company, 1959).

24 For Raffery's view see Max Rafferty, *What They Are Doing to Your Children* (New York: New American Library, 1963).

25 National Commission of Excellence in Education, *A Nation at Risk: The Imperative for Educational Reform* (Washington, DC: U.S. Government Printing Office, 1983).

26 For an example, see Francis Keppel, *The Necessary Revolution in American Education* (New York: Harper and Row, Publishers, 1966).

27 Jerome Bruner, *The Process of Education* (Cambridge: Harvard University Press, 1960).

28 Judson T. Shaplin, "Team Teaching," in Ronald Gross and Judith Murphy, eds., *The Revolution in the Schools* (New York: Harcourt, Brace, and World, Inc., 1964), p. 93.

29 J. Lloyd Trump and Dorsey Baynham, *Focus on Change: Guide to Better Schools* (Chicago: Rand McNally and Co., 1961).

30 Bel Kaufman, *Up the Down Staircase* (Englewood Cliffs, N.J.: Prentice Hall, Inc., 1964).

31 Among the representative romantic critics were: George Dennison, *The Lives of Children* (New York: Random House, 1969); James Herndon, *The way it spozed to be* (New York: Simon and Schuster, 1968); John Holt, *How Children Learn* (New York: Pitman Publishing Co., 1967); Jonathan Kozol, *Death at an Early Age* (Boston: Houghton Mifflin Co., 1967).

32 Charles E. Silberman, *Crisis in the Classroom: The Remaking of American Education* (New York: Random House, 1970).

33 The major source on the British Primary School is Lady Bridget Plowden, et al., *Children and Their Primary Schools: A Report of the Central Advisory Council in Education* (London: Her Majesty's Stationery Office, 1966). Other works on open education are: John Blackie, *Inside the Primary School* (London: Her Majesty's Stationery Office, 1967); Mary Brown and Norman Precious, *The Integrated Day in the Primary School* (New York: Agathon Press, 1970); Lillian S. Stephens, *The Teacher's Guide to Open Education* (New York: Holt, Rinehart and Winston, 1974).

34 Stephen M. Barro, "An Approach to Developing Accountability Measures for the Public Schools," *Phi Delta Kappan*, Vol. LII (December 1970), pp. 196-205. Also see Frank J. Sciara and Richard K. Jantz, *Accountability in American Education* (Boston: Allyn and Bacon, Inc., 1972).

35 For the theory of basic education, see James D. Koerner, ed., *The Case for Basic Education* (Boston: Little, Brown, and Co., 1959).

36 John F. Kennedy, *Message of the President of the United States Relative to an Educational Program*, H.R. Document No. 330 (Washington, DC: U.S. Government Printing Office, 1962), pp. 4-5.

37 The National Commission on Excellence in Education, *A Nation at Risk: The Imperative for Educational Reform* (Washington, DC: U.S. Government Printing Office, 1983), pp. 30-31.

38 Dean C. Corrigan and Kenneth R. Howey, eds., *Special Education in Transition: Concepts to Guide the Education of Experienced Teachers* (Reston, Va.: The Council for Exceptional Children, 1980); also, see *A Common Body of Practice for Teachers: The Challenge of Public Law 94-142 to Teacher Education* (Washington, DC: American Association of Colleges of Teacher Education, 1980).

39 Allan M. West, *The National Education Association: The Power Base for Education* (New York: Free Press, 1980).

[40] The definitive history of the AFT is William E. Eaton, *The American Federation of Teachers, 1916-1961* (Carbondale: Southern Illinois University Press, 1975). Also, see Robert J. Brown, *Teachers and Power: The Story of the American Federation of Teachers* (New York: Simon and Schuster, 1972) and Marshall O. Donley, *Power to the Teacher: How America's Educators Became Militant* (Bloomington: Indiana University Press, 1976).

Selections to Accompany
Chapter 6

The selection below is from Samuel R. Hall's Lectures to School-Masters on
Teaching, *1833. Hall's* Lectures *was one of the first books written in the United
States about teaching. As a lecturer and essayist on teacher education, Hall
drew attention to the problem of preparing enough adequately trained teachers
to staff the common district schools.*

Lectures to School-Masters on Teaching

Having adverted in the preceding Lecture, to certain existing evils, unfriendly
to the character and usefulness of common schools, I shall, in this, call your
attention to *the requisite qualifications of an instructor*. This subject is of
high importance. All who possess the requisite *literary* attainments, are not
qualified to assume the direction of a school. Many entirely fail of usefulness,
though possessed of highly cultivated minds. Other things are required in
the character of a good school-master. Among these, *common sense* is the
first. This is a qualification exceedingly important, as in teaching school one
has constant occasion for its exercise. Many, by no means deficient in intellect,
are not persons of *common* sense. I mean by the term, that faculty by which
things are seen as they are. It implies judgment and discrimination, and a
proper sense of propriety in regard to the common affairs of life. It leads
us to form judicious plans of action, and to be governed by our circumstances,
in the way which men in general will approve. It is the exercise of reason,
uninfluenced by passion or prejudice. It is in man nearly what instinct is in
brutes. Very different from genius or talent, as they are commonly defined,
it is better than either. Never blazing forth with the splendor of noon, but
it shines with a constant and useful light.

SOURCE: Samuel R. Hall, *Lectures to School-Masters on Teaching* (Boston: Carter,
Hendee and Co., 1833), pp. 31-42.

2. *Uniformity of temper* is another important trait in the character of an instructor. Where this is wanting, it is hardly possible to govern or to teach with success. He, whose temper is constantly varying, can never be uniform in his estimation of things around him. Objects change in their appearance as his passions change. What appears right in any given hour may seem wrong in the next. What appears desirable today, may be beheld with aversion tomorrow. An uneven temper, in any situation of life, subjects one to many inconveniences. But when placed in a situation where his every action is observed and where his authority, must be in constant exercise, the man who labors under this malady is especially unfortunate. It is impossible for him to gain and preserve respect among his pupils. No one who comes under the rule of a person of uneven temper, can know what to expect or how to act.

3. A capacity to *understand and discriminate character*, is highly important to him who engages in teaching. The dispositions of children are so various, the treatment and government of parents so dissimilar, that the most diversified modes of governing and teaching need to be employed. The instructor who is not able to discriminate, but considers all alike, and treats all alike, does injury to many. The least expression of disapprobation to one, is often more than the severest reproof to another; a word of encouragement will be sufficient to excite attention in some, while others will require to be urged, by every motive that can be placed before them. All the varying shades of disposition and capacity should be quickly learned by the instructor, that he may benefit all and do injustice to none. Without this, well meant efforts may prove hurtful, because ill-directed, and the desired object may be defeated, by the very means used to obtain it.

4. Teachers should possess much *decision of character*. In every situation of life this trait is important, but in none more so, than in that of which I am treating. The little world, by which he is surrounded, is a miniature of the older community. Children have their aversions and partialities, their hopes and fears, their plans, schemes, propensities and desires. These are often in collision with each other and not unfrequently in collision with the laws of the school, and in opposition to the best interest of themselves. Amidst all these, the instructor should be able to pursue a uniform course. He ought not to be easily swayed from what he considers right. If easily led from his purpose, or induced to vary from established rules, his school must become a scene of disorder. Without decision, the teacher loses the confidence and respect of his pupils. I would not say, that, if convinced of having committed an error, or of having given a wrong judgment, you should persist in the wrong. But I would say, it should be known as one of your first principles in school-keeping, that what is required must be complied with in every case, unless cause can be shown why the rule ought, in a given instance, to be dispensed with. There should *then* be a frank and easy compliance with the

reasonable wish of the scholar. In a word, without decision of purpose in a teacher, his scholars can never be brought under that kind of discipline, which is requisite for his own ease and convenience, or for the improvement in knowledge, of those placed under him.

5. A schoolmaster ought to be *affectionate*. The human heart is so constituted, that it cannot resist the influence of kindness. When affectionate intercourse is the offspring of those kind feelings which arise from true benevolence, it will have an influence on all around. It leads to ease in behavior, and genuine politeness of manners. It is especially desirable in those who are surrounded by the young. Affectionate parents usually see their children exhibit similar feelings. Instructors who cultivate affection, will generally excite the same in their scholars. No object is more important than to gain the love and good will of those we are to teach. In no way is this more easily accomplished than by a kind interest manifested in their welfare; an interest which is exhibited by actions as well as words. This cannot fail of being attended with desirable results.

6. A just *moral discernment*, is of preeminent importance in the character of an instructor. Unless governed by a consideration of his moral obligation, he is but poorly qualified to discharge the duties which devolve upon him. He is himself a moral agent, and accountable to himself, to his employers, to his country and to his God, for the faithful discharge of duty. If he have no moral sensibility, no fear of disobeying the laws of God, no regard for the institutions of our holy religion, how can he be expected to lead his pupils in the way that they should go? The cultivation of virtuous propensities is more important to children than even their intellectual culture. The *virtuous* man, though illiterate, will be happy, while the learned, if *vicious*, must be miserable in proportion to his attainments. The remark of the ancient philosopher, that "boys ought to be taught that which they will most need to practise when they come to be men," is most true. To cultivate virtuous habits, and awaken virtuous principles — to excite a sense of duty to God and of dependence on Him, should be the first objects of the teacher. If he permits his scholars to indulge in vicious habits — if he regard nothing as sin, but that which is a transgression of the laws of the school, if he suffer lying, profaneness, or other crimes, to pass unnoticed and unpunished, he is doing an injury for which he can in no way make amends. An instructor without moral feeling, not only brings ruin to the children placed under his care, but does injury to their parents, to the neighborhood, to the town and, doubtless, to other generations. The moral character of instructors should be considered a subject of very high importance; and let every one, who knows himself to be immoral, renounce at once the thought of such an employment, while he continues to disregard the laws of God, and the happiness of his fellow men. Genuine piety is highly desirable in every one entrusted with the care

and instruction of the young; but morality, at least should be *required*, in every candidate for that important trust.

7. Passing over many topics connected with those already mentioned, I shall now remark on the necessary literary qualifications of a schoolmaster. It will at once be apparent that no one is qualified for this business, who has not a thorough knowledge of the branches required to be taught in common schools. These are Reading, Spelling, Writing, Grammar, Arithmetic, Geography, and in some states the History of the United States. All these branches are necessary, to enable individuals to perform the common business and common duties of life. The four first are requisite in writing a letter on business or to a friend. The fifth is required in the business transactions of every day. The two last are necessary to enable every one to understand what he reads in the common newspapers, or in almost every book which comes within his reach. Of each of these branches, the instructor should certainly have a thorough knowledge; for he ought to have a full knowledge of what he is to teach. As he is to lay the *foundation* of an education, he should be well acquainted with the first principles of science. Of the letters of the alphabet such disposition is made, as to produce an immense number of words, to each of which a distinct meaning is given. The nature and power of letters, and just method of spelling words, should be very distinctly understood. If there be defect in *knowledge* here, there must be a defect in teaching. A man cannot be expected to teach that which he does not know himself. Among all the defects I have witnessed in the literary qualification of instructors, the most common, by far the most common, have been here. Among a great number, both of males and females, I have found *very few* who possessed the requisite knowledge of the nature and power of letters, and rules of spelling. The defect originates in the fact, that these subjects are neglected after childhood, and much that is learned then is subsequently forgotten. Teachers, afterwards, especially of academies, presume that these subjects are familiar, and seldom make the inquiry of scholars, whether they have sufficient knowledge on these points. As a considerable part of every school is composed of those who are learning to spell and read, much importance is attached to the requisite qualifications of the teacher, to lay a proper foundation for subsequent attainments.

Henry Barnard, Superintendent of Common Schools of Connecticut, devoted effort to advancing the cause of popular education. He recognized that the success of the common school movement depended upon well-ordered teacher educational institutions. To advance the cause of the normal school, Barnard collected a number of documents designed to promote the professional education of teachers. The "First Annual Circular of the State Normal School at New Britain," Connecticut was included in Barnard's work on normal schools.

First Annual Circular of the State Normal School at New Britain

The State Normal School or "Seminary for the training of teachers in the art of teaching and governing the Common Schools" of Connecticut was established by act of the legislature, May session, 1849, and the sum of eleven thousand dollars was appropriated for its support for a period of at least four years.

The sum appropriated for the support of the school is derived not from the income of the School Fund, or any of the ordinary resources of the Treasury, but from a bonus of ten thousand dollars paid by the State Bank, at Hartford, and of $1,000 paid by the Deep River Bank, for their respective charters. No part of this sum can be expended in any building or fixtures for the school, or for the compensation of the trustees.

The entire management of the Institution as to the application of the funds, the location of the school, the regulation of the studies and exercises, and the granting of diplomas, is committed to a Board of Trustees, consisting of the Superintendent of Common Schools, ex officio, and one member for each of the eight counties of the state, appointed by the Legislature, two in each year, and to hold their office for the term of four years, and serve without compensation. The Board must submit an annual report as to their own doings, and the progress and condition of the seminary.

The Normal School was located permanently in New Britain, on the 1st of February, 1850, after full consideration of the claims and offers of other towns, on account of the central position of the town in the state, and its

SOURCE: Henry Barnard, *Normal Schools, and Other Institutions, Agencies, and Means Designed for the Professional Education of Teachers* (Hartford: Case, Tiffany and Co., 1851), pp. 47-50.

accessibility from every section by railroad; and also in consideration of the liberal offer on the part of its citizens to provide a suitable building, apparatus, and library, to the value of $16,000 for the use of the Normal School, and to place all the schools of the village under the management of the Principal of the Normal School, as Schools of Practice.

The Building provided for the accommodation of the Normal School, and the Schools of Practice, when completed will contain three large study-halls, with nine classrooms attached, a hall for lectures and exhibitions, a laboratory for chemical and philosophical experiments, an office for the Principal and trustees, a room for the library, and suitable accommodations for apparatus, clothes, furnaces, fuel &c. The entire building will be fitted up and furnished in the most substantial manner, and with special reference to the health, comfort and successful labor of pupils and teachers. In addition to the Normal School building, there are three houses located in different parts of the village for the accommodation of the primary schools belonging to the Schools of Practice.

The immediate charge of the Normal School and Schools of Practice, is committed to Rev. T.D.P. Stone, Associate Principal, to whom all communications relating to the schools can be addressed.

The school was opened for the reception of pupils on Wednesday, the 15th of May, 1850, and the first term closed on Tuesday, October 1st. The number of pupils in attendance during the term was sixty-seven; thirty males, and thirty-seven females.

The second term will commence on Wednesday, the 4th of December, 1850, and continue till the third Wednesday in April, 1851, divided into two sessions as given below.

Terms and vacations. The year is divided into two terms, Summer and Winter, each term consisting of two sessions.

The first session of the winter term commences on the first Wednesday of December, and continues fourteen weeks. The second session of the winter term commences on the third Wednesday of March, and continues six weeks.

The first session of the summer term commences on the third Wednesday of May, and continues twelve weeks. The second session of the summer term commences on the third Wednesday of August, and continues six weeks.

To accommodate pupils already engaged in teaching, the short session of each term will, as far as shall be found practicable, be devoted to a review of the studies pursued in the district schools in the season of the year immediately following, and to a course of familiar lectures on the classification, instruction and discipline of such schools.

Admission of pupils. The highest number of pupils which can be received in any one term, is two hundred and twenty.

Each school society is entitled to have one pupil in the school; and no society can have more than one in any term, so long as there are applicants from any society, at the time unrepresented. Until the whole number of pupils in actual attendance shall reach the highest number fixed by law, the Principal is authorized to receive all applicants who may present themselves, duly recommended by the visitors of any school society.

Any person, either male or female, may apply to the school visitors of any school society for admission to the school, who will make a written declaration that their object in so applying is to qualify himself (or herself) for the employment of a common school teacher, and that it is his (or her) intention to engage in that employment, in this state.

The school visitors are authorized to forward to the Superintendent of Common Schools, in any year, the names of four persons, two of each sex who shall have applied as above, for admission to the school, and who shall have been found on examination by them, "possessed of the qualifications required of teachers of common schools in this state," whom they "shall recommend to the trustees as suitable persons, by their age, character, talents, and attainments, to be received as pupils in the Normal School."

Applicants duly recommended by the school visitors, can forward their certificate directly to the Associate Principal of the Normal School at New Britain, who will inform them of the time when they must report themselves to be admitted to any vacant places in the school.

Persons duly recommended, and informed of their admission, must report themselves within the first week of the term for which they are admitted, or their places will be considered as vacated.

Any persons, once regularly admitted to the Normal School, can remain connected with the same for three years and will not lose their places, by temporary absence in teaching common schools in the state—such experience, in connection with the instruction of the Institution, being considered a desirable part of a teacher's training.

Studies. The course of instruction will embrace: 1. A thorough review of the studies pursued in the lowest grade of common schools. 2. An acquaintance with such studies as are embraced in the highest grade of common schools, authorized by law, and which will render the teaching of the elementary branch more thorough and interesting. 3. The art of teaching and its methods, including the history and progress of education, the philosophy of teaching and discipline, as drawn from the nature of the juvenile mind, and the application of those principles under the ordinary conditions of our common schools.

The members of the school will be arranged in three classes—Junior, Middle and Senior. All pupils on being admitted to the school, will be ranked in the *Junior Class*, until their familiarity with the studies of the lowest grade of common schools have been satisfactorily tested. The *Middle Class* will embrace those who are pursuing the branches usually taught in Public High Schools. The *Senior Class* will comprise those who are familiar with the studies of the Junior and Middle Classes, or who are possessed of an amount of experience in active and successful teaching, which can be regarded as a practical equivalent. All the studies of the school will be conducted in reference to their being taught again in common schools.

Practice in the art of teaching and governing schools. The several schools of the first school district, comprising the village of New Britain, are placed by a vote of the District, under the instruction and discipline of the Associate Principal, as Model Schools and Schools of Practice, for the Normal School. These schools embrace about four hundred children, and are classified into three Primary, one Intermediate and one High School. The course of instruction embraces all the studies pursued in any grade of common schools in Connecticut. The instruction of these schools will be given by pupils of the Normal School, under the constant oversight of the Associate Principal and Professors.

Text books. A Library of the best text books, in the various studies pursued in the schools, is commenced, and already numbers upward of four thousand volumes. Pupils are supplied with text books in such studies as they may be engaged, at a charge, barely sufficient to keep the books in good condition, and supply such as may be injured or lost. Arrangements have also been made to furnish teachers who wish to own a set of text books at the publishers' lowest wholesale price.

Apparatus. The sum of one thousand dollars is appropriated for the purchase of apparatus, which will be procured from time to time, as the wants of the school may require. As far as practicable, such articles of apparatus will be used in the classrooms of the Normal School, as can be readily made by teachers themselves, or conveniently procured at low prices, and be made useful in the instruction of District Schools.

Library. The school is already furnished with the best works on the Theory and Practice of Education, which the Normal pupils are expected to read, and on several of which they are examined. The library will be supplied with Encyclopedias, Dictionaries, and other books of reference, to which free access will be given to members of the school.

Board. Normal pupils must board and lodge in such families, and under such regulations, as are approved by the Associate Principal.

The price of board, including room, fuel, lights and washing, in private families, ranges from $2.00 to $2.50 per week. Persons, expecting to join the school, should signify their intention to the Associate Principal, as early as practicable, before the commencement of a term, that there may be no disappointment in the place and price of board.

Discipline. The discipline of the institution is committed to the Associate Principal, who is authorized to secure the highest point of order and behavior by all suitable means, even to a temporary suspension of a pupil from the schools. The age of the pupils, the objects which bring them to a Normal School, and the spirit of the institution itself will, it is believed, dispense with the necessity of a code of rules. The members are expected to exemplify in their own conduct, the order, punctuality, and neatness of good scholars, and exhibit in all their relations, Christian courtesy, kindness and fidelity.

Examination and inspection. The school will be visited each term by a committee of the trustees, who will report on the results of their examination to the Board.

There will be an examination at the close of each term, before the whole Board, and at the close of the summer term, the examination will be public, and will be followed by an exhibition.

The school is at all times open to inspection, and school visitors, teachers, and the friends of education generally in the state are cordially invited to visit it at their convenience.

Diploma. The time required to complete the course of instruction and practice, which shall be deemed by the trustees a suitable preparation for the business of teaching, and entitle any applicant to a Diploma of the Normal School, will depend on the age, attainments, mental discipline, moral character, and evidence of practical tact in instruction and government of each applicant.

No diploma will be given to any person who does not rank in the Senior Class, and has not given evidence of possessing some practical talent as a teacher in the Schools of Practice, or in the District Schools of the state.

Teachers' Institutes

A portion of the vacation in the spring and autumn, will be devoted by the Officers of the Normal School, to Teachers' Institutes or Conventions, in different parts of the state.

At least two of these Institutes will be held in the spring, for the special benefit of teachers who may be engaged, or expect to teach district schools in the summer following.

County Teachers' Association

The Principal, or one of the Professors of the Normal School, will attend, on invitation and due notice, at every regular meeting of any County Teachers'

Association, which shall continue in session through two evenings and one day, and assist in the lectures, discussions and other exercises of the occasion.

State Teachers' Association

The State Teachers' Association has voted to hold an annual meeting at New Britain during the examination at the close of the summer term of the Normal School, and a special meeting at the dedicatory exercises at the completion of the Normal School in the spring. Arrangements will be made to entertain all members of the Association, during the meeting.

Adopted at a meeting of the Board of Trustees, held at New Britain. Oct. 1, 1850.

Francis Gillette, *President.*

In 1983, A Nation at Risk: The Imperative for Education *was issued by the National Commission on Excellence in Education appointed by Secretary of Education T.H. Bell. The report which was widely disseminated stimulated a nationwide movement for reform. It is significant as one of the important documents relating to education in recent history. The following section excerpted from the report establishes the general tone of the seriousness of the educational problem in the United States and identifies indicators of the educational risk facing the nation.*

A Nation at Risk

Our Nation is at risk. Our once unchallenged preeminence in commerce, industry, science, and technological innovation is being overtaken by competitors throughout the world. This report is concerned with only one of the many causes and dimensions of the problem, but it is the one that undergirds American prosperity, security, and civility. We report to the American people that while we can take justifiable pride in what our schools and colleges have historically accomplished and contributed to the United States and the well-being of its people, the educational foundations of our society are presently being eroded by a rising tide of mediocrity that threatens our very future as a Nation and a people. What was unimaginable a generation ago has begun to occur—others are matching and surpassing our educational attainments.

If an unfriendly foreign power had attempted to impose on America the mediocre educational performance that exists today, we might well have viewed it as an act of war. As it stands, we have allowed this to happen to ourselves. We have even squandered the gains in student achievement made in the wake of the Sputnik challenge. Moreover, we have dismantled essential support systems which helped make those gains possible. We have, in effect, been committing an act of unthinking, unilateral educational disarmament.

Our society and its educational institutions seem to have lost sight of the basic purposes of schooling, and of the high expectations and disciplined effort needed to attain them. This report, the result of 18 months of study, seeks to generate reform of our educational system in fundamental ways and to renew the Nation's commitment to schools and colleges of high quality throughout the length and breadth of our land.

SOURCE: The National Commission on Excellence in Education. *A Nation at Risk: The Imperative for Educational Reform* (Washington, DC: U.S. Department of Education, 1983). pp. 5-11.

That we have compromised this commitment is, upon reflection, hardly surprising, given the multitude of often conflicting demands we have placed on our Nation's schools and colleges. They are routinely called on to provide solutions to personal, social, and political problems that the home and other institutions either will not or cannot resolve. We must understand that these demands on our schools and colleges often exact an educational cost as well as a financial one.

On the occasion of the Commission's first meeting, President Reagan noted the central importance of education in American life when he said: "Certainly there are few areas of American life as important to our society, to our people, and to our families as our schools and colleges." This report, therefore, is as much an open letter to the American people as it is a report to the Secretary of Education. We are confident that the American people, properly informed, will do what is right for their children and for the generations to come.

History is not kind to idlers. The time is long past when America's destiny was assured simply by an abundance of natural resources and inexhaustible human enthusiasm, and by our relative isolation from the malignant problems of older civilizations. The world is indeed one global village. We live among determined, well-educated, and strongly motivated competitors. We compete with them for international standing and markets, not only with products but also with the ideas of our laboratories and neighborhood workshops. America's position in the world may once have been reasonably secure with only a few exceptionally well-trained men and women. It is no longer.

The risk is not only that the Japanese make automobiles more efficiently than Americans and have government subsidies for development and export. It is not just that the South Koreans recently built the world's most efficient steel mill, or that American machine tools, once the pride of the world, are being displaced by German products. It is also that these developments signify a redistribution of trained capability throughout the globe. Knowledge, learning, information, and skilled intelligence are the new raw materials of international commerce and are today spreading throughout the world as vigorously as miracle drugs, synthetic fertilizers, and blue jeans did earlier. If only to keep and improve on the slim competitive edge we still retain in world markets, we must dedicate ourselves to the reform of our educational system for the benefit of all — old and young alike, affluent and poor majority and minority. Learning is the indispensable investment required for success in the "information age" we are entering.

Our concern, however, goes well beyond matters such as industry and commerce. It also includes the intellectual, moral, and spiritual strengths of our people which knit together the very fabric of our society. The people of the United States need to know that individuals in our society who do not possess the levels of skill, literacy, and training essential to this new era will be effectively disenfranchised, not simply from the material rewards that accompany competent performance, but also from the chance to participate fully in our national life. A high level of shared education is essential to a free, democratic society and to the fostering of a common culture, especially in a country that prides itself on pluralism and individual fredom.

For our country to function, citizens must be able to reach some common understandings on complex issues, often on short notice and on the basis of conflicting or incomplete evidence. Education helps form these common understandings, a point Thomas Jefferson made long ago in his justly famous dictum:

> I know no safe depository of the ultimate powers of the society but the people themselves; and if we think them not enlightened enough to exercise their control with a wholesome discretion, the remedy is not to take it from them but to inform their discretion.

Part of what is at risk is the promise first made on this continent: All, regardless of race or class or economic status, are entitled to a fair chance and to the tools for developing their individual powers of mind and spirit to the utmost. This promise means that all children by virtue of their own efforts, competently guided, can hope to attain the mature and informed judgment needed to secure gainful employment, and to manage their own lives, thereby serving not only their own interests but also the progress of society itself.

The educational dimensions of the risk before us have been amply documented in testimony received by the Commission. For example:

- International comparisons of student achievement, completed a decade ago, reveal that on 19 academic tests American students were never first or second and, in comparison with other industrialized nations, were last seven times.
- Some 23 million American adults are functionally illiterate by the simplest tests of everyday reading, writing, and comprehension.
- About 13 percent of all 17-year-olds in the United States can be considered functionally illiterate. Functional illiteracy among minority youth may run as high as 40 percent.
- Average achievement of high school students on most standardized tests is now lower than 26 years ago when Sputnik was launched.
- Over half the population of gifted students do not match their tested ability with comparable achievement in school.
- The College Board's Scholastic Aptitude Tests (SAT) demonstrate a virtually unbroken decline from 1963 to 1980. Average verbal scores fell over 50 points and average mathematics scores dropped nearly 40 points.

- College Board achievement tests also reveal consistent declines in recent years in such subjects as physics and English.

- Both the number and proportion of students demonstrating superior achievement on the SATs (i.e., those with scores of 650 or higher) have also dramatically declined.

- Many 17-year-olds do not possess the "higher order" intellectual skills we should expect of them. Nearly 40 percent cannot draw inferences from written material; only one-fifth can write a persuasive essay; and only one-third can solve a mathematics problem requiring several steps.

- There was a steady decline in science achievement scores of U.S. 17-year-olds as measured by national assessments of science in 1969, 1973, and 1977.

- Between 1975 and 1980, remedial mathematics courses in public 4-year colleges increased by 72 percent and now constitute one-quarter of all mathematics courses taught in those institutions.

- Average tested achievement of students graduating from college is also lower.

- Business and military leaders complain that they are required to spend millions of dollars on costly remedial education and training programs in such basic skills as reading, writing, spelling, and computation. The Department of the Navy, for example, reported to the Commission that one-quarter of its recent recruits cannot read at the ninth grade level, the minimum needed simply to understand written safety instructions. Without remedial work they cannot even begin, much less complete, the sophisticated training essential in much of the modern military.

These deficiencies come at a time when the demand for highly skilled workers in new fields is accelerating rapidly. For example:

- Computers and computer-controlled equipment are penetrating every aspect of our lives—homes, factories, and offices.

- One estimate indicates that by the turn of the century millions of jobs will involve laser technology and robotics.

- Technology is radically transforming a host of other occupations. They include health care, medical science, energy production, food processing, construction, and the building, repair and maintenance of sophisticated scientific, educational, military, and industrial equipment.

Analysts examining these indicators of student performance and the demands for new skills have made some chilling observations. Educational researcher Paul Hurd concluded at the end of a thorough national survey of student achievement that within the context of the modem scientific revolution, "We are raising a new generation of Americans that is scientifically and technologically illiterate." In a similar vein, John Slaughter a former Director of the National Science Foundation, warned of "a growing chasm between a small scientific and technological elite and a citizenry ill-informed, indeed uninformed, on issues with a science component."

But the problem does not stop there, nor do all observers see it the same way. Some worry that schools may emphasize such rudiments as reading and computation at the expense of other essential skills such as comprehension, analysis, solving problems, and drawing conclusions. Still others are concerned that an over-emphasis on technical and occupational skills will leave little time for studying the arts and humanities that so enrich daily life, help maintain civility, and develop a sense of community. Knowledge of the humanities, they maintain, must be harnessed to science and technology if the latter are to remain creative and humane, just as the humanities need to be informed by science and technology if they are to remain relevant to the human condition. Another analyst, Paul Copperman, has drawn a sobering conclusion. Until now, he has noted:

> Each generation of Americans has outstripped its parents in education,
> in literacy, and in economic attainment. For the first time in the history
> of our country, the educational skills of one generation will not surpass,
> will not equal, will not even approach, those of their parents.

It is important, of course, to recognize that *the average citizen* today is better educated and more knowledgeable than the average citizen of a generation ago—more literate, and exposed to more mathematics, literature, and science. The positive impact of this fact on the well-being of our country and the lives of our people cannot be overstated. Nevertheless, *the average graduate* of our schools and colleges today is not as well-educated as the average graduate of 25 or 35 years ago, when a much smaller proportion of our population completed high school and college. The negative impact of this fact likewise cannot be overstated.

Suggestions for Further Reading

Anderson, Lorin W. *The Effective Teacher: Study Guide and Readings.* New York: Random House, 1989.

Barnard, Henry. *Normal Schools, and Other Institutions, Agencies, and Means Designed for Professional Education of Teachers.* Hartford: Case, Tiffany and Co., 1851.

Berube, Maurice R. *Teacher Politics: The Influence of Unions.* New York: Greenwood Press, 1988.

Bestor, Arthur E., Jr. *Educational Wastelands: Retreat from Learning in Our Public Schools.* Urbana: University of Illinois Press, 1953.

Bestor, Arthur E.,Jr. *Restoration of Learning: A Program for Redeeming the Unfulfilled Promise of American Education.* New York: E.P. Dutton and Co., 1959.

Bruner, Jerome. *The Process of Education.* Cambridge: Harvard University Press, 1960.

Conant, James G. *The Education of American Teachers.* New York: McGraw-Hill Book Co., 1963.

Counts, George S. *The Social Foundations of Education.* New York: Charles Scribner's Sons, 1934.

Eaton, William E. *The American Federation of Teachers, 1916-1961.* Carbondale: Southern Illinois University Press, 1975.

Hall, Samuel. *Lectures to School-Masters on Teaching.* Boston: Carter, Hendee and Co., 1833.

Kaufman, Bel. *Up the Down Staircase.* Englewood Cliffs, NJ: Prentice-Hall, Inc., 1964.

Kidder, Tracy. *Among Schoolchildren.* Boston: Houghton Mifflin Co., 1989.

Kohl, Herbert. *The Open Classroom.* New York: Random House, 1970.

Lieberman, Ann. *Building a Professional Culture in Schools.* New York: Teachers College Press, 1988.

Maeroff, Gene I. *The Empowerment of Teachers: Overcoming the Crisis of Confidence.* New York: Teachers College Press, 1988.

Page, David P. *Theory and Practice of Teaching or the Motives and Methods of Good School-Keeping.* New York: A.S. Barnes and Co., 1885.

Parkay, Forrest W. *Becoming a Teacher: Accepting the Challenge of a Profession.* Boston: Allyn and Bacon, 1989.

Rafferty, Max. *What They Are Doing to Your Children.* New York: New American Library, 1963.

Raphael, Ray. *The Teacher's Voice: A Sense of Who We Are.* Portsmouth, NH: Heinemann, 1985.

Rickover, H. G. *Education and Freedom.* New York: E.P. Dutton and Co., 1959.

Silberman, Charles F. *Crisis in the Classroom: The Remaking of American Education.* New York: Random House, 1970.

Warren, Donald, ed. *American Teachers: Histories of a Profession at Work.* New York: Macmillan Publishing Co., 1989.

Chapter 7

Liberalizing Education

The Reformers

Introduction

The earlier chapters in this book have examined the historical development of the key institutions of American education—the elementary school, the high school, and the college and university. Our attention now turns to seven individuals who, by their work as educators, contributed to reforming education. These educators brought about important changes in our view of children, of instruction, of the curriculum, and the general purposes of education. This chapter examines the contributions of: 1. Jean Jacques Rousseau who developed a more natural and permissive view of the child. 2. Johann Heinrich Pestalozzi who devised a new approach to teaching based on using the child's senses. 3. Friedrich Froebel who developed the kindergarten as a setting for early childhood education. 4. Johann Friedrich Herbart who designed a systematic method of instruction that stressed history and literature. 5. Herbert Spencer who argued for a curriculum that emphasized science and technology. 6. Maria Montessori who devised a "prepared environment" for the education of young children. 7. John Dewey who used Pragmatist philosophy to develop an educational method based on problem solving.

Rousseau's *Emile*

Foremost among the European theorists was the French social philosopher, Jean Jacques Rousseau (1712-1778). Like other thinkers of the eighteenth-century Enlightenment, Rousseau sought to discover the laws of nature and to establish a society based on their application. In such a natural society, artificial social conventions would he eliminated and human progress would ensue. Rousseau felt that traditional schools were based on an excessive verbalism which construed education as the mastery of abstract bodies of literature. In his educational novel, *Emile*, Rousseau condemned artificial education and developed a naturalistic theory which rested on three premises: first, that nature was the great educator, instructing man through his senses; second, that instruction should be adapted to the gradually unfolding capacities of the child; third, that instruction should be active and based on the child's experiences.

Rousseau structured his educational method around five clearly defined periods of human growth: infancy, childhood, boyhood, adolescence, and youth. For each stage of development, there was an appropriate set of educational activities. In relating education to these stages, Rousseau was arguing that the whole of childhood be recognized as a legitimate and necessary sequence in human growth: "Childhood has its place in the scheme of human life. We must view the man as a man, and the child as a child."[1] In recognizing the dignity of childhood, Rousseau rejected the Calvinist conception that man was depraved and that children were conceived in sin and born in corruption. This latter concept held that the child should be treated like a miniature adult and that his propensity to evil might be exorcised through harsh discipline and external coercion. Rousseau, considering the child naturally good, held that his interests were also good and should form the basis for his education. In emphasizing the learner's interests and needs, Rousseau was anticipating the child-centered progressive educators of the twentieth century.

During infancy, from birth until age five, Rousseau described Emile as completely helpless and dependent upon others for his needs. Nature had given superabundant energy to the infant in order that he might develop physically through self-activity. Rousseau advised parents to allow the child the greatest possible freedom of movement.

Childhood, from ages five to twelve, constituted Rousseau's second stage of human development. Becoming conscious of his own personal life, the child experienced feelings of happiness and unhappiness. He was a natural egotist motivated by self-love and self-preservation. During this stage, the boy was incapable of reasoning or forming judgments. Such words as obedience, obligation, and duty were meaningless and should have no bearing on the child's education.

ROUSSEAU.

Jean Jacques Rousseau, the author of *Emile*. Charles Carleton Coffin, *Building the Nation* (New York: Harper & Brothers, 1882), p. 44.

In the third state, boyhood, twelve to fifteen, the child's strength increased more rapidly than his needs. This stage of rapid physical development indicated that the time of mental development was approaching. Following his natural curiosity, the child learned by experimenting and by making and doing. As a part of this experimentation, Rousseau urged that Emile be taught a manual skill in order that he have a proper combination of physical and manual labor.

During the fourth stage, from fifteen to eighteen, adolescence, Emile was to come to know and to live in the social order. To live in the world, the adolescent had to know how to live with others; he must be aware of the forces which motivate people. At this stage Emile was now capable of developing moral values. History, biographical exemplars, and religion were introduced as sources of moral values.

During the final stage of education, from eighteen to twenty, Emile broadened his awareness of the world by extensive travels during which he learned foreign languages, studied natural history, diverse peoples, laws and governments. Upon completion of his travels he took a wife, Sophy.

Rousseau's concept of natural education motivated other educational theorists to investigate child growth and development. These theorists, studying under the influence of the eighteenth century Enlightenment, sought to discover in nature a pattern of revealing but inflexible natural patterns of development. Among the many innovators of the period the names of three stand out especially: Johann Heinrich Pestalozzi, Friedrich Froebel, and Johann Friedrich Herbart. These men influenced the educational institutions of Europe tremendously and indirectly helped to shape the emergent American common school. In the early twentieth century, early childhood educators in the United States began to read accounts of the Montessori method of education. The work of Maria Montessori also had an impact on American education as part of the continuing trans-Atlantic interaction of educational ideas.

Johann Heinrich Pestalozzi

The famous Swiss educator was born in 1746, the second of the three surviving children of Johann Baptist Pestalozzi.[2] After his father's early death, he was raised by his mother, Susanna, and a devoted servant, Babeli, Barbara Schmid. During his growing years, young Pestalozzi was carefully sheltered from the outside world. As a result, he was socially inept and as an adult tended to be disorganized when dealing with the practicalities of life. As a youth, he attended the Collegium Humanitatis and the Collegium Carolinum, both classical Swiss schools. Though he enjoyed his studies, he felt that they had not prepared him for the real world.

Upon reaching manhood, Pestalozzi developed a number of interests, each of which absorbed him for short periods of time. His activities ranged from membership in the Helvetic Society, a Swiss patriotic organization, to farming. He was the author of numerous tracts on politics, morals, sociology, and philosophy. As politician, agriculturalist, and industrialist, he was unsuccessful.

After a long process of trial and error, he finally found his life's work in education. Familiar with the naturalistic themes of *Emile*, Pestalozzi sought to educate his son, Jean Jacques, according to Rousseau's principles. As a result of this experience, he was able to identify many of the weaknesses and strengths of Rousseau's ideas. He dedicated himself to the education of the poor and founded schools at Neuhof, Stans, Burgdorf, and Yverdon. At the last one he developed his theory of education, which was based on natural principles of sense experience.

From 1774-1779, Pestalozzi conducted an industrial school for poor children at his estate at Neuhof. He believed that the poverty-ridden Swiss peasants might be educated out of their economic and social deprivation by means of a system of instruction which combined both literacy and useful occupations. His students were engaged in learning farming, spinning, and weaving, as well as reading and arithmetic. Unrealistically, Pestalozzi believed that his primitive school could be economically self-sufficient, but this first educational venture failed. Nevertheless, he remained committed to improving the condition of the poor by developing a methodology of natural education that would regenerate society itself.

Taking a cue from Rousseau, in 1781 he, too, published a novel as a vehicle for his educational theory, *Leonard and Gertrude*.[3] The book depicted the social reformation which took place in the Swiss village of Bonal because of the insight and educational methods of a simple peasant woman, Gertrude. Pestalozzi hoped that what occurred in his mythical village would actually occur in the larger real society.

In 1798 he took charge of an orphanage at Stans, where he tried to combine moral, physical, and intellectual eduction. Unfortunately, Stans soon became a battleground between the French and the Austrians and the school was closed abruptly. The following year Pestalozzi was assigned to the village of Burgdorf where a private school, partially endowed by the Helvetian government, had been established. From 1799 until 1804, Pestalozzi labored at Burgdorf to develop a natural theory of education. As a result of his pedagogical experiments he published *How Gertrude Teaches Her Children* in 1801.[4]

When support was withdrawn from the school at Burgdorf, Pestalozzi went to Yverdon, where he conducted his most famous experimental school from 1804 until 1825. Here he established a gentle environment very different from the harsh modes of traditional schooling. Pestalozzi's school resembled a home where discipline was mild, children were treated as equals, and no one was coerced through fear. Pestalozzi believed that genuine learning could take place only within an institution where children were emotionally secure.

Since Pestalozzi's writing is obscure, systematic treatment of his educational methodology is difficult. However, certain salient features of his work appear. Holding that man was composed of moral, physical, and intellectual powers,

Pestalozzi believed that natural education should develop all three of these powers simultaneously and harmoniously.[5]

Like Rousseau, Pestalozzi believed that all knowledge comes to the human mind through sensation. He believed that conceptualization involved the following stages: one, determining the form and outline of the object; two, determining the number of objects present; three, naming the object. Pestalozzi's much imitated object lesson was based on the teaching of form, number and language and was directed to the development of the skills of measuring, numbering, and speaking rather than to the traditional literary skills of reading and writing. Only after a firm foundation had been established in form, number and language was the learner permitted to go on to these literary skills.

Basically, Pestalozzi urged that all instruction begin with the simplest elements in the learner's immediate environment and then proceed gradually to those more distant and complex, gradually culminating in abstract ideas. Pestalozzi's educational method was a forerunner of the progressive experience curriculum of the twentieth century. Following Dewey, progressive educators emphasized that all education should be based upon the learner's experience. Both Pestalozzi and Dewey opposed an education which was so abstract that it bore no relevance to the child's own experience.

Using his principle of natural education based on sense perception, Pestalozzi inaugurated changes in instructional methodology. In arithmetic, students began learning with concrete objects such as marbles or peas and then moved to an understanding of mathematical symbols and computations. In geography, the lesson began with the child's immediate environment. The child made clay models of local rivers, land forms, and topographical features and gradually began to draw maps. Treating drawing as a prelude to writing, Pestalozzi began with simple lines and then moved to more complex letters. In summary, these are the general principles of Pestalozzian methodology:

1. Sensation is the basis of all instruction.
2. Language should always be related to observation.
3. Instruction should begin with the simplest elements and gradually proceed to the abstract and complex.
4. Teachers should always respect the individuality of the learner.
5. Natural education should harmoniously develop the moral, intellectual, and physical powers of the student.

While Pestalozzi's principles may seem commonplace to the modern teacher, these were revolutionary educational concepts at the beginning of the nineteenth century. Educators flocked to Switzerland to observe the schools at Burgdorf and Yverdon. Pestalozzi's teaching assistants carried his methods to France, England, Germany, and the United States.

Pestalozzian education was first introduced to the United States under the auspices of the American philanthropist William Maclure (1763-1840). During his European travels, Maclure visited Pestalozzi's schools and was impressed with the educational practices conducted in them. Convinced that Pestalozzianism was most suited to American educational needs, Maclure decided to import the method to the United States. He reasoned that the most effective means of introducing Pestalozzian pedagogy was to bring teachers who were trained in the method to the United States from Europe.

Maclure persuaded Joseph Neef (1770-1854) to immigrate to the United States to establish Pestalozzian schools.[6] Neef, who earlier had been an assistant in Pestalozzi's school at Burgdorf, arrived in the United States in 1806. He learned English and wrote his *Sketch of a Plan and Method of Education* (1808), to serve as a prospectus for his school and to acquaint Americans with Pestalozzian education. Neef's *Sketch* had the historical distinction of being the first book on teaching methodology to be published in English in the United States. He later wrote *The Method of Instructing Children Rationally in the Arts of Writing and Reading* (1813) to illustrate further the Pestalozzian theory of education. Neef established several schools in Pennsylvania, Kentucky, and Indiana, which he conducted according to Pestalozzi's method. In 1826, he joined Maclure and the English utopian socialist Robert Owen in the communitarian experiment at New Harmony, Indiana. It was Maclure's plan that the New Harmony schools would be patterned after the Pestalozzian model and serve as an example to American educators. Along with Neef, Maclure brought other Pestalozzian disciples to New Harmony, such as Marie Duclos Fretageot and Phiquepal d'Arusmont. Quarrels between Maclure and Owen and factionalism between the participants brought the effort to a precipitate end in 1828.

Henry Barnard (1811-1900) also worked to popularize Pestalozzian education in the United States. During his European travels, Barnard had visited Pestalozzi's schools and was familiar with his method. In conducting teacher institutes in the United States, Barnard lectured on Pestalozzi's educational theory and practice. He published *Pestalozzi and Pestalozzianism*, which contained a biography of Pestalozzi, a statement of his educational philosophy, and selections from his writings.[7] Barnard also was a member of a New England educational circle that included Amos Bronson Alcott, William C. Woodbridge, and William Russell, who sought to incorporate Pestalozzianism into their educational writing and experiments.

In the second half of the nineteenth century, the work of Edward A. Sheldon (1823-1897), at New York's Oswego Normal School was the major phase of the Pestalozzian movement in the United States.[8] Sheldon, Superintendent of the Oswego Normal School, trained American teachers in the methodology of object training which was based on Pestalozzi's admonition that all knowledge began with sensation and that instruction should be based on real objects. Sheldon and his associates, Margaret Jones, an English Pestalozzian, and Herman Krusi, Jr., the son of one of Pestalozzi's teaching assistants, developed an extensive program of teacher preparation, based on object lessons. Sheldon also published books of lesson plans based on the sensory examination of a number of common objects. Unfortunately, his "lessons on glass, water, and coal" were only very formalized versions of the original Pestalozzian approach. The Oswego method captured the attention of American educators and in 1865 the National Teacher's Association Committee on Object Training reported:

> Whenever this system has been confined to elementary instruction and has been employed by skillful, thorough teachers, in unfolding and disciplining the faculties, in fixing the attention and awakening thought, it has been successful.[9]

For Sheldon, education was to lead children to describe accurately the objects found in their learning environment. He told teachers to base instruction on concrete objects, to use the child's senses actively in the learning process, and to connect concepts gained through sensation to the appropriate words to facilitate the child's mastery of language.[10]

Although the Oswego method was not natural education as it had been conceived of by Pestalozzi and elaborated on by Joseph Neef, Sheldon's influence on teacher training was pronounced. The object lesson, as developed by the Oswego educators, became the dominant educational method used in American schools in the second half of the nineteenth century. Sheldon's work at Oswego improved the preparation of common school teachers. Although it was a formalized version of Pestalozzianism, Sheldon's object lesson was an improvement over the recitation of memorized lessons. The object lesson methodology helped to provide teachers with an organized plan of instruction that gave them greater control over the learning process. Thus Pestalozzi, though often unsuccessful in this other ventures, earned a place in the history of education by developing a methodology that liberalized instruction by rejecting sterile, rote memorization and dogmatic indoctrination, and by placing in its stead an organized, albeit simplified, approach to teaching and learning problems.

Friedrich Froebel

Friedrich Froebel (1782-1852) was another of the many visitors drawn to the Pestalozzian school at Yverdon. A native of southern Germany, Froebel, like his Swiss mentor Pestalozzi, had experienced many "dark nights of the soul" as he sought the vocation which would provide him with direction and purpose. As a youth, he studied religion, and was always somewhat drawn to mysticism. Later, as a university student at Gottingen, he studied physics, chemistry, mineralogy, and natural history. His investigations of natural science produced in him a deep love of nature, which he interpreted within the context of philosophic Idealism. Although he worked variously as a forester, an accountant, a surveyor, and a museum assistant, none of these vocations satisfied him.

At the age of twenty-three, Froebel decided to become a schoolteacher and obtained a position in the Pestalozzian Institute at Frankfort. Here he met Anton Gruner, a disciple of Pestalozzi, and became convinced that an educational career would give meaning to his life. After several years of study with Gruner, Froebel went to Yverdon, where he observed Pestalozzi's educational experiments.

Although impressed with his innovations, Froebel believed the Pestalozzian method needed refinement. In 1816, he founded a school at Keilhau where he hoped to work out his own system. In 1831 he went back to Switzerland to become an instructor in teacher education. In 1837 he returned to Germany, where he established his first kindergarten in the village of Blankenburg. As a result of these experiments he wrote his most important pedagogical work, *The Education of Man*, in which he defined education as "...leading man, as a thinking, intelligent being, growing into self-consciousness, to a pure and unsullied, conscious and free representation of the inner law of Divine Unity, and in teaching him ways and means thereto."[11]

For Froebel, a mystical idealist, there was a spark of the Divine present in all people. The process of child growth and development was the unfolding and the externalization of this essence. Growth was the process of unfolding according to a built-in design in much the same way as the flower bud unfolds as the blossom or the oak tree unfolds from the acorn. The educator was not to interfere with the natural unfolding of the child's self-activity in the environment of the kindergarten—a child's garden.

Froebel regarded the child's play as an important form of self-activity. For children, play was simply their natural way of living. Further, play furnished an important form of socialization of children with their peer group. Hence, the kindergarten was an institution based on play.

Froebel's Gifts and Occupations

Froebel arranged a series of gifts and occupations to provide the core of the kindergarten program. Paramount among the series of gifts to encourage the child's development was the ball. According to Froebel's mystical

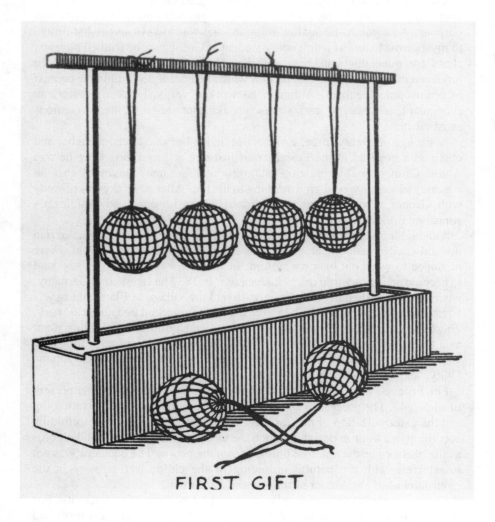

FIRST GIFT

An illustration of Froebel's first kindergarten gift from a nineteenth century catalog of school materials.

conception of child growth, the ball was the first plaything of the child's development. The ball represented the spherical nature of the world and epitomized the concept of the unity of mankind with the Absolute Reality. The sphere was an undifferentiated unity; the other symbols were derived from the ball but still retained a unity of origin in it. Other symbolic gifts were the cube, the brick, the surface, and the point.[12] The Froebelian occupation was designed to involve the child in working with construction materials such as paper, clay, or thread. Occupations such as needlework, sewing, or weaving furnished opportunities for the child to engage in purposeful activity.

The Kindergarten

While the gifts and occupations and their attendant symbolism have been discarded by modern educators as mysticism, major elements of Froebel's ideas have remained to become a definite contribution to education.[13] First, he stressed the spiritual nature of the child as a precious human being. Along with Pestalozzi's work, Froebel's concept of the child as a child helped to render obsolete the doctrine of child depravity. Second, Froebel's emphasis on play, games, and songs liberated school practices. Today, nursery play is designed to awaken in children their first awareness of human relationships and social interaction. Third, Froebelian pedagogy stimulated the examination of child growth and development.

The kindergarten initially was brought to the United States by immigrants who left Germany after the failure of the revolution of 1848. Margarethe Meyer Schurz (1834-1879), the wife of Karl Schurz, is credited with opening the first kindergarten for German-speaking children in Watertown, Wisconsin in 1856. Caroline Louise Frankenburg, who had been trained by Froebel, also established a number of kindergartens in Ohio and Pennsylvania that served German-speaking communities. In cities such as Milwaukee and St. Louis, where the German-American population was concentrated, Froebel's kindergarten principles were used as part of the curriculum for the younger children who attended bilingual schools.

Henry Barnard, who popularized Pestalozzian education in his *American Journal of Education*, also was an enthusiastic advocate of Froebel's kindergarten. While attending the International Exhibit of Educational Systems in London in 1854, Barnard had the opportunity to see a display of kindergarten materials. He afterwards praised Froebel's principles for their usefulness in early childhood education.[14]

Elizabeth Peabody (1808-1898), a leading pioneer in kindergarten education in the United States, established an English language kindergarten in Boston in 1860. After studying Froebelian pedagogy in Europe, she dedicated her life to advancing kindergarten principles through lecturing, writing, and editing the *Kindergarten Messenger*.

William T. Harris, the Superintendent of schools in St. Louis, was attracted to the Froebelian method on both philosophical and educational grounds. Harris, like Froebel, was a philosophical Idealist, who believed that the kindergarten was the ideal institution to externalize the child's potentialities. Due to his advocacy of Froebelian education, the kindergarten became part of the St. Louis public school system in 1873. Susan Blow (1843-1916) worked with Harris in St. Louis, where she assisted in training teachers in kindergarten methods. By the turn of the century, other school systems followed the example set by St. Louis and incorporated the kindergarten as part of the public school. By 1900, it is estimated that approximately 5,000 kindergartens were functioning throughout the United States.[15]

Johann Friedrich Herbart

Still another important educator of the nineteenth century was Johann Friedrich Herbart (1776-1841) a German philosopher and psychologist.[16] He, too, visited Pestalozzi, staying at the Swiss educator's school in Burgdorf in 1799. Herbart was much more emotionally stable than Pestalozzi or Froebel, and not as romantic as they or Rousseau in his educational theory. Herbart devoted himself to the systematic study of philosophy, and applied his keen sense of logic to a critical analysis of the process of education. During his life he was professor of philosophy at the Universities of Gottingen and Konigsburg. As a part of his teaching duties he developed a series of lectures of pedagogy, from which he derived his theory and practice of education. As a university professor, he was most concerned with their usefulness and application to education on the secondary and higher levels. He wrote two books that were major contributions to pedagogy: *The Science of Education*, 1806, and *Outlines of Educational Doctrine*, 1835. Both these sources offer some indications of the elements of his theory.

Like most educational theorists, Herbart regarded the ultimate goal of education as that of moral development. His idea of the end product of education, the "cultured man," comprised five basic elements of morality: freedom, perfection, good will, righteousness, and retribution. To develop as a moral person, the student was provided with the broadest possible range of experience.

Herbart conceived of interest as an internal tendency that facilitated the retention of an idea in consciousness or contributed to its return to consciousness. The power of interests increased with the frequency with which an idea was presented to consciousness and with the association of ideas in what Herbart called the "apperceptive mass." Basing his reasoning upon the doctrine of "many-sidedness of interests" and "apperceptive mass," Herbart arrived at two pedagogical laws: frequency and association. The teachers were to stress by repeated presentation those ideas which they wanted to dominate the student's life, and then point out the similarities between clusters of ideas.

Since he considered morality the final aim of education, Herbart emphasized the humanistic studies of history and literature. If history were taught as the study of the lives of great people, it could provide students with illustrative examples of how to behave. Students could study the historical models and seek to imitate the virtues exemplified by each one. In addition to providing models of value, history and literature also formed a cultural base around which other subject matter was to be correlated. For example, religious events and scientific discoveries could be placed in a historical context. Herbart's concern with literature and history encouraged the inclusion of these studies into the curriculum at a time when secondary education was still dominated by Greek, Latin, and mathematics.

From his logical-psychological researches Herbart concluded that the mind assimilated all ideas in the same way. It was therefore possible to arrive at one methodology of instruction which would be suitable for any subject. Although Herbart's original system was divided into four steps—clarity, association, system, and method—his interpreters established five clearly defined phases of teaching method:[17]

1. *Preparation.* During this first stage, the students' minds were prepared for the assimilation of the new idea into their apperceptive mass. Past ideas, experiences, and other memories were recalled and related to the new idea being introduced in the lesson. This was designed to bring the student into a state of readiness for the lesson.

2. *Presentation.* During the second stage the new idea was actually presented to the student. The teacher's instruction was to be so clear and definite that the student completely understood the new idea.

3. *Association.* The new idea was compared and contrasted with ideas which the student already knew. This step was to facilitate assimilation of the new idea by associating it with familiar and related ideas.

4. *Generalization.* A general definition or principle was formed upon the basis of the combined new and old learning.

5. *Application.* The last step tested the principle with appropriate problems and exercises.

Herbart's educational theory won wide acceptance among American educators during the late nineteenth century. From 1880 to 1900, it was popularized by such leading educators as Charles de Garmo, Charles McMurry, and Frank McMurry. De Garmo's *The Essentials of Method* (1889) and *Herbart and the Herbartians* (1895) were major vehicles in introducing Herbart's ideas to American teachers. In 1895, the National Herbart Society for the Scientific Study of Teaching was launched. The Herbartian influence was most pronounced in the normal schools and teachers colleges where it provided a systematic approach to teacher preparation. As a theoretical rationale for the study of education, it contributed to the academic acceptance of pedagogy as a university discipline. As a practical teaching method, the five Herbartian steps were used by many teachers as a systematic guide to the organization of classroom instruction. During the era in which they dominated teacher education, the American Herbartians introduced several major ideas that had a significant impact on education in the United States. For example, they asserted that the major purpose of education was to develop the sense of ethical character in the young. They emphasized the role of history and literature in conveying ethical concepts in the curriculum.[18] Their approach to the orderly and sequential structuring of instruction led to lesson planning in the form of units.

The positive Herbartian contribution to American education was threefold: their emphasis on history and literature as a cultural core helped to enrich the curriculum; their logically structured methodology encouraged precise lesson planning; they influenced the organization of subject matter content in relationship to educational methodology. On the negative side, Herbartian influence imposed a precise, rigid approach to the process of instruction. Because it emphasized the role of the teacher as planner, presenter of material, and source of information, the student's function became the passive one of receiving information. Herbartianism overemphasized the past to the neglect of the present and its problems. Finally, its exaggeration of formal methodology stifled creativity.

Herbert Spencer

Herbert Spencer (1820-1903) was an English sociologist who enjoyed great popularity in the United States in the late nineteenth century.[19] Spencer sought to apply Charles Darwin's theory of evolution to society and to education. A staunch advocate of the importance of science, he also sought to construct a more modern curriculum that met the needs of an industrial economy and society.

According to Darwin, the various species evolved very slowly over thousands of years. Individuals of certain species who developed favorable characteristics that enhanced their survival were able to successfully adapt to environmental changes. As their offspring inherited these favorable characteristics, they continued the life of the species. The unfit who were unable to adapt successfully eventually perished. Spencer applied Darwin's concept of "survival of the fittest" to the social and economic competition of human beings.

According to Spencer's sociological theory, human society had developed by an evolutionary series of stages that changed it from simple kinship and tribal forms of group life to the complex and modern industrial nation. In a similar manner, human life sustaining activities also evolved from the primitive survival skills of hunting and fishing to the more specialized economic activities required in an industrialized society. Spencer developed his theory of "Social Darwinism" in the last half of the nineteenth century when the industrial revolution was transforming western societies into more complex social systems. An industrialized economy required vocational and professional education of a scientific and technological nature rather than the inherited curriculum based on classical studies.

Spencer's ethical philosophy asserted that the fittest individuals of each generation would survive because of their skill, intelligence, and adaptability to change. Competition would bring about human progress. If allowed to compete without government interference, the fittest would eventually inherit the earth and populate it with their intelligent, diligent, and productive offspring. No action should be taken that interfered with the process of natural selection. The unfit—the lazy, dull, stupid, and weak—like their counterparts among the animals were doomed to eventual extinction. According to Spencer's theory of the survival of the fittest, individual competition would bring about socioeconomic progress.

As a constant advocate of science and technology, Spencer was a persistent critic of the inherited curriculum based on theology, speculative philosophy, and the Greek and Latin classics. For Spencer, the curriculum should be changed to emphasize scientific subjects that facilitated the application of knowledge to practical economic, political, and social affairs. Opposing memorization and rote learning, Spencer argued that the curriculum should prepare people to master the activities needed to earn a living. As a former engineer, he believed that knowledge should be applied to industry, commerce, government, and society. Like Pestalozzi, Spencer wanted learning based on sensory experience that involved the learner with the actual objects found in the environment.

Spencer proposed that the physical, biological, and social sciences be included in the curriculum. Further, his pioneering design for a functional curriculum was based on identifying and classifying the human activities that sustain life. Education should prepare individuals to perform these necessary activities scientifically and efficiently.[20] Spencer's curriculum was organized around five major human activities:

1. Those directly needed for bodily health and self-preservation.

2. Those related to employment and earning a living that indirectly supported self-preservation.

3. Those needed for parenting.

4. Those needed for political and social life.

5. Those of an aesthetic and recreational nature that related to leisure.

Spencer gave a basic emphasis to the activities needed for self-preservation. Since physical health was needed to perform other human activities, students should have knowledge of the human body and its care to combat disease and promote wellness. More indirectly supporting life were the economic, occupational, and professional activities of earning a living. Spencer also recognized that the basic tool skills of reading, writing, and numeracy were indispensable basics in education. Further, people living in industrial societies needed the technical skills and scientific knowledge that contributed to industrial efficiency. Thus, the physical, biological, and social sciences as well as the applied sciences needed to have an important place in the curriculum.

To prepare students for social and political participation, Spencer emphasized the importance of sociology, his own field of expertise. He discounted the importance of narrative history as providing useless information about the succession of kings and queens, accounts of battles, and details of treaties. Much more important, he reasoned, sociology provided useful information about social class, mobility, and change. Sociology held an explanatory and predictive value that could be used in policy-making. Of course, for Spencer, the confirmed Social Darwinist, the best policy was one of noninterference with the process of natural selection. For Spencer, art, poetry, and literature were the least important areas of the curriculum. Such aesthetic activities, he felt, were for leisure and did not relate to earning a living or to economic productivity.

As an educational theorist, Spencer's greatest contribution was as a pioneer in the field of curriculum development. Rather than basing the process of curriculum construction around inherited subject matters, Spencer argued that it should be based on important human activities. His views on curriculum, which were widely circulated in the United States, influenced the work of the NEA Commission on the Reorganization of Secondary Education that published the Seven Cardinal Principles of Education in 1918. Modern curriculum designers still use Spencer's argument that the curriculum should be based on human activities as an organizing principle for their work.

Maria Montessori

The life and career of Maria Montessori (1870-1952) represents an episode in the continuing international interchange of educational ideas. Like Pestalozzi,

Maria Montessori. Dorothy Canfield Fisher, *A Montessori Mother* (New York: Henry Holt and Co.), 1912.

Froebel, Herbart, and Spencer, Montessori was a European educator who exerted an important influence on American education. Born of middle class parents in the town of Chiaravalle in Italy, her early schooling was characterized by her strong desire for technical and scientific education which was then regarded as inappropriate for girls of the upper Italian middle classes. She enrolled in a pre-engineering course in a technical school where she developed an interest in the study of biology and medicine. After completing secondary education, she enrolled in the University of Rome to study medicine and psychology. Montessori had the distinction of being the first woman in Italy to earn the degree of doctor of medicine which was awarded to her in 1896.[21]

Because of her medical background and interest in early childhood education, Montessori came to the attention of the Italian Ministry of Education. She was appointed directress of the state orthophrenic school that was established in Rome in 1899 as an experimental institution to train mentally deficient children. To prepare herself for her work, she carefully reviewed the research of Jean Itard and Eduard Seguin, two French physicians, who had studied the education of mentally impaired children. In particular, she was influenced by Seguin's concept that mentally defective children possessed dormant powers that could be stimulated by activities and materials designed to awaken their muscular and mental faculties.

In 1908, Montessori, at the invitation of the Roman Housing Association, established a children's school, the *Casa dei Bambini*, for the disadvantaged children who lived in the slums of Rome. From her work with these children, Montessori gained a number of pedagogical insights. Her basic working premise was that the educator should recognize and respect the personality of the child. Children, she found, enjoyed order and preferred work over play. They enjoyed repeating actions until they had mastered a given skill.

Montessori developed a biological and psychological perspective into child development. Of particular importance were the years from birth until age six which she identified as the stage of the "absorbent mind." At crucial periods of growth and development in a child's life, certain "sensitive periods" occurred. To train the child during these sensitive periods, she devised a series of exercises of practical life and a set of didactic materials to be used in a structured environment. The activities of practical life consisted of various activities such as washing the hands, hanging up clothing, and serving lunch. These practical activities were to be performed by the child to foster his or her independence and self-reliance. Sensory activities developed the senses and improved muscular coordination. Children were introduced to the alphabet through the use of unmounted, movable sandpaper letters. Reading was taught after writing. Colored rods of various sizes were used to teach measuring and counting.

Montessori also developed a number of didactic, or preplanned instructional materials, to stimulate the child's sensory awareness and muscular coordination. Among these were the lacing and buttoning frames, weights, and packets to be identified by their sound or smell. The didactic materials can be illustrated by the example of sets of cylinders which the children arranged in various ways. Some cylinders were arranged in positions based on their decreasing diameter; others were to be arranged according to decreasing height; and still others according to increasing diameter and height. The materials were self-correcting in that the child, to complete the exercise correctly, had to position the cylinders in the appropriate spaces provided for them.[22] These didactic materials were designed to help the child make comparisons between objects, to form judgments, and to reach decisions.

Since children were really their own self-teachers, the Montessori-trained teacher was called a directress. The directress was to observe children, direct their activities, and facilitate the learning process. Since the child in the Montessori school was involved primarily in individualized activity, the directresses concentrated their attention on each child rather than on group-centered teaching and learning. Most importantly, children were to follow their own spontaneous and natural development.

The first important notice of Montessori's method in the United States came in 1911 when *McClure's Magazine* praised Montessori as "An Educational Wonder-Worker" for her pedagogical insights, her use of sensory training, and her ability to stimulate children to "explode" into reading and writing.[23] A series of articles in *McClure's* on Montessorianism generated an enthusiastic response among American physicians, psychologists, and educators. Also in 1911, Anne E. George, an American teacher, who had studied with Montessori, established a Montessori school in Tarrytown, New York, for children between the ages of two and nine. The acclaim given to Montessorian education stimulated the organization of the Montessori Educational Association in 1913. The Association gained the active support of a number of prominent Americans such as Alexander Graham Bell, A.S. McClure, Dorothy Fisher, and Margaret Wilson, the daughter of the President. Under the auspices of the Association, Maria Montessori came to the United States to lecture on her method.

The initial American interest in Montessorianism occurred at the same time that progressivism was an influential movement in the United States. The progressives were generally critical of the Montessori method; one of their leaders, William H. Kilpatrick, wrote *The Montessori System Examined* (1914) which challenged the method.[24] Kilpatrick charged that Montessori's observations of childhood development were superficial and unscientific. He attacked the method as failing to provide the group work needed to socialize the child. Further, Kilpatrick claimed that the overly structured didactic materials failed to stimulate the child's imagination and creativity. The attack of Kilpatrick and other leading progressives blunted the enthusiasm for the Montessori method in the United States and caused it to lose its popularity.

In the late 1950s, a marked revival of interest in the Montessori method occurred in the United States. A leader in the Montessori renaissance was Nancy Rambusch, who after being trained in the method in Europe, returned to the United States to establish the Whitby School in Greenwich, Connecticut. The revitalization of the Montessori approach gained such a receptive audience that by the early 1970s over one thousand Montessori schools were flourishing throughout the United States.[25]

The renewed popularity of Montessorianism in the United States after a period of dormancy of over forty years is an interesting educational phenomenon. Several explanations can be offered for the Montessori revival. First, the late 1950s were a time of discontent with both traditional and progressive school practices. Many parents were seeking a method that emphasized early intellectual development rather than the socialization that some progressive schools emphasized. There was also dissatisfaction with conventional kindergarten and primary education due to an alleged lack of discipline and neglect of basic academic skills. Second, the growing concern for the education of disadvantaged children in the 1960s was also a stimulus for the Montessori revival. Montessori had worked, herself, among the slum children of Rome and her method seemed well suited to pre-primary and head start programs of early childhood education. It should be pointed out, however, that the Montessori approach is generally found operating at the preschool level among two-to six-year-olds. It has not made any major inroads into the public schools. Nevertheless, the Montessori method is one of the most popular approaches to early childhood education in contemporary America.

John Dewey: Pragmatism and Problem Solving

In addition to the European educators treated in this chapter, the American philosopher, John Dewey (1859-1952) exerted a great influence on the course of American and world education. Dewey was one of the originators of pragmatism, a philosophy that asserted that ideas needed to be tested in human experience and evaluated according to their consequences in affecting human affairs. Dewey's pragmatism, which was also called experimentalism or instrumentalism, was a departure from the more traditional philosophies based on speculative or metaphysical notions about the nature of ultimate reality. The term "experimentalism" meant that human beings should use the laboratory method, or the experimental process of science, in making decisions. "Instrumentalism" meant that the human being was an instrument designer who developed tools to alter or transform the environment. In his books and lectures, Dewey, a professor of philosophy, sought to apply his pragmatic thought to a wide range of issues that included education.

Dewey was a prolific and productive author of books and articles dealing with philosophy, education, and social issues. In 1898, he wrote, *The School and Society*, a description of his experiment at the Laboratory School he founded at the University of Chicago. His *How We Think*, in 1910, stressed problem-solving according to the scientific method as the mode of complete thought. Dewey's *Democracy and Education*, published in 1916, presented his systematic analysis of education in a democratic society. For Dewey, genuine education should be democratic. This view of democracy did not mean that education was intrinsically related to a particular form of political organization. Rather, a democratic milieu for educational activities meant that the learning process was open-ended. The learner was free to experiment, to formulate tentative statements that guided activity, and free from coercion that blocked freedom of inquiry. In Dewey's democratic vista of education, the educational process itself was free of predetermined goals and ends. The sole purpose of education, Dewey wrote, was human growth and development. His *Individualism, Old and New*, written in 1929 on the eve of the Great Depression, was a penetrating study of social change. In modern society, Dewey argued, no person was an island but rather was part of a vast social complex of shared meanings and activities. The role of education in a modern society was to help create a sense of community that reduced the isolation and alienation that many persons experienced in the massiveness of urban life. *Art as Experience*, in 1934, presented Dewey's analysis on the aesthetic dimension of life. Art should not be divided into the fine and practical arts but should be an integrated public expression of human aesthetic expression.

Dewey's Educational Theory

To appreciate Dewey's impact on education, it is necessary to examine some key elements of his philosophy. Dewey's pragmatism, or experimentalism, was influenced in part by his exposure to Hegelian idealism and to Darwinism at formative stages in his own education. As a graduate student in philosophy at the Johns Hopkins University, Dewey studied under the direction of professors who were Hegelian idealists. The philosophy of Hegel, a German idealist, was especially popular in the late nineteenth century. The Hegelians believed that the increasingly complex patterns of social life expressed the unfolding of the Absolute, a great macrocosmic Idea, in the course of human history. Although Dewey later abandoned Hegelian idealism's intricate speculative metaphysics, he continued to believe that human beings were capable of devising more complex and integrated modes of shared experiences and social interrelationships. Education should, he argued, contribute to creating a great society, a complete human community.

Even more important than Hegelianism in Dewey's emerging philosophy was Darwin's evolutionary theory. Darwin's theory postulated an ever-changing environment in which the organism lives, adjusts, and adapts in order to survive. The terms "organism" and "environment" were used by Dewey in structuring his educational philosophy. The organism is an active creature, physiologically composed of living tissue, which possesses a set of drives or impulses that seek to maintain life. Every organism lives in an environment, a habitat, that contains elements that nourishes and sustains its life but also threatens it.

The terms organism and environment, for Dewey, were applicable to all forms of life, including human life. Physiologically and psychologically, the human being as an organism had some advantages in interacting with the environment. Possessing a highly developed brain, walking upright, and having a thumb and movable forefinger, the human being was capable of transforming the environment and not merely reacting to environmental changes. The drives and impulses that were life sustaining could be reflected upon and used to make the environment more satisfying and hospitable. The human being was also an instrument and toolmaker who could use thought and action to alter, transform, and reconstruct the environment. Life was, in Dewey's view, an ongoing episodic series of transformative interactions between human beings and their environment. These interactions constituted what Dewey called "experience." Education was a process of intelligently and reflectively using experience for human growth and development. Followers of Dewey's pragmatic philosophy would translate his ideas into pedagogical strategies such as "learning through experience," "learning by doing," and using the experimental method as the basic instructional strategy.

Dewey's philosophy of education was highly social. The human being inhabits a social as well as physical environment. Humans are communicating social creatures who have formed groups that cooperatively work at transforming the environment. This shared human experience, based on mutuality of interests, creates a social intelligence that enriches and adds to the fund of human experience. For Dewey, human beings with their mutual interests and needs have common problems. In solving these common problems, they create common instruments. Language, or shared communication, is a means of discussing the interests and needs of common life. It is upon the commonality or mutuality of interests that community itself arises. Dewey described the school as a little or "embryonic" community which would lead the young to life and participation in the larger community. Schooling, in Experimentalist terms, meant that children by sharing their ideas and working to resolve mutual problems would become community creators.

For Dewey, education, especially organized education or schooling, is an agency of cultural continuity, reconstruction, and renewal. Schools are deliberately created social institutions by which a particular society transmits its inherited cultural heritage or experience from its mature, or adult, members, to its immature members, its children. Without this deliberate cultural transmission from adult to child, each generation would be forced to begin its cultural life anew. Organized education is, in Dewey's terms, the process of introducing children to their culture by providing them with the skills and knowledge needed for communication and participation in the group's cultural life. While this transmission implied a function for schooling that was culturally conservative, Dewey's version of the school was not meant to perpetuate the cultural status quo. Dewey also perceived education as a force for bringing about cultural renewal, change, and reform.

For Dewey, the school, as society's organized education for the enculturation of the young, has a threefold function to simplify, purify, and balance the cultural heritage which it transmits to the immature. In simplifying the complexity of the cultural heritage, the school selects those cultural elements that are valuable for children to know and experience. It reduces their complexity into units that children can experience according to their readiness and previously acquired fund of knowledge. The school acts to purify by identifying and transmitting those elements of the culture that have the greatest educational and social value and eliminating those that are personally and socially detrimental to human growth. It, then, balances the selected and purified cultural elements by integrating them into a harmonious totality.

The Complete Act of Thought

For Dewey, the scientific method, broadly conceived, is the most effective and intelligent process of thinking and of learning. Dewey called the scientific method the "complete act of thought." As a pragmatist, he believed that ideas could be validated only by testing them in action and judging them by their consequences on human experience. He structured the "complete act of thought," or problem-solving according to the scientific method, into a process of five sequential steps. Just as the scientific method was the most effective way to think, it was equally effective as an instructional method. Dewey's problem-solving method follows:

1. *The problematic situation.* The individual experiences perplexity, confusion, and doubt as a result of involvement in an incomplete situation whose full character is undetermined. The individual's activity is blocked by an obstacle which is new and different from prior experience.

2. *Defining the problem.* To resolve the problem, the individual needs to locate and identify the obstacle or difficulty and determine its particular characteristics.

3. *Analyzing and researching the problem.* The individual now undertakes to analyze the problem by careful research. This kind of research involves reflection on previous experience, the consultation of sources, and the general gathering of appropriate information that relates to the problem.

4. *Conjecturing hypothetical and tentative solutions to the problem.* Based upon research into the problem, the individual thinks of or conjectures possible actions that can be taken to resolve the problem. These tentative solutions take the form of hypothetical solutions. Such tentative statements usually are expressed in hypothetical terms, such as, if I do this, then the following is likely to result.

5. *Testing the preferred solution.* The individual now selects and acts on the plan that promises a preferred solution to the problem. If the problem is solved, then the individual resumes activity until encountering another problem.[26]

Educators who used Dewey's complete act of thought often referred to it as "learning by doing," the "activity method," or the "laboratory method." Students were to be involved in solving problems that arose from their interests and experience rather than predigested academic subject matters. In using the problem-solving method, however, students, through their research into problems, were led to investigate and use bodies of knowledge. Teachers who used the problem-solving method anticipated that students would learn to use the process as a mode of thinking that could be applied to situations in school and in life. As they used the process, they would investigate and use knowledge by applying it to solving problems. Thus, both the process of thinking and the content of thought would be fused and integrated rather than compartmentalized.

As students used the scientific approach to problem solving, they were disciplining themselves. According to Dewey's view, discipline was internal to the task being performed or came from what was required to solve a problem rather than from an external source. In traditional school settings, discipline was often administered by teachers in the form of rewards or punishments that were external to the task or problem. Traditional educators held that such externally administered discipline would eventually be internalized by the students. Disagreeing, Dewey argued that genuine discipline was intrinsic to the task and came from the requirements needed to solve the problem. Rather than providing external coercion, the teacher who followed Dewey's approach to learning acted as a guide and facilitator by suggesting resources that could be used to solve problems.

As students learned to discipline themselves by using the scientific method, they also learned to work together in groups. The importance of shared experience and the mutuality of interests in solving common problems was important in developing a sense of community. This social dimension was an important part of the democratic process. As a member of the group, the individual learned to cooperate with others, to discuss, to deliberate, and to act in concert with others. The cooperative act, based on open discussion, was at the heart of the democratic method.

Dewey believed that education had no external ends. For him, the end of education was simply human growth that led to still more growth and development. Growth involved the ability to interrelate particular experiences into a totality or a network of experience. Knowledge gained through experience in solving problems meant that education, like life, was a process of a continuous reconstruction of experience.

Dewey's Laboratory School

The implementation of Dewey's experimentalism can be seen in his work at the Laboratory School of the University of Chicago which he directed from 1896 to 1904. Here, Dewey operationalized his philosophy by using it to establish the curriculum of the school and to guide the learning of the children who attended it. Dewey's own books, *The School and Society*, 1899, and *The Child and the Curriculum*, 1902, provide some insights into the method used at the Laboratory School. Dewey wanted his students to explore and to gain control over their environment. By solving personal, social, and intellectual problems, children developed their intelligence and problem-solving capabilities. In an important sense, the Laboratory School was also a true educational laboratory. It was a place where educational ideas could be tested in practice and disseminated to the larger community of educators.[27]

Dewey detailed three levels of learning activities to be used at the Laboratory School. In the first level, children were to exercise their senses and develop physical coordination. The second level involved children in using materials and tools that were part of the environment. The school's environment needed to have an abundant store of the materials and resources that excited children's interests and stimulated them in constructive, experimental, and creative activities. The third stage found children actively using their intelligence to discover, examine, and use ideas. Through these three levels of learning, children moved from impulsive behavior to a more reflective mode of observing situations, planning activities, and conjecturing the consequences of possible actions.[28]

The children enrolled in Dewey's Laboratory School investigated a variety of problems. For example, the seven-year-old children examined ores and metals and constructed their own kiln. Those who were eight years old engaged in natural science experiments with air currents, gravitation, weights and measures and examined the relationship of the earth to the sun. The nine-year-olds extended their concepts of space by working on projects that related to the topography and river systems of the United States, problems of soil erosion, and geological formations.

An interesting firsthand account of Dewey's work at the Laboratory School has been provided by Katherine Mayhew and Anna Edwards who were teachers at the school. In their book, *The Dewey School*, they wrote ". . . the chief object is to secure a free and informal community life in which each child will feel that he has a share and his own work to do." In the school, the emphasis was on "forms of practical and constructive activity" that appealed to the children's "social sense" and "regard for thorough and honest work."[29]

At the Laboratory School, several key features of Dewey's experimentalism were evident. First, the emphasis on shared participation, discussion, and decision-making was important. Group discussion led to a sharing or pooling of experience. Second, the ideas developed in discussion were actually tested in the children's experiments. Third, teachers acted to facilitate the problem solving process.

After Dewey left the University of Chicago and its Laboratory School, he devoted himself to teaching and writing in philosophy and philosophy of education. As a professor at Columbia University, he wrote many of his books and articles on experimentalism. Dewey's philosophy of education exerted a profound influence on American education and on the new directions that education was taking in the twentieth century.

Conclusion

The educational ideas of Rousseau, Pestalozzi, Froebel, Herbart, Montessori and Dewey were important sources of educational change. While there were others who contributed to shaping the contours of educational theory and practice, these individuals, in many respects, were pioneering figures who developed important insights into the field. Rousseau, for example, developed new insights into child nature and stages of development. Pestalozzi designed instructional methods that redirected teaching and learning into more naturalistic patterns that stressed children's direct sensory experience. Froebel's kindergarten focused attention on the importance of early childhood as a formative period in human growth and development. Herbart's formal instructional steps provided teachers, especially those being prepared in normal schools, with a useful and effective teaching strategy. Spencer's work was a pioneering statement of sociology of education and of a design for a more functional type of curriculum. Montessori was an educator whose approach to education found a worldwide audience. John Dewey, America's preeminent philosopher of education, developed experimentalism as an educational philosophy that emphasized the laboratory method and problem solving. These theorists produced fundamental changes in how we think about education.

Notes

[1] William Boyd, *The Emile of Jean Jacques Rousseau: Selections* (New York: Teachers College Press, Teachers College, Columbia University, 1966), p. 34.

[2] An account of Pestalozzi's career is Robert B. Downs, *Heinrich Pestalozzi: Father of Modern Pedagogy* (Boston: Twayne Publishers, 1975).

[3] Johann H. Pestalozzi, *Leonard and Gertrude*, trans. Eva Channing (Boston: D.C. Heath and Co., 1907).

[4] Johann H. Pestalozzi, *How Gertrude Teaches Her Children*, trans. Lucy E. Holland and Francis Turner (London: Swan Sonnenschein and Co., 1907).

[5] Gerald L. Gutek, *Pestalozzi and Education* (New York: Random House, Inc., 1968), p. 95.

[6] For a treatment of Neef's career, see Gerald L. Gutek, *Joseph Neef: The Americanization of Pestalozzianism* (University, AL: University of Alabama Press, 1978).

[7] Henry Barnard, *Pestalozzi and Pestalozzianism* (New York: F.C. Brownell Co., 1862).

[8] Ned H. Dearborn, *The Oswego Movement in American Education* (New York: Teachers College, Columbia University, 1925).

[9] Will Seymour Monroe, *History of the Pestalozzian Movement in the United States* (Syracuse, NY: C.W. Bardeen Publisher, 1907), pp. 183-184.

[10] Edward A. Sheldon, *Lessons on Objects* (New York: Charles Scribner's Sons, 1863), p. 22.

[11] Friedrich Froebel, *The Education of Man*, trans. W.N. Hailmann (New York: Appleton and Co., 1896), p. 1.

[12] Kate D. Wiggin and Nora A. Smith, *Froebel's Gifts* (Boston: Houghton Mifflin Company, 1896), pp. 6-30.

[13] William Heard Kilpatrick, *Froebel's Kindergarten Principles: Critically Examined* (New York: The Macmillan Company, 1916), pp. 195-200.

[14] Evelyn Weber, *The Kindergarten: Its Encounter with Educational Thought in America* (New York: Teachers College Press, Columbia University, 1969), p. 24.

[15] Nina C. Vandewalker, *The Kindergarten in American Education* (New York: Arno Press and The New York Times, 1971), p. 195.

[16] For an analysis of Herbart and his method, see Harold B. Dunkel, *Herbart and Education* (New York: Random House, 1969).

17 Johann Friedrich Herbart, *Outlines of Educational Doctrine* trans. Alexis F. Lange, annot. Charles de Garmo (New York: The Macmillan Company, 1901).

18 Charles de Garmo, *Herbart and the Herbartians* (New York: Charles Scribner's Sons, 1895), p. vi.

19 Richard Hofstadter, *Social Darwinism in American Thought* (Boston: Beacon Press, 1955). Also see, Harold Y. Vanderpool, ed., *Darwin and Darwinism: Revolutionary Insights Concerning Man, Nature, Religion, and Society* (Lexington, MA: D.C. Heath and Co., 1973).

20 For Spencer's views on education see, Herbert Spencer, *Education: Intellectual, Moral and Physical* (New York: D. Appleton Co., 1881) and Andreas Kazamias, *Herbert Spencer on Education* (New York: Teachers College Press, Columbia University, 1966).

21 E.M. Standing, *Maria Montessori: Her Life and Work* (New York: New American Library, 1962).

22 Maria Montessori, *The Montessori Method*, trans. by Anne E. George (New York: Schocken Books, 1971), pp. 170-171.

23 Josephine Tozier, *An Educational Wonder-Worker, The Methods of Maria Montessori,'' McClure's Magazine*, XXXVII, (May 1911), pp. 3-19.

24 William H. Kilpatrick, *The Montessori System Examined* (New York: Houghton-Mifflin Co., 1914).

25 Paula P. Lillard, *Montessori: A Modern Approach* (New York: Schocken Books, 1973), p. 16.

26 John Dewey, *Democracy and Education* (New York: Macmillan Co., 1964), p. 150. (Published originally in 1916).

27 An excellent account of the Laboratory School can be found in Arthur G. Wirth, *John Dewey as Educator: His Design and Work in Education (1894-1904)* (New York: John Wiley and Sons, 1966). Herbert M. Kliebard, *The Struggle for the American Curriculum 1893-1958* (Boston: Routledge/Kegan Paul, 1986) places Dewey's work at the Laboratory School into the history of curriculum development in the United States.

28 Wirth, *John Dewey as Educator*, pp. 96-99, 154-160.

29 Katherine Camp Mayhew and Anna Camp Edwards, *The Dewey School* (New York: D. Appleton-Century Co., 1936).

Selections to Accompany
Chapter 7

Johann Heinrich Pestalozzi, one of the leading educational reformers of the nineteenth century, had a profound influence upon both European and American education. His educational methodology, which emphasized sense realism, directly contributed to the reorganization of the Prussian schools. The ideas of many American educators such as Henry Barnard, Edward A. Sheldon, and others were also greatly affected by Pestalozzi's methodology. Trying to explain his new approach to education, Pestalozzi wrote the following report to the "Friends of Education," a Swiss society organized to support his reformed pedagogy.

The Method: A Report by Pestalozzi

I am trying to psychologize the instruction of mankind; I am trying to bring it into harmony with the nature of my mind, with that of my circumstances and my relations to others. I start from no positive form of teaching, as such, but simply ask myself: —

"What would you do, if you wished to give a single child all the knowledge and practical skill he needs, so that by wise care of his best opportunities, he might reach inner content?"

I think, to gain this end, the human race needs exactly the same thing as the single child.

I think, further, the poor man's child needs a greater refinement in the methods of instruction than the rich man's child.

Nature, indeed, does much for the human race, but we have strayed away from her path. The poor man is thrust away from her bosom, and the rich destroy themselves both by rioting and by lounging on her overflowing breast.

SOURCE: Johann H. Pestalozzi, *How Gertrude Teaches Her Children*, trans. Lucy E. Holland and Francis C. Turner (London: Swan Sonnenschein and Co., 1907), pp. 199-211. The report has been abridged by the author.

The most essential point from which I start is this: —

Sense impression of Nature is the only true foundation of human instruction, because it is the only true foundation of human knowledge.

All that follows is the result of this sense impression, and the process of abstraction from it. Hence in every case where this is imperfect, the results also will be neither certain, safe nor positive; and in any case, where the sense impression is inaccurate, deception and error follow.

I start from this point and ask: — "What does Nature herself do in order to present the world truly to me, so far as it affects me? That is, — By what means does she bring the sense impressions of the most important things around me, to a perfection that contents me?" And I find, — She does this through my surroundings, my wants, and my relations to others.

Thus all the Art (of teaching) men is essentially a result of physicomechanical laws, the most important of which are the following: —

1. Bring all things essentially related to each other to that connection in your mind which they really have in Nature.

2. Subordinate all unessential things to essential, and especially subordinate the impression given by the Art to that given by Nature and reality.

3. Give to nothing a greater weight in your idea than it has in relation to your race in Nature.

4. Arrange all objects in the world according to their likeness.

5. Strengthen the impressions of important objects by allowing them to affect you through different senses.

6. In every subject try to arrange graduated steps of knowledge, in which every new idea shall be only a small, almost imperceptible addition to that earlier knowledge which has been deeply impressed and made unforgettable.

7. Learn to make the simple perfect before going on to the complex.

8. Recognize that as every physical ripening must be the result of the whole perfect fruit in all its parts, so every just judgment must be the result of a sense impression, perfect in all its parts, of the object to be judged. Distrust the appearance of precocious ripeness as the apparent ripeness of a worm-eaten apple.

9. All physical effects are absolutely necessary; and this necessity is the result of the art of Nature, with which she unites the apparently heterogeneous elements of her material into one whole for the achievement of her end. The Art, which imitates her, must try in the same way to raise the results at which it aims to a physical necessity, while it unites its elements into one whole for the achievement of its end.

10. The richness of its charm and the variety of its free play cause the results of physical necessity to bear the impress of freedom and independence. Here, too, the Art must imitate the course of Nature, and by the richness of its charm and the variety of its free play, try to make its results bear the impress of freedom and independence.

11. Above all, learn the first law of the physical mechanism, the powerful, universal connection between its results and the proportion of nearness or distance between the object and our senses. Never forget this physical nearness or distance of all objects around you has an immense effect in determining your positive sense impressions, practical ability and even virtue. But even this law of your nature converges as a whole towards another. It conveys towards the centre of our whole being, and we ourselves are this centre. Man! never forget it! All that you are, all you wish, all you might be, comes out of yourself. All must have a centre in your physical sense impression, and this again is yourself. In all it does, the Art really only adds this to the simple course of Nature. — That which Nature puts before us, scattered and over a wide area, the Art puts together in narrower bounds and brings nearer to our five senses, by associations, which facilitate the power of memory, and strengthen the susceptibility of our senses, and make it easier for them, by daily practice, to present to us the objects around us in greater numbers, for a longer time and in a more precise way.

Pestalozzi.

Burgdorf, June 27th, 1800.

Friedrich Froebel, who developed the Kindergarten, presented his most systematic work on educational theory in The Education of Man. *Although the style of this work is complicated by the mystical overtones of Froebel's philosophic idealism, the book provides valuable insight into his concepts of man, the child, and education.*

Froebel: The Education of Man

In all things there lives and reigns an eternal law. To him whose mind, through disposition and faith, is filled, penetrated, and quickened with the necessity that this cannot possibly be otherwise, as well as to him whose clear, calm mental vision beholds the inner in the outer and through the outer, and sees the outer proceeding with logical necessity from the essence of the inner, this law has been and is enounced with equal clearness and distinctness in nature (the external), in the spirit (the internal), and in life which unites the two. This all-controlling law is necessarily based on an all-pervading, energetic, living, self-conscious, and hence eternal Unity. This fact, as well as the Unity itself, is again vividly recognized, either through faith or through insight, with equal clearness and comprehensiveness; therefore, a quietly observant human mind, a thoughtful, clear human intellect, has never failed, and will never fail, to recognize this Unity.

This Unity is God. All things have come from Divine Unity, from God, and have their origin in the Divine Unity, in God alone. God is the sole source of all things. In all things there lives and reigns the Divine Unity, God. All things live and have their being in and through the Divine Unity, in and through God. All things are only through the divine effluence that lives in them. The divine effluence that lives in each thing is the essence of each thing.

It is the destiny and life-work of all things to unfold their essence, hence their divine being, and, therefore, the Divine Unity itself—to reveal God in their external and transient being. It is the special destiny and life-work of man, as an intelligent and rational being, to become fully, vividly, and clearly conscious of his essence, of the divine effluence in him, and, therefore, of

SOURCE: Friedrich W. Froebel, *The Education of Man*, trans. W.M. Hailmann (New York: D. Appleton and Company, 1887). Hailmann was a well-known lecturer on education in the United States and at the time he translated Froebel's work was Superintendent of Public Schools at LaPorte, Indiana. *The Education of Man* was a volume in the series edited by W.T. Harris, U.S. Commissioner of Education. The author has selected representative selections from the text.

God; to become fully, vividly, and clearly conscious of his destiny and life-work; and to accomplish this, to render it (His essence) active, to reveal it in his own life with self-determination and freedom.

Education consists in leading man, as a thinking, intelligent being, growing into self-consciousness, to a pure and unsullied, conscious and free representation of the inner law of Divine Unity, and in teaching him ways and means thereto.

The knowledge of that eternal law, the insight into its origin, into its essence, into the totality, the connection, and intensity of its effects, and knowledge of life in its totality, constitute *science, the science of life*; and, referred by the self-conscious, thinking, intelligent being to representation and practice through and in himself, this becomes *science of education*.

The system of directions, derived from the knowledge and study of that law, to guide thinking, intelligent beings in the apprehension of their life-work and in the accomplishment of their destiny, is *the theory of education*.

The self-active application of this knowledge in the direct development and cultivation of rational beings toward the attainment of their destiny, is *the practice of education*.

The object of education is the realization of a faithful, pure, inviolate, and hence holy life.

Knowledge and application, consciousness and realization in life, united in the service of a faithful, pure, holy life, constitute the wisdom of life, pure wisdom.

To be wise is the highest aim of man, is the most exalted achievement of human self-determination.

To educate one's self and others, with consciousness, freedom, and self-determination, is a twofold achievement of wisdom: it *began* with the first appearance of man upon the earth; it *was manifest* with the first appearance of full self-consciousness in man; it *begins now* to proclaim itself as a necessary, universal requirement of humanity, and to he heard and heeded as such. With this achievement man enters upon the path which alone leads to life; which surely tends to the fulfillment of the inner, and thereby also to the fulfillment of the outer requirement of humanity; which, through a faithful, pure, holy life, attains beatitude.

By education, then the divine essence of man should be unfolded, brought out, lifted into consciousness, and man himself raised into free, conscious obedience to the divine principle that lives in him, and to a free representation of this principle in his life.

Education, in instruction, should lead man to see and know the divine, spiritual, and eternal principle which animates surrounding nature, constitutes the essence of nature, and is permanently manifested in nature; and, in living reciprocity and united with training, it should express and demonstrate the fact that the same law rules both (the divine principle and nature), as it does nature and man.

Education as a whole, by means of instruction and training, should bring to man's consciousness, and render efficient in his life, the fact that man and nature proceed from God and are conditioned by him—that both have their being in God.

Education should lead and guide man to clearness concerning himself and in himself, to peace with nature, and to unity with God; hence it should lift him to a knowledge of himself and of mankind, to a knowledge of God and of nature, and to the pure and holy life to which such knowledge leads.

Froebel's Kindergarten

Would you, O parents and educators, see in miniature, in a picture, as it were, what I have here indicated, look into this education-room—of eight boys, seven to eight years old.

This unifying and, at the same time, self-reliant spirit unites all things that come near and seem adapted to its nature, its wants, and inner status—unites stones and human beings in a common purpose, a common endeavor. And thus each one soon forms for himself his own world; for the feeling of his *own power* implies and soon demands also the possession of his *own space* and his *own material* belongings exclusively to him.

Be his realm, his province, his land, as it were, a corner of the courtyard, of the house, or of the room; be it the space of a box, of a chest, or of a closet; be it a grotto, a hut, or a garden—the human being, the boy at this age, needs an external point, if possible, chosen and prepared by himself, to which he refers all his activity.

When the room to be filled is extensive, when the realm to be controlled is large, when the whole to be represented or produced is complex, then brotherly union of similar-minded persons is in place. And when similar-minded persons meet in similar endeavor, and their hearts find each other, then either the work already begun is extended, or the work begun by one becomes a common work.

On the large table of the much-used room there stands a chest of building-blocks, in the form of bricks, each side about one sixth of the size of actual bricks, the finest and most variable material that can be offered a boy for purposes of representation. Sand or sawdust, too, have found their way into the room, and fine, green moss has been brought in abundantly from the last walk in the beautiful pine-forest.

It is intermission, and each one has begun his own work. There in a corner stands a chapel quite concealed, a cross and an altar indicate the meaning of the structure: it is the creation of a small, quiet boy. There on a chair two boys have united to undertake a considerably greater piece of work: it is a building of several stories, and probably represents a castle, which looks down from the chair as from a mountain into a valley. But what has quietly grown under the hands of that boy at the table? It is a green hill crowned by an old, ruined castle. The others, in the meanwhile, have erected a village in the plain below.

Now, each one has finished his work; each one examines it and that of the others. In each one rises the thought and the wish to unite all in a connected whole; and scarcely has this wish been recognized as a common one, when they establish common roads from the village to the ruin, from this to the castle, and from the castle to the chapel, and between them lie brooks and meadows.

At another time some had fashioned a landscape from clay, another had constructed from pasteboard a house with doors and windows, and a third had made miniature ships from nutshells. Each one examines his work: it is good, but it stands alone. He sees his neighbor's work: it would gain so much by being united. And immediately the house, as a castle, crowns the hills, and the tiny ship floats on the small artificial lake, and, to the delight of all, the youngest brings his shepherd and sheep to graze between the mountain and the lake. Now they all stand and behold with pleasure and satisfaction the work of their own hands.

Again, what busy tumult among those older boys at the brook down yonder! They have built canals and sluices, bridges and seaports, dams and mills, each one intent only on his own work. Now the water is to be used to carry vessels from the higher to the lower level: but at each step of progress one trespasses on the limits of another realm, and each one equally claims his right as lord and maker, while he recognizes the claims of the other. What can serve here to mediate? Only *treaties*, and like states, they bind themselves by strict treaties. Who can point out the varied significance, the varied results of these plays of boys? Two things, indeed, are clearly established. They proceed from one and the same spirit of boyhood and the playing boys made good pupils, intelligent, and quick to learn, quick to see and to do, diligent and full of zeal, reliable in thought and feeling, efficient and vigorous. Those who played thus are efficient men, or will become so.

Particularly helpful at this period of life is the cultivation of gardens owned by the boys, and their cultivation for the sake of the produce. For here man for the first time sees his work bearing fruit in an organic way, determined by logical necessity and law — fruit which, although subject to the inner laws of natural development, depends in many ways upon his work and upon the character of his work!

This work fully completes, in many ways, the boy's life with nature, and satisfies his curiosity concerning her workings, his desire to know her — a desire that urges him again and again to give thoughtful and continuous attention and observation to plants and flowers. Nature, too, seems to favor these promptings and occupations, and to reward them with abundant success; for a glance upon these gardens of children reveals at once the fact that, if a boy has given his plants only moderate care and attention, they thrive remarkably well; and that the plants and flowers of the boys who attend to them with special care live in sympathy with these boys, as it were, and are particularly healthy and luxuriant.

If the boy cannot have the care of a little garden of his own, he should have at least a few plants in boxes or pots, filled not with rare and delicate or double plants, but with common plants that have an abundance of leaves and blossoms, and thrive easily.

The child, or boy, who has guarded and cared for another living thing, although it be of a lower order, will be led more easily to guard and foster his own life. At the same time the care of plants will gratify his desire to observe other living things, such as beetles, butterflies, and birds, for these seek the vicinity of plants.

In John Dewey's short book entitled Experience and Education, *written in 1938, he took to task the defenders of educational traditionalism and extremist advocates of educational progressivism as well. Both schools of thought, he observed, were laboring under the difficulties of an "either-or" attitude. He urged progressives to develop a positive plan of action, a genuine philosophy of education, rather than being content with maintaining a purely negative attitude to traditional schooling. In the selection which follows, Dewey discusses the nature of freedom.*

Experience and Education

. . . The only freedom that is of enduring importance is freedom of intelligence, that is to say, freedom of observation and of judgment exercised in behalf of purposes that are intrinsically worth while. The commonest mistake made about freedom is, I think, to identify it with freedom of movement, or with the external or physical side of activity. Now, this external or physical side of activity cannot be separated from the internal side of activity; from freedom of thought, desire, and purpose. The limitation that was put upon outward action by the fixed arrangements of the typical traditional schoolroom, with its fixed rows of desks and its military regimen of pupils who were permitted to move only at certain fixed signals, put a great restriction upon intellectual and moral freedom. Strait-jacket and chain-gang procedures had to be done away with if there was to be a chance for growth of individuals in the intellectual springs of freedom without which there is no assurance of genuine and continued normal growth.

But the fact still remains that an increased measure of freedom of outer movement is a *means*, not an end. The educational problem is not solved when this aspect of freedom is obtained. Everything then depends, so far as education is concerned, upon what is done with this added liberty. What end does it serve? What consequences flow from it? Let me speak first of the advantages which reside potentially in increase of outward freedom. In the first place, without its existence it is practically impossible for a teacher to gain knowledge of the individuals with whom he is concerned. Enforced quiet and acquiescence prevent pupils from disclosing their real natures. They enforce artificial uniformity. They put seeming before being. They place a

SOURCE: John Dewey, *Experience and Education* (New York: The Macmillan Company, 1938), pp. 69-76. Used by permission of Kappa Delta Pi, An Honor Society in Education, owners of the copyright.

premium upon preserving the outward appearance of attention, decorum, and obedience. And everyone who is acquainted with schools in which this system prevailed well knows that thoughts, imaginations, desires, and sly activities ran their own unchecked course behind this facade. They were disclosed to the teacher only when some untoward act led to their detection. One has only to contrast this highly artificial situation with normal human relations outside the schoolroom, say in a well-conducted home, to appreciate how fatal it is to the teacher's acquaintance with and understanding of the individuals who are, supposedly, being educated. Yet without this insight there is only an accidental chance that the material of study and the methods used in instruction will so come home to an individual that his development of mind and character is actually directed. There is a vicious circle. Mechanical uniformity of studies and methods creates a kind of uniform immobility and this reacts to perpetuate uniformity of studies and of recitations, while behind this enforced uniformity individual tendencies operate in irregular and more or less forbidden ways.

The other important advantage of increased outward freedom is found in the very nature of the learning process. That the older methods set a premium upon passivity and receptivity has been pointed out. Physical quiescence puts a tremendous premium upon these traits. The only escape from them in the standardized school is an activity which is irregular and perhaps disobedient. There cannot be complete quietude in a laboratory or workshop. The nonsocial character of the traditional school is seen in the fact that it erected silence into one of its prime virtues. There is, of course, such a thing as intense intellectual activity without overt bodily activity. But capacity for such intellectual activity marks a comparatively late achievement when it is continued for a long period. There should be brief intervals of time for quiet reflection provided for even the young. But they are periods of genuine reflection only when they follow after times of more overt action and are used to organize what has been gained in periods of activity in which the hands and other parts of the body beside the brain are used. Freedom of movement is also important as a means of maintaining normal physical and mental health. We have still to learn from the example of the Greeks who saw clearly the relation between a sound body and a sound mind. But in all the respects mentioned freedom of outward action is a means to freedom of judgment and of power to carry deliberately chosen ends into execution. The amount of external freedom which is needed varies from individual to individual. It naturally tends to decrease with increasing maturity, though its complete absence prevents even a mature individual from having the contacts which will provide him with new materials upon which his intelligence may exercise itself. The amount and the quality of this kind of free activity as a means of growth is a problem that must engage the thought of the educator at every stage of development.

There can be no greater mistake, however, than to treat such freedom as an end in itself. It then tends to be destructive of the shared cooperative activities which are the normal source of order. But, on the other hand, it turns freedom which should be positive into something negative. For freedom from restriction, the negative side, is to be prized only as a means to a freedom which is power: power to frame purposes, to judge wisely, to evaluate desires by the consequences which will result from acting upon them; power to select and order means to carry chosen ends into operation.

Natural impulses and desires constitute in any case the starting point. But there is no intellectual growth without some reconstruction, some remaking, of impulses and desires in the form in which they first show themselves. This remaking involves inhibition of impulse in its first estate. The alternative to externally imposed inhibition is inhibition through an individual's own reflection and judgment. The old phrase "stop and think" is sound psychology. For thinking is stoppage of the immediate manifestation of impulse until that impulse has been brought into connection with other possible tendencies to action so that a more comprehensive and coherent plan of activity is formed. Some of the other tendencies to action lead to use of eye, ear, and hand to observe objective conditions; others result in recall of what has happened in the past. Thinking is thus a postponement of immediate action, while it effects internal control of impulse through a union of observation and memory, this union being the heart of reflection. What has been said explains the meaning of the well-worn phrase "self-control." The ideal aim of education is creation of power of self-control. But the mere removal of external control is no guarantee for the production of self-control. It is easy to jump out of the frying-pan into the fire. It is easy, in other words, to escape one form of external control only to find oneself in another and more dangerous form of external control. Impulses and desires that are not ordered by intelligence are under the control of accidental circumstance. It may be a loss rather than a gain to escape from the control of another person only to find one's conduct dictated by immediate whim and caprice; that is, at the mercy of impulses into whose formation intelligent judgment has not entered. A person whose conduct is controlled in this way has at most only the illusion of freedom. Actually he is directed by forces over which he has no command.

Suggestions for Further Reading

Barlow, Thomas A. *Pestalozzi and American Education*. Boulder, CO: Este Es Press, 1977.

Boyd, William. ed. *The Emile of Jean Jacques Rousseau: Selections*. New York: Teachers College Press, Columbia University, 1966.

Dearborn, Ned. H. *The Oswego Movement in American Education*. New York: Teachers College, Columbia University, 1925.

de Garmo, Charles. *Herbart and the Herbartians*. New York: Charles Scribner's Sons, 1895.

Dewey, John. *The Child and the Curriculum*. Chicago: University of Chicago Press, 1902.

Dewey, John. *Democracy and Education*. New York: Macmillan Co., 1916.

Dewey, John. *Experience and Education*. New York: Macmillan Co., 1938.

Dewey, John. *How We Think*. New York: D.C. Heath and Co., 1933.

Dewey, John. *The School and Society*. Chicago: University of Chicago Press, 1899.

Downs, Robert S. *Heinrich Pestalozzi: Father of Modern Pedagogy*. Boston: Twayne Publishers, 1975.

Dunkel, Harold B. *Herbart and Education*. New York: Random House, 1969.

Dunkel, Harold B. *Herbart and Herbartianism: An Educational Ghost Story*. Chicago: University of Chicago Press, 1970.

Froebel, Friederich. *The Education of Man*. W.N. Hailmann, trans. New York: Appleton and Co., 1896.

Grimsely, Ronald. *Jean-Jacques Rousseau*. Sussex, Eng.: Harvester Press, 1983.

Gutek, Gerald L. *Joseph Neef: The Americanization of Pestalozzianism*. University, AL: University of Alabama Press, 1978.

Gutek, Gerald L. *Pestalozzi and Education*. New York: Random House, 1968.

Herbart, Johann Friedrich. *Outlines of Educational Doctrine*. Alexis F. Lange, trans. New York: Macmillan Co., 1901.

Kazamias, Andreas M., ed. *Herbert Spencer on Education*. New York: Teachers College Press, Columbia University, 1966.

Kennedy, James B. *Herbert Spencer on Education*. New York: G.K. Hall and Co., 1978.

Kilpatrick, William H. *Froebel's Kindergarten Principles: Critically Examined*. New York: Macmillan Co., 1916.

Kilpatrick, William H. *The Montessori System Examined*. New York: Houghton-Mifflin Co., 1914.

Lillard, Paula P. *Montessori: A Modern Approach*. New York: Schocken Books, 1973.

Lilley, Irene M. *Friedrich Froebel: A Selection from his Writings*. Cambridge: Cambridge University Press, 1967.

Misenheimer, Helen Evans. *Rousseau on the Education of Women*. Lanham, MD: University Press of America, 1981.

Montessori, Maria. *The Discovery of the Child*. New York: Ballantine Books, 1948.

Monroe, Will S. *History of the Pestalozzian Movement in the United States*. Syracuse, NY: C.W. Bardeen Publisher, 1907.

Pestalozzi, Johann H. *How Gertrude Teaches Her Children*. Lucy E. Holland and Francis Turner, trans. London: Swan Sonnenschein and Co., 1907.

Pestalozzi, Johann H. *Leonard and Gertrude*. Evan Channing, trans. Boston: D.C. Heath and Co., 1907.

Silber, Kate. *Pestalozzi: The Man and His Work*. London: Routledge and Kegan Paul, 1960.

Spencer, Herbert S. *Essays: Scientific, Political, and Speculative*. New York: D. Appleton Co., 1910.

Standing, E.M. *Maria Montessori: Her Life and Work*. New York: New American Library, 1962.

Vandewalker, Nina C. *The Kindergarten in American Education*. New York: Arno Press and the New York Times, 1971.

Weber, Evelyn. *The Kindergarten: Its Encounter with Educational Thought in America*. New York: Teachers College Press, Columbia University, 1969.

Wirth, Arthur. *John Dewey as Educator: His Design for Work in Education (1894-1904)*. New York: John Wiley and Sons, 1966.

Education and Integration

Introduction

Horace Mann and Henry Barnard believed that the common school should promote the integration of Americans into a national community. Children of varied social, racial, ethnic, economic, and religious backgrounds would share in a democratic system of education which would unite these several peoples into one, indivisible union. Throughout the nineteenth century the common school assimilated more than thirty-five million immigrants into American life. Yet, the common school failed to realize completely the goal of social integration. Large numbers of Americans were still excluded from full economic, political, and social participation in their nation's life. Although American educators theorized about equality of educational opportunity, many American children were still educationally disenfranchised because of race and poverty.

The military victory of the northern armies in the Civil War liberated almost four million slaves. In 1865, ratification of the Thirteenth Amendment to the Constitution abolished slavery in the United States; in 1866, the Fourteenth Amendment specified that no state should "deprive any person of life, liberty, or property, without due process of law." While these Constitutional amendments formally ended black servitude, the effects of over two hundred years of slavery remained to plague both black and white in the years after the Civil War.

Although they were legally free, many American blacks were excluded from the national democratization by the doctrine of "separate but equal" which legalized practices of racial segregation. After 1875, southern states enacted laws which segregated public transportation, accommodations, and other facilities. In 1896, the Supreme Court in the *Plessy v. Ferguson* decision upheld these practices. The "separate but equal" doctrine had a particularly pernicious effect upon the theory of equal educational opportunity. Although the states claimed that white and black schools received equal support, some spent more money to educate the white than the black children. The following pages outline the struggle of American blacks to take part in the common promise of American life by describing some of the major events that helped to overturn the "separate but equal" doctrine.

The Origins of the South's Problems

Historically, the existence of African slavery as a part of the plantation economy made southern social developments different from those in the northern states. Slavery came to be regarded as the South's peculiar institution. Some southern leaders during the revolutionary and early national periods regarded slavery as a necessary evil. A few, like Jefferson, favored the gradual emancipation of the slaves and their resettlement in Africa. In 1793, Eli Whitney invented a cotton gin that made it possible to easily separate the cotton fibers from the seeds. This made it economically efficient to cultivate cotton on a large scale in the South, and a vast area of land extending from Georgia and South Carolina westward to Texas was opened to "King Cotton" and the plantation system. The growth of the textile industry in England and in the North gave the cotton planters a market for their produce which stimulated the southern economy and led to a rapid increase in the number of African slaves.

Until the 1840s, southern leaders had apologized for slavery as a necessary evil. When northern abolitionists such as William Lloyd Garrison and Horace Greeley attacked slavery in the decade before the Civil War, southerners went further and began to try to justify it. Articles in *De Bow's Review*, a leading southern publication, contained a positive defense of slavery. Edmund Ruffin, a noted agriculturalist, argued that African slavery had produced a well-ordered society based on the model in Plato's *Republic*. Other writers, such as Governor Hammond of South Carolina, found it justified in the Old Testament. Although the Civil War, fought from 1861 to 1865, destroyed slavery by armed force, some southerners continued to accept the doctrine of black inferiority that had been part of the rationale used to justify the South's "peculiar institution."

The southern blacks faced hostility from whites who had been raised from birth on the theory of white supremacy. In addition to this racial hostility, they were victimized by the debilitating effects of the slave system in other ways. Since slave marriages had no legal status, there was no reliable family structure. Many southern states had made it a legal offense to teach blacks to read during the slave period and as a result most of them were illiterate. Further, the system was such that most of them were forced into a condition of dependence upon white masters.

At the close of the Civil War the black population, nearly four and a half million, was located almost entirely in the South. Only about 300,000 blacks lived in northern states. It has been estimated that only three per cent of the black population were literate. Since blacks had been denied education during slavery, the task of teaching them was enormous.

As the Union Army entered the South, northern charitable and religious groups sent funds and teachers to educate the newly freed former slaves. Schools were established and staffed by the "New England school marms" who were much maligned by some white southerners. Although these voluntary and charitable efforts made some inroads, they were inadequate to deal with the magnitude of the problem of black education. In 1865, the federal government established the Freedmen's Bureau under the direction of General Oliver O. Howard. From its founding until 1870, the Bureau maintained a school system which enrolled almost a quarter of a million black students.

During the Reconstruction period, which began with the Confederate defeat in 1865 and lasted in some southern states until 1877, blacks had their first encounters with representative government. During these years, southern state governments were controlled by black representatives in coalition with radical Republicans. Although some historians have interpreted Reconstruction as an era of political corruption and graft on the part of blacks, "scalawags," and "carpetbaggers," there has been in recent years a revision and reinterpretation of the times. Critics of the Reconstruction legislatures neglected to mention their constructive contributions such as abolition of property requirements for suffrage, reform of penal institutions, construction of roads and highways, and most significantly the establishment of free public schools. Prior to the Civil War, most southern states had not established common schools. It was not until Reconstruction that these states inaugurated systems of public education.

After the post-Civil War period of Reconstruction ended in 1877, the blacks' position was determined by the economic and political conflicts among the divided white southerners. Three major socioeconomic classes had emerged in the post-war era: the land-owning and industry-owning white leadership, the socioeconomically disadvantaged "poor whites," and the blacks. The only thing separating the black and the "poor white" was the color line. The "poor white" had been antagonistic toward the black before the Civil War, and emancipation only served to harden his hatred of the latter as an economic competitor.

Toward the end of the nineteenth century, racial rivalries intensified as political fuel was added to the burning embers of antagonism. Until the 1880s, the Democratic Party was the sole political force in the South. In the late 1880s and 1890s, the Populist Party was organized. Thus the blacks became the balance of power between the two hostile white groups who were seeking political power among the voters. Gradually the "poor white" agriculturalists gained control, and determined that blacks should never again exercise the role of political balance in the South.

At first, by restricting the primaries to white voters only, black voters were excluded but not actually disenfranchised. By the late 1890s and early 1900s, however, rigid segregation laws had been enacted, and blacks were actively disenfranchised by property qualifications, literacy tests, poll taxes, and the white primary. Every area of southern life became segregated, to the point of maintaining separate drinking fountains and transportation requirements. The disenfranchisement took place with little protest from the northern white community. Many northern progressives failed to include a place for black citizens in their programs of social reform. The prevailing mood of social Darwinism, with its emphasis on white Anglo-Saxon superiority, produced a climate of opinion that tolerated and tacitly approved the segregation legislation. The growth of these attitudes reinforced the already existing pattern of separate schools for the races.

Booker T. Washington

After the Reconstruction period, the task of black leadership fell to an Alabama educator, Booker T. Washington (1856-1915), president of Tuskegee Institute. Concerning himself with educating blacks in vocations and trades, Washington urged them to avoid the political arena. Thus, at the very time when blacks were being disenfranchised and excluded from sharing the growing opportunities of American life, their own leading spokesman urged caution and patience. Washington felt that blacks had tried to move too quickly into professional and political life and first needed to establish a solid economic base as skilled workers and craftsmen.

Washington worked to cultivate amicable relations between members of both races. His autobiography, *Up From Slavery*, recounts his own career and the difficult early history of Tuskegee.[1] Some idea of Washington's social theory can be gained from his famous Atlanta Exposition Address, which he delivered at the opening of the Cotton States Exposition in Atlanta in 1895. In this address, which has been referred to as the Atlanta Compromise, Washington urged blacks to cultivate friendly relations with southern whites. He expressed regret that some blacks believed participation in politics more important than property ownership or the acquisition of skills. He urged blacks to improve themselves by seeking occupations in agriculture, mechanics, commerce, domestic service, and the professions.[2] Washington also believed that they should remain in the South, where they should work out their destiny with the cooperation of the white community:

> As we have proved our loyalty to you in the past, in nursing your children, watching by the sick bed of your mothers and fathers, and often following them with tear-dimmed eyes to their graves, as in the future, in our humble way, we shall stand by you with a devotion that no foreigner can approach, ready to lay down our lives, if need be, in defense of yours, interlacing our industrial, commercial, civil, and religious lives with yours in a way that shall make the interests of both races one. In all things that are purely social we can be as separate as the fingers, yet one as the hand in all things essential to mutual progress.[3]

As a practical educator, Washington sought to make Tuskegee Institute into a national example of successful educational effort. He recognized a close relationship between theory and practice, building a curriculum that combined industrial work and academic training as complementary subjects, and teaching that "working with the hands" was a source of uplifting moral power. Washington designed Tuskegee's educational program to teach the dignity of labor, to thoroughly and effectively teach the trades, to supply the demand for trained leaders, and to help students meet their educational expenses.[4]

In assessing Washington's social and political influence on the course of black-white racial relations, it must be remembered that he contributed to a climate of opinion that prevailed until the time when African-Americans began to struggle for equality. Washington labored at a time when he could have counted on few white or northern voices to aid him had he attempted to lead a struggle for racial equality. Washington's speech and attitude was at best an uneasy compromise with the racial *status quo*.

Black Self-Assertion

Washington's Atlanta Compromise may have represented temporary acceptance of the *status quo* by some blacks, but not for all. The noted African-American historian W.E.B. Du Bois became a strong critic of Washington's rationale for black social progress. According to Du Bois, Washington's position involved a triple paradox:

> . . . . Is it possible, and probable, that nine millions of men can make effective progress in economic lines if they are deprived of political rights, made a servile caste, and allowed only the most meagre chance for

Carnegie Hall, Tuskegee University, Tuskegee, Alabama. One of the buildings of Tuskegee Institute, now University, created by Booker T. Washington. Photo by Patricia A. Gutek.

developing their exceptional men? If history and reason give any distinct answer to these questions, it is an emphatic No. And Mr. Washington thus faces the triple paradox of his career:

1. He is striving nobly to make Negro artisans business men and property owners; but it is utterly impossible, under modern competitive methods, for workingmen and property owners to defend their rights and exist without the right of suffrage.

2. He insists on thrift and self-respect, but at the same time counsels a silent submission to civic inferiority such as is bound to sap the manhood of any race in the long run.

3. He advocates common-school and industrial training, and depreciates institutions of higher learning; but neither the Negro common schools, nor Tuskegee itself could remain open a day were it not for teachers trained in Negro colleges or trained by their graduates.[5]

As a result of criticism from Du Bois and others, interested individuals, both black and white, who were concerned with the advancement of racial equality organized the Niagara Movement in 1905. Among the principles of the new movement were freedom of speech and criticism, abolition of distinctions based on race, recognition of human brotherhood, and the right of all to education.

The first decade of the twentieth century witnessed a number of violent race riots. In August of 1908, a bloody race riot occurred in Springfield, Illinois, within view of Lincoln's home. Between 1880 and 1920 more than 3,000 lynchings occurred in the United States, 70 per cent of whom were black victims. In the light of these events the Atlanta Compromise was not a working agreement.

In 1910, under the leadership of the constitutional lawyer Moorfield Storey and Du Bois, the National Association for theAdvancement of Colored People was founded. The NAACP rejected the submissiveness of Washington's Atlanta Compromise and advocated:

1. The strict enforcement of the civil rights guaranteed by the Fourteenth Amendment;
2. Equal educational opportunities for all and in all the states, and the same public school expenditure for the black and the white child;
3. In accord with the Fifteenth Amendment, that the right of the black to vote on the same terms as other citizens be recognized in all parts of the country.

Committee on Civil Rights

After World War II, national attention turned to civil rights. Returning black veterans who had fought for freedom abroad did not intend to accept second class citizenship in their own country. In 1946, President Truman appointed a Presidential Committee on Civil Rights which made recommendations to the President and to Congress for needed legislation. The Committee's report, *To Secure These Rights*, sought to educate Americans about racial discrimination in hiring practices, health care, voting rights, and education. In condemning racially segregated schooling as unfair to black children, the Committee pointed out that segregated schools attended by blacks had lower per pupil expenditures and teachers' salaries and had less adequate physical facilities than schools attended by white children. Among the recommendations of the Committee were:

1. The reestablishment of the Fair Employment Practices Committee,
    FEPC;
2. The appointment of an ongoing national civil rights commission;
3. The denial of federal aid to states that segregated schools and public
    facilities;
4. A federal anti-lynching law;
5. Federal protection of voting rights and abolishing of the poll tax;
6. Ending racial discrimination in the armed forces, health care
    facilities, housing, and interstate transportation.[6]

President Truman, a strong supporter of civil rights, was unable to get
enough support for the enactment of the recommendations in Congress. By
executive order, in 1948 he ended racial segregation in the armed forces and
prohibited discrimination in federal agencies.

In the 1950s, a concerted effort was made to remove the legal obstacles
that kept blacks from enrolling in colleges, and universities in the states where
higher and professional education was segregated by law. The National
Association for the Advancement of Colored People, NAACP, began a carefully prepared series of challenges in the courts to end the *de jure* racial
segregation which had received judicial sanction in the *Plessy v. Ferguson*
case in 1896.

In 1896, the U.S. Supreme Court in *Plessy v. Ferguson* upheld a Louisiana
law that racially segregated railroad passengers on the basis of the "separate
but equal" doctrine was used to segregate a range of facilities, including
schools.[7] In fact, however, segregated facilities, especially schools, were not
equal. Educational expenditures per pupil were greater for white than for black
students. Salaries paid to teachers were generally higher, the school year longer,
and physical facilities better for the schools attended by whites than those
attended by blacks.

Legal Action Against Segregation

By a series of court cases involving segregation in professional and graduate
schools, the NAACP established the ground work that would be used to achieve
desegregation in elementary and secondary education.

In 1938, the U.S. Supreme Court heard the case of Lloyd L. Gaines, a
black, who sought admission to the University of Missouri Law School, which
was then attended only by whites.[8] Since Missouri did not have a "separate
but equal" law school, the Court ruled that Gaines was being denied equality
of the privileges provided for "separated groups" within the state and should
be admitted to the Law School.

In 1948, Ada L. Sipuel, a black, sought admission to the all-white University of Oklahoma Law School. She was advised by university officials to delay her application until the state built a separate law school for blacks. Finding that Oklahoma was denying Sipuel's rights under the "equal Protection clause" of the Fourteenth Amendment, the Court ruled that she was entitled to a legal education within the same period of time that applicants from other groups received such an education.[9]

In 1950, Herman M. Sweatt, a black, was denied admission to the all-white University of Texas Law School. Texas had established a small segregated law school in which Sweatt was the only student. The U.S. Supreme Court ruled that the alternative law school did not match the facilities, faculty, and academic quality of the University of Texas Law School and did not provide an equal education.[10]

Brown v. Board of Education

After the legal foundations for the admission of blacks to racially segregated graduate and professional schools had been established the NAACP challenged segregation in the public schools. In *Brown v. Board of Education, 1954*, the NAACP attorneys, led by Thurgood Marshall, challenged the "separate but equal" precedent established by *Plessy v. Ferguson* in 1896. Using sociological and psychological evidence as well as legal precedents, Marshall argued that racially segregated schools: (1) violated the due process clause of the Fourteenth Amendment; (2) denied black children equality of educational opportunity; (3) caused psychological damage to black children.

The Supreme Court in *Brown v. Board of Education* ruled that segregated schools were "inherently unequal" and violated the Fourteenth Amendment of the Constitution. Chief Justice Earl Warren stated:

> Segregation of white and colored children in public schools has a detrimental effect upon the colored children. The impact is greater when it has the sanction of the law; for the policy of separating the races is usually interpreted as denoting the inferiority of the Negro group. A sense of inferiority affects the motivation of a child to learn. Segregation with the sanction of law, therefore, has a tendency to retard the education and mental development of Negro children and to deprive them of some of the benefits they would receive in a racially integrated school system.[11]

The civil rights movement had two major lines of development in relation to the schools. At first civil rights advocates concentrated on the schools of the old South and the border states, where segregation had the force of longstanding law as well as custom. Although the decision of 1954 reversed the "separate but equal" doctrine, much actual legal spadework had to be done to make enforcement of the decision a reality. The second area concerned the schools of the northern states, especially in the large cities, where there had been an influx of black migration from the South. In these northern metropolitan areas the patterns of racial segregation took a more subtle form. Here segregation came to be referred to as *de facto*, having its basis usually in the residential patterns that developed rather than in actual legislation.[12]

The Southern Reaction

The southern white reaction to the events of 1954 was at first one of disbelief and defiance of the Supreme Court's decision, and then of token acceptance. Almost immediately, certain southern white politicians resurrected the "states' rights" argument against the anti-segregation decision. The legislature of South Carolina passed a Resolution on February 16, 1954, "condemning and protesting the usurpation and encroachment on the Reserved Powers of the States by the Supreme Court." On March 12, 1956, seventeen United States Senators and seventy-seven Representatives to Congress presented this statement:

> Without regard to the consent of the governed, outside agitators are threatening immediate and revolutionary changes in our public school systems. If done, this is certain to destroy the system of public education in some of the States.

Grudgingly, politicians in some of the southern states complied with the Court's decision, but not without testing the federal government's willingness to implement it. In 1957, Governor Faubus of Arkansas attempted to block the desegregation of the Little Rock schools. President Eisenhower met the Governor's tactics with an executive order which authorized the use of federal troops. In 1962, Governor Barnett of Mississippi attempted to halt the enrollment of James Meredith, a black, in the University of Mississippi. Governor Barnett claimed to base his action of interposition on the Tenth Amendment of the United States Constitution. He alleged that the interests of order and safety required him to "interpose and invoke the police powers of the state." The use of the word "interpose" harked back to John C. Calhoun's long buried but equally futile doctrine of "interposition." President Kennedy ordered federal troops into the state of Mississippi to end violence in Oxford, and to secure Meredith's admission to the University.

Civil Rights and Desegregation Enforced

Since the Brown case, the process of school desegregation and ensuring of civil rights in the United States continued. In September 1957, Congress passed a civil rights act, the first federal legislation enacted in this area in eighty-two years. The 1957 Civil Rights Act established a commission with power to investigate the denial of voting rights and equal protection of the laws on account of color, race, religion, or national origin. In 1960, another civil rights act was passed which empowered federal courts to appoint referees to examine state voting qualifications whenever a petitioner had been denied the right to vote because of race or color.

The Civil Rights Act of 1964, proclaimed as the most far-reaching law of its kind, not only protected voting rights but sought to guarantee civil rights in employment and education. It guaranteed equal access to public accommodations and strengthened the machinery for preventing employment discrimination by contractors holding government contracts. It also established a community relations service to help localities resolve racial tensions and disputes. Significant for education, the Act empowered the federal government to file school desegregation suits and to withhold federal funds wherever discrimination was practiced in applying federal programs.

The Civil Rights Act of 1968 continued the series of federal laws that prohibited racial discrimination. It protected civil rights workers and provided several penalties for interfering with the rights of attending school or working. A significant provision of the Act prohibited discrimination in the sale or rental of public and private housing.

Along with the civil rights acts, a series of Supreme Court decisions continued the process to desegregate public schools. An important decision was that of *Griffin v. the School Board of Prince Edward County* in 1964.[13] In Prince Edward County, Virginia, the Board of Supervisors had refused to levy taxes for the 1959-1960 school year with the result that the public schools were forced to close. A private association, called the Prince Edward School Foundation, was formed to operate private schools for white children. In the 1960-1961 school year, the major financial support for the foundation came from state and county tuition grants. The Supreme Court ruled that the closing of the Prince Edward County public schools denied black students the equal protection of the laws guaranteed by the Fourteenth Amendment. The County Supervisors' action had forced children to attend racially segregated schools which, although designated as private schools, received county and state support.

In 1969, the Supreme Court in *Alexander v. Holmes County Board of Education* discarded the "all deliberate speed" criterion for school desegregation.[14] It reversed lower court decisions that allowed some Mississippi school districts to delay desegregation. The Court ruled that every school district in the land was to terminate racially segregated systems "at once."

In 1971 in *Swann v. Charlotte-Mecklenburg Board of Education*, the Supreme Court ruled that busing was an acceptable means of achieving school desegregation.[15] It also stated that future school construction must not be used to perpetuate or reestablish segregated schools. Following the Swan decision, district courts began attacking *de facto* segregation in northern and western urban areas such as San Francisco, Philadelphia, Pittsburgh, Detroit, Los Angeles, Denver, and Boston. The first phase of the legal thrust against racial inequality was directed against *de jure* segregation in the South. The second phase of the movement toward racial equality was launched against *de facto* segregation in the large northern cities.

De Facto Segregation

A number of cities such as Chicago, New York, Philadelphia, Los Angeles, and others had a growing black community that was enlarged by continuing in-migration from the South. These population centers required a complicated readjustment of racial relations. The integration of blacks into urban life was often complicated by socioeconomic factors. One of the consequences of racial discrimination was economic disadvantagement. Lower economic status usually resulted in lack of educational opportunity and little social mobility. Several factors contributed to the complexity of achieving racial integration in education:

1. The northern metropolitan schools were not segregated by law as they had been in the South. However, they were segregated in fact.

2. The large northern city was generally composed of a variety of residential neighborhoods. Many of these communities were populated by people of similar socioeconomic and ethnic backgrounds. In many large cities, the various communities were racially segregated into black or white sections. Genuinely racially integrated residential areas, although they existed, were not common. The black population tended to live in the inner city areas. The white population was located on the peripheral sections of the city or in adjacent suburbs. The typical demographic pattern of the late 1960s and 1970s was a movement of the black population outward from the central city. The white population was moving to the fringes of the city or to the adjacent suburbs. Examples of such racial patterns occurred in Chicago, New York, Los Angeles, and other large northern metropolitan areas.

3. The schools which had been the scene of racial segregation in the South now became a focal point of desegregation efforts in the North. Civil rights leaders saw public schools as agencies for improving social and economic mobility as well as racial

integration. The northern public school became a focal agency for the movement toward racial integration.

4. The public school in the United States has usually been located in the residential area of the children who attend it. The locally based school attendance concept encouraged local public schools as "neighborhood schools." Since there were very few racially integrated neighborhoods in many large northern cities and since residential patterns were often either white or black, neighborhood schools reflecting the population of a specific residential area were often attended by either white or black children. Civil rights leaders attacked the *status quo* in northern education as *de facto* segregation and urged efforts to racially integrate schools.

In the 1960s, there were concerted legal and political efforts to integrate northern schools. While still using the judicial process, some civil rights organizations turned to more activist methods of achieving their goals such as demonstrations or school boycotts. Superintendents, principals, and other school administrators found themselves in the center of such activism. In cities such as Chicago and Milwaukee, school boycotts were used to protest *de facto* segregation as black parents kept their children out of school for limited periods of time to enforce their demand for policy changes.

During the 1960s and 1970s, the various civil rights organizations developed strategies to integrate the public schools. In a common pursuit, major civil rights organizations remained committed to the ideal of equality or educational opportunity for all children. They further believed that equality could best be achieved through genuinely integrated education. Both the National Urban League and the NAACP recommended that: 1) inner city children be taught by qualified teachers; 2) special reading programs and other forms of educational assistance be instituted where needed; 3) integrated education was a national opportunity for all American children regardless of color. In addition to sharing these goals, the Southern Christian Leadership, headed by Dr. Martin Luther King, Jr., expressed a special commitment to improved educational programs and preferential programs to overcome learning deficits. Most of the civil rights organizations favored including African-American history in the curriculum and other activities in the school program that would recognize the black contribution to American life.

Although they have generally agreed on educational goals, some differences surfaced over specific programs designed to integrate education. Some suggested the interdistrict busing of students from one area to another within the large cities to achieve racially integrated classrooms. Others recommended overlapping school districts that included both black and white residential areas. Civil rights leaders also charged that the quality of education provided in inner

city schools was inferior to that of other schools. To improve education in
the inner city schools, compensatory programs, recruitment of qualified
teachers, increased expenditures, an extended school year, smaller class size,
and expanded vocational programs were urged.

During the 1960s, the public focus was directed to issues of school
desegregation and integration. The mood of the late 1960s and early 1970s

The Ebenezer Baptist Church of Atlanta, Georgia, the home church of Dr. Martin Luther
King, Jr., leader of the civil rights movement. Photo by Patricia A. Gutek.

produced controversy and spawned some groups which resisted the movement. The Ku Klux Klan, the White Citizen's Council, and Black Nationalists advocated racial supremacist ideologies. Other groups, like the Southern Christian Leadership Conference, the National Association for the Advancement of Colored People, and the Urban League, saw school integration as a part of a much larger economic, social, and political issue.

Education and the Urban Crisis of the 1960s

By the late 1960s, a socially tense and potentially explosive situation had developed in America's urban areas. Rising social and economic expectations had been largely unfilled in the nation's big cities. Among black youth in northern cities, unemployment rates remained high despite the programs of the "war on poverty." In the summer of 1967, violent civil disorders erupted in Newark, New Jersey and Detroit, Michigan. Again, following the assassination of Dr. Martin Luther King Jr., in the spring of 1968, civil disorders occurred in several cities, including Chicago and the nation's capital, Washington, DC, with a loss of lives and property.

On July 28, 1967, President Lyndon Johnson established a National Advisory Commission of Civil Disorders, headed by Governor Otto Kerner of Illinois as chairman and Mayor John Lindsay of New York City as vice-chairman. The Kerner Commission examined the racial disorders in terms of their historical, sociological, economic, legal, and educational causes. The Commission member's who were aware of the interrelationship of the urban school with its society, found that, despite the progress made in racial desegregation, the quality of education in many inner-city schools was inadequate and unequal to that received by many white children. According to the Commission's report:

> ...for many minorities, and particularly for the children of the racial ghetto, the schools have failed to provide the educational experiences which could help overcome the effects of discrimination and deprivation.

> This failure is one of the persistent sources of grievance and resentment within the Negro community. The hostility of Negro parents and students toward the school system is generating increasing conflict and causing disruption within many city school districts.[16]

The Kerner Commission recommended several broad strategies to improve urban education. The most pressing problem was to eliminate *de facto* racial segregation. Compensatory education was needed to improve instruction in urban schools. It also recommended expanded opportunities for inner city youth to enter vocational training programs and college. Along with more effective instructional programs, the Commission urged improvement of school-community and parental participation in the school system.

In its specific recommendations, the Kerner Commission urged increased funding for innovative programs to eliminate *de facto* racial segregation. For example, model or magnet schools might be established on an integrated basis, offering special programs to attract students of varying racial and socioeconomic backgrounds. Year-round schooling might be provided for students with learning problems. Such extended programs would include activities to improve verbal skills and provide job training. Early childhood education programs would include activities to improve verbal skills and provide job training. Early childhood education programs, such as Head Start, should continue to receive support to develop learning readiness. Textbooks and curricula should be revised to include recognition of the culture, history, and contributions of minority groups to American civilization. In particular, the Commission urged emphasis on programs to improve reading and writing as the necessary foundations for later education.

The Report of the Kerner Commission gave added support to the national effort at "compensatory education" which was already underway. The federal government, the states, school districts, and many schools of education were involved in designing and implementing education programs to provide added educational services to children of low-income families to compensate for learning deficits that were believed to come from disadvantaged backgrounds. Among the major compensatory education programs was the federally funded Head Start, initiated in 1965, under the Economic Opportunity Act. Children eligible to enroll in Head Start programs ranged in age from three to six and were members of families with annual incomes under three thousand dollars. The goal of the Head Start program was to help economically disadvantaged children to begin school on terms equal to those of their more advantaged peers. Along with Head Start, other federally financed projects were Vista, the Job Corps, the Teacher Corps, and Upward Bound. Job Corps centers were established to provide vocational training to high school dropouts. Upward Bound was designed to prepare disadvantaged youth for college. Federal funds also were used to provide more teachers, buildings, and equipment in areas with concentrations of low-income children.

Reassessing Compensatory Education

While the President's Commission on Civil Disorders was urging more compensatory education programs, a major study conducted under the auspices of the federal government warned against exaggerating the impact of these programs in improving the academic achievement of disadvantaged children.

Mandated by Congress when it passed the Civil Rights Act of 1964, Professor James Coleman's report on the *Equality of Educational Opportunity* was the product of the largest statistical survey ever made of American education.[17] Coleman and his staff used standardized achievement tests to measure the skills of 645,000 students in problem solving, reading, writing, and arithmetic in 4,000 schools throughout the United States.

Coleman's initial working assumption supported the rationale of compensatory education that the unequal achievement of children from lower socioeconomic groups resulted from their unequal access to educational facilities. The advocates of compensatory education had claimed that such factors as the condition of school buildings, the quality of textbooks and libraries, class size, and the preparation of teachers were education "inputs" that directly determined the school's "outputs," namely students' achievements. If the school "inputs" for disadvantaged students were improved, it was assumed that achievement also would improve. Thus, Coleman had expected to find that differences in the quality of the school attended by majority and minority group students would explain inequalities in academic achievement.

Coleman found that children's achievement was highly dependent on their family and socioeconomic background. Differences in achievement among poor children correlated highly with the socioeconomic status of the peer group with whom they attended school. Children of low socioeconomic status had higher academic achievement when they attended a middle-class school than when they attended one composed largely of children from their own background. Family background and socioeconomic class had a more important impact on academic achievement than had been thought. While quantitative improvements in the condition of schooling were important, the school was but one factor in academic success. Indeed, socioeconomic factors had a more persuasive impact.

Another important study was Christopher Jencks' *Inequality: A Reassessment of the Effect of Family and Schooling in America* which examined the long-standing assumption that a correlation existed between schooling and future socioeconomic success.[18] Using highly sophisticated empirical procedures, Jencks concluded that impact on reducing the gap between rich and poor was not as powerful as believed. School achievement, Jencks argued, was largely determined by the student's socioeconomic status and family background. His major conclusion was that genuine equality of opportunity depended on a redistribution of income.

The educational implications that come forth from the research of Coleman and Jencks did much to shatter the optimistic view that schools alone could end the poverty cycle that had victimized lower socioeconomic classes in the United States. The various programs of compensatory education that had relied so heavily on the power of the school to effect social change had promised more than could be delivered.

Conclusion

While the movement for equality of educational opportunity in the United States has been continuous, it has encountered a number of obstacles. Of these, one of the most oppressive has been the legacy of discrimination based upon race. Racial discrimination has had a long history in the United States that dates back to the introduction of the practice of African slavery into North America. The residues of racism continued long after the emancipation of the slaves as a result of the Civil War, Lincoln's Emancipation Proclamation, and the ratification of the Thirteenth Amendment. Indeed, *de jure* segregation under the guise of the "separate but equal" doctrine of the *Plessy v. Ferguson* decision of 1896 seemed to give legal sanction to discrimination based on race. It was not until the historic decision in the Brown case in 1954 that racism in the form of the "separate but equal doctrine" was overturned. One of the great transformations of the twentieth century in the United States has been the movement first to desegregate and then to integrate American society and its schools. As is true of many of the great movements in our history, the goal of a truly free and equal society still remains a sought after prize. However, the legacy of the Civil Rights movement of the 1950s and 1960s makes the realization of that democratic goal a distinct possibility as we prepare as a nation to enter the twenty-first century.

Notes

[1] Booker T. Washington, *Up From Slavery* (New York: Doubleday and Co., 1938).

[2] E. Davidson Washington, ed., *Selected Speeches of Booker T. Washington (New York: Doubleday, Doran, and Co., 1932), pp. 31-36.*

[3] *Ibid.*, p. 34

[4] Booker T. Washington, *Working with the Hands* (New York: Doubleday, Page, and Co., 1904), pp. 80-81.

[5] W. E. Burghardt Du Bois, *The Souls of Black Folk: Essays and Sketches* (Chicago: A.C. McClurg and Co., 1903), pp. 51-52.

[6] Committee on Civil Rights, *To Secure These Rights: the Report of the President's Committee on Civil Rights* (New York: Simon and Schuster, 1947).

[7] *Plessy v. Ferguson*, 163 U.S. 537 (1896).

[8] *Missouri Ex Rel Gaines v. Canada*, 305 U.S. 337 (1938).

[9] *Sipuel v. Oklahoma Board of Regents*, 332 U.S. 631 (1948).

[10] *Sweatt v. Painter*, 339 U.S. 629 (1950).

[11] *Brown v. Board of Education*, 347 U.S. 483 (1954).

[12] The terms *de jure* and *de facto* are Latin phrases which are descriptively applied to certain legal situations. *De jure* means by right, or by lawful title. *De jure* segregation refers to a separation of the races which is enforced by law. *De facto* means actually, in fact, or in reality. *De facto* segregation has come to refer to racial separation, accidental or deliberate, which exists but without the sanction of law.

[13] *Griffin v. School Board of Prince Edward County*, 377 U.S. 218 (1964).

[14] *Alexander v. Holmes County Board of Education*, 396 U.S. 19 (1969).

[15] *Swann v. Charlotte-Mecklenburg Board of Education*, 402 U.S. 554 (1971).

[16] The National Advisory Commission of Civil Disorders, *Report of the National Advisory Commission on Civil Disorders* (New York: Bantam Books, Inc., 1968) pp. 424-25.

[17] James S. Coleman, et al., *Equality of Educational Opportunity* (Washington, DC: U.S. Government Printing Office, 1966).

[18] Christopher Jencks, et al., *Inequality: A Reassessment of the Effect of Family and Schooling in America* (New York: Basic Books, Inc., 1972).

Selections to Accompany
Chapter 8

Booker T. Washington, the black educator who first attempted to lead African-Americans up from slavery, believed that social improvement would follow if they had a solid economic base. He urged blacks to seek economic betterment through the trades and crafts rather than through political means. By nature Washington seems to have been a gradualist, a conservative, and a practical man. Although his attitude is not widely accepted today, it does represent an important historical attitude on the gradualistic method of bringing about social and economic change through education. In the selection below, taken from The Future of the American Negro, *Washington discusses the role of education in that future.*

The Future of the American Negro

One of the main problems as regards the education of the Negro is how to have him use his education to the best advantage after he has secured it. In saying this, I do not want to be understood as implying that the problem of simple ignorance among the masses has been settled in the South; for this is far from true. The amount of ignorance still prevailing among the Negroes, especially in the rural districts, is very large and serious. But I repeat, we must go farther if we would secure the best results and most gratifying returns in public good for the money spent than merely to put academic education in the Negro's head with the idea that this will settle everything.

In his present condition it is important, in seeking after what he terms the ideal, that the Negro should not neglect to prepare himself to take advantage of the opportunities that are right about his door. If he lets these opportunities slip, I fear they will never be his again. In saying this, I mean always that

SOURCE: *Booker T. Washington, The Future of the American Negro* (Boston: Small, Maynard, and Co., 1900), pp. 67-69, 78-82.

the Negro should have the most thorough mental and religious training; for without it no race can succeed. Because of his past history and environment and present condition it is important that he be carefully guided for years to come in the proper use of his education. Much valuable time has been lost and money spent in vain, because too many have not been educated with the idea of fitting them to do well the things which they could get to do. Because of the lack of proper direction of the Negro's education, some good friends of his, North and South, have not taken that interest in it that they otherwise would have taken. In too many cases where merely literary education alone has been given the Negro youth, it has resulted in an exaggerated estimate of his importance in the world, and an increase of wants which his education has not fitted him to supply.

But, in discussing this subject, one is often met with the question, Should not the Negro be encouraged to prepare himself for any station in life that any other race fills? I would say, Yes; but the surest way for the Negro to reach the highest positions is to prepare himself to fill well at the present time the basic occupations. This will give him a foundation upon which to stand while securing what is called the more exalted positions. The Negro has the right to study law; but success will come to the race sooner if it produces intelligent, thrifty farmers, mechanics, and housekeepers to support the lawyers. The want of proper direction of the use of the Negro's education results in tempting too many to live mainly by their wits, without producing anything that is of real value to the world. Let me quote examples of this.

• • •

. . . the skilled labour has been taken out of the Negro's hands; but I do mean to say that in no part of the South is he so strong in the matter of skilled labour as he was twenty years ago, except possibly in the country districts and the smaller towns. In the more northern of the Southern cities, such as Richmond and Baltimore, the change is most apparent; and it is being felt in every Southern city. Wherever the Negro has lost ground industrially in the South, it is not because there is prejudice against him as a skilled labourer on the part of the native Southern white man; the Southern white man generally prefers to do business with the Negro mechanic rather than with a white one, because he is accustomed to do business with the Negro in this respect. There is almost no prejudice against the Negro in the South in matters of business, so far as the native whites are concerned; and here is the entering wedge for the solution of the race problem. But too often, where the white mechanic or factory operative from the North gets a hold, the trades-union soon follows, and the Negro is crowded to the wall.

But what is the remedy for this condition? First, it is most important that the Negro and his white friends honestly face the facts as they are; otherwise the time will not be very far distant when the Negro of the South will be crowded to the ragged edge of industrial life as he is in the North. There is still time to repair the damage and to reclaim what we have lost.

I stated in the beginning, that industrial education for the Negro has been misunderstood. This has been chiefly because some have gotten the idea that industrial development was opposed to the Negro's higher mental development. This has little or nothing to do with the subject under discussion; we should no longer permit such an idea to aid in depriving the Negro of the legacy in the form of skilled labour that was purchased by his forefathers at the price of two hundred and fifty years of slavery. I would say to the black boy what I would say to the white boy, Get all the mental development that your time and pocketbook will allow of, — the more, the better; but the time has come when a larger proportion — not all, for we need professional men and women — of the educated coloured men and women should give themselves to industrial or business life. The professional class will be helped in so far as the rank and file have an industrial foundation, so that they can pay for professional service. Whether they receive the training of the hand while pursuing their academic training or after their academic training is finished, or whether they will get their literary training in an industrial school or college, are questions which each individual must decide for himself. No matter how or where educated, the educated men and women must come to the rescue of the race in the effort to get and hold its industrial footing. I would not have the standard of mental development lowered one whit; for, with the Negro, as with all races, mental strength is the basis of all progress. But I would have a large measure of this mental strength reach the Negroes' actual needs through the medium of the hand. Just now the need is not so much for the common carpenters, brick masons, farmers, and laundry women as for industrial leaders who, in addition to their practical knowledge, can draw plans, make estimates, take contracts; those who understand the latest methods of truck-gardening and the science underlying practical agriculture; those who understand machinery to the extent that they can operate steam and electric laundries, so that our women can hold on to the laundry work in the South, that is so fast drifting into the hands of others in the large cities and towns.

One of the most significant decisions of the United States Supreme Court affecting public education was that of the 1954 decision in Brown v. the Board of Education of Topeka. *Prior to this decision, state laws requiring or permitting racial segregation in public schools were presumed constitutional, according to the "separate but equal" provisions of the* Plessy v. Ferguson *case in 1896. In 1954 the Court heard cases from Delaware, Kansas, South Carolina, and Virginia which questioned the constitutionality of the "separate but equal" provision. The decision of 1954, quoted below, declared that racially segregated public schools had no place in American life. This decision was one of far-reaching social, political, legal, and educational significance.*

Brown v. Board of Education of Topeka

These cases come to us from the States of Kansas, South Carolina, Virginia, and Delaware. They are premised on different facts and different local conditions, but a common legal question justifies their consideration together in this consolidated opinion.

In each of the cases minors of the Negro race, through their legal representatives, seek the aid of the courts in obtaining admission to the public schools of their community on a nonsegregated basis. In each instance, they have been denied admission to schools attended by white children under laws requiring or permitting segregation according to race. This segregation was alleged to deprive the plaintiffs of the equal protection of the laws under the Fourteenth Amendment. In each of the cases other than the Delaware case, a three-judge federal district court denied relief to the plaintiffs on the so-called "separate but equal" doctrine announced by this Court in *Plessy v. Ferguson*, 163 U.S. 537. Under that doctrine, equality of treatment is accorded when the races are provided substantially equal facilities, even though these facilities be separate. In the Delaware case, the Supreme Court of Delaware adhered to that doctrine, but ordered that the plaintiffs be admitted to the white schools because of their superiority to the Negro schools.

The plaintiffs contend that segregated public schools are not "equal" and cannot be made "equal," and that hence they are deprived of the equal protection of the laws. Because of the obvious importance of the question presented, the Court took jurisdiction. Argument was heard in the 1952 Term, and reargument was heard this Term on certain questions propounded by the Court.

SOURCE: *Brown v. Board of Education of Topeka,* 347 U.S. 483 (1954).

Reargument was largely devoted to the circumstances surrounding the adoption of the Fourteenth Amendment in 1868. It covered exhaustively consideration of the Amendment in Congress, ratification by the states, then existing practices in racial segregation, and the views of proponents and opponents of the Amendment. This discussion and our own investigation convince us that, although these sources cast some light, it is not enough to resolve the problem with which we are faced. At best, they are inconclusive. The most avid proponents of the post-War Amendments undoubtedly intended them to remove all legal distinctions among "all persons born or naturalized in the United States." Their opponents, just as certainly, were antagonistic to both the letter and the spirit of the Amendments and wished them to have the most limited effect. What others in Congress and the state legislatures had in mind cannot be determined with any degree of certainty.

An additional reason for the inconclusive nature of the Amendment's history, with respect to segregated schools, is the status of public education at that time. In the South, the movement toward free common schools, supported by general taxation, had not yet taken hold. Education of white children was largely in the hands of private groups. Education of Negroes was almost nonexistent, and practically all of the race were illiterate. In fact, any education of Negroes was forbidden by law in some states. Today, in contrast, many Negroes have achieved outstanding success in the arts and sciences as well as in the business and professional world. It is true that public education had already advanced further in the North, but the effect of the Amendment on Northern States was generally ignored in the congressional debates. Even in the North, the conditions of public education did not approximate those existing today. The curriculum was usually rudimentary; ungraded schools were common in rural areas; the school term was but three months a year in many states; and compulsory school attendance was virtually unknown. As a consequence, it is not surprising that there should be so little in the history of the Fourteenth Amendment relating to its intended effect on public education.

In the first cases in this Court construing the Fourteenth Amendment, decided shortly after its adoption, the Court interpreted it as proscribing all state-imposed discriminations against the Negro race. The doctrine of "separate but equal" did not make its appearance in this Court until 1896 in the case of *Plessy v. Ferguson, supra,* involving not education but transportation. American courts have since labored with the doctrine for over half a century. In this Court, there have been six cases involving the "separate but equal" doctrine in the field of public education. In *Cumming v. Board of Education of Richmond County,* 175 U.S. 528, and *Gong Lum v. Rice,* 275 U.S. 78, the validity of the doctrine itself was not challenged. In more recent cases, all on the graduate school level, inequality was found in that specific benefits enjoyed by white students were denied to Negro students of the same educational qualifications. *State of Missouri ex rel. Gaines v. Canada*, 305 U.S. 337; *Sipuel v. Board of Regents of University of Oklahoma*, 332 U.S. 631; *Sweatt v. Painter*, 339 U.S. 629; *McLaurin v. Oklahoma State Regents*, 339 U.S. 637. In none of these cases was it necessary to reexamine the doctrine to grant relief to the Negro plaintiff. And in *Sweatt v. Painter, supra*, the Court expressly reserved decision on the question whether *Plessy v. Ferguson* should be held inapplicable to public education.

In the instant cases, that question is directly presented. Here, unlike *Sweatt v. Painter*, there are findings below that the Negro and white schools involved have been equalized, or are being equalized, with respect to buildings, curricula, qualifications and salaries of teachers, and other "tangible" factors. Our decision, therefore, cannot turn on merely a comparison of these tangible factors in the Negro and white schools involved in each of the cases. We must look instead to the effect of segregation itself on public education.

In approaching this problem, we cannot turn the clock back to 1868 when the Amendment was adopted, or even to 1896 when *Plessy v. Ferguson* was written. We must consider public education in the light of its full development and its present place in American life throughout the Nation. Only in this way can it be determined if segregation in public schools deprives these plaintiffs of the equal protection of the laws.

Today, education is perhaps the most important function of state and local governments. Compulsory school attendance laws and the great expenditures for education both demonstrate our recognition of the importance of education to our democratic society. It is required in the performance of our most basic public responsibilities, even service in the armed forces. It is the very foundation of good citizenship. Today it is a principal instrument in awakening the child to cultural values, in preparing him for later professional training, and in helping him to adjust normally to his environment. In these days, it is doubtful that any child may reasonably be expected to succeed in life if he is denied the opportunity of an education. Such an opportunity where the state has undertaken to provide it, is a right which must be made available to all on equal terms.

We come then to the question presented: Does segregation of children in public schools solely on the basis of race, even though the physical facilities and other "tangible" factors may be equal, deprive the children of the minority group of equal educational opportunities? We believe that it does.

In *Sweatt v. Painter, supra* (339 U.S. 629, 70 S.Ct. 850), in finding that a segregated law school for Negroes could not provide them equal educational opportunities, this Court relied in large part on "those qualities which are incapable of objective measurement but which make for greatness in a law school." In *Mclaurin v. Oklahoma State Regents, supra* (339 U.S. 637, 70 S.Ct. 853), the Court, in requiring that a Negro admitted to a white graduate school be treated like all other students, again resorted to intangible considerations: ". . . his ability to study, to engage in discussions and exchange views with other students, and, in general, to learn his profession." Such considerations apply with added force to children in grade and high schools. To separate them from others of similar age and qualifications solely because of their race generates a feeling of inferiority as to their status in the community that may affect their hearts and minds in a way unlikely ever to be undone. The effect of this separation on their educational opportunities was well stated by a finding in the Kansas case by a court which nevertheless felt compelled to rule against the Negro plaintiffs:

"Segregation of white and colored children in public schools has a detrimental effect upon the colored children. The impact is greater when it has the sanction of the law; for the policy of separating the races is usually interpreted as denoting the inferiority of the Negro group. A sense of inferiority affects the motivation of a child to learn. Segregation with the sanction of law, therefore, has a tendency to retard the educational and mental development of Negro children and to deprive them of some of the benefits they would receive in a racially integrated school system."

Whatever may have been the extent of psychological knowledge at the time of *Plessy v. Ferguson*, this finding is amply supported by modern authority. Any language in *Plessy v. Ferguson* contrary to this finding is rejected.

We conclude that in the field of public education the doctrine of "separate but equal" has no place. Separate educational facilities are inherently unequal. Therefore, we hold that the plaintiffs and others similarly situated for whom the actions have been brought are, by reason of the segregation complained of deprived of the equal protection of the laws guaranteed by the Fourteenth Amendment. This disposition make unnecessary any discussion whether such segregation also violates the Due Process Clause of the Fourteenth Amendment.

Because these are class actions, because of the wide applicability of this decision, and because of the great variety of local conditions, the formulation of decrees in these cases presents problems of considerable complexity. On reargument, the consideration of appropriate relief was necessarily subordinated to the primary question—the constitutionality of segregation in public education. We have now announced that such segregation is a denial of the equal protection of the laws. In order that we may have the full assistance of the parties in formulating decrees, the cases will be restored to the docket, and the parties are requested to present further argument. . . . The Attorney General of the United States is again invited to participate. The Attorneys General of the states requiring or permitting segregation in public education will also be permitted to appear as *amici curiae* upon request to do so by September 15, 1954, and submission of briefs by October 1,1954.

It is so ordered.

Suggestions for Further Reading

Coleman, James S., et al. *Equality of Educational Opportunity.* Washington, DC: U.S. Government Printing Office, 1966.

Cruse, Harold. *Plural but Equal: A Critical Study of Blacks and Minorities and America's Plural Society.* New York: William Morrow and Co., 1987.

Du Bois, W.E. Burghardt. *The Souls of Black Folk: Essays and Sketches.* Chicago: A.C. McClurg and Co., 1903.

Harlan, Louis R. *Booker T. Washington: The Wizard of Tuskegee, 1901-1915.* New York: Oxford University Press, 1983.

Fox-Genovese, Elizabeth. *Within the Plantation Household: Black and White Women of the Old South.* Chapel Hill: University of North Carolina Press, 1988.

Jencks, Christopher, et al. *Inequality: A Reassessment of the Effect of Family and Schooling in America.* New York: Basic Books, Inc., 1972.

Lofgren, Charles A. *The Plessy Case: A Legal-Historical Interpretation.* New York: Oxford University Press, 1987.

Marable, Manning. *W.E.B. Du Bois: Black Radical Democrat.* Boston: Twayne Publishers, 1986.

McLaurin, Melton A. *Separate Pasts: Growing Up White in the Segregated South.* Athens: University of Georgia Press, 1987.

National Advisory Commission of Civil Disorders. *Report of the National Advisory Commission on Civil Disorders.* New York: Bantam Books, 1968.

Schwartz, Bernard. *Swann's Way: The Second Busing Case and the Supreme Court.* New York: Oxford University Press, 1986.

Taylor, D. Garth. *Public Opinion and Collective Action: The Boston School Desegregation Conflict.* Chicago: University of Chicago Press, 1986.

Tushnet, Mark V. *The NAACP's Legal Strategy Against Segregated Education, 1925-1950.* Chapel Hill, NC: University of North Carolina Press, 1987.

Washington, Booker T. *Up From Slavery.* New York: Doubleday and Co., 1938.

Washington, Booker T. *Working with the Hands.* New York: Doubleday, Page, and Co., 1904.

Washington, E. Davidson. ed. *Selected Speeches of Booker T. Washington.* New York: Doubleday, Doran, and Co., 1932.

The Recent Past
An Era Of Reform

Recent events are always difficult to place in historical perspective. Some events which seem of great importance when they occur, lose their significance over time. Other events which are passed over lightly may be the truly important ones that have a pronounced impact in the light of history. In this chapter, the climate of educational reform of the 1980s is examined. The long range impact of these reforms will need further assessment.

The Climate of the 1980s

The 1980s, in sharp contrast to the 1960s, saw a conservative resurgence in politics, economics, and education. During Ronald Reagan's term as President, from 1981 to 1989, the conservative ideology was applied to the nation's economy, social issues, and educational philosophy. The "back-to-the-basics" movement which had gathered momentum in many local school districts throughout the 1970s found national expression in the educational policies of the Reagan administration. A current that ran through the 1980s was the issuing of a series of reports that expressed alarm over the declining academic quality of American education and urged concerted efforts to raise the standards in the nation's public schools.

Terrel H. Bell, Secretary of Education in the Reagan cabinet, focused national attention on the quality of American elementary and secondary education through *A Nation at Risk*, the report of the National Commission on Excellence in Education. Under Bell's leadership, the Department of Education encouraged educational reform in the various states and acted as a national vehicle for disseminating information about successful state and local programs. Taking a basic education position, the Reagan administration endorsed the Commission on Excellence's call for an emphasis on basic academic subjects. President Reagan, himself, urged a return to old-fashioned discipline and values in the schools. When Bell resigned as Secretary of Education in 1984 to become a professor of school administration at the University of Utah, he was succeeded by William J. Bennett, the chairman of the National Endowment for the Humanities. Bennett issued a number of recommendations that emphasized basic academic subject matter.

During the 1970s, a movement for "basic education," had enlisted the support of citizen's groups, politicians, and other interested parties. In some regions of the country, school administrators endorsed and implemented a basic education approach describing the basic education movement of the 1970s. Diane Ravitch, an educational historian, commented that a generalized public opinion existed that believed academic standards of American education had deteriorated because: (1) basic skills and academic subject matter were de-emphasized in the curriculum; (2) social promotion rather than mastery of academic skills and subjects was practiced by many schools. Ravitch, herself, reflected a basic education orientation based on the liberal arts and sciences.[1]

The basic education movement of the 1970s set the stage for many of the criticisms and recommendations that would be developed in the reports of the 1980s. Among the criticisms were:

1. Experimentation, social promotion, and neglect of standards had caused a decline in the academic quality of many public schools.

2. Educators had not attempted to reverse a perceived decline in fundamental moral, ethical, and civic values, indeed, programs of "values clarification" and ethical humanism had contributed to that decline.

3. The quality of instruction had deteriorated because of lack of effective classroom management by inadequately prepared teachers.

4. American schools had become top heavy with administrators; non-instructional costs should be cut by concentrating on academic

subjects rather than non-academic ones.
5. Student achievement was measured imprecisely; achievement tests
   that measured mastery of basic academic skills and subjects should
   be used for promotion.[2]

In addition to the basic education climate of opinion in the early 1980s, several national commissions were conducting periodic re-examinations of the purposes, organization, and curriculum of American schools. For example, such examinations had been conducted in the past by the Committee of Ten in 1873, the Commission on the Reorganization of Secondary Education in 1918, and James B. Conant in 1959. Among the important reports of the 1980s were: *High School: A Report on Secondary Education in America*, sponsored by the Carnegie Foundation for the Advancement of Teaching; *Horace's Compromise: The Dilemma of the American High School*, co-sponsored by the National Association of Secondary School Principals and the Commission on Educational issues of the National Association of Independent Schools; and *Academic Preparation for College: What Students Need to Know and Be Able to Do*, sponsored by the College Board.[3]

There was also an economic dimension to the climate of opinion that fostered the atmosphere for school reform. In the 1970s, the United States appeared to be losing its economic pre-eminence as the world's leading economic power. Critics from the business community charged that many graduates of American schools lacked the fundamental skills needed for productivity in the workplace of the 1980s. The success of foreign competitors, especially the West Germans and Japanese, was attributed to the superiority of the educational system in those countries. Declining American productivity was attributed to the failure of American schools to prepare competently trained individuals who possessed the creativity and discipline demanded in rapidly changing and highly competitive world economy. By the early 1980s, a pervasive climate of public opinion existed that supported educational reform. In 1983, *A Nation at Risk* found a generally receptive audience.

A Nation At Risk

The report of the National Commission on Excellence began with the dramatic warning, "Our Nation is at risk. Our once unchallenged preeminence in commerce, industry, science, and technological innovation is being overtaken by competitors throughout the world." It continued, "The educational foundations of our society are presently being eroded by a rising tide of mediocrity that threatens our very future as a Nation and a people."[4]

In rapid order, the Commission's report identified the indicators of the nation's risk. Among them were:

1. Some 23 million adults were functionally illiterate.

2. 13 percent of 17-year olds were functionally illiterate.

3. A virtually unbroken decline on the Scholastic Aptitude Tests from 1963 to 1980.

4. A steady decline in U.S. science achievement scores.

Based upon these indicators, the report contended that ''The average graduate of our schools and colleges today is not as well-educated as the average graduate of 25 or 35 years ago, when a much smaller proportion of our population completed high school and college.''[5]

A Nation at Risk made a series of recommendations. It recommended that high school students be required to take four years of English, three years of mathematics, three years of science, three years of social studies, and one-half year of computer science.[6] Calling this recommendation on emphasis the ''Five New Basics,'' the report addressed the improvement of academic content. It was further recommended that more time be provided for students to learn the ''New Basics'' by lengthening the school day or year.

To raise academic standards, the authors of the report urged schools, colleges, and universities to ''adopt more rigorous and measurable standards, and higher expectations, for academic performance and student conduct.'' Institutions of higher education were advised to raise their admission requirements.[7]

A Nation at Risk also carried several recommendations designed to improve teaching. Among them were:

1. Prospective teachers should ''meet high academic standards,'' have an aptitude for teaching, and be competent in an academic discipline.

2. Teachers' salaries should be competitive and ''performance-based.'' Salary, promotion and tenure decisions should be based on effective evaluation systems that include peer review.

3. Career ladders should be developed to distinguish between the ''beginning instructor, the experienced teacher, and the master teacher.''

4. The shortage of teachers in the critical areas of mathematics and science should be addressed by facilitating ''nonschool personnel'' who hold appropriate degrees into teaching.[8]

A Nation at Risk attracted national attention, especially in the media. To create a national forum for the report, Secretary of Education Bell arranged twelve regional meetings, followed by a national conference under the auspices of the Department of Education. The regional forums, attended by public and private school educators, school board members, and political leaders, were designed to: (1) keep the report of the Commission of Excellence in the news; (2) stimulate state and local district implementation efforts; (3) highlight and disseminate models of effective reform efforts; (4) define the federal government's role as stimulating educational reform and disseminating information but not providing extensive funding.[9]

As the national discussion about educational reform continued, certain key issues emerged. Among them were:

1. The development of alternatives to single teachers' salary schedules such as merit pay and career ladders.

2. The modification of the conventional teacher education programs in departments and colleges of education.

3. Raising high school graduation and college admission requirements and increasing the length of the school day and school year.

4. Encouraging partnerships between business and schools to improve the quality of education.[10]

An important element in Bell's strategy was to use the federal government as a pulpit for education reform but not as a funding source. The Department of Education's effort to publicize "model programs" was compatible with the administration's general direction.

Critics of *A Nation at Risk*

While *A Nation at Risk* enjoyed national media coverage and a generally receptive audience, the "reform" efforts were criticized by teachers' organizations and educators who believed that: (1) teachers were unfairly being made the scapegoat for national problems which were beyond the capability of schools to solve; (2) reductions in federal support had weakened efforts at equity or equality of educational opportunity for women, members of minority groups and persons with handicaps.

The National Education Association's *Teacher's Views of Equity and Excellence* identified the achievements that had promoted equality of educational opportunity. For example:

1. As of 1979, "85 percent of white students" and "75 percent of black students" were earning high school diplomas — "three times the percentage" of 1949.

2. The "median educational level of blacks" had increased "from eighth grade in 1960 to twelfth grade in 1980."

3. "Black students had registered gains in "reading, writing, and arithmetic skills" and "the gap between blacks and whites on standardized test scores" had been reduced.

In addition, the NEA indicated that disadvantaged children in federally-aided programs had made significant gains in reading and mathematics achievement and that bi-lingual education had provided "millions of youngsters an equal chance to learn and participate in American society." Further, Title IX, prohibiting sex discrimination in education, had increased women's educational opportunities. The NEA then charged that these important achievements were being jeopardized by the "serious erosion" of the national commitment "to quality and equality."[11] Specifically, the NEA condemned policies that relaxed the application of "anti-discrimination statutes" and that reduced the funding of programs to improve the education of economically disadvantaged children.[12]

Generally suspicious of merit pay and career ladder proposals, the NEA developed its own recommendations for improving the condition of teachers, which included:

1. Reducing class size and improving educational materials.

2. Attracting and retaining talented teachers by "competitive entry-level salaries" and rewards that did not "selectively raise the pay of a few teachers at the expense of many."

3. Including teachers in instructional decision-making and reducing their non-educational tasks.

4. Establishing constructive teacher evaluation systems.

5. Creating more opportunities for professional development designed by professional educators and supported by school districts.

6. Improving teacher education programs resting on standards that teachers "believe are basic to success in the classroom."[13]

The American Federation of Teachers (AFT) responded to the issues generated by *A Nation at Risk* with position papers that stated the organization's position.[14] The AFT developed broad recommendations on teacher recruitment and retention which advocated general salary increases for teachers, more rigorous teacher certification requirements, improved teacher evaluation, improved school discipline, improved teaching conditions and smaller class size. The AFT also urged a reform of teacher education and certification practices which emphasized higher admission standards, an inquiry-based curriculum with more emphasis on the liberal arts and sciences, written entry examinations, and an extended internship prior to certification.

The AFT policy called for "stricter high school graduation requirements in academic subjects including math, science, English, history and foreign languages, though not at the expense of other essentials like music, art, and vocational education." [15]

Action For Excellence

Action for Excellence, the report of the Task Force on Education for Economic Growth, sponsored by the Education Commission of the States, was issued in 1983. Motivated by concerns similar to those of the Commission of Excellence in Education, the Task Force was particularly concerned with declining U.S. economic growth and productivity in the face of growing international competition. The Task Force sought to develop partnerships between business and education designed to make American schooling more effective and responsive to economic change. The Task Force stated that, "Technological change and global competition make it imperative to equip students in public schools with skills that go beyond the basics." [16]

For the authors of *Action for Excellence*, American schools had been weakened by lowered standards, educational deficits and "blurred goals." Other nations, especially Japan and West Germany, were challenging America's position as a scientific and technological leader. To regain America's threatened technological supremacy, the Task Force identified two imperatives: (1) expanding and upgrading the definition of basic skills beyond reading, writing, and arithmetic, and (2) mobilizing the educational system to teach the required new skills effectively.

Analyzing America's educational crisis under the heading of "Educational Deficits and Blurred Goals," the Task Force, like the Commission on Excellence, identified such problems as:

1. Deficits in student achievement, especially in reading, writing, comprehension, and mathematics skills.

2. Serious educational mathematics and science deficits, the disciplines most closely related to technological progress, manifested by "a lack of general scientific and mathematical literacy" and by projected shortages of skilled scientists and engineers; this educational deficit was aggravated by an obsolete science curriculum.

3. Serious shortages of qualified teachers in such critical subjects as science and mathematics.

4. Inadequate teachers' salaries based on "rigid salary schedules" rather than rewarding exceptional teachers for superior performance. [17]

The Task Force devised a strategy to improve the nation's education. It recommended that the governor of each state, along with that state's legislators, state and local boards of education, business and other leaders, should develop and implement an action plan to improve the state's schools, from kindergarten through grade 12. Each state plan should seek to prepare a "well-educated work force" with the "changing skills" needed for economic productivity. It should develop community, business, labor, government and education alliances to improve education for economic growth. The Task Force recommendations closely paralleled the strategies of the Commission on Excellence by suggesting that the state governor should act as the chief agent of educational reform.

The Task Force urged partnerships between business and education. The goals of business-school partnerships were to: (1) encourage business leaders to share "their expertise in planning, budgeting, and management" with school administrators; (2) to develop job training programs; (3) to prepare students to use the skills, techniques, and equipment actually used in businesses. The "Action for Excellence" agenda revealed a major trend of the 1980s—that the nation's businesses should help to shape educational policies.

The Task Force called upon local communities and states "to assign higher budget priority" to education and to ensure that resources were used more effectively and efficiently to promote educational quality. As did other national reports, the Task Force recommended improving teachers' preparation, status and salaries. It also endorsed the "career ladder" concept, by which teachers would assume more responsibility and receive salary increments as they advanced upward through various career stages or steps.

The Task Force followed the trend to more rigorous academic content that was found in *A Nation at Risk*. Local school districts were advised to establish "firm, explicit and demanding requirements concerning discipline, attendance, homework, grades and other essentials of effective schooling." The curriculum should be made more academically rigorous. Non-essential, non-academical courses should be eliminated.

Action for Excellence introduced the concept of "quality assurance" by which state boards of education were to establish objective evaluation procedures to assess and reward effective teacher performance. While the application of quality assurance evaluation would reward effective teachers, it would also identify teachers whose performance was inadequate and who needed remediation. Public schools were advised to institute "periodic testing of general achievement and specific skills" and colleges and universities were to "upgrade their entrance requirements."[18]

Current Trends

To place *A Nation at Risk, Action for Excellence*, and the other national reports on education into a broad historical perspective requires a sufficient perspective to assess the impact of their recommendation on the nation's schools. As the United States and its schools entered the 1990s, it was possible, however, to identify several trends that the reform era had generated.

The educational emphasis of the federal, state, and local governments appeared to be shifting. While basic constitutional and legal changes in the educational responsibilities of these government units did not occur, the states — the governor, legislature, and office of education — were taking an increased leadership role in raising requirements and standards and increasing funding. The federal government is likely to continue to urge reform efforts and to disseminate information about model programs. For example, federal efforts to combat the illegal use of drugs is likely to have an educational component.[19] Both Congress and the Bush administration are likely to enact legislation providing increased funding for early childhood education.

The various states which enacted more rigorous academic requirements and teacher competency tests are likely to remain the focal centers of educational change. Governors, who assumed the role of educational change agents in the 1980s are likely to remain as key figures in efforts to improve education. In the early 1990s, it is likely that efforts to improve teachers' salaries either by general increments, career ladders, or merit pay will continue. Teacher education programs can be expected to require more courses in the liberal arts and sciences and academic subjects. The states that require entry and probationary period examinations can be expected to continue this requirement.

The American high school can also be expected to experience curricular change. Vocational programs and elective courses are likely to decrease while basic academic subjects, such as mathematics, science, and English will receive more emphasis. The early 1990s will see the continuing impact of computers and technology upon the educational system. Computer literacy will become a common basic skill along with the traditional reading, writing, and arithmetic.

Notes

[1] Diane Ravitch, "Why Basic Education," *Conference on Basic Education, Council on Basic Education*, (Portland, Oregon, April 27, 1978).

[2] Gerald L. Gutek, *Basic Education: A Historical Perspective* (Bloomington, IN: Phi Delta Kappa Educational Foundation, 1981), pp. 9-13.

[3] For the reports, see Ernest L. Boyer, *High School: A Report on Secondary Education in America* (New York: Harper & Row, 1983); Theodore R. Sizer,

Horace's Compromise: The Dilemma of the American High School (Boston: Houghton Mifflin Co., 1984); The College Board, *Academic Preparation for College: What Students Need to Know and Be Able to Do* (New York: The College Board, 1983).

4 The National Commission of Excellence in Education, *A Nation At Risk: The Imperative for Educational Reform* (Washington, DC: U.S. Government Printing Office, 1983), p. 5.

5 *Ibid.*, p. 11.

6 *Ibid.*, p. 24.

7 *Ibid.*, p. 27.

8 *Ibid.*, pp. 30-31.

9 T.H. Bell, *Report by the Secretary on the Regional Forums on Excellence in Education* (Washington, DC: U.S. Department of Education, 1983), p. 4.

10 *Ibid.*, pp. 9-19. Also, see Staff of the National Commission on Excellence in Education, *Meeting the Challenge: Recent Efforts to improve Education Across the Nation* (Washington, DC: U.S. Department of Education, 1983).

11 National Education Association, *Teachers' Views on Equity and Excellence* (Washington, DC: National Education Association, 1983), pp. 3-4.

12 *Ibid.*, pp. 4-6.

13 National Education Association, *The Teaching Profession* (Washington, DC: National Education Association, 1983), pp. 2-6.

14 AFT Issues Papers on "Length of School Day and School Years," "Incentive Schemes and Pay Compensation Plans," "Teacher Recruitment and Early Career Incentives," "Teacher Preparation and Certification," "Standards, Curriculum, and Testing," "Elementary and Secondary Teacher Evaluation," "School Improvement," (Washington, DC: American Federation of Teachers, 1983).

15 AFT Issues Paper on "Length of School Day and School Year," p. 2.

16 Task Force on Education for Economic Growth, *Action for Excellence* (Denver: Education Commission of the States, 1983), pp. 9, 22-30.

17 *Ibid.*, pp. 22-30.

18 *Ibid.*, pp. 34-41.

19 *What Works: Schools Without Drugs.* (Washington, DC: U.S. Department of Education, 1986).

Selections to Accompany
Chapter 9

As the decade of the 1980s came to an end, the professional educators were stressing the need for effective schools, principals, and teachers. Much of the literature of the 1980s reiterated the theme of educational effectiveness. In the following selection from What Works: Research About Teaching and Learning, *the theme of effective education is highlighted.*

Effective Schools, Principals, and Teachers

Effective Schools

Research Finding:

The most important characteristics of effective schools are strong instructional leadership, a safe and orderly climate, school-wide emphasis on basic skills, high teacher expectations for student achievement, and continuous assessment of pupil progress.

Comment:

One of the most important achievements of education research in the last 20 years has been identifying the factors that characterize effective schools, in particular the schools that have been especially successful in teaching basic skills to children from low-income families. Analysts first uncovered these characteristics when comparing the achievement levels of students from different urban schools. They labeled the schools with the highest achievement as "effective schools."

Schools with high student achievement and morale show certain characteristics:

- vigorous instructional leadership,

SOURCE: *What Works: Research About Teaching and Learning.* (Washington, DC: U.S. Department of Education, 1986), pp. 45, 47, 50, 52, 59. The excerpts used have been selected by the author. Footnote citations have been deleted.

- a principal who makes clear, consistent, and fair decisions,
- an emphasis on discipline and a safe and orderly environment,
- instructional practices that focus on basic skills and academic achievement,
- collegiality among teachers in support of student achievement,
- teachers with high expectations that all their students can and will learn, and
- frequent review of student progress.

Effective schools are places where principals, teachers, students, and parents agree on the goals, methods, and content of schooling. They are united in recognizing the importance of a coherent curriculum, public recognition for students who succeed, promoting a sense of school pride, and protecting school time for learning.

Discipline

Research Finding:

Schools contribute to their students' academic achievement by establishing, communicating, and enforcing fair and consistent discipline policies.

Comment:

For 16 of the last 17 years, the public has identified discipline as the most serious problem facing its schools. Effective discipline policies contribute to the academic atmosphere by emphasizing the importance of regular attendance, promptness, respect for teachers and academic work, and good conduct.

Behavior and academic success go together. In one recent survey, for example, high school sophomores who got "mostly A's" had one-third as many absences or incidents of tardiness per semester as those who got "mostly D's." The same students were 25 times more likely to have their homework done and 7 times less likely to have been in trouble with the law. Good behavior as a sophomore led to better grades and higher achievement as a senior.

The discipline policies of most successful schools share these traits:

- Discipline policies are aimed at actual problems, not rumors.
- All members of the school community are involved in creating a policy that reflects community values and is adapted to the needs of the school.
- Misbehavior is defined. Because not everyone agrees on what behavior is undesirable, defining problems is the first step in solving them. Students must know what kinds of behavior are acceptable and what kinds are not.
- Discipline policies are consistently enforced. Students must know the consequences of misbehavior, and they must believe they will be treated fairly.

• A readable and well-designed handbook is often used to inform parents and students about the school's discipline policy.

Effective Principals

Research Finding:

Successful principals establish policies that create an orderly environment and support effective instruction.

Comment:

Effective principals have a vision of what a good school is and systematically strive to bring that vision to life in their schools. School improvement is their constant theme. They scrutinize existing practices to assure that all activities and procedures contribute to the quality of the time available for learning. They make sure teachers participate actively in this process. Effective principals, for example, make opportunities available for faculty to improve their own teaching and classroom management skills.

Good school leaders protect the school day for teaching and learning. They do this by keeping teachers' administrative chores and classroom interruptions to a minimum.

Effective principals visibly and actively support learning. Their practices create an orderly environment. Good principals make sure teachers have the necessary materials and the kind of assistance they need to teach well.

Effective principals also build morale in their teachers. They help teachers create a climate of achievement by encouraging new ideas; they also encourage teachers to help formulate school teaching policies and select textbooks. They try to develop community support for the school, its faculty, and its goals.

In summary, effective principals are experts at making sure time is available to learn, and at ensuring that teachers and students make the best use of that time.

Teacher Supervision

Research Finding:

Teachers welcome professional suggestions about improving their work, but they rarely receive them.

Comment:

When supervisors comment constructively on teachers' specific skills, they help teachers become more effective and improve teachers' morale. Yet, typically, a supervisor visits a teacher's classroom only once a year and makes only general comments about the teacher's performance. This relative lack of specific supervision contributes to low morale, teacher absenteeism, and high faculty turnover.

Supervision that strengthens instruction and improves teachers' morale has these elements:

- agreement between supervisor and teacher on the specific skills and practices that characterize effective teaching,
- frequent observation by the supervisor to see if the teacher is using these skills and practices,
- a meeting between supervisor and teacher to discuss the supervisor's impressions
- agreement by the supervisor and teacher on areas for improvement, and
- a specific plan for improvement, jointly constructed by teacher and supervisor.

Principals who are good supervisors make themselves available to help teachers. They make teachers feel they can come for help without being branded failures.

Rigorous Courses

Research Finding:

The stronger the emphasis on academic courses, the more advanced the subject matter, and the more rigorous the textbooks, the more high school students learn. Subjects that are learned mainly in school rather than at home, such as science and math, are most influenced by the number and kind of courses taken.

Comment:

Students often handicap their intellectual growth by avoiding difficult courses. In order to help young people make wise course choices, schools are increasingly requiring students to take courses that match their grade level and abilities; schools are also seeing to it that the materials used in those courses are intellectually challenging.

The more rigorous the course of study, the more a student achieves, within the limits of his capacity. Student achievement also depends on how much the school emphasizes a subject and the amount of time spent on it: the more time expended, the higher the achievement. Successful teachers encourage their students' best efforts.

In 1990, President George Bush launched a "war on drugs" designed to combat the growing problem of drug abuse in the United States. The war on drugs is being fought against international and domestic suppliers of illegal drugs. Education represents another dimension in the war on drugs. In 1986, the U.S. Department of Education issued What Works: Schools Without Drugs. *Its recommendations have been excerpted in the following selection which identifies a major problem facing the nation and its schools.*

Schools Without Drugs: Recommendations

Parents

Instilling Responsibility

Recommendation #1:

Teach standards of right and wrong and demonstrate these standards through personal example.

Children who are brought up to value individual responsibility and self-discipline and to have a clear sense of right and wrong are less likely to try drugs than those who are not. Parents can help to instill these ideals by:

- Setting a good example for children and not using drugs themselves.
- Explaining to their children at an early age that drug use is wrong, harmful, and unlawful, and reinforcing this teaching throughout adolescence.
- Encouraging self-discipline through giving children everyday duties and holding them accountable for their actions.
- Establishing standards of behavior concerning drugs, drinking, dating, curfews, and unsupervised activities, and enforcing them consistently and fairly.
- Encouraging their children to stand by their convictions when pressured to use drugs.

SOURCE: *What Works: Schools Without Drugs.* (Washington, DC: U.S. Department of Education, 1986), pp. 13, 15, 17, 19, 21, 23, 27, 29, 31, 33, 37, 39. The excerpts used have been selected by the author.

Parents

Supervision

Recommendation #2:

Help children to resist peer pressure to use drugs by supervising their activities, knowing who their friends are, and talking with them about their interests and problems.

When parents take an active interest in their children's behavior, they provide the guidance and support children need to resist drugs. Parents can do this by:

• Knowing their children's whereabouts, activities, and friends.

• Working to maintain and improve family communications and listening to their children.

• Being able to discuss drugs knowledgeably. It is far better for children to obtain their information from their parents than from their peers or on the street.

• Communicating regularly with the parents of their children's friends and sharing their knowledge about drugs with other parents.

• Being selective about their children's viewing of television and movies that portray drug use as glamorous or exciting.

In addition, parents can work with the school in its efforts to fight drugs by:

• Encouraging the development of a school policy with a clear no-drug message.

• Supporting administrators who are tough on drugs.

• Assisting the school in monitoring students' attendance and planning and chaperoning school-sponsored activities.

• Communicating regularly with the school regarding their children's behavior.

Parents

Recognizing Drug Use

Recommendation #1:

Be knowledgeable about drugs and signs of drug use. When symptoms are observed, respond promptly.

Parents are in the best position to recognize early signs of drug use in their children. In order to prepare themselves, they should:

- Learn about the extent of the drug problem in their community and in their children's schools.
- Be able to recognize signs of drug use.
- Meet with parents of their children's friends or classmates about the drug problem at their school. Establish a means of sharing information to determine which children are using drugs and who is supplying them.

Parents who suspect their children are using drugs often must deal with their own emotions of anger, resentment, and guilt. Frequently they deny the evidence and postpone confronting their children. Yet the earlier a drug problem is found and faced, the less difficult it is to overcome. If parents suspect their children are using drugs, they should:

- Devise a plan of action. Consult with school officials and other parents.
- Discuss their suspicions with their children in a calm, objective manner.
- Do not confront a child while he is under the influence of drugs.
- Impose disciplinary measures that help remove the child from those circumstances where drug use might occur.
- Seek advice and assistance from drug treatment professionals and from a parent group.

Schools

Assessing the Problem

Recommendation #4:

Determine the extent and character of drug use and establish a means of monitoring that use regularly.

School personnel should be informed about the extent of drugs in their school. School boards, superintendents, and local public officials should support school administrators in their efforts to assess the extent of the drug problem and to combat it.

In order to guide and evaluate effective drug prevention efforts, schools need to:

- Conduct anonymous surveys of students and school personnel and consult with local law enforcement officials to identify the extent of the drug problem.
- Bring together school personnel to identify areas where drugs are being used and sold.
- Meet with parents to help determine the nature and extent of drug use.

- Maintain records on drug use and sale in the school over time, for use in evaluating and improving prevention efforts. In addition to self-reported drug use patterns, records may include information on drug-related arrests and school discipline problems.

- Inform the community, in nontechnical language, of the results of the school's assessment of the drug problem.

Schools

Setting Policy

Recommendation #5:

Establish clear and specific rules regarding drug use that include strong corrective actions.

School policies should clearly establish that drug use, possession, and sale on the school grounds and at school functions will not be tolerated. These policies should apply to both students and school personnel, and may include prevention, intervention, treatment, and disciplinary measures.

School policies should:

- Specify what constitutes a drug offense by defining (1) illegal substances and paraphernalia, (2) the area of the school's jurisdiction, for example, the school property, its surroundings, and all school-related events, such as proms and football games, and (3) the types of violations (drug possession, use, and sale).

- State the consequences for violating school policy; as appropriate, punitive action should be linked with treatment and counseling. Measures that schools have found effective in dealing with first-time offenders include:
  —a required meeting of parents and the student with school officials, concluding with a contract signed by the student and parents in which (1) they acknowledge a drug problem, (2) the student agrees not to use drugs, and to participate in drug counseling or a rehabilitation program.
  —suspension, assignment to an alternative school, in-school suspension, after-school or Saturday detention with close supervision and demanding academic assignments.
  —referral to a drug treatment expert or counselor.
  —notification of police.
  —penalties for repeat offenders and for sellers may include expulsion, legal action, and referral for treatment.

- Describe procedures for handling violations, including:

—legal issues associated with disciplinary actions—confidentiality, due process, and search and seizure—and how they apply.

—responsibilities and procedures for reporting suspected incidents that identify the proper authorities to be contacted and the circumstances under which incidents should be reported.

—procedures for notifying parents when their child is suspected of or caught with drugs.

—procedures for notifying police.

- Enlist legal counsel to ensure that the policy is drafted in compliance with applicable Federal, State, and local laws.

- Build community support for the policy. Hold open meetings where views can be aired and differences resolved.

Schools

Enforcing Policy

Recommendation #6:

Enforce established policies against drug use fairly and consistently. Implement security measures to eliminate drugs on school premises and at school functions.

Ensure that everyone understands the policy and the procedures that will be followed in case of infractions. Make copies of the school policy available to all parents, teachers, and students, and take other steps to publicize the policy.

Impose strict security measures to bar access to intruders and prohibit student drug trafficking. Enforcement policies should correspond to the severity of the school's drug problem. For example:

- Officials can require students to carry hall passes, supervise school grounds and hallways, and secure assistance of law enforcement officials, particularly to help monitor areas around the schools.

- For a severe drug problem, officials can use security personnel to monitor closely school areas where drug sale and use are known to occur; issue mandatory identification badges for school staff and students; request the assistance of local police to help stop drug dealing; and, depending on applicable law, develop a policy that permits periodic searches of student lockers.

Review enforcement practices regularly to ensure that penalties are uniformly and fairly applied.

Schools

Teaching About Drug Prevention

Recommendation #7:

Implement a comprehensive drug prevention curriculum from kindergarten through grade 12, teaching that drug use is wrong and harmful and supporting and strengthening resistance to drugs.

A model program would have these main objectives:

- To value and maintain sound personal health.
- To respect laws and rules prohibiting drugs.
- To resist pressures to use drugs.
- To promote student activities that are drug free and offer healthy avenues for student interests.

In developing a program, school staff should:

- Determine curriculum content appropriate for the school's drug problem and grade levels.
- Base the curriculum on an understanding of why children try drugs in order to teach them how to resist pressures to use drugs.
- Review existing materials for possible adaptation. State and national organizations—and some lending libraries—that have an interest in drug prevention make available lists of materials.

In implementing a program, school staff should:

- Include all grades. Effective drug education is cumulative.
- Teach about drugs in health education classes, and reinforce this curriculum with appropriate materials in such classes as social studies and science.
- Develop expertise in drug prevention through training. Teachers should be knowledgeable about drugs, be personally committed to opposing drug use, and be skilled at eliciting participation by students.

Schools

Enlisting the Community

Recommendation #8:

Reach out to the community for support and assistance in making the school's antidrug policy and program work. Develop collaborative arrangements in which school personnel, parents, school boards, law enforcement officers, treatment organizations, and private groups can work together to provide necessary resources.

School officials should recognize that they cannot solve the drug problem alone. They need to get the community behind their efforts by taking action to:

- Increase community understanding of the problem through meetings, media coverage, and education programs.
- Build public support for the policy; develop agreement on the goals of a school drug policy, including prevention and enforcement goals.
- Educate the community about the effects and extent of the drug problem.
- Strengthen contacts with law enforcement agencies through discussions about the school's specific drug problems and ways they can assist in drug education and enforcement.
- Call on local professionals, such as physicians and pharmacists, to share their expertise on drug abuse as class lecturers.
- Mobilize the resources of community groups and local businesses to support the program.

Students

Learning the Facts

Recommendation #9:

Learn about the effects of drug use, the reasons why drugs are harmful, and ways to resist pressures to try drugs. Students can arm themselves with the knowledge to resist drug use by:

- Learning about the effects and risks of drugs.
- Learning the symptoms of drug use and the names of organizations and individuals who are available to help when friends or family members are in trouble.
- Understanding the pressures to use drugs and ways to counteract them.
- Knowing the school rules on drugs and ways to help make the school policy work.
- Knowing the school procedures for reporting drug offenses.
- Knowing the laws on drug use and the penalties, for example, for driving under the influence of drugs and alcohol. Understanding how the laws protect individuals and society.
- Developing skill in communicating their opposition to drugs and their resolve to say no.

Students

Helping Fight Drug Use

Recommendation #10:

Use an understanding of the danger posed by drugs to help other students avoid them. Encourage other students to resist drugs, persuade those using drugs to seek help, and report those selling drugs to parents and the school principal.

Although students are the primary victims of drug use in the schools, drug use cannot be stopped or prevented unless students actively participate in this effort.

Students can help fight drug use by:

• Participating in open discussions about the extent of the problem at their own school.

• Supporting a strong school antidrug policy and firm, consistent enforcement of rules.

• Setting a positive example for fellow students and speaking forcefully against drug use.

• Teaching other students, particularly younger ones, about the harmful effects of drugs.

• Encouraging their parents to join with other parents to promote a drug-free environment outside of school. Some successful parent groups have been started by the pressure of a son or daughter who was concerned about drugs.

• Becoming actively involved in efforts to inform the community about the drug problem.

• Starting a drug-resistance club or other activity to create positive, challenging ways for young people to have fun without drugs. Obtaining adult sponsorship for the group and publicizing its activities.

• Encouraging friends who have a drug problem to seek help and reporting persons selling drugs to parents and the principal.

Communities

Providing Support

Recommendation #11:

Help schools fight drugs by providing them with the expertise and financial resources of community groups and agencies.

Law enforcement agencies and the courts can:

- Provide volunteers to speak in the schools about the legal ramifications of drug use. Officers can encourage students to cooperate with them to stop drug use.
- Meet with school officials to discuss drug use in the school, share information on the drug problem outside of school, and help school officials in their investigations.

Social service and health agencies can:

- Provide volunteers to speak in the school about the effects of drugs.
- Meet with parents to discuss symptoms of drug use and to inform them about counseling resources.
- Provide the schools with health professionals to evaluate students who may be potential drug users.
- Provide referrals to local treatment programs for students who are using drugs.
- Establish and conduct drug counseling and support groups for students.

Businesses can:

- Speak in the schools about the effects of drug use on employment.
- Provide incentives for students who participate in drug prevention programs and lead drug-free lives.
- Help schools obtain curriculum materials for their drug prevention program.
- Sponsor drug-free activities for young people.

Parent groups can:

- Mobilize others through informal discussions, door-to-door canvassing, and school meetings to ensure that students get a consistent no-drug message at home, at school, and in the community.
- Contribute volunteers to chaperone student parties and other activities.

Print and broadcast media can:

- Educate the community about the nature of the drug problem in their schools.
- Publicize school efforts to combat the problem.

Communities

Tough Law Enforcement

Recommendation #12:

Involve local law enforcement agencies in all aspects of drug prevention: assessment, enforcement, and education. The police and courts should have well-established and mutually supportive relationships with the schools. Community groups can:

- Support school officials who take a strong position against drug use.
- Support state and local policies to keep drugs and drug paraphernalia away from schoolchildren.
- Build a community consensus in favor of strong penalties for persons convicted of selling drugs, particularly for adults who have sold drugs to children.
- Encourage programs to provide treatment to juvenile first-offenders while maintaining tough penalties for repeat offenders and drug sellers.

Law enforcement agencies, in cooperation with schools, can:

- Establish the procedures each will follow in school drug cases.
- Provide expert personnel to participate in prevention activities from kindergarten through grade 12.
- Secure areas around schools and see that the sale and use of drugs are stopped.
- Provide advice and personnel to help improve security in the school or on school premises.

Suggestions for Further Reading

Bell, T.H. *Report by the Secretary on the Regional Forums on Excellence in Education.* Washington, D.C.: U.S. Department of Education, 1983.

Boyer, Ernest L. *High School: A Report on Secondary Education in America.* New York: Harper & Row, 1983.

College Board. *Academic Preparation for College: What Students Need to Know and Be Able to Do.* New York: The College Board, 1983.

Coombs, Philip H. *The World Crisis in Education: The View from the Eighties.* New York: Oxford University Press, 1985.

Goodlad, John I. *A Place Called School: Prospects for the Future.* New York: McGraw-Hill Book Co., 1983.

Gutek, Gerald L. *Basic Education: A Historical Perspective.* Bloomington, Ind.: Phi Delta Kappa Education Foundations, 1981.

Sizer, Theodore R. *Horace's Compromise: The Dilemma of the American High School.* Boston: Houghton-Mifflin Co., 1984.

Staff of the National Commission on Excellence in Education. *Meeting the Challenge: Recent Efforts to Improve Education Across the Nation.* Washington, D.C.: U.S. Department on Education, 1983.

National Commission on Excellence in Education. *A Nation at Risk: The Imperative for Educational Reform.* Washington, D.C.: U.S.Government Printing Office, 1983.

National Education Association. *The Teaching Profession.* Washington, D.C.: National Education Association, 1983.

National Education Association. *Teachers' Views on Equity and Excellence.* Washington, D.C.: National Education Association, 1983.

Roberts, Arthur D. and Cawelti, Gordan. *Redefining General Education in the American High School.* Alexandria, VA: Association for Supervision and Curriculum Development, 1984.

Task Force on Education for Economic Growth. *Action for Excellence.* Denver, CO: Education Commission of the States, 1983.

Chapter 10

Toward a Conclusion

I t is always challenging for an historian to conclude a book. The writing of the last chapter is no exception to this problem of historical writing. The history of American education is an ongoing one that will require new chapters, new interpretations, and new revisions in the future. This closing chapter provides a summary and identifies some continuing challenges that will face American education.

A Summing Up

The record of education is an unfinished account. As a public experience, the history of American education includes the contributions of many individuals. Some are famous historical personages such as Horace Mann, Henry Barnard, and John Dewey. In addition, however, the dedicated service of school administrators and teachers is also part of the record.

A particularly American educational institution is the common school, whose evolution is closely related to the concept of equality of educational opportunity. From Mann and Barnard through Dewey to the present, educational leaders have defined the common school as a publicly controlled and publicly responsible institution accessible to children of all races, religions, and socioeconomic backgrounds.

The single-track American school structure also reflects the democratic concept of education. The "educational ladder" extends from elementary school through the high school, college, and university. Although socioeconomic status has a great impact on school success, the formal school structure, at least, does not impede equality of opportunity.

Like America's history in general, American educational experience resulted from the interaction of the American people and their environment. American education, developing in the equalitarian spirit of its pioneers, has reflected a broadly based commitment to the democratic ethic. Since public education is responsible to the public and its demands, control has been vested at the local level in elected boards of education.

The concept of local control, which originated in New England, became an integral element in the nineteenth century common school movement. Since the framers of the United States Constitution made no specific reference to education, state governments under the tenth amendment's reserved powers clause assumed the role of educational authorities and delegated substantial powers to local boards.

Although local control has persisted to the present, many twentieth century trends have limited it. State governments have exercised an influence by distributing funds to local schools which must meet various state-imposed criteria or mandates. The federal programs have brought with them guidelines to be met by the schools receiving funds. State and federal decisions have shaped educational policies and practices. Despite the federal and state roles, public schools, their facilities and their programs, still vary tremendously throughout the United States.

The contemporary school system has evolved as the nation evolved from a rural and frontier environment into a complex, industrialized, technological society. Reflecting this socioeconomic transformation, education, too, has become a large-scale enterprise, and the teaching profession has grown with it. Today's teacher is better prepared in both academic subject matter and instructional methodology than the pioneer teacher of the "little red schoolhouse" ever dreamed of being.

Persistent Concerns

The sections that follow examine some persistent concerns of American education. Some of the concerns treated are: (1) achieving greater equality of educational opportunity for all Americans; (2) enhancing multicultural pluralism; (3) improving the quality of American education.

An important concern in American education is that of extending equality of educational opportunity and enhancing the cultural richness of a pluralistic society. The struggle for equality of opportunity has been waged most dramatically by African-Americans who have worked to achieve racial integration and civil rights. The civil rights movement served as both a model and a stimulus to other groups such as Amer-Indians, Hispanic-Americans, handicapped persons, and women who have organized to seek greater socioeconomic and educational opportunities.

American women have also become conscious of sex discrimination in educational and economic opportunities. Although the history of the women's movement in the United States dates back to the early nineteenth century, the crusade for women's rights gained an added momentum in the 1960s, 1970s, and 1980s. Surfacing as "Women's Liberation" in the 1960s, it has grown into an articulate and well-organized movement for equal rights for women.

In education, the efforts of blacks, Hispanic-Americans, and other groups have taken several directions. One decided thrust has been for members of minority groups to secure more positions in schools, colleges, and universities as administrators and teachers. School districts, colleges, and universities have developed affirmative action programs to provide more employment opportunities to minority group members. Educational institutions have also developed policies to encourage the admission of more members of underrepresented groups.

Simultaneously with the struggle for equal rights, educators have acknowledged the importance of recognizing and preserving America's multicultural heritage. The theories of Americanization and the melting pot have been subjected to sociological scrutiny and have been generally discarded for a revitalized cultural pluralism.[1] In the past, educators such as Ellwood P. Cubberley saw the public school as an agency of Americanizing immigrants into a common national identity that was defined specifically in English and Protestant terms. Cubberley wrote that the task of American public schools was "to break up" ethnic settlements and "to implant" in the children of immigrants the "Anglo-Saxon conceptions of righteousness, law and order, and popular government."[2]

A more generous theory was that of the "melting pot" which held that the United States was a crucible in which a new American identity was being forged. According to the "melting pot" theory, the American character was still in the process of becoming. It would be a new nationality to which peoples of different languages, races, and ethnic backgrounds would contribute.[3]

A third alternative was presented by the advocates of cultural pluralism, such as Horace Kallen, who envisioned a mosaic of people living in a common national society.[4] The contemporary era has witnessed the re-emergence of the theory of cultural pluralism in several forms. In its cultural manifestations, the revival of cultural pluralism stimulated members of racial, ethnic, and language groups to rediscover their own identity by retracing their historical roots. The desire for ethnic identity has led to courses and programs in schools and colleges designed to heighten racial and ethnic consciousness. There are, for example, programs in African-American, and Polish-American studies to name only a few.

The movements for equality of opportunity and ethnic and language uniqueness have merged in the various bilingual and bicultural programs of education that are found throughout the United States. Although such programs have been designed for various ethnic and language groups, the Spanish-speaking Hispanic-Americans are the largest groups involved in them. Since the inception of these programs, a debate has waged over their purpose. Should they be designed as transitional or as maintenance programs? A transitional program is to aid children whose first language is one other than English to use that language as a bridge to the learning of English; a maintenance program seeks to preserve the child's native language by providing ongoing instruction in it.

The twin movements for equality and uniqueness pose problems but also create new opportunities for American education. If equality is defined as a common opportunity and experience that is shared by all, then an education for equality tends to reduce the differences that separate people. Thus, if American public schools pursued the common school concept—as they have generally done historically—then the future will require more pervasive equalizing tendencies. On the other hand, if schools emphasize programs that stress racial, ethnic, and language uniqueness, it becomes necessary to broaden and make less specific the core of common experience. Since equality and uniqueness are values that are worthy of schools operating in a democratic society, the American educational future requires a synthesis of both values. In the 1970s and 1980s, various professional associations of educators, including those involved in teacher preparation, have emphasized the need to maximize equality of opportunity and to emphasize the multicultural character of American society.

In examining American education in its historical perspective, many of the great challenges that faced American education in the past were quantitative. The demand was for more schools, more programs, and more teachers to serve the needs of an ever-growing student population. The evolution of the common school in the early nineteenth century, the growth of the high school at the turn of the century, and the rapid expansion of the community college in the twentieth century were products of the effort to extend educational opportunities to more Americans. After World War II, in particular, the educational institutions of the United States faced the quantitative challenge of providing education for a massive student population.

As the United States enters the twenty-first century, the major challenge facing American education will be qualitative rather than quantitative. This and future generations of Americans will need to answer anew Herbert Spencer's question, "What Knowledge is of Most Worth?" What knowledge will help to prepare American children to live rewarding and productive lives in the post-industrial society that is growing more massive, more technological, and more complex?

As one surveys American educational history, especially in curriculum and instruction, a pendulum appears to be swinging back and forth between the poles of continuity and change. In the 1920s and 1930s, progressives who stressed learning by projects and problem-solving activities debated Essentialists who emphasized basic subject matter disciplines. The debate of the 1950s was between the proponents of life adjustment education and those, like Arthur Bestor, who wanted fundamental intellectual disciplines stressed in the school curriculum. During the 1960s, innovations such as the non-graded school, team teaching, and open space education were introduced. The 1970s saw a movement for basic education, which rejected many innovations of the previous decade. Rarely has the curricular pendulum rested in the center between the poles of continuity and change.

If the study of educational history could accomplish but a single goal, it might be one that cultivates a sense of perspective that avoids both a rigid traditionalism that regards change as anathema and also a naive enthusiasm for panaceas that promise success through untested and frequently misunderstood innovations. Hopefully, a sense of educational balance will encourage a synthesis that embraces the positive features of the past and the promising experimentation of the future. Such a synthesis would recognize the cultivation of literacy and knowledge as the special task of the school and would seek to find humane and efficient means of educating persons to the fullness of their human potentiality.

This book is intended primarily to describe selected topics in the development of American education in historical perspective. Some of the major challenges facing public education have been examined in that context, and their definition, analysis and resolution in the future will constitute the next chapters in its story. Persistent challenges for the future will be:

1. Redefinitions of goals so that the broad purposes of education can realize the democratic promise of American life.

2. Continued efforts to develop strategies to resolve the problems of racial, gender, social, and economic alienation and discrimination so that educational opportunities are available for all.

3. Identification and investigation of the problems of life in a mass society so that education can be carried on as a quest for the cultivation of individual and national excellence.

4. The development of curricular and instructional programs designed to solve the problems of racial discrimination, social isolation, and cultural deprivation.

5. More intensive efforts to help the growing child become more independent, more creative, and freer to develop his or her own intelligence, personality and capabilities to the fullest possible extent.

6. A restructuring of American schools so that they will be more human, more personal, and less bureaucratic.

The American Educational Commitment

The major challenges raised here are only a few of the issues, problems, and conflicts facing contemporary American education. The successful response of both the American people and their schools in meeting these challenges rests in the last analysis on their continued commitment to education, its potential excellence, and the ideal of equal educational opportunity. Perhaps the greatest contribution that the study of the history of American education can make is a greater understanding of the origins and development of this commitment.

Arriving in the New World wilderness, the transplanted European colonists established schools to preserve their civilization. During the early years of the American Republic, common education throughout the country built loyalties to the new nation. Throughout the nineteenth century, the public school assimilated the streams of immigrants who came to the United States, and forged their loyalty likewise. As industry and technology transformed rural America into an urban society, the public high school extended educational opportunity at the secondary level. After World War II, the opportunities for college attendance were extended to larger numbers of American youth. Approaching the twenty-first century, the greatest goal of education is still to make equality of educational opportunity a reality for the disadvantaged youth in both urban and rural areas. As educational opportunities are extended to more and more individuals, the teaching profession, as well as the public, need to remain firmly committed to the highest standards in education. Thus, equal opportunity and excellence continue to be the twin goals which sustain the American educational commitment.

Notes

[1] Nathan Glazer and Patrick Moynihan, *Beyond the Melting Pot* (Cambridge, Mass.: M.I.T. Press, 1963).

[2] Ellwood P. Cubberley, *Changing Conceptions of Education* (New York: Riverside Educational Monographs, 1909), pp. 15-16.

[3] For a careful discussion of the differences between Americanization, the melting pot, and cultural pluralism, see Mark Krug, *The Melting of Ethnics: Education of the Immigrants, 1880-1914* (Bloomington, Indiana: Phi Delta Kappa Educational Foundation, 1976), pp. 1-16.

[4] Horace M. Kallen, *Cultural Pluralism and the American Idea* (Philadelphia: University of Philadelphia Press, 1956).

Suggestions for Further Reading

Banks, James A. and Banks, Cherry A. McGee. *Multicultural Education: Issues and Perspectives*. Boston: Allyn and Bacon, Inc., 1989.

Bennett, Christine I. *Comprehensive Multicultural Education: Theory and Practice*. Boston: Allyn and Bacon, Inc., 1986.

Glazer, Nathan, and Moynihan, Patrick. *Beyond the Melting Pot*. Cambridge, Mass.: M.I.T. Press, 1963.

Kallen, Horace M. *Cultural Pluralism and the American Idea*. Philadelphia: University of Philadelphia Press, 1956.

Krug, Mark. *The Melting of the Ethnics: Education of the Immigrants, 1880-1914*. Bloomington, Indiana: Phi Delta Kappa Educational Foundation, 1976.

Rich, John Martin. *Innovations in Education: Reformers and Their Critics*. Boston: Allyn and Bacon, Inc., 1988.

Index